Perspectives on Justice, Indigeneity, Gender, and Security in Human Rights Research

"This edited collection of "Perspectives in Human Rights" by Laura E. Reimer, Ph.D. and Katerina Standish, Ph.D. is a thought-provoking examination of contemporary human rights issues, grounded in academic research. The contributors delve into subjects such as justice, Indigeneity, gender, and security, and provide insightful and inspiring perspectives on the futures of human rights. With a focus on hope and dignity, the collection offers a unique look at the expanding margins of human rights research and a collective effort to resist the decline of human flourishing, expression, and dignity. The deeper themes of hope and dignity pervade throughout the book, making it a must-read for anyone interested in human rights and the role of meaningful research in developing pathways forward in modern human rights contexts."

—Dr. Richard Jochelson, *Dean of Law at the Faculty of Law, University of Manitoba*

"An impressive collection of perspectives on a broad range of cutting-edge human rights issues from both well-known and respected scholars, and emerging voices from the Master of Human Rights program at the University of Manitoba. This collection will undoubtedly influence the debates and practice in these areas, making it an incredible resource to both human rights practitioners and academics alike."

—Dr. Nathan Derejko, *Assistant Professor; Mauro Chair in Human Rights and Social Justice*

"This collection of essays furthers discussions of human rights issues on a wide range of contemporary topics relevant locally and globally. From restorative justice to Indigeneity, to gender-based violence, to cyber operations, to environmental justice and beyond, this edited volume contributes an expansive research base for teaching human rights. Each chapter provides an opportunity for rich dialogue when teaching contemporary human rights, making *Perspectives on Justice, Indigeneity, Gender, and Security in Human Rights Research* an important and timely contribution to human rights research pedagogy."

—Karlee Sapoznik Evans, BAH, M.A., Ph.D., *Deputy Manitoba Advocate for Children and Youth*

Laura E. Reimer · Katerina Standish
Editors

Perspectives on Justice, Indigeneity, Gender, and Security in Human Rights Research

palgrave
macmillan

Editors
Laura E. Reimer
Faculty of Law
University of Manitoba
Winnipeg, MB, Canada

Katerina Standish
National Centre for Peace
and Conflict Studies
University of Otago
Dunedin, Otago, New Zealand

ISBN 978-981-99-1929-1 ISBN 978-981-99-1930-7 (eBook)
https://doi.org/10.1007/978-981-99-1930-7

Cover illustration: Eduardo Estellez/500px

This Palgrave Macmillan imprint is published by the registered company Springer Nature Singapore Pte Ltd.
The registered company address is: 152 Beach Road, #21-01/04 Gateway East, Singapore 189721, Singapore

Foreword

When Dr. Arthur Mauro, the founder of the Centre for Peace and Justice at the University of Manitoba in Canada delivered his now rather famous speech "Winnipeg – the New Geneva" on November 21, 2009 (copied at the end of this collection), the standing ovation of those in attendance of the packed ballroom at the Westin Hotel was immediate, heartfelt, and lengthy. We had witnessed a master storyteller weaving a well-crafted narrative focusing on the province of Manitoba's human rights challenges and opportunities from our history, the present, and the future.

From Manitoba's past, Dr. Mauro spoke about the well documented Winnipeg General Strike of 1919. The forces between that of the labour movement and the immigration population versus capitalism. Through violent confrontation, there was an ability to find resolve. We now have laws that recognize workers rights and a propitiatory attitude towards labour and management.

For the present, Mauro used the image of the Canadian Museum for Human Rights, under construction in 2009, and spoke of how it would change the Canadian human rights landscape. And of the future, Dr. Mauro challenged all of us to build on past and present experiences, to work together to find a collective path forward to create the Geneva of the Prairies in Winnipeg.

And it is because of Dr. Mauro's passionate challenge that I believe Dr. Laura Reimer has strategically chosen each of the authors who are writing a chapter for *Perspectives on Justice, Indigeneity, Gender and Security in*

Human Rights Research. Each author is exploring human rights issues. And while some of the authors in the book focus on human rights issue outside of Canada, all the basic foundational human rights find a home in the Geneva of the Prairies in Winnipeg.

Further, I believe Dr. Laura Reimer asked me to participate in this project because I have known Dr. Arthur Mauro for close to 40 years. Most of those 40 years would be deemed to be social. We crossed paths while attending both public and private gatherings. However, there are two specific milestones that are germane to my writing this foreword and my relationship with Dr. Mauro.

The first milestone was when I was Leader of her Majesty's Loyal Opposition in the provincial Manitoba Legislature in the early 2000s, Dr. Mauro was somebody whom I consulted on a regular basis. His close ties to Manitoba's 14th Premier Duff Roblin (1958–1967) made him one of my most invaluable advisors and confidant. His ability to grasp an issue and provide a logical solution along with his marvellous sense of humour kept me grounded and was greatly appreciated.

The second one revolved around my appointment as the Inaugural President & CEO of the Canadian Museum for Human Rights in 2009. Once again, I found myself engaging Dr. Mauro in conversation on a variety of topics that were grounded in human rights discourse. One of our ongoing dialogues was discussing whether basic rights and freedoms that belong to every person in the world were more fundamental than governments, civil society, and communities working together to implement lasting solutions to reduce violence, deliver justice, combat corruption, and ensure inclusive participation.

After I completed the Official Opening of the Canadian Museum for Human Rights in 2014, Dr. Mauro's vision became the catalyst that allowed me to bring together the following Winnipeg Community Leaders for a working dinner at Ralph Connor House: Chair of the Truth and Reconciliation Commission, Murray Sinclair; Community Leaders Dr. Lloyd Axworthy, Ida Albo, Art DeFehr, Gerry Labosier; President & CEO of the Winnipeg Foundation, Richard Frost; Executive Director of the Ma Mawi Wi Chi Itata Centre, Inc., Diane Redsky; former Winnipeg Chief of Police, Devon Clunis; President & CEO the Catholic Health Corporation of Manitoba, Dan Lussier; the President of the University of Winnipeg, Annette Trimbee, the President of the University of Manitoba, David Barnard, to discuss how to pursue the question of advancing Dr. Mauro's vision of the Geneva on the Canadian Prairies.

That evening was energetic, consultative, and informative. Above all, it was a clear opportunity to see the depth of knowledge, the diversity, and the passion that exists in Winnipeg about human rights. The leadership in the room felt that Winnipeg could take the pulpit and start to share the human rights organizations we have here that are focused on making lives better for all people.

That meeting was the catalyst that led to the establishment of the City of Human Rights Education. The City of Human Rights Education is focused on exploring international human rights issues and raising the profile of local grassroots human rights people and organizations making a difference on those international issues.

Dr. Arthur Mauro is the son of Italian Immigrants and was born in Fort William, Ontario. He went on to get academic providence studying at St Paul's College in Winnipeg. One of the biggest impacts on Dr. Mauro's life, while studying at St. Paul's College was the intellectual tradition and moral aptitude that the Jesuits brought to their teaching. Dr. Mauro developed a keen sense of debate and realized early on that the best way to explore issues was out in the open- through spirited debate and dialogue. It was because of this spirited debate and dialogue that Dr. Mauro in his later years to spoke openly against the anti-sematic attitudes he witnessed against Winnipeg's entrepreneurial and hardworking Jewish Community.

Dr. Arthur Mauro is well known for his vast community leadership. In private enterprise and in voluntary service, Arthur Mauro has contributed to the economic, civic, and cultural life of Manitoba. His contributions span the law, higher education, charities, health services, advanced research, national and provincial aspects of public policy sport, aboriginal affairs, community development, business development, the fine arts, and national unity. It was with this backdrop that Dr. Mauro was awarded the Order of Manitoba, the Order of Canada, and established the Mauro Centre for Peace and Justice.

Dr. Mauro has been a guest speaker and guest lecturer to many different social gatherings, both public and private. He speaks passionately about Winnipeg as a city that cares. He cites that Winnipeg established the first Community Foundation in Canada, and that the United Way in Winnipeg has risen to the highest levels of success because labour and management collectively saw the need to improve the lives of all citizens by building a stronger community, together.

I highly recommend you read the entirety of Dr. Mauro's speech "Winnipeg- the New Geneva" located within this collection. It will serve you well as you explore the chapters of this human rights odyssey. If learning and hope are high on your bucket list, then you will undoubtedly find a good measure of both as you turn the pages of *Perspectives on Justice, Indigeneity, Gender, and Security in Human Rights Research.*

Winnipeg, Manitoba, Canada
2023

Stuart A. Murray. O. M.

Stuart Murray is the current President & CEO of the City of Human Rights Education (The COHRE) and the Human Rights Hub of Winnipeg (The Hub). Murray is a member of the City of Winnipeg's Human Rights Committee of Council. He was appointed as the first Chief Executive Officer (CEO) of the new Canadian Museum for Human Rights, Canada's fifth national museum.

Contents

Notes on Contributors

Rhéal Cenerini B.A., Ag (Dip.), M.A., Canada, is a multifaceted franco-Manitoban writer who explores universal themes through theatre, poetry, and prose. From the quest for identity, in particular through the lens of the UNDRIP, to an examination of human relations in all their forms and notions of power and success, his work has been presented in Winnipeg, in eastern Canada, and in France. He is motivated by a passion for agriculture and is also a market gardener.

Brandi Chartier B.A., MHR, Canada, Brandi's bachelor degree in international development and conflict resolution furthered her desire to navigate and understand the world we live in. She is interested in the intersectionality of gender, class, and human rights. Her previous experience has seen her complete two trips to Africa: the first to Kenya was on a youth mission trip to build a school, the second was a 2-month trip to Ghana aiding in the advancement of women's education and quality of life. These significant experiences, along with regular non-profit work locally, are experiences along a larger journey of her goal to make the world a better place.

Ha Bich Dong B.A., M.P.A., M.A., Vietnam, Ha's current research interests focus on the decolonization and internationalization in education. She seeks to challenge the legacies of colonialism in Southeast and East

Asia and explores how schools may contribute to peacebuilding citizenship. Ha is a board member of The Mama Ada Foundation and a mentor at Volunteer for Peace Vietnam.

Dr. Albert Evrard LL.D, L.L.M., M.S.T, M.C.A, M.P.A., STB, LL.B, GDCL, France, currently holds a chair on Aging at the School of Law in Institut Catholique de Toulouse (France). Attorney in Brussels (Belgium), he moved to university research on Aging, with regular inside stay in nursing home. In Canada, the focus was on representations of Old Age in Art (National Gallery of Ontario), on theological, spiritual, and anthropological approaches (Regis College, University of Toronto 2013–2015), on Elder Law at the Legal Clinic (McGill University), on international law, ethics at U of M Law School, and the Jesuit Center for Catholic Studies (2019–2021). From 2019 to 2021 he was a Visiting Scholar at St Paul's College, University of Manitoba, extending his important research in human rights in matters of aging.

Christa C. Gilliam Ph.D., MSW, USA, is an Associate Professor and Chairperson in the Department of Social Work at Coppin State University in Baltimore, M.D. A California native, she moved to Baltimore, M.D. to pursue her Ph.D. after more than 10 years of practising in the public sector serving children and families. She earned her Ph.D. in social work from Morgan State University and her MSW from the University of California, Berkeley. Her interests are rooted in her experience as a practitioner turned academic. Dr. Gilliam has worked in higher education since 2005, advancing the mission of social work through teaching, service to the profession and community, and research on topics addressing racial and gender oppression. Her current scholarship focuses on social work workforce development, leadership, professional mentoring, social work policy and practice in urban communities, and social, economic, political, and environmental justice.

Carlos Godoy B.A., M.A., M.B.A., M.A., Brazil, is a retired Brazilian Army Officer who has been participating in peacekeeping training, support, and field activities for fifteen years. His formal education is a B.A. in Law, M.A. in Military Operations, M.B.A. in Financial Management, M.A. in Peace and Conflict Studies. His study focuses on international aid and how effective it should be to promote emancipatory peacebuilding. Further, peacekeeping as an early phase of post-conflict reconstruction is also another of his areas of interest.

Ashley Haller B.A., MHR, Canada, Ashley's research is dedicated to advancing gender equality and advocating for the human rights of women. Through her writing and advocacy, Ashley hopes to provide an interdisciplinary perspective to gendered issues, while also presenting concrete solutions for change. She is currently working on human rights education projects in Winnipeg, Manitoba.

Will Jordan B.A., MHR, Canada, holds a Master of Human Rights and bachelor of Human Justice from the University of Regina. Will's work incorporates restorative justice practices into Canada's judicial system.

Sydney Laurin B.A., MHR, Canada, is a Calgary native holding an undergraduate degree in Criminal Justice from Mount Royal University (MRU) and Master of human rights from the university of Manitoba. Sydney is passionate about supporting survivors of sexual violence and is knowledgeable regarding LGBTQ, victims, and women's rights. Throughout her educational journey, Sydney has received numerous scholarships including the Harvey and Sandra Sector Master of Human Right Fellowship and a full-ride athletic scholarship to play women's varsity hockey at MRU. Throughout her playing career, she was vital in the creation of a mandatory sexual consent module on campus. Sydney completed her master's practicum with the government of Manitoba's Status of Women Office, where she took on a massive research project examining the impacts of COVID-19 on women and marginalized groups. After producing a comprehensive report with recommendations for recovery, Sydney was offered a senior policy analyst position with the Government of Manitoba's Department of Families. She currently works to develop and draft legislation pertaining to critical human rights issues and social service program delivery for the province.

Stephen Lunn B.A., MHR, Canada, holds a Bachelor of Arts (Honours) in Political Studies, and a Master of Human Rights from the University of Manitoba. He has an interest in International Law applicable to cyberspace, International Humanitarian Law, and International Human Rights Law.

Abigail Myles B.A., MHR, Canada, Abigail/Abby Myles is a graduate of the first cohort of Canada's only Master of Human Rights program, located at the University of Manitoba in the Faculty of Law. Her research has focused on children's rights in African contexts, and inter-group allyship to foster diversity, equity, and inclusion. As a result, her professional and volunteer experiences have centred upon human rights, diversity and inclusion, peace and conflict studies, youth leadership, and curriculum development.

Dr. Laura E. Reimer MPA, Ph.D., Canada, Dr. Laura Reimer is currently the Academic Program Development Director for the Faculty of Law at the University of Manitoba, where she was formerly the inaugural Practicum and Professional Development Coordinator of Canada's first Master of Human Rights program. Her diverse education and expertise include public administration, governance, Indigenous education, peace and conflict studies, and human rights. As a result, she has held numerous adjunct teaching positions in five North American universities and been awarded for her teaching excellence. She has published six books, two of which were doctoral research collections from the Arthur V Mauro Institute for Peace and Justice at the University of Manitoba, co-edited with Dr. Katerina Standish and Dr. Chuck Thiessen.

Dr. Cathryne L. Schmitz Ph.D., MSW, United States, is a Professor Emerita in the Department of Social Work at the University of North Carolina Greensboro (UNCG). Her scholarship focuses on critical multiculturalism, environmental justice, human rights, analysis of the privilege/oppression nexus, leadership, global engagement, interdisciplinary education, organizational development and community building, and peacebuilding. She has been engaged in intercultural global education, environmental education, knowledge building, and curriculum development. She has numerous publications and is currently focusing in the areas of environmental justice, identity, and culture, interdisciplinary knowledge building, and organizational/community transformation. She has expanded her focus through her cross-disciplinary appointments with the Department of Peace and Conflict Studies and the Program in Women and Gender Studies. She also contributes to and learns from her work in the community and with the UNCG Center for New North Carolinians.

Korellia Schneider B.A., M.A., USA, is from the United States and currently resides in Canada. Her travels have carried her to several countries, where she has worked as an educator, translator, editor, and researcher. She is particularly interested in the intersections between social justice and human rights in an international context. She has conducted research in the areas of gender, environmental justice, nuclear disarmament, and Japanese history. She considers herself a lifelong learner both in and outside of the classroom.

Dr. Lacey Sloan Ph.D., MSSW, United States, is an Associate Professor and MSW Director at Auburn University at Montgomery. She received her BSW from the University of Mississippi and her MSSW and Ph.D. in social work from The University of Texas at Austin. Her three intertwining areas of scholarship are sexual rights and gender-based violence; social work education and practice in Islamic contexts; and environmental justice. Since 2001, using local and Indigenous knowledge, she facilitated the development and/or accreditation of 3 MSW programs (University of Southern Maine; College of Staten Island, and Zayed University in the United Arab Emirates) and 3 BSW programs (College of Staten Island; Somalia; and Qatar), and a diploma and a certificate program in social work (Somalia). Dr. Sloan was a steering committee member for development of Council on Social Work Education's specialized practice in Environmental Justice.

Dr. Katerina Standish Ph.D., Canada/New Zealand, is the Director of Research at the National Centre for Peace and Conflict Studies and active board member of the Canadian Peace Research Association. She is currently the Chief Editor of *Peace Review: A Journal of Social Justice*, and has guest lectured and participated in webinars at the Mauro Institute for Peace and Justice at the University of Manitoba. She is a Senior Lecturer and sits on the editorial boards of the *Journal for Peace Education, In Factis Pax: Journal of Peace Education and Social Justice, International Journal of Advanced Peace and Gandhian Studies, Global Journal of Peace Research and Praxis and Sustainability: Journal of Sustainable Development*. She is a member of multiple Peace and Justice and Human Rights organizations and associations. Dr. Standish holds a doctoral degree in Peace and Conflict Studies from the University of Manitoba, a Master's Degree in Human Security and Peacebuilding from Royal Roads University, a post-baccalaureate in Communications from Simon Fraser University, an undergraduate degree in Sociology, Anthropology, and Humanities from Simon Fraser University and is currently completing a Masters in Indigenous Studies from the University of Otago.

Dr. Annette Trimbee Ph.D., Canada, is the president and vice-chancellor of MacEwan University, having previously served as president and vice-chancellor of The University of Winnipeg. Dr. Trimbee is Red River Metis, originally from Winnipeg and spent over 25 years in Edmonton building a distinguished career with the Government of Alberta. During this period, she held several senior leadership positions, including appointments as Deputy Minister of Advanced Education and Technology and of Treasury Board and Finance. Annette's academic field is aquatic ecology. She is a member of the International Red River Water Basin Board and currently serves as the Chair of the Council of Post-Secondary Presidents of Alberta and Chair of the Canadian Research Knowledge Network. She received the Indspire Laureate award for Education in 2022.

Introduction

Laura E. Reimer

Hope. Late on December 10 1948, in Paris, France, a small delegation signed the *United Nations Declaration of Human Rights* and the world changed. In a world that had suffered unspeakably, hope for a world of dignity was formally established. Under the leadership of Eleanor Roosevelt of the United States, the primary purpose of the United Nations was international security. Both hope and commitment burned brightly as the major world powers of the time determined that the atrocities of war in Europe—economic, personal, and environmental—would never again take place on such a large scale. Almost a century later, human rights and human rights issues have become the central and unifying narrative across the globe, and the work that began with a small delegation of visionaries now guides one of the fastest growing and expanding fields of study.

Within this collection of research-based perspectives, readers will recognize the unifying beacons of hope and dignity based in academic research. Not only do the authors provide enlightenment into the

L. E. Reimer (✉)
Faculty of Law, University of Manitoba, Winnipeg, MB, Canada
e-mail: Laura.Reimer@umanitoba.ca

L. E. Reimer and K. Standish (eds.), *Perspectives on Justice, Indigeneity, Gender, and Security in Human Rights Research*,
https://doi.org/10.1007/978-981-99-1930-7_1

growing edges of human rights research, but they have also engaged their interests, hearts, and scholarship to provide a unique exploration of the hope for the future situated at the core of human rights literature.

Perspectives on Justice, Indigeneity, Gender, and Security in Human Rights Research was born out exceptional research at the University of Manitoba, home to Canada's first Master of Human Rights program, and in Winnipeg, the city that houses the unique and world-renowned Canadian Museum of Human Rights. Winnipeg's human rights history runs deep. Many Canadian language rights, voting rights, Indigenous rights, and labor rights were established for the first time in Winnipeg and enshrined in legislation. The scholars who have identified the human rights issues and challenges on the following pages take their rightful place among those who have pioneered the field. The central contribution of this collected work is that as scholars, the authors have recognized obscured human rights issues and offer concrete solutions through recommendations for effective public policy. When human rights scholarship enters the realm of government policy with influence and research-based recommendations, the protection of human dignity can be more certainly assured.

The perspectives in this collection present major themes in human rights and contextualize them in modernity. The cases range from a Canadian university campus to the factories of Bangladesh and cybersecurity in the Ukraine. Human rights, justice, indigeneity, gender, and security are explored through the lenses of hope, dignity, and actionable address. The collection includes a speech delivered by Dr. Arthur Mauro, former Chancellor of the University of Manitoba and benefactor of the Arthur V. Mauro Institute for Peace and Justice on the University of Manitoba campus. It is from the vision and philanthropy of Dr. Mauro that the meaningful study of human rights takes place at the University of Manitoba. In one of his most important speeches, Dr. Mauro calls upon the passions and vision that characterize the leading edges of social justice and human dignity to explain why Winnipeg could well be "the new Geneva." He outlines the rules for peace and justice, just as the Geneva Convention outlined the rules of war.

The first section of the collection presents four key aspects of human rights and social justice. "Access to Justice" presents readers with a fulsome expose of the many ways restorative justice offers access to justice through ways and means that are accessibly, dignifying, and can transform conflict meaningfully while upholding human rights. The chapter on "Allyship and Equality in Youth Organizations" presents a case study of a Canadian youth leadership organization and how it has transformed to ensure that human rights issues are not issues for its community. Readers are then provided a container in which to encapsulate a human rights/social justice education praxis that emerged from coursework on Human Rights and Social Justice, delivered to third-year medical students in Aotearoa/New Zealand. The first section concludes with a provocative theoretical chapter, in which readers are guided to ponder the question "Are human rights universal?" In each of these chapters, readers are coached, through evidence-based research, to recognize that although justice and access to justice are human rights in liberal democracies, the daily practices that operationalize these cherished values face severe challenges.

The second section explores themes that encircle human rights in the Indigenous context, though readers will quickly recognize both the discouragements to, and the hope for, reconciliation and dignity offered by each of the authors. "The United Nations Declaration on the Rights of Indigenous People: A Prototype for Reconciliation?" argues that the UNDRIP is, first and foremost, a political document seeking to strike a balance between the collective rights of Indigenous people and the public interest of nations that have greatly benefitted at the expense of these same people. "Indigenous Rights and the University" outlines a proven leadership strategy from a Canadian university president for Indigenizing the university while remaining true to its purpose as an institution of higher learning. Both chapters offer readers the opportunity to consider not just the rights of Indigenous people, but the rights of all of us to know one another and respect our differences while exploring dignifying ways to craft our shared future.

No collection about human rights issues would be complete without an exploration of gender, and the four chapters offered take readers into deeper explorations of issues that some may have thought long-ago resolved. "Transgender Healthcare in Canada" poses questions about dignity and health that have not yet been voiced in most human rights literature. "Femicide in Mexico" demonstrates that for some governments, human rights to do not extend to everyone. Exploring the murder and persecution of women in the largely patriarchal country of Mexico, this chapter highlights the world-wide phenomena of the oppression of women. In a completely different context, the author of "Women Workers in the Ready-made Garment Industry in Bangladesh" explores human rights and social justice in the context of exploited, impoverished women and children, a widely documented world-wide problem. In the final chapter of the section, "Extremism, Terrorism and Misogyny" the author draws on two tragic mass shootings in Canada to make her argument to both the public and lawmakers that misogynistically motivated attacks targeting women are not merely the result of mental illness and must be recognized in law and in fact as extremist acts of terrorism.

The final collection of chapters presents human rights research in the area of security. "Hope with Charity: Human Rights, the Law, and Aging" forces readers to carefully consider the potential bifurcation of human rights, dignity, and aging—as supported by law. Reflecting on the concept of hope in the understanding and evolution of human rights among the elderly the author explores the obligations of lawmakers to preserve human dignity. Then, "Human Security and the Digital Threat: Russia and Ukraine" explores human security in the context of cyber-warfare, along with its implications for the rest of the world. Readers are then challenged to look inside Canada's public school system and the efforts of local schools to apply imposed yet apparently ineffective higher-level government policies to the volatile issue of bullying in schools. How the issues of hope and dignity are reflected is explored, based in carefully collected data. The final chapter explores the emerging frontier of environmental security and human rights. The authors of "Climate Change: Environment Justice, Human Rights, and Peaceful Practices" demonstrate compellingly how the three are inextricably linked and that sustainable development is not possible without equity and justice. Furthermore, readers are compelled to consider that in order to successfully address climate change, we must recognize the interconnected relationships between climate change; human caused environmental degradation; and racial, social, economic, and environmental injustice.

Perspectives on Justice, Indigeneity, Gender, and Security in Human Rights Research is about human rights issues with research-based solutions in a collective effort to resist virtue-signaling and further deterioration of human dignity. The deeper themes of dignity and hope emerge from each of the chapters as readers are awakened to contemporary human rights issues currently being researched in the areas of justice, indigeneity, gender, and security.

Acknowledgements The Editors wish to thank Mr. Kyle Chemerika for his outstanding editing work during the final stages of this collection.

Human Rights and Justice

Access to Justice

Will Jordan

When it comes to discussion of access to justice within the context of human rights, conversation is often focused on a narrow understanding of what access to justice means. Within international legal frameworks, access to justice has often been defined through Articles that can be found in the *International Convention on Civil and Political Rights* (ICCPR). Some examples include Article 14(1), which provides that all are equal before the courts and tribunals and must be afforded a fair hearing; Article 14(2), which outlines each person's right to the presumption of innocence; and Article 14(3), which highlights each person's rights to legal counsel, time to prepare an adequate defence, and a trial without undue delay, among other guarantees.[1]

Within the Canadian context, access to justice is often understood in a very similar light as those highlighted in international legal frameworks. The *Canadian Charter of Rights and Freedoms* provides many of the standards of access to justice that are guaranteed to all Canadians. For example, equality rights provided under section 15(1) of the *Canadian*

W. Jordan (✉)
University of Regina, Regina, Canada
e-mail: wjordan@sasktel.net

L. E. Reimer and K. Standish (eds.), *Perspectives on Justice, Indigeneity, Gender, and Security in Human Rights Research*, https://doi.org/10.1007/978-981-99-1930-7_2

Charter of Rights and Freedoms state that "[e]very individual is equal before and under the law and has the right to the equal protection and equal benefit of the law without discrimination."[2] While this is one of the most common definitions of access to justice in Canada, other significant figures such as Chief Justice of the Canadian Supreme Court, Richard Wagner, have argued that access to justice is best summarized as the following:

> "Access to justice" can mean many things. Having the financial ability to get legal assistance when you need it. Being informed of your right to counsel when your liberty is at stake. Having courts that can resolve your problem on time. But it also means knowing what tools and services are available, and how to get to them. It means knowing your rights and knowing how our legal systems work. It can even mean seeing people like yourself represented in all parts of the legal system. And it means having confidence that the system will come to a just result – knowing you can respect it, and accept it, even if you don't agree with it. Ultimately, it is about getting good justice for everyone, not perfect justice for a lucky few.[3]

While the meaning of access to justice can include a wide range of different meanings, the importance of access to justice is consistent. According to Currie, nearly half of the Canadian population will experience some kind of law-related problem over a given three-year period.[4] With this significant number of Canadians encountering some sort of legal issue, it is important that individuals understand how to access justice appropriately. Unsurprisingly, legal issues can have major implications on numerous facets of an individual's life. For example, employment and housing are both important parts of an individual's life which be negatively impacted by way of having a criminal history. In more extreme circumstances, individuals accused of serious criminal offences can be deprived of their rights and freedoms by way of incarceration. Being able to access justice by way of legal representation, being informed of your rights, and having access to fair processes in a timely manner can help to ensure people's rights are protected.

When it comes to access to justice and achieving "good justice for everyone," an emerging perspective that has been gaining traction in the international community has been promoting access to practices that are considered alternative philosophies of justice. In many jurisdictions, different philosophies of justice such as Restorative Justice (RJ) and Indigenous legal practices have been implemented as a means of diverting cases from retributive Western legal systems or transforming the justice system in its entirety. While practices such as RJ have increased in popularity due to their "victim-oriented nature,"[5] RJ and other legal philosophies have often been overshadowed or pushed to the side by Western legal traditions. Examples of this phenomenon have been well documented at both the international and national level. In the aftermath of International Criminal Tribunal for the former Yugoslavia (ICTY) and the International Criminal Tribunal for Rwanda (ICTR), commentators have noted that individuals who participated in the tribunals criticized the procedures for "a lack of emphasis on restorative justice."[6] Further to this point, academics have also noted that institutions such as the International Criminal Court (ICC) that claim to have "a restorative justice mandate," do very little in the way of carrying out practices grounded in alternative justice philosophies like RJ.[7]

This paper will argue that we should expand narrow definitions of access to justice to include access to "alternative forms of justice" when applicable. Several legislative tools such as the *Criminal Code*,[8] the *Youth Criminal Justice Act* (YCJA),[9] and the *Canadian Victims Bill of Rights* (CVBR)[10] would support an expansion of the Canadian understanding of access to justice to include alternative philosophies of justice. In addition to expanding understandings of access to justice in the Canadian context, this paper will explore the various challenges alternative philosophies of justice face in terms of having access to their programs being recognized as a human right. Within the Canadian framework, co-option of alternative forms of justice by provincial and federal governments present significant barriers to accessing alternative justice programming. Other barriers to accessing alternative philosophies of justice include the displacement of alternative practices by more dominant Western legal principles such as retribution. By highlighting these barriers, this study looks to address some of the concerns practitioners of alternative philosophies of justice have regarding promoting access to justice within the Canadian legal framework.

Understanding Alternative Philosophies of Justice

What Are Alternative Philosophies of Justice?

Defining what constitutes an alternative philosophy of justice can be a difficult task given the large range of practices that fall under this label. To provide a better understanding of what makes an approach to justice an alternative philosophy of justice, it is useful to understand how they contrast with Western criminal justice systems and how practitioners define alternative philosophies. Westernized criminal justice systems are primarily understood as frameworks that are offender-focused, attempt to assign blame to achieve punitive outcomes, and offer little support to victims in addressing their needs in the aftermath of a criminal offence.[11] Generally, criminal justice systems that prioritize determining guilt and assigning punishments as the primary outcome of the justice process are referred to as retributive justice systems. For some academics, retributive justice systems are considered "clumsy" or "ineffective" as they pay significant attention to identifying perpetrators and collecting evidence of their criminal behaviour, rather than identifying causes of and sustainable solutions to crime.[12]

Given retributive justice's limited capacity to identify and address the root causes of criminal behaviour, advocates of justice reform have pushed for alternative philosophies of justice to fill the gaps left by retributive systems, or completely replace the retributive system in more extreme circumstances. These philosophies that have emerged to address the shortcomings of retributive systems have often been referred to as restorative justice practices. According to Maglione, RJ refers to three distinct but overlapping objects that include the following:

> (1) a justice reform movement emerging in the 1970s in the Western world and then spreading globally, advocating for a (2) largely non-punitive and participatory approach to harmful behaviours (3) mainly implemented by facilitated and voluntary encounters between direct stakeholders, geared toward addressing those harms and their consequences.[13]

Further to this point, Maglione also suggests that alternative philosophies that fall under the category of RJ have taken different forms and adopted different practices based on the geographical, political, and social context in which the RJ movement took place.[14] While Maglione's understanding of RJ as a non-punitive approach that emphasizes encounters between stakeholders is not new, his acknowledgement that RJ and alternative philosophies of justice are influenced by the systems in which they emerge is an important point.

It is in considering the influence of specific justice systems that many academics in the field of RJ have had issues coming to a consensus definition of alternative philosophies. For some academics, there has been a desire to define RJ based on the processes that are commonly practised. An example includes Dünkel et al.'s definition which argues RJ "has come to be used to describe processes and practices that seek to employ a different approach to resolving conflicts."[15] For experts who support definitions of RJ that emphasize processes, there are often certain caveats that must be met. Generally, those who support process-oriented definitions stipulate that offenders, victims, and community members must voluntarily come together to resolve harm caused by the offender in the wake of a criminal offence. This is best exemplified by Marshal's definition of RJ that states RJ is "a process whereby all the parties with a stake in a particular offense come together to resolve collectively how to deal with the aftermath of the offense and its implications for the future."[16]

While some commentators are satisfied with process-oriented definitions, others have identified problems with these definitions. Those who oppose process-oriented approaches, such as Doolin, suggest that Marshal's popular understanding of RJ is too vague. Doolin suggests that process-oriented definitions do little to indicate which stakeholders ought to be included in the restorative process, what is meant by appropriate processes to achieve resolutions, and what the outcomes of RJ processes should be.[17] Contrarily, understandings of RJ that emphasize restorative outcomes over the types of processes used allow for a greater range of practices to fall under the category of RJ, while still ensuring some degree of restoration occurs for those who decide to participate in RJ processes. Although Doolin does not offer a standard definition of RJ, Doolin explains that RJ processes should be evaluated based on the outcomes of restorations sought with an emphasis on achieving the most restorative outcome possible.[18] Restorative outcomes can vary largely based on the specifics of the offence that brought the stakeholders together and can range from an apology to reparations being paid to the victim. With these types of definitions of RJ, practices where a victim or offender decide not to participate can still be considered a restorative process. These types of processes will often use a surrogate victim or offender so that some degree of restorative outcome is available for stakeholders who do want to participate.

Of course, outcome-oriented definitions present their own unique challenges when it comes to understanding RJ. Commentators have noted that outcome-oriented definitions are restrictive as RJ outcomes will vary based on the specific desires of stakeholders participating in the process with some participants achieving a greater sense of restoration than others.[19] This criticism recognizes that a victim and an offender may meet to participate in RJ but leave the process without coming to a resolution. Even though an outcome has not been reached, it would be inaccurate to suggest that no RJ process has occurred at all. What can be made of this difficulty in determining what constitutes a restorative practice is that RJ needs to be understood in the context of the jurisdiction in which it is being practised and the policy which enables RJ processes to occur.

Because of difficulties attempting to define RJ, authors such as Woolford and Nelund and Van Ness and Strong have moved away from formal definitions of RJ and adopted a more appropriate and flexible understanding. These authors have attempted to establish understandings of RJ through core elements of restorative processes. For example, Van Ness and Strong identify three pillars of restorative processes which include an encounter, reparation or amends, and transformation or reparation.[20] For any process to be considered a restorative process under Van Ness and Strong's (2015) conceptualization of RJ, the process needs to include an encounter between stakeholders, amends need to be made in some way by the offender towards the victim, and steps need to be taken to ensure the seamless reintegration of both the offender and victim back into society.[21] Similarly, Woolford and Nelund suggest that there are several significant traits of restorative processes that include open and active participation, empowering participants, and offering satisfying relational healing processes.[22]

While both Woolford and Nelund and Van Ness and Strong lay out defining traits for restorative processes, they are also flexible in their understandings of RJ. This is ultimately one of the most important features in a definition of RJ as RJ processes are highly adaptable to fit the needs of those participating. In recognizing this important feature of RJ, Woolford and Nelund state that "[i]n any specific application of restorative justice, moments may arise when these ideals are unreachable or temporarily suspended."[23] This is because authors with flexible understanding of RJ recognize that RJ is a living model that is a "continuously evolving body of ideas intended to articulate a method of justice built upon the active participation of stakeholders."[24] This means that RJ will evolve or be revised to "meet future challenges."[25] Ultimately, it is clear that these versions of understanding RJ are more appropriate as they represent a more dynamic and flexible definition of RJ.

RJ in the Canadian Context

RJ and alternative philosophies of justice have a long history in Canada. The Canadian justice system is often accredited with the first use of RJ in tandem with the traditional criminal justice system. In 1974, two teens living in Elmira, Ontario engaged in a vandalism spree that led to numerous victimizations in the small community. As a result of the spree, a probation officer named Mark Yantzi took the teens to confront their victims and listen to how their actions affected them. This process was the first instance of a victim-offender mediation (VOM) and ultimately led to many communities establishing victim-offender reconciliation programs across Canada with the support of Mennonite communities.[26] While this was the first instance of VOM being used for RJ, it is important to note that many modern RJ practices have been significantly influenced by Indigenous legal traditions. Authors such as Tomporowski et al. have explained that Indigenous practices such as sentencing circles predate Canada's legal framework but have been worked into Canada's judicial system as commonly used restorative practices.[27]

Restorative practices have become widespread in Canada as a result of s.717(1)(a) of the *Criminal Code* which came into effect through sentencing reforms in 1996. Tomporowski et al. (2011) have noted that the lack of national data collection on RJ has made it difficult to measure the impact of the sentencing reforms on the increase of RJ on Canada (p. 826).[28] However, recent data collection of RJ referrals indicate that 22,576 referrals were made to RJ programs across 18 ministries in 2017/18 because of the provision.[29] S.717(1)(a) reads:

> **717 (1)** Alternative measures may be used to deal with a person alleged to have committed an offence only if it is not inconsistent with the protection of society and the following conditions are met:
>
> > **(a)** the measures are part of a program of alternative measures authorized by the Attorney General or the Attorney General's delegate

> or authorized by a person, or a person within a class of persons, designated by the lieutenant governor in council of a province...[30]

Because of the language used in s.717(1)(a) of the *Criminal Code*, alternative philosophies of justice such as restorative justice practices are often referred to as alternative measures in the context of adult offenders. Young offenders can be afforded similar opportunities in the aftermath of a criminal offence by way of the YCJA. In a similar vein to alternative measures, provisions in the YJCA allow young offenders access to alternative philosophies of justice to address concerns of "overuse of the courts and incarceration in less serious cases, disparity and unfairness in sentencing, a lack of effective reintegration of young people released from custody, and the need to better take into account the interests of victims."[31] Unlike adult offenders, however, when young offenders are referred to alternative justice processes the youth is being assigned to an extrajudicial sanction.

There are several important points to note about alternative measures and extrajudicial sanctions in terms of their relationship with alternative philosophies of justice and restorative practices. The first point is that alternative measures and extrajudicial sanctions include a range of practices that can be a part of restorative practices but do not result from a restorative process. For example, the Public Prosecution Services of Canada has stated that alternative measures can range from rehabilitative programming for offenders to paying restitution to victims and community through means such as community service.[32] While these can be outcomes of restorative processes, they can also be a disposition without having the victim and offender engaging in a restorative process. Rather, it is possible that the sentencing justice mandated an outcome based on the traditional criminal process alone. Despite this consideration, it is not uncommon for the Government of Canada to identify these alternative measures and restorative processes as one and the same.[33]

The second point to highlight regarding alternative measures and extrajudicial sanctions is that the practices and policy can vary by province. Although s.717 of the *Criminal Code* and the YCJA give legislative authority for the use of RJ processes, provinces are ultimately responsible for developing, funding, and regulating their respective RJ programs.[34] As a result, the range of restorative processes available in a province can vary wildly and there is no federally legislated understanding of RJ to create consistency across provinces. However, it is important to note there have been efforts to establish some uniformity for RJ across the nation through federal, provincial, and territorial (FPT) working groups. As a part of their work, the FPT Working Group on Restorative Justice has established a definition for RJ in Canada which explains that RJ is "an approach to justice that seeks to repair harm by providing an opportunity for those harmed and those who take responsibility for the harm to communicate about and address their needs in the aftermath of a crime."[35] Furthermore in 2018, the FPT Working Group on Restorative Justice has also committed "to increase the use of restorative justice processes by a minimum target of 5% per jurisdiction, where possible, over the next 3 years."[36] With clear interest in expanding access to RJ across Canada, it is worthwhile examining other legislative tools that can be used to support further access to RJ in the nation.

Tools for Expanding RJ as a Right to Access to Justice in Canada

The Criminal Code

When it comes to expanding understanding of access to justice to include access to alternative philosophies of justice and their practices, the *Criminal Code* is one of the pieces of Canadian legislation that needs to be at the centre of the conversation. As previously mentioned, s.717 is often identified as the most important section in terms of enabling RJ and alternative philosophies of justice to take place in the Canadian criminal justice framework. However, s.717 is far from the only piece of enabling policy that should be considered when making an argument for accessing alternative philosophies of justice as a right. While alternative measures speak (albeit not in direct fashion) to the use of RJ processes, s.718 of the *Criminal Code* outlines both the purpose and principles of sentencing with respect to Canada's legal system. Of course, several of these sentencing principles include more punitive aspects of Western legal systems, such as the need to denounce unlawful conduct, to deter the offender from committing crime, and to separate offenders from society.[37] In contrast to these more retributive principles, s.718(2) of the *Criminal Code* includes several principles which speak to the importance of restorative principles in Canadian legal frameworks. These principles read as follows:

> **718(2)** A court that imposes a sentence shall also take into consideration the following principles:
>
> **(d)** an offender should not be deprived of liberty, if less restrictive sanctions may be appropriate in the circumstances; and
>
> **(e)** all available sanctions, other than imprisonment, that are reasonable in the circumstances and consistent with the harm done to victims or to the community should be considered for all offenders, with particular attention to the circumstances of Aboriginal offenders...[38]

In many respects, the acknowledgement of restorative principles in Canadian legal frameworks is a recent development. Commentators such as Roach have pointed out that, during the 1990s, the Canadian House of Commons expressed interest in RJ while federal and provincial Ministers of Justice "recognized the 'holistic' and 'healing' approach of aboriginal justice as essential to reform."[39] These interests and admissions led to significant sentencing reform in 1996 through the introduction of Bill C-41 to Parliament that introduced the previously highlighted principles in s.718(2). Additionally, the 1996 sentencing reforms also entrenched other RJ principles within the *Criminal Code*, which indicated provisions of "reparations to victims and the community are legitimate goals of sentencing" by way of s.718(e)–(f).[40]

Shortly after their introduction into Canadian legislation, several pieces of Bill C-41 became a topic of controversy within the Canadian Supreme Court. In 1999, a case called *R v. Gladue* came to the attention of the Canadian Supreme Court and justices hearing the case were asked to comment on s.718(2)(e) of the *Criminal Code*. At the heart of the case was the appellant Mrs. Gladue who was looking to have her sentence reduced because of the trial judge's comments that the defendant shouldn't be given any special considerations in terms of a sentence as it related to her Indigenous heritage.[41] Upon considering that s.718(2)(e) of the *Criminal Code* reads that all sanctions other than imprisonment should be considered with particular attention being paid to Indigenous persons, it appeared that Gladue had grounds to appeal her sentence. Despite this, the Supreme Court dismissed her case. However, what did emerge from *R v. Gladue* was important history on the development of Bill C-41 and commentary on the importance of RJ in Canada.

Upon reviewing the criminal justice system in the *R v. Gladue* case, the presiding justices noted that Canada's incarceration rate of approximately 130 inmates per 100,000 population places it second or third highest among industrialized democracies.[42] As a means of responding to the Canadian reliance on incarceration, the justices explained that Parliament passed the first codification of sentencing reform with two objectives in mind: "(i) reducing the use of prison as a sanction, and (ii) expanding the use of restorative justice principles in sentencing."[43] Further to this point, the justices state that "[t]he 1996 sentencing reforms embodied in Part XXIII, and s. 718.2(e) in particular, must be understood as a reaction to the overuse of prison as a sanction, and must accordingly be given appropriate force as remedial provisions."[44] Finally, the justices argued that "Parliament's choice to include (e) and (f) alongside the traditional sentencing goals must be understood as evidencing an intention to expand the parameters of the sentencing."[45]

When it comes to reflecting on the 1996 sentencing reforms established through Bill C-41, it is clear that both Parliament and justices of the highest court in Canada agree that restorative outcomes are necessary within the Canadian legal framework. In response to the *R v. Gladue*, the Canadian criminal justice system has taken measure to provide processes in which Indigenous offenders can have their historical circumstances considered by courts to become eligible for alternative justice processes such as Indigenous-run healing lodges.[46] While provisions such as s.718(2)(e) have been criticized as being "unfair for non-Indigenous offenders because it was a 'race-based discount' on sentencing"[47] they should not be understood in this light. At their core, the principles established through the 1996 sentencing reforms reflect the need to rely less on the use of incarceration in exchange for restorative outcomes for all Canadians. This is made clear by previously highlighted comments of the justices in the *R v. Gladue* case as well as the following statement by the same justices:

> The next question is the meaning to be attributed to the words "with particular attention to the circumstances of aboriginal offenders". The phrase cannot be an instruction for judges to pay "more" attention when sentencing aboriginal offenders. It would be unreasonable to assume that Parliament intended sentencing judges to prefer certain categories of offenders over others. Neither can the phrase be merely an instruction to a sentencing judge to consider the circumstances of aboriginal offenders just

> as she or he would consider the circumstances of any other offender. There would be no point in adding a special reference to aboriginal offenders if this was the case.[48]

Ultimately it is clear that through the 1996 sentencing reforms, Parliament intended to make alternative philosophies of justice more accessible for all Canadian and not just a particular group. With this in mind, advocates for alternative philosophies of justice need to leverage the comments of Parliament, justices of the Supreme Court of Canada, and Canadian legislation as they clearly indicate processes such as RJ are fundamental in accessing better justice in Canada.

The Youth Criminal Justice Act

In a similar vein to provisions included in the 1996 sentencing reforms for the *Criminal Code*, the YCJA was a response on the behalf of the Canadian Parliament to address issues pertaining to the extremely punitive *Young Offenders Act*. This is made clear in the "Preamble" of the YCJA that articulates the following points:

- Society has a responsibility to address the developmental challenges and needs of young persons.
- Communities and families should work in partnership with others to prevent youth crime by addressing its underlying causes, responding to the needs of young persons.
- The youth justice system should reserve its most serious interventions for the most serious crimes and reduce the over-reliance on incarceration.[49]

To be able to meet the objective of reducing over-reliance on incarceration, s.10 of the YJCA allows prosecutors and sentencing judges to consider the aforementioned extrajudicial sanctions for youth offenders when appropriate. Under the YCJA, the number of custody charges and incarcerated youth dropped by 64% and 50% respectively between 2002–2003 and 2009–2010.[50] Criteria that would qualify young offenders for an extrajudicial sanction include the fully informed and free consent of the youth to participate in the process, opportunity for the youth to consult with legal counsel throughout the process, acceptance of responsibility by the youth for their actions that resulted in an offence, and authorization of the program of sanctions by the Attorney General.[51]

Much like alternative measures and s.717 of the *Criminal Code*, a significant amount of attention is given to s.10 of the YCJA when looking to increase access to alternative practices and philosophies of justice. However, the YCJA contains numerous other provisions that support the increased right to access alternative measures, some of which include alternative practices of justices. The most notable of these provisions include s.38(2) of the YCJA, which emphasizes the following sentencing principles in terms of young offenders:

> **38(2)** A youth justice court that imposes a youth sentence on a young person shall determine the sentence in accordance with the principles set out in section 3 and the following principles:
>
> **(d)** all available sanctions other than custody that are reasonable in the circumstances should be considered for all young persons, with particular attention to the circumstances of aboriginal young persons;
>
> **(e)** subject to paragraph (c), the sentence must
>
> > **(i)** be the least restrictive sentence that is capable of achieving the purpose set out in subsection (1),
> > **(ii)** be the one that is most likely to rehabilitate the young person and reintegrate him or her into society, and
> > **(iii)** promote a sense of responsibility in the young person, and an acknowledgement of the harm done to victims and the community.[52]

S.38(2)(d) closely resembles the provisions for adult offenders found in s.718(2)(e) of the *Criminal Code*, and thusly, has also been subjected to the same criticism of racial favouritism in sentencing. Commentators such as Anand have noted in the wording of s.38(2)(d) of the YJCA that Indigenous young offenders are not subjected to the same standard of proportionality as other offenders.[53] As a result of this consideration, it is possible to conclude that youth court judges "can impose disproportionately lenient youth sentences" regarding Indigenous young offenders.[54] To a degree, there is some merit to this argument as Anand notes that, during debates on this section of the YCJA, Members of Parliament insisted that "that such an amendment was needed in order to address the overrepresentation of Aboriginal young people in youth custody centres."[55]

Despite specific intentions from Members of Parliament to establish differential treatment in sentencing Indigenous young offenders, s.50(1) of the YCJA pushes back against this narrative as it stipulates that s.718(e) of the *Criminal Code* and all relevant jurisprudence applies to the sentencing with respect to Indigenous youth. With the inclusion of s.50(1) in the YCJA, this means that the decisions and considerations from watershed cases such as *R v. Gladue* also apply to youth sentencing. As a result of s.50(1) of the YCJA, unique sentencing innovations and diversions methods specific to Indigenous offenders established through the *R v. Gladue* also need to be considered for youth. The inclusion of s.50(1) within the YCJA means that the comments made by the justices in the *R v. Gladue* case about *Gladue* sentencing principles not being "race-based" or favouring certain groups through restorative sentencing are also relevant with young offenders. Rather, s.50(1) suggests that both s.718(2)(e) of the *Criminal Code* and s.38(2)(d) of the YCJA should be understood as looking to apply greater use of extrajudicial sanctions for all youth accused of committing a criminal offence as opposed to relying on incarceration. This is especially true for s.38(2)(d) of the YCJA when one considers that outcomes for youth sentencing are meant to be "the least restrictive" while imposing meaningful consequences for young offenders under s.38(2)(e)(i) of the YJCA.[56] Extrajudicial sanctions that rely on restorative processes such as conferencing have been demonstrated to lower youth incarceration rates in Canada while adequately holding youth accountable for their actions.[57] Advocates looking to explore greater use of restorative philosophies should keep these considerations as they serve as clear examples for increased use of alternative philosophies of justice in the Canadian legal framework.

The Canadian Victim Bill of Rights

The CVBR is by far one of the most interesting of the legislative tools that can be used to advocate for expanding understandings of access to justice to include access to alternative philosophies of justice. This is in large part due to the CVBR containing several sections that specifically mention the use of RJ which other key legislation does not. According to s.6(b) of the CVBR, every victim has the right to request information about "the services and programs available to them as a victim, including restorative justice programs."[58] While this section mentions RJ and restorative programs specifically, it is also important to note that this section does not guarantee victims a right to partake in restorative processes. Rather, this particular section only guarantees victims the right to request information pertaining to restorative program. However, victims right to access RJ programs becomes more concrete when considering s.47 of the CVBR, which states that all victims registered under the *Corrections and Conditional Release Act* will be provided with information about RJ programs and, upon the victim's request, measures for victims to participate in RJ processes.[59]

Although s.6(b) of the CVBR does not specifically outline a right to access alternative philosophies of justice, it is still important to examine in some detail. This is because when victims have access to information pertaining to restorative programs, they can make informed decisions and push for justice processes they prefer given their own circumstances. This is best exemplified by an individual named Marlee Liss who participated in what may have been Canada's first instance of using RJ to resolve a sexual assault crime, rather than adjudication. Liss was the victim of a sexual assault that was initially assigned to be dealt with through the traditional justice system. Throughout the process, however, Liss shared with her legal team that she felt that prison would not benefit her assaulter and that the court process would only serve to re-traumatize her.[60] Upon researching alternatives to the traditional justice system, Liss discovered RJ processes and requested that a VOM take place between herself and her assailant. Initially, prosecutors resisted Liss's request until she threatened to drop all charges against her assailant unless a restorative process was granted. Eventually, Liss was granted the restorative process and has gone on to advocate for greater use of RJ in the criminal justice system by way of her Re-Humanize Movement.[61]

There are several points to take away Liss's experience and the CVBR as a tool for advocating for greater access to alternative philosophies of justice. The first point is that, although the CVBR makes it a right for victims to be able to request information about RJ processes, the onus is on the victim to make the request for information and to understand what RJ is in the first place. In returning to Liss's experience, Liss indicates that she had no prior knowledge of RJ or alternative processes until she researched them herself.[62] Further to this point, it is clear that Liss's right to information by way of s.6(b) of the CVBR (2015) could never be accessed as Liss had no knowledge about RJ to ask for information pertaining to restorative processes. The problem that Liss faced regarding her rights as a victim is emblematic of a problem most victims similarly face. According to a study conducted by the Department of Justice, 52% of Canadians reported a low familiarity with RJ with an additional 30% saying they only had a moderate understanding.[63]

This transition to the second point to highlight with regard to Liss and the CVBR as a tool for expanding access to justice. When Canadians are informed of RJ processes, they are generally favourable towards these processes and would support greater education regarding the processes. In the same study conducted by the Department of Justice, a majority of Canadians supported the use of RJ after receiving an explanation of what RJ is. In addition to this, 80% of Canadians agreed that "criminal justice officials should be required to inform victims, survivors and accused of the availability of RJ processes."[64] What should be taken away from this is that, even though s.6(b) of the CVBR only guarantees access to information, Canadians with information pertaining to RJ are very likely to pursue RJ processes. Given this information, advocates for expanding access to justice to include access to alternative philosophies and criminal justice professionals need to raise greater awareness around the CVBR. Furthermore, it is crucial that advocates push criminal justice officials to uphold their obligations under both s.6(b) and s.47 of the CVBR (2015) to ensure access to alternative philosophies are better understood as a right within the Canadian legal framework.

Barriers to Accessing Alternative Philosophies

Co-Option of Alternative Philosophies

One of the most significant barriers to greater access to alternative philosophies of justice within the Canadian legal framework is government co-option of alternative philosophies of justice. Commentators such as Christie have explained that lawyers and the state have been known to steal conflict, so much so that conflict becomes their "property" and not that of any other person or group.[65] At their core, restorative philosophies of justice attempt to address this concern outlined by Christie by allowing greater victim and community participation in the wake of an offence. In its most simple form, co-option of alternative philosophies of justice is the fear that, "through legislated standards of practice, the government will be re-exerting its influence over [restorative processes]."[66]

The fear that government will exert influence over restorative processes is not unfounded and can be seen throughout the Canadian legal framework. One of the most troubling ways in which government can reclaim its possession over criminal matters is through establishing policy that significantly limits who can qualify for processes. While some advocates for alternative philosophies of justice may argue that RJ can be used for any type of offence if the participants are willing, federal, and provincial policy significantly limits the types of offences that can be referred to RJ programs. Within federal government policy, it is a general principle that RJ is "most suitable for offenders with no record, who have committed less serious offences and are unlikely to reoffend."[67] In addition to this, the following circumstances strictly exclude RJ from being used at the federal level:

- the offence involved the use of, or threatened use of, violence reasonably likely to result in harm that is more than merely transient or trifling in nature;
- a weapon was used or threatened to be used in the commission of the offence
- the offence is a sexual offence;
- the offence had a serious impact upon the victim or victims (physical, psychological or financial);
- the conduct demonstrated sophisticated planning (for example, the offence was part of an ongoing criminal enterprise).[68]

Although this list of circumstances that preclude RJ is not exhaustive, it is obvious that these restrictions are meant to both protect vulnerable victims and denounce serious criminal offences. While these are necessary considerations, it is important to note that victims such as Marlee Liss may find RJ processes more empowering while viewing traditional justice systems more traumatizing. By not allowing certain victims to choose whether RJ processes would be appropriate for them, government effectively "steals" conflict from victims.

In addition to "stealing conflict" by limiting which offences can be referred to restorative programs, in rare circumstances, governments have engaged in developing their own restorative programs and then deciding which community programs receive certain cases. Across a majority of Canadian provinces, it is most common that prosecutors, judges, and defence counsel work together to determine whether an offender qualifies for an alternative measure. If the Crown counsel approves the offender to receive an alternative measure, a referral for the offender will usually be sent directly to a community organization that is being contracted to by a provincial ministry of justice.[69] However, in what might be one of the most egregious examples of government co-option, the Government of Manitoba has established its own restorative program called the Restorative Justice Centre.

According to the Government of Manitoba, the Restorative Justice Centre is meant to be a part of their "Criminal Justice Modernization Strategy" that aims to "more effectively use restorative justice options to improve public safety, reduce delay in the court system and ultimately reduce reliance on incarceration."[70] The Restorative Justice Centre receives all referrals from the criminal justice system and has the capacity to either mediate the referral itself or delegate the referral to the proper restorative program "to better address risk and underlying causes of criminal behaviour."[71] In reality, what has actually occurred through the development of the Restorative Justice Centre is that the involvement of community programs in RJ are pushed to the side. By conducting their own mediations through the Restorative Justice Centre, the Government of Manitoba has effectively removed conflict resolution from the capable hands of community organizations that specialize in restorative processes and claimed it as their own. Authors such as Gavrielides have noted that government-run programs tend to be less effective than community organizations as government programs rely on "1–3 day training packages" for police officers, probations staff, and prison guards with no practical experience in the field of RJ.[72] Gavrielides adds that governments have expiration dates that incentivize quick and cheap programming whereas community organizations do not have these same deadlines and have often been well established in communities for long periods of time.[73]

Furthermore, by being the arbiter of which community programs can be delegated the remaining RJ referrals, the Restorative Justice Centre (and the Government of Manitoba by proxy) wields significant power over community organizations which rely on referrals for funding. What can stem from this is a dynamic where "facilitators are forced to meet arbitrary training and credentialing criteria in order to be placed on an 'approved list to practice'" RJ that forces community organizations to alter this manner of practice to fit into the government's definition of appropriate practice.[74] Ultimately, it is clear that government co-option can vary in the degree it harms access to alternative philosophies of justice, but nonetheless significantly limits who can participate in these highly desirable programs.

Even though practitioners of RJ such as Christie[75] and Braithwaite[76] frequently highlight criticisms of criminal justice systems usurping power from victims and local communities, many practitioners have not imagined RJ as operating independently from the criminal justice system. Pavlich highlights this notion among RJ practitioners and suggests that theories of RJ often see themselves as possessing a different rationale from the criminal justice system all while still entrenching their visions of RJ inside that system.[77] According to Pavlich, RJ and the criminal justice system contain two separate "governmentalities," a term that can best be understood as "the 'mentalities' that establish apparatuses of understanding, meaning horizons, to enable particular methods of ruling."[78] More specifically, Pavlich focuses on "the 'mentalities' of governance that supporters use to make sense of the practices claiming the name 'restorative justice'."[79]

To Pavlich, restorative governance is understood as "future-directed, pragmatic, problem-solving processes designed to repair, restore and effectively redress the harms of crime" as opposed to criminal justice governance that "focuses its adversarial methods on past events to determine guilt."[80] Furthermore, Pavlich notes that governors of criminal justice processes (i.e., police, lawyers, judges, correctional officers, etc.) fundamentally oppose those who govern restorative processes (stakeholders such as victims and other community agents) by way of the state's ability to exert dominate restorative processes.[81] Even though restorative and criminal justice governance fundamentally oppose one another, Pavlich notes that "[RJ] also predicates itself on key concepts within the criminal justice system" that produces a phenomenon called an "*imitor* paradox."[82] Pavlich describes the RJ "*imitor* paradox" as "a seemingly singular, internally consistent entity even though it is simultaneously committed to two opposing foundations: namely, as substitute for and imitator of criminal justice concepts and institutions."[83]

While Pavlich points out that recognizing the paradox RJ finds itself in does not discredit the achievements or claims RJ has made, Pavlich suggests that there is a need to address the consequences the paradox presents RJ through its need to replicate itself within the criminal justice framework.[84] In many respects, the paradox Pavlich highlights carries many of the same consequences previously outlined through government co-option. Unlike government co-option of RJ that identifies criminal justice governing bodies as actively seeking to establish control over RJ processes, the "*imitor* paradox" identifies proponents of RJ as already imagining RJ as an appendage to the criminal justice system because they tend to think and practice RJ within the terms and delimitations of the criminal justice system.[85] By suggesting that RJ operate as an alternative to certain criminal justice processes but remain embedded within the criminal justice system, Pavlich argues that RJ practitioners "enhance (perhaps even expand) existing criminal justice and/or legal institutions" through a self-inflicted form of co-option.[86] Although Pavlich concedes there are political advantages to "maintaining the paradoxical stance" RJ finds itself in, it is also important for proponents of RJ to reflect on the paradox as opportunity to imagine RJ independent from the criminal justice system, or more radically, becoming the system itself.[87] This is to suggest that, in order to move beyond both the consequences of both government and self-inflicted co-option, RJ practitioners need to adhere to the common notion that RJ is an independent philosophy of justice and begin identifying potential avenues that RJ can use to operate independently.

Institutionalization of Alternative Philosophies

Although the inclusion of alternative philosophies within Western criminal justice frameworks represents important progress in terms of establishing more holistic justice systems, it is important to recognize that this can come at a cost to restorative values. In a variety of Western justice systems, RJ and other alternative philosophies of justice have been worked into these legal frameworks as both an afterthought and as way to supplement traditional justice processes. This is obviously the case in the Canadian context as the 1996 sentencing reforms to the *Criminal Code* and the reforms to youth sentencing by way of the YCJA emphasize the need to use more restorative outcomes rather than relying on incarceration. However, authors such as Maglione (2021) have noted that combining restorative and traditional justice policy into one framework often results in "sterilizing the transformative potential of RJ due to the conflicting values underpinning criminal justice and RJ."[88] In his studies, Maglione presents three examples of different jurisdictions where RJ values are diluted into penal policy. According to Maglione (2021), with penal policy "one is either a 'victim' or an 'offender', there is no room for (social, personal, cultural) overlaps between those two positions."[89] This is fundamentally opposed to core values of RJ practices as they often look to address the history of victimization within those who caused harm to better address root causes of criminal behaviour. However, Maglione (2021) notes that in jurisdictions such as England and Wales, France and Norway, their RJ processes are often set up in a way where the "'victim' appears as disempowered and vulnerable whilst the 'offender' is presented as the harm-maker/wrongdoer neatly separated from their victim."[90] Further to this point of institutionalization, Maglione notes that "community members" participating in these processes are often reduced to social workers and police officers.[91] This presents a significant loss to RJ values as other significant stakeholders that would typically fall under the "community member" category, such as neighbours or family members, are barred from participating through a sort of criminal justice gatekeeping.[92]

Commentators on this phenomenon have pointed out that when RJ is situated within traditional criminal justice systems, the effectiveness of RJ practices are often measured against traditional criminal justice objectives such as offender rehabilitation and lowered recidivism rates rather than restorative values of repairing harm or meeting victim needs.[93] Maglione suggests this occurs as adopting the terminology of the criminal justice system "is a crucial condition for 'mainstreaming'" RJ practices.[94] While lower recidivism rates can be a positive by-product of restorative processes, Pavlich notes that RJ practitioners should be fundamentally concerned with focusing on upholding core values of RJ such as "helping stakeholders to define, and develop ways to heal, the harms of crime."[95] Pavlich argues such as over-emphasizing values traditionally held by the criminal justice system plays into the previously highlighted "*imitor* paradox."

Canadian legislation often reinforces the notion of institutionalization of RJ as many of the enabling frameworks for alternative philosophies of justice also emphasize the importance of criminal justice objectives. For example, among the various restorative sentencing principles outlined by the *Criminal Code*, the following retributive sentencing principles also appear:

718 The fundamental purpose of sentencing is to protect society and to contribute, along with crime prevention initiatives, to respect for the law and the maintenance of a just, peaceful and safe society by imposing just sanctions that have one or more of the following objectives:

(a) to denounce unlawful conduct and the harm done to victims or to the community that is caused by unlawful conduct;

(b) to deter the offender and other persons from committing offences;

(c) to separate offenders from society, where necessary;

(d) to assist in rehabilitating offenders;...[96]

Further to this point, the YCJA also includes numerous objectives that emphasize retributive objectives such as ensuring accountability of young offenders through meaningful consequences, rehabilitation, and reintegration.

The consequences of "mainstreaming" processes with traditional criminal justice systems have also been explored extensively. Authors such as Marder have argued that the hybridization of restorative processes and criminal justice processes often results in stakeholders losing the capacity to make decisions collectively through the restorative processes while consolidating the control justice systems can impose on citizens engaging in these processes.[97] For commentators such as Daly, the hybridization of RJ and criminal justice processes can be used to explain why RJ programs often produce more modest results than advocates of RJ expect.[98] Further to this point, Laxminarayan explains that "the mainstreaming of restorative justice may lead to a clash between safeguarding the quality of restorative justice and institutionalising these programmes."[99]

At its worst, the institutionalization of RJ can allow processes that are meant to have restorative elements to be completely overtaken or dominated by traditional justice processes. This is extremely apparent when one considers the use of conditional sentences in the Canadian justice system. The Department of Justice defines a conditional sentence as a term of imprisonment that the offender serves within the community, and that is aimed at reducing the use of incarceration.[100] Although the restorative nature of conditional sentences could be debated, Justice Lamer of the Supreme Court of Canada in the case *R v. Proulx* determined conditional sentences possess restorative traits and are "better than incarceration at achieving the restorative objectives of rehabilitation, reparations to the victim and the community, and promotion of a sense of responsibility in the offender and acknowledgment of the harm done to the victim and the community."[101] Despite this admission, Roberts notes that Justice Lamer avoids giving primacy of importance to either punishment or restorative elements of sentencing when it comes to understanding conditional sentencing in the *R v. Proulx* case.[102] As a result, conditional sentences can be seen as the epitome of hybridization of RJ and traditional criminal justice process in Canada.

Even though conditional sentences were conceived as a means of achieving restorative outcomes with punitive outcomes acting as a type of insurance policy to guarantee good behaviour of offenders who receive them, studies have demonstrated that punitive outcomes tend to occur more frequently. In a study conducted by Roach (2015), he discusses the implications conditional sentences have in the Canadian legal framework and how restorative values are often undermined by conditional sentences through an effect called "net-widening."[103] According to Roach, net-widening can be understood as "any process in which offenders are subject to more intrusive sanctions than before. Thus net widening would occur if offenders who would be fined or subject to a probation order are now subject to a conditional sentence."[104] When an offender is serving a conditional sentence, they are subjected to a number of potentially demanding conditions, such as curfews, in which any unjustified breach of the conditions can result in the offender being incarcerated.[105]

Roach's study reveals that, in the first two years of their existence, 28,000 conditional sentences were ordered but statistics show that no meaningful reduction in the number of incarcerated persons occurred.[106] In a similar national study of Canadian use of conditional sentences, Reid and Roberts found that conditional sentences only resulted in decarceration in 2008, and in the twelve years after this, resulted in a 3% increase in custodial admissions.[107] What can be made of this information is that the requirements of conditional sentences are often being breached by those who receive them and are resulting in incarceration. Roach argues that breaches of conditional sentences occur with great frequency as sentencing judges are not reserving conditional sentences for the most serious cases, but rather, giving out conditional sentences to less-serious offenders with "draconian breach provisions" that seek to provide reparations for the victims and community.[108] What is observed in Roach's study is the effect of net-widening and institutionalization of

RJ. Although conditional sentences are supposed to contain restorative elements and reduce incarceration, the onerous nature of the punitive elements of the conditional often overpower or outweigh any potential benefits conditional sentences have to offer. Of course, this is an example at its worst, but should nonetheless serve as a cautionary example of how restorative philosophies of justice can be sterilized when operating too closely to traditional criminal justice processes.

Conclusion

When it comes to expanding access to justice to include access to alternative philosophies of justice, influential Canadian legislation provides clear avenues for establishing alternative justice processes as a means of accessing justice and as a right within the Canadian justice framework. In both the *Criminal Code* and the YCJA, Canada has established provisions that establish frameworks for alternative processes of justice such as RJ to take place, as well as entrenched various restorative principles within their sentencing principles for both adult and young offenders. Further to this point, the CVBR has established information pertaining to RJ and RJ processes as a right for all victims in the Canadian justice system. Although the means for victims accessing these rights can be challenging as a result of the nature of the CVBR, it does not diminish the importance of these rights and places a greater need to address the provisions that make the right difficult to access. If the Canadian legislative framework leaves any room to doubt the importance RJ plays in terms of access to justice in Canada, decisions from Canada's Supreme Court largely put the intent behind these provisions to rest by explaining how they should be interpretated moving forward. The reasoning behind the justices' interpretation also speaks highly of the importance of access to RJ as their decision relies heavily on the comments of Parliament regarding the purpose of several legislative provisions within the *Criminal Code* and the YCJA.

Despite the importance RJ carries both historically and in the present Canadian context, it is clear that there exist several significant barriers which can limit access to alternative philosophies of justice, and in turn, access to justice. Both co-option and institutionalization of RJ processes present a similar challenge to RJ in Canada. On one hand, co-option of RJ through government exerting its influence over RJ or through practitioners attempting to consolidate RJ within the criminal justice typically results in criminal justice governing bodies dominating these processes. The power these governing bodies exert over RJ processes ultimately goes against the core principles of RJ which seek to allow stakeholders outside of the criminal justice governing bodies resolve crime. Through government and self-inflicted co-option, these principles are largely pushed to the side. In a similar vein to co-option, the institutionalization of RJ examines the potential contributions RJ can have to increasing punitive outcomes such as incarceration when hybridizing RJ processes with criminal justice processes. While RJ is not fundamentally opposed to punitive outcomes (reparations can be understood as a form of punishment), the institutionalization of RJ sees RJ values completely overlooked to produce harsher outcomes than RJ would typically prescribe. Ultimately, this results in the sanitization of RJ processes.

Two recommendations can be made in terms of correcting the course for RJ. First, more funding needs to be allocated to community organizations. Academics such as Gavrielides have highlighted the capacity of community organizations to handle caseloads of around 100 offences on a budget of $100,000 (less than $1000 per case).[109] This increase in funding can support community organizations' ability to take on larger caseloads and return conflict resolution back to community. Secondly, policy that governs restorative frameworks need to be less restrictive to ensure greater access to RJ. Governments can enact policy that can limit which offences are eligible for RJ and who can conduct restorative processes. For these procedures to be changed, government and the criminal justice institutions need to be willing to let go of power they have traditionally held over this policy which may prove to be a challenge moving forward. What can be made of these barriers should be examined through the lens Pavlich offers in his work. In order to increase access to justice through alternative philosophies of justice, it may be time to imagine how RJ can exist independently of the criminal justice system to better serve individuals requesting these processes.

Notes

1. United Nation General Assembly, "International Covenant on Civil and Political Rights," *United Nations, Treaty Series*, 999 (16 December 1966): 171.
2. *Canadian Charter of Rights and Freedoms*, Part 1 of the Constitution Act, 1982, being Schedule B to the Canada Act 1982 (UK), 1982, c. 11.

3. Richard Wagner, "Access to Justice: Societal Imperative," Supreme Court of Canada, May 14, 2019. https://www.scc-csc.ca/judges-juges/spe-dis/rw-2018-10-04-eng.aspx.
4. Ab Currie, "The Legal Problems of Everyday Life: The Nature, Extent and Consequences of Justiciable Problems Experienced by Canadians," Department of Justice Canada, 2007. https://publications.gc.ca/collections/collection_2010/justice/J3-2-2007-5-eng.pdf.
5. Jo-Anne Wemmers, "Restorative Justice for Victims of Crime: A Victim-Oriented Approach to Restorative Justice," *International Review of Victimology* 1, no. 9 (2002): 43–59.
6. Charles Trumbull, "The Victims of Victim Participation in International Criminal Proceedings," *Michigan Journal of International Law* 29, no. 4 (2008): 777–826.
7. Claire Garbett, "The International Criminal Court and Restorative Justice: Victims, Participation and the Processes of Justice," *Restorative Justice* 5, no. 2 (2017): 198–220.
8. *Criminal Code*, R.S.A. 1985, c. C-46.
9. *Youth Criminal Justice Act*, SC 2002. c. 1.
10. *Canadian Victims Bill of Rights,* SC 2015, c. 13.
11. Susan Szmania and Daniel Mangis, "Finding the Right Time and Place: Case Study Comparison of the Expression of Offender Remorse in Traditional Justice and Restorative Justice Contexts," *Marquette Law Review* 89, no. 2 (2005): 335–58.
12. Morten Pedersen, "The ICC, the Rohingya and the Limitations of Retributive Justice," *Australian Journal of International Affairs* 73, no. 1 (2019): 9–15.
13. Giuseppe Maglione, "Restorative Justice and the State. Untimely Objections Against the Institutionalisation of Restorative Justice," *British Journal of Community Justice* 17, no. 1 (2021): 4–22.
14. Maglione, "Restorative Justice and the State," 5.
15. Freider Dünkel, Phillip Horsfield, and Andrea Parosanu, "Introduction," In *European Research on Restorative Juvenile Justice—Vol. 1, Research and Selection of the Most Effective Juvenile Restorative Justice Practices in Europe: Snapshots from 28 EU Member States*, eds. Frieder Dünkel, Philip Horsfield, and Andrea Parosanu (Brussels: International Juvenile Justice Observatory, 2015), 1–17.
16. Tony Marshall, *Restorative Justice: An Overview* (London: Home Office, 1999).
17. Katherine Doolin, "But What Does It Mean? Seeking Definitional Clarity in Restorative Justice," *The Journal of Criminal Law* 71, no. 5 (2007): 427–44.
18. Doolin, "But What Does It Mean" 427–44.

19. Kathleen Daly, "What is Restorative Justice? Fresh Answers to a Vexed Question," *Victims & Offenders* 11, no. 1 (2016): 9–29.
20. Daniel Van Ness, and Karen Strong. *Restoring Justice: An Introduction to Restorative Justice* (New York: Routledge, 2015).
21. Van Ness and Strong, *Restoring Justice.*
22. Andrew Woolford, and Amanda Nelund, *The Politics of Restorative Justice: A Critical Introduction* (Halifax & Winnipeg: Fernwood Publishing, 2019).
23. Woolford and Nelund, *The Politics of Restorative Justice*, 11.
24. Ibid., 13.
25. Ibid., 13–14.
26. Ted Watchel, "Defining Restorative Justice," International Institute for Restorative Practices, 2016. https://www.iirp.edu/images/pdf/Defining-Restorative_Nov-2016.pdf.
27. Barbara Tomporowski, Manon Buck, Catherine Bargen, and Valarie Binder, "Reflections on the Past, Present, and Future of Restorative Justice in Canada," *Alberta Law Review* 48, no. 4 (2011): 815–29.
28. Tomporowski, Buck, Bargen and Binder, "Reflections," 826.
29. Public Safety Canada, "Increasing the Use of Restorative Justice in Criminal Matters in Canada—Baseline Report," Government of Canada, 2020, https://www.publicsafety.gc.ca/cnt/rsrcs/pblctns/2020-resjus-jusrep/index-en.aspx.
30. *Criminal Code*, s.717(1)(a).
31. Government of Canada. "Youth Criminal Justice Act Summary and Background," 2021. https://www.justice.gc.ca/eng/cj-jp/yj-jj/tools-outils/back-hist.html.
32. Public Prosecution Services of Canada. "Public Prosecution Services of Canada Deskbook," Government of Canada, 2015. https://www.ppsc-sppc.gc.ca/eng/pub/fpsd-sfpg/fps-sfp/tpd/p3/ch08.html.
33. Government of Canada. "Restorative Justice—Legislation and Policy," 2021. https://www.justice.gc.ca/eng/cj-jp/rj-jr/lp.html.
34. Government of Saskatchewan. "The Alternative Measures and Extrajudicial Sanctions: Policies," Ministry of Justice, 2013. https://www.saskatchewan.ca/residents/justice-crime-and-the-law/courts-and-sentencing/alternatives-to-going-to-court/alternative-measures-extrajudicial-sanctions-programs.
35. Public Safety Canada, "Increasing the Use of Restorative."
36. Ibid.
37. *Criminal Code*, s.718(a)–(c).
38. *Criminal Code*, s.718(2)(d)–(e).
39. Kent Roach, "Changing Punishment at the Turn of the Century: Restorative Justice on the Rise," *Canadian Journal of Criminology* 42, no. 3 (2000): 249–80.

40. Roach, "Changing Punishment at the Turn of the Century," 253–54.
41. *R. v. Gladue*, [1999] 1 S.C.R. 688 at para. 18.
42. Ibid., para. 52.
43. Ibid., para. 48.
44. Ibid., para. 57.
45. Ibid., para. 43.
46. Correctional Services Canada, "Indigenous Healing Lodges," Government of Canada, 2021. https://www.csc-scc.gc.ca/002/003/002003-2000-en.shtml.
47. Department of Justice, "Spotlight on Gladue: Challenges, Experiences, and Possibilities in Canada's Criminal Justice System," Research and Statistics Division, 2017. http://publications.gc.ca/collections/collection_2018/jus/J4-46-2017-eng.pdf.
48. *R v. Gladue* at para. 37.
49. *Youth Criminal Justice Act*, "Preamble."
50. Government of Canada, "Youth Criminal Justice Act Summary and Background."
51. *Youth Criminal Justice Act*, s.10.
52. *Youth Criminal Justice Act*, s.38(2)(d)-(e).
53. Sanjeev Anand, "Crafting Youth Sentences: The Roles of Rehabilitation, Proportionality, Restraint, Restorative Justice, and Race under the Youth Criminal Justice Act," *Alberta Law Review* 40, no. 4 (2003): 943–64.
54. Anand, "Crafting Youth Sentences," 959.
55. Ibid., 960.
56. *Youth Criminal Justice Act*, s.38(2)(e)(i).
57. Government of Canada, "Youth Criminal Justice Act Summary and Background."
58. *Canadian Victims Bill of Rights*, s.6(b).
59. *Canadian Victims Bill of Rights*, s.47.
60. Kim Zarzour, "How a Markham Sex Assault Survivor Found Justice—and Peace," *Toronto Star*, November 2, 2019. https://www.thestar.com/news/gta/2019/11/02/how-a-markham-sex-assault-survivor-found-justice-and-peace.html?rf.
61. Marlee Liss, "Marlee Liss," 2021. https://www.marleeliss.com/.
62. Zarzour, "How a Markham Sex Assault Survivor Found Justice."
63. Department of Justice, "Research at a Glance—Restorative Justice," Research and Statistics Division, 2018. https://www.justice.gc.ca/eng/rp-pr/jr/rg-rco/2018/mar08.pdf.
64. Department of Justice, "Research at a Glance—Restorative Justice."
65. Nils Christie, "Conflicts as Property," *The British Journal of Criminology* 17, no. 1 (1997): 1–15.
66. Reed Leverton, "The Case for Best Practice Standards in Restorative Justice Processes," *American Journal of Trial Advocacy* 31, no. 3 (2008): 501–30.

67. Public Prosecution Services of Canada, "Public Prosecution Services of Canada Deskbook."
68. Ibid.
69. Government of Saskatchewan, "Alternative Measures and Extrajudical Sanctions—Program Manual," Ministry of Justice, 2013. https://www.saskatchewan.ca/residents/justice-crime-and-the-law/courts-and-sentencing/alternatives-to-going-to-court/alternative-measures-extrajudicial-sanctions-programs.
70. Government of Manitoba. "Criminal Justice System Modernization Strategy," 2018. https://www.gov.mb.ca/justice/pubs/criminaljusticereform.pdf.
71. Government of Manitoba, "Criminal Justice System Modernization Strategy," 5.
72. Theo Gavrielides, "Where is Restorative Justice Heading?" *Probations Junior* 2, no. 4 (2013): 79–95.
73. Gavrielides, "Where is Restorative Justice Heading?".
74. Leverton, "The Case for Best Practice," 526.
75. Christie, "Conflicts as Property."
76. John Braithwaite, *Restorative Justice and Responsive Regulation*. Oxford: OUP, 2002.
77. George Pavlich, *Governing Paradoxes of Restorative Justice*. London: GlassHouse Press, 2005.
78. Pavlich, *Governing Paradoxes of Restorative Justice*, 10.
79. Ibid.
80. Ibid., 13.
81. Ibid.
82. Ibid, 14.
83. Ibid.
84. Ibid, 15.
85. Ibid.
86. Ibid, 18.
87. Ibid, 23.
88. Maglione, "Restorative Justice and the State," 5.
89. Ibid., 13.
90. Ibid.
91. Ibid., 14.
92. Ibid.
93. Pavlich, *Governing Paradoxes of Restorative Justice*.
94. Maglione, "Restorative Justice and the State," 13.
95. Pavlich, *Governing Paradoxes of Restorative Justice*, 13.
96. *Criminal Code*, s. 718(a)-(d).
97. Ian Marder, "Institutionalising Restorative Justice in the Police: Key Findings from a Study of Two English Police Forces," *Contemporary Justice Review* 23, no. 4 (2020): 500–26.

98. Kathleen Daly, "Mind the Gap: Restorative Justice in Theory and Practice," in *Restorative Justice and Criminal Justice: Competing or Reconcilable Paradigms?* eds. Andreas Von Hirsch, Julian Roberts, Anthony Bottoms, Kent Roach, and Mara Schiff (Australia: Hart Publishing, 2003), 219–36.
99. Malini Laxminarayan, "Accessibility and Initiation of Restorative Justice," European Forum for Restorative Justice, 2014. https://www.euforumrj.org/sites/default/files/2019-11/accessibility_and_initiation_of_rj_website_0.pdf.
100. Department of Justice. "The Future of Conditional Sentencing: Perspectives of Appellate Judges," Government of Canada, 2015. https://www.justice.gc.ca/eng/rp-pr/csj-sjc/ccs-ajc/rr04_8/p1.html.
101. R. *v.* Proulx, [2000] 1 S.C.R. 61 at para. 127.
102. Julian Roberts, "The Changing Face of Conditional Sentencing," Department of Justice, 2015. https://www.justice.gc.ca/eng/rp-pr/csj-sjc/jsp-sjp/op00_3-po00_3/p4.html#foot148.
103. Kent Roach, "The Changing Face of Conditional Sentencing," Department of Justice, 2015. https://www.justice.gc.ca/eng/rp-pr/csj-sjc/jsp-sjp/op00_3-po00_3/p3.html.
104. Roach, "The Changing Face of Conditional Sentencing," para. 6.
105. Andrew Reid, and Julian Roberts, "Revisiting the Conditional Sentence of Imprisonment After 20 Years: Is Community Custody Now an Endangered Species?" *Canadian Criminal Law Review* 24, no. 1 (2019): 1–37.
106. Roach, "The Changing Face of Conditional Sentencing."
107. Reid and Roberts, "Revisiting the Conditional Sentence," 28.
108. Roach, "The Changing Face of Conditional Sentencing," para. 13–14.
109. Gavrielides, "Where is Restorative Justice Heading?" 83.

Bibliography

Anand, Sanjeev. "Crafting Youth Sentences: The Roles of Rehabilitation, Proportionality, Restraint, Restorative Justice, and Race under the Youth Criminal Justice Act." *Alberta Law Review* 40, no. 4 (2003): 943–64.

Braithwaite, John. *Restorative Justice and Responsive Regulation.* Oxford: OUP, 2002.

Canadian Charter of Rights and Freedoms, Part 1 of the Constitution Act, 1982, being Schedule B to the Canada Act 1982 (UK), 1982, c 11.

Canadian Victims Bill of Rights, SC 2015, c 13.

Christie, Nils. "Conflicts as Property." *The British Journal of Criminology* 17, no. 1 (1997): 1–15.

Correctional Services Canada. "Indigenous Healing Lodges." Government of Canada, 2021. https://www.csc-scc.gc.ca/002/003/002003-2000-en.shtml.

Criminal Code, R.S.A. 1985, c. C-46.

Currie, Ab. "The Legal Problems of Everyday Life: The Nature, Extent and Consequences of Justiciable Problems Experienced by Canadians." Department of Justice Canada, 2007. https://publications.gc.ca/collections/collection_2010/justice/J3-2-2007-5-eng.pdf.

Daly, Kathleen. "Mind the Gap: Restorative Justice in Theory and Practice." In *Restorative Justice and Criminal Justice: Competing or Reconcilable Paradigms?*, edited by Andreas Von Hirsch, Julian Roberts, Anthony Bottoms, Kent Roach, and Mara Schiff, 219–36. Australia: Hart Publishing, 2003.

———. "What is Restorative Justice? Fresh Answers to a Vexed Question." *Victims & Offenders* 11, no. 1 (2016): 9–29.

Department of Justice. "The Future of Conditional Sentencing: Perspectives of Appellate Judges." Government of Canada, 2015. https://www.justice.gc.ca/eng/rp-pr/csj-sjc/ccs-ajc/rr04_8/p1.html.

———. "Research at a Glance – Restorative Justice." Research and Statistics Division, 2018. https://www.justice.gc.ca/eng/rp-pr/jr/rg-rco/2018/mar08.pdf.

———. "Spotlight on Gladue: Challenges, Experiences, and Possibilities in Canada's Criminal Justice System." Research and Statistics Division, 2017. http://publications.gc.ca/collections/collection_2018/jus/J4-46-2017-eng.pdf.

Doolin, Katherine. "But What Does It Mean? Seeking Definitional Clarity in Restorative Justice." *The Journal of Criminal Law* 71, no. 5 (2007): 427–44.

Dünkel, Freider, Phillip Horsfield, and Andrea Parosanu, "Introduction." in *European Research on Restorative Juvenile Justice—Vol. 1, Research and Selection of the Most Effective Juvenile Restorative Justice Practices in Europe: Snapshots from 28 EU Member States*, edited by Frieder Dünkel, Philip Horsfield, and Andrea Parosanu, 1–17. Brussels: International Juvenile Justice Observatory, 2015.

Garbett, Claire. "The International Criminal Court and Restorative Justice: Victims, Participation and the Processes of Justice." *Restorative Justice* 5, no. 2 (2017): 198–220.

Gavrielides, Theo. "Where is Restorative Justice Heading?" *Probations Junior* 2, no. 4 (2013): 79–95.

Government of Canada. "Restorative Justice—Legislation and Policy." 2021. https://www.justice.gc.ca/eng/cj-jp/rj-jr/lp.html.

———. "Youth Criminal Justice Act Summary and Background." 2021. https://www.justice.gc.ca/eng/cj-jp/yj-jj/tools-outils/back-hist.html.

Government of Manitoba. "Criminal Justice System Modernization Strategy." 2018. https://www.gov.mb.ca/justice/pubs/criminaljusticereform.pdf.

Government of Saskatchewan. "Alternative Measures and Extrajudical Sanctions—Program Manual." Ministry of Justice, 2013. https://www.saskatchewan.ca/residents/justice-crime-and-the-law/courts-and-sentencing/alternatives-to-going-to-court/alternative-measures-extrajudicial-sanctions-programs.

———. "The Alternative Measures and Extrajudicial Sanctions: Policies." Ministry of Justice, 2013. https://www.saskatchewan.ca/residents/justice-crime-and-the-law/courts-and-sentencing/alternatives-to-going-to-court/alternative-measures-extrajudicial-sanctions-programs.

Laxminarayan, Malini. "Accessibility and Initiation of Restorative Justice." European Forum for Restorative Justice, 2014. https://www.euforumrj.org/sites/default/files/2019-11/accessibility_and_initiation_of_rj_website_0.pdf.

Leverton, Reed. "The Case for Best Practice Standards in Restorative Justice Processes." *American Journal of Trial Advocacy* 31, no. 3 (2008): 501–30.

Liss, Marlee. "Marlee Liss." 2021. https://www.marleeliss.com/.

Marder, Ian. "Institutionalising Restorative Justice in the Police: Key Findings from a Study of Two English Police Forces." *Contemporary Justice Review* 23, no. 4 (2020): 500–26.

Marshall, Tony. *Restorative Justice: An Overview*. London: Home Office, 1999.

Maglione, Giuseppe. "Restorative Justice and the State. Untimely Objections Against the Institutionalisation of Restorative Justice." *British Journal of Community Justice* 17, no. 1 (2021): 4–22.

Pavlich, George. *Governing Paradoxes of Restorative Justice*. London: GlassHouse Press, 2005.

Pedersen, Morten. "The ICC, the Rohingya and the Limitations of Retributive Justice." *Australian Journal of International Affairs* 73, no. 1 (2019): 9–15.

Public Prosecution Services of Canada. "Public Prosecution Services of Canada Deskbook." Government of Canada, 2015. https://www.ppsc-sppc.gc.ca/eng/pub/fpsd-sfpg/fps-sfp/tpd/p3/ch08.html.

Public Safety Canada. "Increasing the Use of Restorative Justice in Criminal Matters in Canada—Baseline Report." Government of Canada, 2020. https://www.publicsafety.gc.ca/cnt/rsrcs/pblctns/2020-resjus-jusrep/index-en.aspx.

Reid, Andrew, and Julian Roberts. "Revisiting the Conditional Sentence of Imprisonment After 20 Years: Is Community Custody Now an Endangered Species?" *Canadian Criminal Law Review* 24, no. 1 (2019): 1–37.

Roach, Kent. "The Changing Face of Conditional Sentencing." Department of Justice, 2015. https://www.justice.gc.ca/eng/rp-pr/csj-sjc/jsp-sjp/op00_3-po00_3/p3.html.

———. "Changing Punishment at the Turn of the Century: Restorative Justice on the Rise." *Canadian Journal of Criminology* 42, no. 3 (2000): 249–80.

Roberts, Julian. "The Changing Face of Conditional Sentencing." Department of Justice, 2015. https://www.justice.gc.ca/eng/rp-pr/csj-sjc/jsp-sjp/op00_3-po00_3/p4.html#foot148.

R. v. Gladue, [1999] 1 S.C.R. 688.

R. v. Proulx, [2000] 1 S.C.R. 61.

Szmania, Susan, and Daniel Mangis. "Finding the Right Time and Place: Case Study Comparison of the Expression of Offender Remorse in Traditional Justice and Restorative Justice Contexts." *Marquette Law Review* 89, no. 2 (2005): 335–58.

Tomporowski, Barbara, Manon Buck, Catherine Bargen, and Valarie Binder. "Reflections on the Past, Present, and Future of Restorative Justice in Canada." *Alberta Law Review* 48, no. 4 (2011): 815–29.

Trumbull, Charles. "The Victims of Victim Participation in International Criminal Proceedings." *Michigan Journal of International Law* 29, no. 4 (2008): 777–826.

United Nation General Assembly. "International Covenant on Civil and Political Rights." *United Nations, Treaty Series* 999 (16 December 1966): 171. https://www.refworld.org/docid/3ae6b3aa0.html.

Van Ness, Daniel and Karen Strong. *Restoring Justice: An Introduction to Restorative Justice*. New York: Routledge, 2015.

Wagner, Richard. "Access to Justice: Societal Imperative." Supreme Court of Canada, May 14, 2019. https://www.scc-csc.ca/judges-juges/spe-dis/rw-2018-10-04-eng.aspx.

Watchel, Ted. "Defining Restorative Justice." International Institute for Restorative Practices, 2016. https://www.iirp.edu/images/pdf/Defining-Restorative_Nov-2016.pdf.

Wemmers, Jo-Anne. "Restorative Justice for Victims of Crime: A Victim-Oriented Approach to Restorative Justice." *International Review of Victimology* 1, no. 9 (2002): 43–59.

Woolford, Andrew, and Amanda Nelund. *The Politics of Restorative Justice: A Critical Introduction*. Halifax & Winnipeg: Fernwood Publishing, 2019.

Youth Criminal Justice Act, SC 2002. c. 1.

Zarzour, Kim. "How a Markham Sex Assault Survivor Found Justice—and Peace." *Toronto Star*. November 2, 2019. https://www.thestar.com/news/gta/2019/11/02/how-a-markham-sex-assault-survivor-found-justice-and-peace.html?rf.

Allyship and Equality in Youth Organizations: A Case Study of HOBY Canada

Abigail Myles

Allyship is a necessary tool to combat discrimination and implement greater accessibility, diversity, and inclusion (ADI) in human rights. Allies or allyship refer to individuals that desire to support or engage with social movements protesting or combating injustice that impacts individuals belonging to a different identity group.[1] Allies do not personally experience the injustice and, therefore, hold privilege and isolation from the oppression being combatted.[2] As out-group members within the movement, allies must continually seek guidance, support autonomy, and amplify voices of those in the impacted group to avoid recreating harm, co-optation, or serving self-interest.[3] Through networking, collaboration, and the sharing of ideas, barriers can be removed for sustainable peace and an environment where human rights can be fully realized.[4] Many organizations, such as Hugh O'Brian Youth Leadership (HOBY) Canada,[5]

A. Myles (✉)
University of Manitoba, Winnipeg, MB, Canada
e-mail: abigail.s.myles@gmail.com

L. E. Reimer and K. Standish (eds.), *Perspectives on Justice, Indigeneity, Gender, and Security in Human Rights Research*,
https://doi.org/10.1007/978-981-99-1930-7_3

ignite hope for equality as they are disrupting standard practices by intentionally addressing inequality and discrimination in their operations. The HOBY Canada case study demonstrates how all people and organizations can be optimized to create space for allyship action and provide a model for ADI transformation.

HOBY Canada's journey of expanding the youth empowerment movement to ongoing allyship action and dismantling discrimination is outlined in this chapter. Their allyship model presents a practical process that all organizations can utilize for greater inclusion. It follows a frame stemming from stages of generation, conceptualization, application, and ongoing action. The stages do not aim to act as a one-size-fits-all method of increasing ADI but provide insights for enacting relevant and practical allyship action in individual and organizational settings. Allyship for human rights implementation requires attention to contextual and cultural realities for effectiveness. A central theme of hope and empowerment is intended to inspire action and provide a roadmap to use when incorporating allyship in daily life. It is through a posture of collaboration, humility, and perseverance that average individuals can enact extraordinary change. All individuals and organizations have a societal responsibility to engage in allyship action to improve ADI and address discrimination, facilitating the realization of dignity, equality, and human rights through cumulative participation.

Key Language

The key language used throughout this chapter is defined because it holds power due to present and historical dynamics that are continually evolving and being reconstructed.[6] When describing these constructs, the language chosen must be assessed as it is an active reinforcement or resistance of the power hierarchies.[7] When power hierarchies and injustice are recognized and addressed, trust and progress are expanded.[8] As language is evaluated, a multitude of preferences is used by groups to define roles and relationships.[9] The key language is chosen to provide clarity and outline distinctions, recognizing that it will be preferred by some while contested by others; however, it is not intended to offend.

Accessibility, Diversity, and Inclusion (ADI)

HOBY Canada brands their allyship through the lens of ADI to incorporate accessibility within diversity and inclusion. It is more representative of socioeconomic barriers, the shared understandings, and organizational goals in allyship. This aims to expand the focus of allyship to include more impacted groups that face barriers to opportunity in the organization.

Dominant Culture and Oppressive Systems

Dominant culture refers to the norms and narratives that advantage a dominant group over all others, creating distinctions of an in-group and out-groups.[10] The dominant group is given the power to contain control and set the standards for and over all other groups.[11] These norms marginalize out-groups, and as they combine with in-group societal power, they facilitate discrimination, inequality, and oppression based on group membership.[12] Systems of oppression are hidden by societal patterns and sentiments of universality, even when one identity is represented in positions of power and control.[13] Therefore, terminology of dominant and impacted are used in reference to current power dynamics to accurately address social reality, inspire transformation, and avoid further diversion among communities. As these roots of inequality and privilege are revealed, barriers to inter-group relationships and activities can be reduced for collaboration in pursuit of correcting injustice.[14]

What is HOBY Canada?

The HOBY origin story recounts an experience in 1958 with German Nobel Peace Prize winner Albert Schweitzer, where American actor, Hugh O'Brian, witnessed actions and programs that pursued justice in Africa. At the end of this experience, O'Brian was challenged by Schweitzer to use what he had learned in his life and actions when returning home.[15] Youth were not empowered, and O'Brian considered youth to be the greatest potential for enacting positive change.[16] Schweitzer's teachings inspired O'Brian to create and implement HOBY youth leadership opportunities for high school students with opportunities for continued involvement.

HOBY Canada develops leadership experiences that range from single-day to 3-Day workshops and seminars across Canada. Youth are promoted in HOBY Canada as capable and powerful advocates in allyship that are empowered to cultivate change for human rights. HOBY Canada challenges traditional understandings of leadership, believing that it spurs from action that goes beyond titles or skills.[17] Instead, it is believed that all people have the potential to become leaders and use their influence and actions for transformation through their everyday interactions and responses.[18]

All HOBY Canada operations are completed by previous HOBY alumni that volunteer their time to support the continuation of these opportunities within their communities.[19] Volunteerism and participation bridge generational and demographic differences between volunteers and participants to frame a learning environment of exploration and collaboration.[20] The curriculum delivered at HOBY Canada programs empowers ambassadors to confront problems and increase exposure to new perspectives.[21] Emphasis on participation and youth voice in HOBY Canada programs breaks down traditional power dynamics that limit capacity by fostering space to build shared meaning among participants.[22] HOBY Canada strives for a better tomorrow through the investment in leaders of today.

Why HOBY Canada?

HOBY Canada shapes the youth leadership movement through dedication to core values of volunteerism, integrity, excellence, diversity, innovative thinking, community partnerships, and lifelong learning opportunities.[23] These are reinforced by guiding principles of empowering "how to think and not what to think."[24] These are the themes grounding the organization in authentic leadership that informs discussion and action.[25] Further, individual senses of meaning, purpose, and identity are positively recognized in the organization as motivations for action and change. HOBY Canada invests in individual motivation to cultivate a passion that produces innovation and transformation in leadership and change.[26] Dedication to these organizational foundations is envisioned in program elements, such as diversity panels that seek to increase perspectives and representation at events. HOBY Canada is committed to programs and curricula that display what leadership should be and are not confined by normalized practices of dominant narratives. This fosters an organizational culture of support to remove barriers related to ADI. The resulting innovative and ever-changing nature of the organization has created a reputation of progression and open-mindedness. Thus, the organization's alumni and networks expect a response and allyship action in the face of social injustice.

When confronted with divisive topics in media and popular culture discourse, HOBY Canada claims a sense of responsibility to use their platform for justice and inclusion. HOBY Canada models transparency by openly displaying its allyship action to encourage alumni to begin their personal allyship journeys. HOBY Canada's alumni predominantly identify with the dominant culture and are looking to be involved in transformational change. Therefore, social movements provide opportunities for organizational education and action alongside alumni. All identity groups should be involved in realizing equality and human rights because all groups are impacted by dominant systems and the inequalities they cause.[27] HOBY Canada shifts mindsets of denial in the dominant culture to inquiry and opportunity for identifying and correcting injustice. By reframing this mindset, barriers of confidence lessen, and the potential for good is increased to facilitate a space of collaboration, humility, and perseverance. This generates hope for a continued legacy of increasing ADI and allyship at all levels and sites of the organization.

Case Context

There are various contributing factors that spark the development of intentional ADI evaluation in HOBY Canada. COVID-19 leads to a reality of uncertainty, ongoing change, and new structures in all realms of life. As a result, all in-person HOBY Canada affiliated events were canceled, and the organization restructured its priorities to introspection and structural assessment. Further, the large-scale resurgence of the Black Lives Matter movement ignited public discourse and political action bringing attention to racism and discrimination across North America. The HOBY Canada board of directors released a statement of solidarity in support of BIPOC communities. The statement explicitly called out and condemned actions rooted in white supremacy and discrimination that are engrained in the dominant culture, including within HOBY Canada. However, the board of directors and alumni were not content with ending their allyship at this point and pursued further evaluation and action.

In preliminary discussions, the impacts of the Black Lives Matter movement generated a focus on pursuing greater ADI in solidarity with BIPOC alumni. This sparked exploration of allyship, what it means to the organization, and their ability to set an example for alumni that desire to respond to injustice. Themes of representation and recruitment took forefront positions in the focus of ADI discussions. The HOBY Canada leadership agreed that the organization lacked an accurate representation of the Canadian landscape, which needed to be addressed. Upcoming hiring for the Board of Directors was approaching and seemed to be a natural focal point for beginning the change processes within the organization.

HOBY Canada Response

The process of HOBY Canada's allyship journey is categorized into four main stages: generation, conceptualization, application, and ongoing action. First, the generation of ideas initiates the process and supports the identification of problems and solutions. Second, conceptualization begins to define specific problems and solutions to take abstract ideas into practical plans. Third, the application outlines the actions implemented to initiate transformation within HOBY Canada. Finally, ongoing actions that occur throughout and following the process are revealed. These stages provide overarching frameworks to spark and support allyship action.

Generation

HOBY Canada shapes their vision of allyship with brainstorming and possibilities. This incites a sense of unrestricted production to maximize potential. An educational focus supports the development of foundational knowledge to ground understanding and increases awareness of current discourse. Brainstorming and reflection are paired with ongoing research to expand the identification of areas in the organization that contain ADI barriers. Moreover, areas of confidence in ADI throughout the organization are highlighted as likely blind spots in evaluation. This collection begins the process of identifying all potential actions to increase ADI at all levels and aspects of the organization.

The brainstorm list of action items is categorized to support the application. Tasks are intentionally placed under specific portfolios to reduce becoming overwhelmed and to aid in the execution of developed plans. Briefs outlining positional and site responsibility are drafted with support notes to inform members of the organization's expectations and partnerships for implementation. The unassigned tasks are specified as unaddressed gaps and barriers in the organization. Exposure of limitations is utilized as a guide for building potential infrastructure for ongoing evaluation, implementation, and accountability within the organization.

Conceptualization

Central to the conceptualization stage is processing the generated ideals into practical strategies for preparation and application. To mobilize action in the organization, a proposed action plan is drafted with avenues that encompass the outlined barriers. The intention to address the long-term vision of barrier removal in association with immediate and practical responses supports the initiation and continuity of the allyship journey.[28] Three avenues are provided for achieving greater ADI in HOBY Canada. Creating and hiring a Director of Diversity and Inclusion is the first avenue of consideration in the proposal. This position is tasked with the evaluation of organizational programs and operations through an ADI lens. This includes providing proposals for correction and improvement in operations or partnering with specific sites and committees that have ADI requests or concerns. Second, an internal ADI evaluation is proposed where the board of director members are involved in a systematic ADI audit of the organization. Inclusion of positionality and bias training, volunteer diversity inventory, program review, and policy analysis would produce a foundational understanding to prepare board members. Third, an external ADI evaluation is presented to hire a third-party consultant. They would conduct an organizational review and provide steps needed to be taken for improvement. This base would outline a customized, realistic, and effective plan for the organization and its capacity. As a volunteer organization, consideration of the capacity and limitations of volunteers is required at the forefront of change processes to reduce procrastination or partial implementation. This approach cultivates hope for expansive improvement across the organization over time while ensuring direct action that avoids delays in an application.

To support the conceptualization approach, the board of directors provides opportunities for alumni to voice their concerns and contribute. A survey is created to collect alumni feedback on operations, their experience, barriers, and concerns that they witness or experience within the organization. Further, virtual focus groups open to all alumni and volunteers increase opportunities for alumni to engage with, shape, and be represented in the change processes.

HOBY Canada prioritizes the lived experiences of alumni and participants. The planning and facilitation of interactive and collaborative learning environments engage the knowledge and experience of alumni as a resource.[29] This enhances the ability of the board of directors to accurately represent the HOBY Canada alumni base, their diverse experiences, and identities.[30] Reducing hierarchy in the learning process welcomes larger exploration, risk, and challenging discussion to support transformation.[31] In allyship and human rights action, this encourages innovative thinking and critique necessary for new developments and inspiration.

Application

The engagement of local and impacted populations is central to allyship and human rights processes for greater expansion, impact, and ownership.[32] Therefore, the survey outlines key aspects of all programs and operations in HOBY Canada: programming, recruitment, training, volunteerism, and general concerns. Each category allows an open opportunity for alumni to identify barriers they encounter, witness, or foresee across operations and initiatives. Next, alumni identify or suggest improvements for that sector of the organization. These responses are compiled for the board of directors to review. Second, the focus groups follow the survey structure to highlighting barriers and suggested solutions for improvement. Alumni contributions are developed through brainstorming and inquiry in the focus group. Insights and data collected from alumni are cultivated by the board of directors into a Diversity Action Plan for strategic ADI enhancement throughout the organization.

The HOBY Canada board of directors vote upon specific, actionable items for implementation that include the recruitment and facilitation of an ADI task force. This task force is composed of alumni passionate about pursuing ongoing ADI education, evaluation, and action within the organization. The Directors of Diversity and Inclusion are responsible for overseeing and facilitating the ADI task force, managing allocated ADI funds, and organizing large-scale ADI evaluation projects. In setting this precedent, the current HOBY Canada leaders are shifting organizational priorities that increase ADI intentionality and emphasize its significance.

This hopes to ensure that complicity is avoided, and core values of excellence and innovative thinking are infused in all operations of HOBY Canada.

Ongoing Action

The board of directors primarily identifies as members of the dominant culture, being majority white, able-bodied, middle class, etc. Therefore, continual education must be at the cornerstone of every step of the HOBY Canada allyship journey. HOBY Canada board members are continually encouraged to diversify their learning outlets and resources to cultivate an understanding of those with lived experience. This aims to support the amplification of diverse perspectives when they are not physically represented within the alumni network or the board of directors' team. Expansion of knowledge and perspectives require continual dialogue for the full realization of potential in the organization. Brainstorming sessions and allotted time in meetings dedicated to ADI allow for discussion that explores personal experience, researched understanding, and differing interpretations. Shared understanding and knowledge among the organization's leadership develop an evolving foundation for action. This generates greater acceptance and belief in the allyship process. From these roots, HOBY Canada identifies barriers to equality and accumulates tools for change and ADI improvements throughout the organization. Incorporating transparency throughout the process for alumni via various platforms and updates increases engagement and invites alumni to join the allyship journey. Creating space for alumni representation and interaction supports the connection of abstract concepts directly into practical action.

HOBY Canada sets an example of daily and practical steps that can be taken by individuals or organizations to engage with anti-discrimination and creating hope for a just and equal future. In the field of human rights, the ongoing actions of diversifying resources, shared knowledge, dialogue, transparency, and accountability are similarly central to effectiveness. Progression and enhancement in the field are optimized when these tenets are valued, as it expands the accesses and possibilities to combat injustice. As displayed in the case of HOBY Canada, these themes can be practically incorporated into the routines of organizations. Further, it provides opportunities to bridge the theoretical and practical approaches emerging to maximize possibilities for human rights realization.

Key Takeaways

Collaboration

Individual inquiry and opportunity in HOBY Canada spark a communal conversation that produces expansive changes. By voicing concern and interest to the director team, a network of invested members is cultivated to pursue change. When concerns and passions are not voiced, opportunities for positive action are missed. In this case, the support and investment of HOBY Canada volunteers and alumni are crucial in ideation to actionable change. Without a significant commitment to this pursuit and the agreement of upper-level leadership, this process would look extremely different. Therefore, the discovery of community within organizations and those completing similar work elsewhere is central. This broadens the influence of the project within the organization and expands the network of ideas available to the team. HOBY Canada provides an example of individual passions influencing sustainable, collective action with the ability to transform societal structures.[33] Collaboration must be held at the center of progress to foster an atmosphere of restoration and interconnectedness that recognizes the inherent dignity and worth of everyone's story.[34] Reconciliation and common purpose are achieved for transformation through restoration and the building of relationships. This is crucial to the pursuit of human rights and social justice as all groups and identities are empowered and enlisted in the process, not just those that are negatively affected by discrimination. This provides a holistic approach with greater interaction that produces far-reaching societal impact, involvement, and influence.[35]

Humility

Evaluation of oneself and personal passions is a difficult and emotionally taxing responsibility. Continued involvement in HOBY Canada by alumni spurs from positive associations and experiences within the organization that embeds obstacles in the ability of alumni to honestly critique the organization. Combatting these realities demands a posture of humility for effectiveness. Humility requires an openness and willingness to address fault and limitation in one's abilities and understanding. Vulnerability requires greater risk to evaluate personal contributions that recreate oppression to dismantle and resist it moving forward.[36] HOBY Canada continues to use critique and evaluation as an outlet to display a commitment to the organization and avoid fault-finding or discouragement.

Positionality becomes fundamental to this mindset when evaluating and internalizing new knowledge and perspectives. Each member must be willing to reflect upon their personal identity, biases, and resulting blind spots. Clear boundaries and limitations are required in a posture of humility to encourage continuation and reduce fear or doubt. Willingness to accept progress over perfection keeps HOBY Canada open to criticism and accountable to alumni networks. HOBY Canada displays that upholding integrity and setting a positive example is just as inherent to the process as receiving feedback, acknowledging mistakes, and correcting errors. Human rights realization mirrors this sentiment as elitism and entitlement stunt growth and progress under facades of confidence and denial. When status and reputation are set aside for honesty and reflection, the realities of progress and involvement are more accessible and less intimidating.

Perseverance

Allyship is not a destination. There is not a point when one arrives or a checklist to complete to achieve a permanent ally distinction. Conversely, allyship requires dedication and an ongoing commitment to equality and justice that is enacted daily.[37] Dominant narratives and systems thrive when unchallenged and, therefore, promote silence and complicity. Meaningful, productive dialogue unpacking ADI and injustice in dominant culture must be continuous for change to be realized.[38] It is in each action and response that solidarity and allyship are built and displayed. Social justice and equality are long-standing pursuits that have been advocated across generations. In human rights, continued perseverance and courage fuel dedication that advance equality.

Conclusion

The realization of equality, dignity, and human rights require allyship action that all individuals and organizations can enact to address discrimination and improve their ADI. It is through this practice that all people are invited to affect real, societal change with a hope for a better future.[39] HOBY Canada demonstrates an inclusive approach to allyship for the realization of human rights and the pursuit of greater

ADI. Roles and responsibilities for all identity groups are incorporated in transformation throughout stages of generation, conceptualization, application, and ongoing action. By maintaining a posture of collaboration, humility, and perseverance, action is facilitated, and all people can be empowered to advocate for equality.[40] Through interconnectedness and restoration of relationships among groups, openness to criticism and feedback for improvement, and continuous, intentional decision-making, increased possibilities are realized.[41] Through their outlined allyship journey, HOBY Canada provides a pillar of hope within human rights. All individuals and organizations working toward a common purpose can combat oppression and pursue equality within the individual, community, and organizational life.

Discussion Questions

1. Define allyship. What strategies can be used to effectively support groups facing injustice?
2. Explore the relationship between personal identity, ADI, and conflict.
3. What considerations are necessary to implement this framework across sectors (individually, public sector, private sector, etc.)?
4. Select a current ethnic conflict outside of the North American context. How can this allyship framework be applied to advocacy and conflict transformation in that case?

Notes

1. Kendrick T. Brown, "Perceiving Allies from the Perspective of Non-Dominant Group Comparisons to Friends and Activists," *Current Psychology* 34, no. 4 (2015): 713; Lisa Droogendyk, Stephen C. Wright, Micah Lubensky and Winnifred R. Louis. "Acting in Solidarity: Cross-Group Contact between Disadvantaged Group Members and Advantaged Group Allies." *Journal of Social Issues* 72, no. 2. (2016): 321; J. E. Sumerau, TehQuin D. Forbes, Eric Anthony Grollman and Lain A. B. Mathers. "Constructing Allyship and the Persistence of Inequality." *Social Problems*. (2020): 3; Shaun Wiley, and Christine Dunne. "Comrades in the Struggle? Feminist Women Prefer Male Allies Who Offer Autonomy—not Dependency-Oriented Help." *Sex Roles*, 80 (2018): 662.

2. Droogendyk, "Acting in Solidarity," 14; bell hooks, *Where We Stand: Class Matters* (New York: Routledge, 2000), 127; Michael Alan Sacks, and Marika Lindholm. "A Room Without a View: Social Distance and the Structuring of Privileged Identity," in *Working Through Whiteness: International Perspectives*, ed. Cynthia Levine-Rasky (Albany: University of New York Press, 2002), 130; Sumerau et al., "Constructing Allyship," 2; Wiley and Dunne, "Comrades in the Struggle," 656.
3. Juliana Carlson, Cliff Leek, Erin Casey, Rich Tolman and Christopher Allen, "What's in a Name? A Synthesis of "Allyship" Elements from Academic and Activist Literature," *Journal of Family Violence*. (2019): 896; Erin A. Casey, and Kristin Ohler. "Being a Positive Bystander: Male Antiviolence Allies' Experiences "Stepping Up." *Journal of Interpersonal Violence*, 27, no. 1 (2012): 65; Droogendyk, "Acting in Solidarity," 10–12, 21; Jodi Dueck-Read, "Transnational Activism: Intersectional Identities and Peacebuilding in the Border Justice Movement" (Ph.D. Thesis, University of Manitoba, 2016); Jenalee Kluttz, Jude Walker and Pierre Walter. "Unsettling Allyship, Unlearning and Learning Towards Decolonising Solidarity." *Studies in the Education of Adults* 52, no. 1 (2019): 51; Sumerau et al., "Constructing Allyship," 3–4; Wiley and Dunne, "Comrades in the Struggle," 656–657.
4. Casey and Ohler, "Being a Positive Bystander," 63.
5. "About HOBY Canada," HOBY Canada, accessed August 28, 2020, https://www.hobycanada.com/about.
6. Shannon Cormier, *Walk With Me: Sharing Space Along the Path* (M.A. Thesis, University of Manitoba, 2017), 97; Kluttz et al., "Unsettling allyship," 51; Sumerau et al., "Acting in Solidarity," 2–3; Beverley Daniel Tatum, *Why Are All The Black Kids Sitting Together In The Cafeteria? And Other Conversations About Race: Revised and Updated* (New York: Basic Books, 2017), 333.
7. Cormier, "Walk With Me," 97; Carlson et al., "What's in a Name," 4; Wiley and Dunne, "Comrades in the Struggle," 656.
8. Brown, "Perceiving Allies," 714; Cormier, "Walk With Me," 83, 99; Droogendyk, "Acting in Solidarity," 7; Kluttz et al., "Unsettling Allyship," 50; Sacks and Lindholm, "A Room Without," 146.
9. Cormier, "Walk With Me," 97; Tatum, "Why Are All," 97; Sacks and Lindholm, "A Room Without," 129.
10. Casey and Ohler, "Being a Positive Bystander," 63, 75; Bush, 2002, 31; hooks, "Where We Stand," 2000, 127.
11. Cormier, "Walk With Me," 98; Dueck-Read, "Transnational Activism," 112; Paulo Freire, *Pedagogy of the Oppressed* (New York: Bloomsbury Publishing, 1970), 59; Sacks and Lindholm, "A Room Without," 130; Tatum, "Why Are All," 103.

12. Haneen Ghabra, and Bernadette Marie Calafell, "From Failure and Allyship to Feminist Solidarities: Negotiating our Privileges and Oppressions Across Borders." *Text and Performance Quarterly* 21, no. 3 (2018): 48; Sacks and Lindholm, "A Room Without," 129; Wiley & Dunne, "Comrades in the Struggle," 656.
13. Cormier, "Walk With Me," 82; Droogendyk, "Acting in Solidarity,", 8–9; Ghabra and Calafell, "From Failure and Allyship," 45; Sumerau et al., "Constructing Allyship," 2–3.
14. Brown, "Perceiving Allies," 714; Freire, "Pedagogy of the Oppressed," 68; Ghabra and Calafell, "From Failure and Allyship," 52; hooks, *Where We Stand*, 127; John Paul Lederach, *Preparing for Peace: Conflict Transformation Across Cultures* (New York: Syracuse University Press, 1995), 30; Sacks and Lindholm, "A Room Without," 145.
15. Vicki Ferrence Ray, "Hugh O'Brian Youth Leadership: Using a Theoretical Model at the Intersection of Youth Leadership Education and Service-Learning," *New Direction for Student Leadership*, no. 150 (2016): 99–100.
16. Ray, "Hugh O'Brian Youth," 101.
17. Ray, "Hugh O'Brian Youth," 97–98.
18. Peter G. Northouse, *Leadership: Theory and Practice* (Thousand Oaks, California: SAGE Publications, 2016), 71, 161.
19. Ray, "Hugh O'Brian Youth," 101.
20. Casey and Ohler, "Being a Positive Bystander," 63; Freire, "Pedagogy of the Oppressed," 81; Lederach, "Preparing for Peace," 59–61.
21. Lederach, "Preparing for Peace," 80.
22. Lindsey Pointer, Kathleen McGoey and Haley Farrar. *The Little Book of Restorative Teaching Tools: Games, Activities, and Simulations for Understanding Restorative Justice Practices* (New York: Good Books, 2020), 17.
23. "About HOBY Canada," HOBY Canada, accessed August 28, 2020, https://www.hobycanada.com/about.
24. Ray, "Hugh O'Brian Youth," 99.
25. Northouse, *Leadership: Theory and Practice*, 195.
26. Lisa Schirch, *The Little Book of Strategic Peacebuilding: A Vision and Framework for Peace with Justice* (New York: Good Books, 2004), 14–15.
27. Tatum, "Why Are All," 196.
28. Schirch, "The Little Book," 9.
29. Lederach, "Preparing for Peace," 83, 120–1.
30. Droogendyk, "Acting in Solidarity," 6.
31. Schirch, "The Little Book," 40.
32. Schirch, "The Little Book," 21.
33. Droogendyk, "Acting in Solidarity,"5; Lederach, "Preparing for Peace," 61.

34. Pointer et al., "The Little Book," 33.
35. Lederach, "Preparing for Peace," 82.
36. Casey and Ohler, "Being a Positive Bystander," 63; Droogendyk, "Acting in Solidarity," 6; Pointer et al., "The Little Book," 35.
37. Casey and Ohler, "Being a Positive Bystander," 77; Droogendyk, "Acting in Solidarity," 13.
38. Tatum, "Why Are All," 331.
39. Carlson et al., "What's In A Name," 4; hooks, "Where We Stand," 121.
40. Brown, "Perceiving Allies," 714; Freire, "Pedagogy of the Oppressed," 68; Ghabra and Calafell, "From Failure and Allyship," 52; Kluttz et al., "Unsettling Allyship," 62.
41. Droogendyk, "Acting in Solidarity," 10–2, 21; Sumerau et al., "Constructing Allyship," 3–4; Wiley and Dunne, "Comrades in the Struggle," 656–57.

Bibliography

"About HOBY Canada," HOBY Canada. Accessed August 28, 2020. https://www.hobycanada.com/about

Brown, Kendrick T. Perceiving Allies from the Perspective of Non-Dominant Group Comparisons to Friends and Activists. *Current Psychology* 34, no. 4 (2015): 713–722.

Carlson, Juliana, Cliff Leek, Erin Casey, Rich Tolman, and Christopher Allen. What's In a Name? A Synthesis of "Allyship" Elements from Academic and Activist Literature. *Journal of Family Violence* 35 no. 8 (2019): 889–898.

Casey, Erin A., and Kristin Ohler. Being a Positive Bystander: Male Antiviolence Allies' Experiences "Stepping Up". *Journal of Interpersonal Violence* 27, no. 1 (2012): 62–83.

Cormier, Shannon. *Walk With Me: Sharing Space Along the Path.* M.A. Thesis, University of Manitoba, 2017.

Droogendyk, Lisa, Stephen C. Wright, Micah Lubensky, and Winnifred R. Louis. "Acting In Solidarity: Cross-Group Contact Between Disadvantaged Group Members and Advantaged Group Allies." *Journal of Social Issues* 72, no. 2 (2016): 315–334.

Dueck-Read, Jodi. "Transnational Activism: Intersectional Identities and Peacebuilding In the Border Justice Movement." Ph.D. Thesis, University of Manitoba, 2016.

Freire, Paulo. *Pedagogy of the Oppressed.* New York: Bloomsbury Publishing, 1970.

Ghabra, Haneen, and Bernadette Marie Calafell. "From Failure and Allyship to Feminist Solidarities: Negotiating Our Privileges and Oppressions Across Borders." *Text and Performance Quarterly* 21, no. 3 (2018): 38–54.

Hooks, bell. *Where We Stand: Class Matters*. New York: Routledge, 2000.

Kluttz, Jenalee, Jude Walker, and Pierre Walter. Unsettling Allyship, Unlearning and Learning Towards Decolonising Solidarity. *Studies in the Education of Adults* 52, no. 1 (2019): 49–66.

Lederach, John Paul. *Preparing for Peace: Conflict Transformation Across Cultures*. New York: Syracuse University Press, 1995.

Northouse, Peter G. *Leadership: Theory and Practice*. Thousand Oaks, California: SAGE Publications, 2016.

Pointer, Lindsey, Kathleen McGoey, and Haley Farrar. *The Little Book of Restorative Teaching Tools: Games, Activities, and Simulations for Understanding Restorative Justice Practices*. New York: Good Books, 2020.

Ray, Vicki Ferrence. Hugh O'Brian Youth Leadership: Using a Theoretical Model at the Intersection of Youth Leadership Education and Service-Learning. *New Direction for Student Leadership,* 150 (2016): 97–101.

Sacks, Michael Alan, and Marika Lindholm. "A Room Without a View: Social Distance and the Structuring of Privileged Identity." In *Working Through Whiteness: International Perspectives*, edited by Cynthia Levine-Rasky Albany: University of New York Press, 2002.

Schirch, Lisa. *The Little Book of Strategic Peacebuilding: A Vision and Framework for Peace with Justice*. New York: Good Books, 2004.

Sumerau, J. E., TehQuin D. Forbes, Eric Anthony Grollman, and Lain A.B. Mathers. "Constructing Allyship and the Persistence of Inequality." *Social Problems* (2020): 1–16.

Tatum, Beverly Daniel. *Why Are All The Black Kids Sitting Together In The Cafeteria? And Other Conversations About Race: Revised and Updated*. New York: Basic Books, 2017

Wiley, Shaun, and Christine Dunne. Comrades In the Struggle? Feminist Women Prefer Male Allies Who Offer Autonomy—Not Dependency-Oriented Help. *Sex Roles* 80, no. 11–12 (2018): 656–666.

Teaching Human Rights and Social Justice

Katerina Standish

Teaching is a form of academic inquiry where the 'data' emerges from the creation, delivery, experience, and reflection of fostering learning. Moreover, while Boyer called this the *Scholarship of Teaching,*[1] something that occurs in all learning delivery environments where an educator is actively participating in the discipline, something becomes 'real' scholarship when it is disseminated.[2] Transformative peace pedagogy is about changing world views, shifting violent or apathetic behavior, and re: rendering one's consciousness of purpose.[3] This chapter aims to provide a container to encapsulate a peace education *praxis* that emerged from coursework on Human Rights and Social Justice (HR & SJ) delivered to third-year medical students in Aotearoa/New Zealand. This work seeks to connect the value of reflective practice to the 'work' of transformative peace pedagogy. Teacher's self-study is a methodology for probing expert practice. There is 'no one way, or correct way, of doing self-study,'[4] but it can be helpful to have a detailed methodology to follow; with this in mind,

K. Standish (✉)
Canadian Peace Research Association, London, ON, Canada
e-mail: Katerina.standish@umanitoba.ca

L. E. Reimer and K. Standish (eds.), *Perspectives on Justice, Indigeneity, Gender, and Security in Human Rights Research*,
https://doi.org/10.1007/978-981-99-1930-7_4

using curriculum and field notes[5] or, post-class reflection, this chapter will un enmesh the dynamic and tangible outcomes that emerged from the cross-disciplinary delivery of a unit on HR and SJ.

Context

I taught the intensive course as part of teaching exchange from the Humanities/Social Sciences (H/SS) into the Medical/Sciences.[6] In their third year of General Practitioner (GP) Medical Training, students had an opportunity to study outside their professional credential learning spaces; to embark upon intellectual and scholarly investigation.

Out of 16 students, 12 were females, and four were males. Most of the class was in their early 20s, and two individuals were in their early 30s. None of the students were parents, had childcare responsibilities, had visible disabilities, and all were domestic students. The students' cultural backgrounds included Pacific Islander, Indonesian, Chinese, Arab, Indigenous, South Asian, and European.

Of 16 possible course options, 16 students in the GP program attended my class. I will mention that students in this teaching exchange have 1st, 2nd, and third choices for their desired H/SS course. It might also be pertinent to note that of the 16 students in this class, only one selected it as the first choice. The majority had picked my class *at least* third (students who did not get their first, second, or third choices were assigned to learning units and my sense was that many students attended my elective as mandatory).

The department gave students a course teaser on the class that included the following information:

HUMAN RIGHTS AND SOCIAL JUSTICE
Course Instructor: Dr. Katerina Standish

The United Nations tells us that Human rights are inherent to all human beings, regardless of race, sex, nationality, ethnicity, language, religion, or any other status. Human rights include the right to life and liberty, freedom from slavery and torture, freedom of opinion and expression, the right to work and education, and many more. Everyone is entitled to these rights without discrimination. However, we know that simply having a 'right' to something does not ensure its existence. The United Nations also tells us that there is an 'inequality gap' and that social justice is an underlying principle for peaceful and prosperous coexistence within and among nations. We uphold the principles of social justice when we promote gender equality or the rights of indigenous peoples and migrants. We advance social justice when we remove barriers people face because of sex, age, race, ethnicity, religion, culture, or disability.

On one hand, we are told we all have a right to human dignity. However, on the other, human actions within society result in people being treated unfairly or unjustly with unequal access to economic, political, and social opportunities. This course will provide students with a conceptual appreciation of Human Rights and Social Justice, how they cohabit cultural space and diverge.

Medical Professionals encounter and engage with people in a variety of social/cultural, and political circumstances. The goal of this elective will be to promote the awareness of how two equality structures cohabit within social and cultural spaces. This class will appreciate notions of 'universal' Human rights alongside 'inequality' of opportunity, resources, and privileges.

Learning Units

1. *Introduction to Human Rights*
2. *Instruments and aspects of the right to human dignity*
3. *HR and Identities*
4. *The Concept of Justice*
5. *Social Justice: equity, access, participation, and rights.*
6. *Denial of Human Rights and Injustice.*

The class included lectures, seminars, and interactive learning labs. Students were assigned readings for each teaching unit as prep, then we met weekly to engage and encounter course materials. Each unit resulted in a reflective learning log entry that permitted the students to consider content, express challenges, or surprises, and offer a curiosity or question to stimulate discussion at the next session.

The format of most sessions began with curiosities offered by the students, followed by lectures, knowledge support in the form of handouts, videos, films, and activities that utilize experiential practices to stimulate learning. Two quizzes established a baseline of knowledge about *Human Rights* (in unit 1) and *Justice* (in unit 4). In these quizzes, students sat in groups of 6 and then 4 (the group decided smaller dialogue sizes worked better after our first class) and worked collaboratively in dialogue to go through set questions. Several students opened their laptops to 'find' answers to the 1st quiz questions. They were asked, instead, to 'mine' their understanding for answers.

The learning setup involved working collaboratively at the start and end of each class to move tables and chairs around to reconfigure the traditional classroom (all chairs facing the front of the room). There were no set seating assignments, and the students were free to sit anywhere, with anyone, as the course progressed. Students decided that they preferred to end the class session early rather than take a scheduled fifteen-minute break in class one. However, they were invited and welcomed to take comfort breaks (for any reason), including leaving the classroom.

Pedagogy

Medical students are used to a very different learning environment than H/SS students, and one of the goals of the learning exchange is to expose them to different styles of investigation and inquiry. In the departmental pre-class sessions, instructors (there were 16 of us) were told that this would be a chance for GP students to 'not know,' to get comfortable with the fact that there are 'no right answers' in the humanities and to value having personal perception, reflection, and experience as a learning outcome. Students were provided with guidance and suggestions regarding in and out of class practices, and the following class pedagogy was shared in my course syllabus:

In each session, students will critically consider their personal, national, and 'group' perceptions of various rights, instruments, and concepts related to Human Rights and Social Justice in a reflective dialogue session. Reflective dialogue is an interactional and interpersonal encounter whereby students are taught and practice active listening skills. This dialogue practice aims to create a broader discussion of personal reflection using questions and focused inquiry. The dialogue-based exploration of what we 'think' these rights, instruments, and concepts entail will be followed by a brief lecture of shared understandings of these terms and facets and then an invitation for students to challenge, problematize, critique, and reflect upon the class content.

> **How to class:** in this elective, I will invite you to critically engage with the content and materials we peruse. Criticality is a skill you develop when you inquire, problematize, challenge, assess, and describe. Critically evaluating

something, a topic, a film, a piece of writing, or an idea is a practice where we challenge ourselves to 'see' deeply. We do not read; we *consider*. We do not watch; we *investigate*. We do not acquire knowledge; we *construct* it through interaction.

Furthermore, we do not impose our views on others. We can come to a consensus…we can agree. Nevertheless, we recognize that our position is likely distinct from a person who sees the same thing through critical analysis. We all bring different experiences, expertise, and intelligence to our critiques. Finally, a critique is not BAD (it is not a criticism); it is a way of intellectually engaging with material and content in such a way as to perceive and challenge ourselves.

*When we **read**, we ask: what views are being presented in this argument? What views are included or excluded? What is missing? What more can be said? Am I persuaded?*

*When we **watch**, we ask: whose perspective is being used, who is, or is not being included, and what is the purpose of the communication (e.g., entertainment, recruitment)? Is it delivering a message (or multiple messages), and am I convinced? We ask, what do I think about this topic now that I did not before? What purpose does the style of presentation hold? Am I informed, interested, bored? Could they have done something more engaging? How?*

*When we **discuss**, we speak and listen to learn, help others learn, and increase **the room's** understanding of something. Critical engagement is an act of generosity: to read, watch, and discuss, pays attention to the 'other.' So, thank you all for being generous!*

Curriculum and *Field-Notes*

The following section will present some of the core curricula of the teaching units, followed by my teaching field notes (captured in *italicized* text). Field notes are an ethnographic method of documenting and analyzing critical reflection that enables the participant/observer (in my case, teacher/learner) to consider and illuminate outcomes of interaction and observation (Majaraj, 2016). While not a formalized research study, the novelty of teaching content 'at home' in my discipline of peace and conflict studies (PACS) to a new and not necessarily compatible student group encouraged me to begin a process of professional reflection that I share here. As a PACS scholar/practitioner, and peace educator, I position my educative offerings as opportunities to foster critical consciousness. The consciousness of reality is used to impact or alter reality as a liberatory and therefore humanizing practice. In teaching for critical consciousness (termed *conscientization* by Freire[7] and *engaged pedagogy* by hooks,[8] we not only find out how 'we' see the world, but we also learn how 'others' do too. Through the peace pedagogies of reflective dialogue, collaboration, shared experiences, and active listening, this curriculum becomes a co-creation of understanding and experience. The following learning units are described and then deliberated in *field-note* reflections.

Class 1: Introduction to Human Rights

To open the learning space, students were encouraged to participate in a preliminary round of sharing. The students were not only strangers to me, but primarily unacquainted with one another. While I teach in a small unit, the medical school is enormous, and most of the students in our elective did not know one another. They were asked to answer (written on the board): Q1 What is your name and what should we call you? Q2 Where were you born, and where do you live now? Q3 Have you studied Human Rights or Social Justice before? Q4 What did you have for dinner last night?

I find the students very reserved (compared to H/SS students at least), and after the first person skipped over Qs 2 and 3, the rest only answered Q1 and 4. The dinner question was offered to initiate students to the notion that their experience 'builds' the learning outcomes of the class. Everyone answered this question, and a wide variety of meals were communicated (many I had not heard of). I had gone first (as I had with Qs1-3), and when I said, 'burnt toast,' several smiled (though no one laughed out loud) as I volunteered that I was not much at cooking. My takeaway from the questions was that all the students who had offered their nativity and domicile were from places far away from the city they were studying medicine in and that no one had studied HR & SJ; this will be an opportunity to teach them content that was essentially new to them.

After the introductions, we moved the tables and chairs, and students were separated into facing groups of 6. The HR quiz was handed out, and students spent time discussing answers until all 24 questions were complete.[9]

As I walked around the classroom, I saw several students immediately open laptops or iPads to find the 'correct' answer to the quiz questions. I repeated the instructions that the quiz's purpose was not to find out the answers to provide us with a baseline of how 'we' understand these terms and concepts. The goal was to 'mine' perception, not to locate facts.

When I looked around, I saw many students engaging with the test in lively discussion, while others sat back and looked bored. One table seemed only to have two speakers, which I considered a sign of their unfamiliarity with one another and the quiz content. After much discussion, and after they had completed all the questions to the best of their ability, I put the quiz presentation up, and we went through each one, answering group responses then offering the 'correct' answers to the queries. When we completed all the questions, it was the end of the session, and I reminded students about their learning log assignments, offering their curiosity by email. We ended class with a handout of the Universal Declaration of Human Rights and a forecast for the next session. As the students had elected to leave early (rather than take their break), the students left with no one remaining behind to put tables back (though I had asked that any that could stay a moment to help shuffle).

I had asked for the learning logs (3-500 words) to be sent by email before midnight on the day of class so that reflections were recent and would not require recollection. When I received the logs, I was confident that the reason that the students had left class so abruptly was twofold; firstly, all but one student communicated that they were shocked and embarrassed by their ignorance about Human Rights. Secondly, I realized that these students were TOP science students who had competed with hundreds of other candidates to enter medical school; in one in-class quiz and in front of their peers, they had had their confidence wholly devastated. I remind myself that it is vital to share with the students that 'what you know does not define your worth or entitle you to a more significant share of respect or deference. All people are equal in dignity, and ignorance is simply an opportunity to learn.' Hopefully, they show up to the second class…

NEXT TIME: *Ahhhhh!!! I mistimed the end of class (I had forgotten that class was ending earlier because we did not take a break), so we missed circle talk (debriefing). The class ended abruptly, and we need to ease out of these topics much more intentionally next time. Change your timing page for the rest of the classes!*

Class 2: Instruments and Aspects of the Right to Human Dignity

The silence of the first-class contrasted with the cornucopia of expression in the learning logs. Students did not stick to 3-500 words, and I received over 1000 words from six different students—lots of thought, appreciation, and percolation in these missives. The students again wrote of how sub-par their HR education was and how clear it was that the HR statement from the Minister of Foreign Affairs only talked about HR abuses overseas and ignored those in NZ.

CURRICULUM: In the second teaching unit, we embarked upon a brief exploration of the difference between 'Nationalism' and 'Citizenship,' followed by a curated exploration of the core six Human Rights Instruments:

1. International Convention on the Elimination of All Forms of Racial Discrimination (1965)
2. International Covenant on Civil and Political Rights (1966)
3. International Covenant on Economic, Social and Cultural Rights (1966)
4. Convention on the Elimination of All Forms of Discrimination against Women (1979)
5. Convention against Torture and Other Cruel, Inhuman or Degrading Treatment or Punishment (1984)
6. Convention on the Rights of the Child (1989).

These sessions aimed to understand the difference between nations and citizens, expose the instruments to the students (though some were quite dull to read), and elevate parts of the corpus that showed greater scope than the Universal Declaration of Human Rights written in 1948. The aim was to introduce the Human Rights project as an emerging ideal or incomplete project that exits conceptually between International and State Law and social norms and conventions. I asked students to self-inquiry of their status as members of 'nations' or holders of 'citizenship' and what that meant to them.

Nationalism: a group of people who share cultural characteristics comprise a 'nation;' such groups can be civic, ethnic, religious, ideological, or linguistic, and are entitled to self-government.

Citizen(ship): A person who resides and is recognized by a state as having legal rights to a passport, to leave and return to that country, to live in that country, to work there.

The secondary ambition of this sessions' curriculum was to articulate (connect) their understanding of the tenets of citizenship in this country to sources in the HR Instruments. Students were then invited to watch a video of the current Foreign Affairs Minister's statement regarding Human Rights in 2021. Afterward, they were offered a snapshot of New Zealand HR by the recent UN Human Rights Committee, who found multiple shocking concerns regarding HR violations in New Zealand.

Finally, though content analysis is not a huge part of scientific research (at least not for medical students studying to become GPs), we concluded this class with a learning/practice session of 'mining' HR case studies from New Zealand to 'decode' HR violations. In groups of 4, students were asked to pick one of 9 case studies and identify HR violations. National case studies included child poverty, homelessness, disability, resource deserts, health inequity, unemployment, domestic violence, incarceration, and racial discrimination.

They came back! Big class today, and I felt the students both struggled and shone! We went through the curiosities from last week. They seemed relieved that so many of them had the same sense of ignorance and bewilderment, that they were fundamentally uninformed, and that this seems very important that they know this. The overwhelming question (11 of the 16) was: 'why were we not taught this?' I asked them if they could think of a reason. I suggested that in addition to limited space in the curriculum or teachers' inability to teach such a specialized topic (which they had volunteered), there might be a reason we are 'not' taught about our human rights.

If you know your rights, you may hold your government responsible for satisfying them, which government's do not.

We discussed the fact that while they overall possess Civil and Political rights, they and their fellow citizens enjoy much more limited facets of Economic, Cultural and Social rights such as guaranteed employment, fair wages, opportunities for promotion, adequate standards of living, freedom from hunger, right to the highest attainable standard of physical and mental health, any needed medical services, Human Rights Education, and equal access, available and accessible to all, of higher learning.

This was not easy to fathom for many. In black and white, it looked like unemployment, poverty, untreated illness or injury, and fee-based training and education were violations of HR espoused by their government. This is the beginning of critical consciousness, where students begin to see their reality more fully. To move our thinking forward and receive the information arriving in everyone's mind, I asked them to consider that a possible reason that HR are NOT being taught was that their ignorance, as citizens, is a way for the government to skirt HR obligations to which they are obligated.

Before breaking, I reminded the students that the goal of the course was exposure, not saturation, that there are whole classes on just one covenant. In contrast, they were dashing over dozens of articles to gain exposure. I think the heavy lifting paid off when they got to decode case studies and use the articles to learn more about the reality of HR in their nation.

During circle talk, at the end of class, the students were mostly silent. I am starting to perceive that dialogue space 'as a class' is far less comfortable. They talk in small groups, but only one or two contribute when the whole class is listening.

NEXT TIME: *Good session but too much with all 6 Core Instruments. Next time I will offer the Bill of Human Rights (Universal Declaration, Intl. Cov. on Civil & Political Rights, and Intl. Cov. on Economic, Social & Cultural Rights) only. Case studies worked well. Lots of meaningful learning today, and although I think it might feel awkward, I will try circle talk next week again, one more time.*

Class 3: HR and Identities

The session began with our curiosities, and students began to ask more institutional and structural questions regarding civil rights and national responsibilities. Students asked how HR was supposed to protect people from inequality but that it was not being enforced. They asked 'why poverty is permitted to exist in such a *rich* country.'

After the content-driven classes 1 and 2, today was a learning workshop that permitted us to begin to scaffold (layer and ascend) our understanding of how identity, inequality, and injustice are connected. We are gearing up to switch from HR to SJ next week. It will be necessary for the students to hold a space in their new consciousnesses for self-concept, social identity, economic and legal inequality, and injustice.

CURRICULUM: The class curriculum began by inquiring how identity (personal and group membership) impacts HR. After sharing content on the components of personal identity (including career, political views, religious beliefs, relationships, cultural identity, personality, body image, possessions, interests, work/hobbies, practices/habits, appearance, family structure, values, life choices, sex, gender, education, age, race/ethnicity, ability, sexual orientation, and socio-economic status), we ventured into Social Identity Theory (SIT). SIT says the groups we belong to are essential sources of pride and self-esteem.[10] There are two ways we gain a sense of belonging in the social world: by enhancing the status of the group we belong to (in-group) and denigrating or discriminating against a group to which we do not belong (out-group). This often leads to dehumanization, where the prejudices of dominant groups can lead to unequal life chances, circumstances, and experiences of social subordination for those in an out-group. We ventured into inequality: the state of not being considered economically or legally equal and how those with unequal political power in a society experience enshrined inequality. This cultural attitude leads to acts of injustice. We first appreciated how the HR system sought/seeks to create a fair starting point for all but that inequality (the experience of being unequal) becomes injustice when social/cultural prejudice leads to acts and attitudes that result in discrimination: injustice deprives a person of experiencing the HR they are entitled.

We then ruminated on the relationship between inequality and injustice to reflect that people in unequal societies trust each other less; they experience larger material precarity and greater feelings of humiliation (violating *dignity* needs), leading to violence. We then regarded statistics on inequality in New Zealand, connecting inequality (via injustice) to violence.

This was arresting for students to learn. Most thought that New Zealand (NZ) was a safe, stable, and secure nation. I shared stats that showed otherwise.

1 in 4 kids is growing up in poverty. NZs child wellbeing rank for developed nations is 35 out of 41. 1 in 3 NZ women experiences violence. Indigenous women are twice as likely as non-Indigenous to experience violence. 1 in 5 children experiences sexual violence. NZ ranked worst for domestic violence in the OECD. Every 8th homicide victim in NZ is a child (more than two-thirds of whom are under age 2). NZ has

the highest teen suicide rate in the OECD. Half of all homicides in NZ are committed by family members. Moreover, 76% of family violence incidences are NOT reported to the police.

We needed to come up from the dark matter of this lecture, so we looked at the Frans de Waal *Fairness Study* YouTube video of the capuchin monkeys.[11] This is a great clip that shows how hard-wired we are to perceive inequality as injustice by showing how enraged a capuchin monkey gets when the task they are doing in a controlled experiment is 'paid' by a piece of cucumber. In contrast, their fellow capuchin, visible in the next cage, gets rewarded with a grape. The video is hilarious, and the class, as expected, laughed out loud and then asked to watch it again.

The monkey experiment video was the bridge between the lecture content and an Identity bead workshop. In this workshop, students are given raw wooden beads of various sizes, a short piece of leather string (to make a bracelet), and a multitude of colored felts to color the beads if they wish. The instructions are easy, we go through a list of identity features, and I ask them to pick a bead size that corresponds to how *vital* that identity facet is to them personally, which they can then decorate. We then repeat the activity; this time, I ask them to pick a bead size corresponding to how *vital* that identity facet is to their 'group.' There is a long list of identity features. However, due to the time, I pick the following categories (considering we must go through it twice): sex/ *gender*, *education*, *age*, *race/ethnicity*, *ability*, *sexual orientation*, and *socio-economic status*. This is a classic art therapy exercise that accesses personal expression through creative activity. We then concluded the class with a forecast of the next week and another silent circle talk.

> NEXT TIME*: no circle-talk. These students are incredibly expressive in their learning logs, and I do not think this peace praxis adds anything valuable to the learning space.*

Class 4: The Concept of Justice

Despite the couple of people who looked annoyed by the project, which made me question my pedagogical choice, the learning logs showed how insightful and enjoyable they found the art project was. Many said it was the first time they had ever considered how their group identity beads compared to their personal identity choices. Some wrote it was a nice 'break' from all the academic stuff…which I confess, after three sessions of life-changing (critical consciousness-raising) coursework, I had intended. This stuff is hard; I know it is arresting. I dearly hope I am not traumatizing these students with reality. I know this stuff is standard in my field, but medical trainees are not taught this.

I could identify two streams of response in the learning logs; some students focused on the art therapy and how the project made them think deeply about culture and identity. Other students focused on HR abuses in New Zealand which they termed 'VERY depressing.' Many wrote that they were utterly shocked about the violence statistics. One student said she was glad that the other students were 'waking up' to her reality. As a person who grew up disadvantaged, she wrote that she often felt like an outsider among the medical students, many of whom were from very privileged backgrounds.

CURRICULUM: Our class curriculum began, in an echo of the first session, with a quiz.[12] Again, students were informed that this was looking for how these terms are understood or appreciated, not 'correct' answers. The Justice Quiz is short, and students spent more time paring down their answers together in their groups instead of trying to get the 'right' answers. We came together and shared our responses, and students were much more comfortable saying 'I have no idea' than in the first round. This is good; the point of this kind of learning is to use our knowledge as the base of understanding; we do not have to be correct to ask ourselves what experience we would need to be in to 'know' the answers to these questions. None of us are lawyers (me included), but we cannot understand injustice without learning how justice is comprised.

This class introduced Justice Studies, and we started with notions of social order and crime. Then, we focused our investigation on four kinds of justice: distributive, procedural, retributive, and restorative. There are dozens of 'kinds' of justice out there, but we focused on the big four looking at type and goal. A snapshot of our learning included content minimally fleshed out this rubric:

Retributive Justice
Procedural Justice
Retributive Justice
Restorative Justice

We viewed a video about the NZ Justice system, which both delighted and surprised the students. This was illustrative that many people 'hold' ideas about justice based on TV shows.[13] The amusing video showed the reality of 'justice' in the NZ court system, and we followed this with a greater appreciation of alternative and restorative forms of justice. In this content, we explored the role of community and responsibility in achieving just outcomes, including how restorative processes differ from court processes, particularly considering the empowerment of victims and the reintegration of offenders. We followed this with a short video on restorative justice in A/NZ from Lower Hutt.[14]

Our session on justice concluded with a short unit and video on Transformative Justice. This model is concerned with transforming the structural conditions that create crime and violence 'without creating more violence.' As a peace praxis, transformative processes seek to transform the conditions that allow harm to be normalized by working outside the civil and restorative justice paradigms. We watched a short film to help students relate to the project, and then we talked about 'who' deserves justice and who gets left out of justice in the various models.[15]

The class closed with a forecast of next week's social justice class and a reminder to send learning logs.

> NEXT TIME: *This class was a joy to facilitate. The timing was almost perfect (yeah, me), and lots of good in-class reflection. There was a spontaneous circle-talk at the end, which kept several students talking together about medical justice. No changes!*

Class 5: Social Justice: Equity, Access, Participation, and Rights

> *After learning about types of justice last class, many of the students were concerned that the only people who get 'justice' in A/NZ are those who can pay for it. They were glad to see that restorative processes are getting more attention but questioned whether transformative justice was possible in a nation with court-based justice. There were also some honest questions about 'what can we do?'*

CURRICULUM: We began by talking about what 'we' think social justice is. There were a few circular definitions, '*social justice is justice for society,*' and '*social justice is justice that is socially just.*' We agreed that there was some fuzziness to the term, which made us want an actual definition. I offered Margot Hurlbert's definition:

> A set of ideas, values, and social practices ensures that all persons and groups enjoy economic security, can participate effectively in democratic decision-making, exercise mutual respect and caring for one another, and live their lives in ways that protect and sustain the natural environment for future generations.[16]

We then considered several other ways of thinking about 'what' social justice is: *promotion of just societies, eliminating hunger, reducing poverty, distributing resources fairly, ability to live with good health and full employment, living free from discrimination.* We then talked about approaches to social justice, including equal rights, equal opportunity, and equal treatment for all. This led us to talk about the 'who' of social justice identifying how activism exists to foster political and social change in a variety of people, including *Students, Teachers, Lawyers, Politicians, Social Service Agents, Grassroots Community Group members, Medical Professionals, Entrepreneurs, Researchers, Analysts, Social Workers, Citizen/Voters.*

We discussed examples of how social justice is considered at different levels, including the *Local*: homelessness, youth crime, homophobia, ageism, racism, sexism, ableism; *National*: Indigenous injustice, unemployment, health, and educational inequity; and the *International*: world poverty, slavery, human trafficking, genocide. We brainstormed how social justice is a way to aid the most vulnerable in society and that the goals of social justice change depending on the place, people, and needs of the time.

Because these students are all future doctors, at this point, I geared the class toward perceiving health inequity as a form of social injustice. We learned about how our identities and prejudices about our bodies and lives can lead to lethal outcomes. We watched Dr. David Williams's compelling TED Talk about how 'Racism makes us sick.'[17] This was a challenging (troubling) watch, so we followed this with visual literacy queries to take us out of the emotional impact of the video and focus our critical thinking skills on the video as a *vessel* of meaning. Our visual literacy questions included:

1. What was the purpose of this TED Talk?
2. What do you think about the evidence Dr. Williams presented?

3. Did this talk convince you that systemic bias impacts health?
4. Do you think this could be relevant in Aotearoa/New Zealand?

Dr. Williams's video and visual literacy content was followed by an echo of the national statistics shown in class 3; this time, we looked at the health statistics of people in the A/NZ. We looked at sobering mortality rates, dental diseases, maternal morbidity rates, psychological and psychiatric admissions, and life expectancy. This led us to a presentation of the four principles of Social Justice for Health, including *Equity*: To ensure fair distribution of available resources across society. *Access*: Ensure all people have access to goods and services regardless of, for example, age, sex/gender, ethnicity. *Participation*: Enable people to participate in decisions that affect their lives. *Rights*: To protect individual liberties to information about circumstances and decisions affecting them and appeal to decisions people feel are unfair.

The penultimate section of the session was a viewing of a segment on healthcare inequity in NZ.[18] This film showed the challenges and opportunities being used to address health inequity in A/NZ. Among the great strides toward Social Justice for Heath include increased self-determination for *Māori*.[19] Lastly, we explored the *Waitangi* Tribunal principles for primary health care. The *Waitangi* Tribunal is a permanent commission concerned with the Government and *Māori* under the Treaty of *Waitangi*: A/NZ's founding document.

We closed with a reminder that it was our last session next week, that we would have a final chance to offer our curiosities, and that the bulk of the session would be exploring the gravest violation of HR (genocide) and the darkest form of 'bad medicine' in a documentary on illegal organ harvesting in hospitals in mainland China.

I was the only one putting chairs and tables back today, but it gave me a chance to think over the session. I am relieved that this class is almost over. While I cannot think of what I would do differently—everything we did before this class made us ready to move into health inequity as an abuse of HR and avenue of SJ—I am not from this country. I worried that my limited exposure to the national/cultural conversations around health would show. As teachers, we often must balance what our students want to know with our sense of expertise and experience. I was comfortable with the HR and SJ content, whereas the students attended the content of this session. Of course, they did…as future doctors and people 'learning' about the reality of their national health inequity landscape; this was stimulating and served to recruit the whole room to the work of social justice for health.

Class 6: Denial of Human Rights and Injustice

The curiosities presented for this final class were almost uniform; the words were varied, but the sentiment was identical: 'as a future doctor, what can I do to improve Māori health outcomes?'

CURRICULUM: our 'darkest' curriculum began with exploring the worst abuse form in humanity: crimes against people. The class looked at 'deliberate destruction of a national, racial, political, religious or cultural group' via either instrumental or cultural genocide. We talked about the 'anatomy' of genocide that victims are identified based on identities (some of which you are born with or into). I shared Stanton's warning stages of genocide: *Classification*, *Symbolization*, *Dehumanization*, *Organization*, *Polarization*, *Preparation*. The *Extermination* stage, followed finally by the last stage: *Denial*.[20]

We took a comfort break, and then we talked about self-care in the classroom. Students were informed that the film we were about to watch was difficult to see and that they needed to self-manage. We talked about what stress in the body feels like, how to breathe when we feel confronted by troubling material (low belly), and they were encouraged to leave the classroom at any time. To give them an idea of where we were going after the short documentary, I mentioned that we would conduct another visual literacy unit afterward, similar to what we did with Dr. Williams's TED Talk.

The documentary 'Human Harvest,' director Leon Lee's award-winning film, features Nobel Peace Prize nominees David Matas and David Kilgour and their investigation of organ harvesting from Falun Gong practitioners in China. The film shows medical 'crimes against humanity,' and we viewed this on a streaming service Kanopy. The film is replete with compelling witness testimony access, evidence, and outcomes of live-organ transfers. It includes expert and intimate statements of the systematic and sinister dehumanization, mutilation, and extermination of prisoners.

The goal of this viewing was to connect the ideas (and ideals) of HR from class 1 to the realities of injustice. The students, including the one

Chinese/Kiwi[21] student, communicated that they had no idea this had occurred in their learning logs. The film was several years old (2014), but new concerns were rising about incarcerations of Uyghur Muslims in China, with overtones of dehumanization and worse.

After the film was over, we turned the lights on and moved into the analysis. We talked about *evidence*, *persuasiveness*, whether the students were *convinced*, and then I asked them to determine whether what they have seen comprised a 'genocide.' All agreed, yes.

We then took another comfort break and came back together to share class reflections. I summarized our journey by moving through the class as if there were six geographical sections. I began at the door, then moved around until I ended up at the door again. I then asked, 'what now?' The majority sentiment was *I have learned so much in this class, and where before I could say 'I had no idea, now that I do, I am going to be an agent for change and make sure I work for social justice in my life, my work, and my country.'* A final comment by one of the older students '*well, I guess I have to start voting now'* was met with a round of laughter. Students asked many times what they could 'do' to support HR and SJ. A baseline action I suggested was to 'vote, vote, vote' to use some of those political and civic rights enshrined in A/NZ to participate in the country's democracy. These doctors are the future, and we need every one of them to join in.

Final Reflection:

> *My intention in crafting this class was to provide a supportive space to introduce and elevate HR and SJ discourse into the minds of future medical professionals. The class was an intensive and intense mix of content, experience, critical reflection, and exposure. The main difference that I can see between teaching this content to non-medical students is that they do not seem to practice intellectual distancing in the same way as the future GPs. If I teach this again, I will do less HR content and more case study exploration. The students each had different areas of interest, and it would be good, in the future delivery of this material, to conduct more research to share with the group.*

Conclusions

This chapter began as an academic inquiry of the delivery, experience, and reflection of teaching Human Rights (HR) and Social Justice (SJ) content to GP trainees in Aotearoa/New Zealand. As a self-study, the focus of this chapter was to capture curriculum and professional reflection on the course conveyance, student feedback, and perceived change in consciousness. This class was a challenge to teach, I certainly had to work harder than usual to simulate dialogue, but inevitably the content and workshop aspects resulted in a communicated desire to support HR and SJ initiatives, to use the platform of professional medical practice to recognize inequity in health outcomes, and to aid vulnerable peoples to have their rights upheld.

As a vehicle for critical consciousness-raising and transformative peace pedagogy, this teaching unit on HR and SJ was an opportunity to share the social impact of professional practice for future GPs and final reflections from students (learning logs) communicated an evident dedication that '*now that I know, I want to help.*' Hopefully, the teaching curriculum and insights gleaned in this chapter will inspire other teachers to utilize transformative peace pedagogy in their work.

Discussion Questions

1. What is the difference between Nationalism and Citizenship?
2. What is a general definition of Human Rights?
3. What are the (6) core HR instruments?
4. What is Social Justice?
5. How do Human Rights relate to Social Justice?
6. How do you encounter new material 'critically?'

Notes

1. Ernest Boyer, *Scholarship Reconsidered: Priorities for the Professoriate* (San Francisco: Jossey-Bass, 1990).
2. Lee S. Shulman, "Taking Learning Seriously," *Change: The Magazine Of Higher Learning* 31, no. 4 (1999): 10–17. https://doi.org/10.1080/00091389909602695.
3. Tony Jenkins "Transformative Peace Pedagogy: Fostering a Reflective, Critical, and Inclusive Praxis for Peace Studies," *In Factis Pax* 10, no. 1 (2016): 1–7.
4. John Loughran, "Researching Teacher Education Practices: Responding to the Challenges, Demands, and Expectations of Self-Study," *Journal of Teacher Education* 58, no. 1 (January 2007): 15.

5. Nandini Maharaj, "Using Field Notes to Facilitate Critical Reflection," *Reflective Practice* 17, no. 2 (2016): 114–24.
6. The New Zealand university where this course was delivered is a nationally and internationally highly ranked 'full' institution that grants medical, dental, law, STEM, and humanities/social science degrees (Undergraduate, Master's, and Doctoral).
7. Paulo Freire, *The Pedagogy of the Oppressed* (New York: Continuum, 2003).
8. Bell Hooks, *Teaching to Transgress* (New York: Routledge, 1994).
9. The HUMAN RIGHTS QUIZ:

    1. What can be defined as human rights? (a) Those benefits granted to any adult person. (b) Those entitlements for those lawfully residing in a given country. (c) Those rights are inherent to all human beings.
    2. What makes the Universal Declaration of Human Rights so unique? (a) It was drafted by people from all over the world. (b) Sets common standards on human rights protection. (c) Both previous answers.
    3. Which of the following is not a part of the International Bill of Human Rights? (a) Universal Declaration of Human Rights, (b) International Covenant on Civil and Political Rights, (c) Convention on the Elimination of all Forms of Discrimination Against Women.
    4. Is Human Rights Education relevant? (a) It is only relevant for those working in the legal profession. (b) It is only relevant for those presenting complaints on human rights violations, (c) It is relevant for all human beings.
    5. Who served as the Chairperson of the drafting committee of the Universal Declaration of Human Rights? A. Eleanor Roosevelt, B. René Cassin, C. Winston Churchill.
    6. How many languages has the Universal Declaration of Human Rights been translated into? A. 520 languages, B. 300 languages, C. 150 languages.
    7. Everyone has the same human rights everywhere. True or False.
    8. Women have equal rights with men? True or False.
    9. What is the leading entity in the UN system for the promotion and protection of human rights? A. The Economic and Social Council, B. Human Rights Council, C. The Office of the High Commissioner for Human Rights.
    10. Do you lose your rights if you are forced to abandon the country you live in? Yes or No.
    11. Are sexual and reproductive health issues protected by international human rights? True or False.
    12. When was the Universal Declaration of Human Rights adopted?
    13. How many articles does the Universal Declaration of Human Rights contain?

14. What are the (after 1948) six international human rights treaties monitored by the treaty bodies?
15. When was the United Nations Founded?
16. What was the first document that asserted individual rights, and when was it drafted?
17. What is the charter called that was drafted in 1948?
18. What is DISCRIMINATION?
19. What is EQUALITY?
20. What is TORTURE?
21. What is a VIOLATION?
22. What is SLAVERY?
23. When was the NZ Bill of Rights Drafted?
24. What does it cover?

10. Henry Tajfel and John Turner, "An Integrative Theory of Intergroup Conflict," in *The Social Psychology of Intergroup Relations*, eds. W. G. Austin, and S. Worchel (Monterey, CA: Brooks/Cole, 1979): 33–7.
11. Frans de Waal, *Two Monkeys were Paid Unequally: Excerpt from Frans de Waal's TED Talk*, TED Blog Video, April 4, 2013, video, 2:43, https://www.youtube.com/watch?v=meiU6TxysCg.
12. THE JUSTICE QUIZ:

    1. What is Justice?
    2. What is the purpose of justice?
    3. What is punitive justice?
    4. What is retributive justice?
    5. What is reparative justice?
    6. What is restorative justice?
    7. What is transformative justice?
    8. What is social justice?
    9. Where did the idea of 'justice' come from?
    10. Who is entitled to justice?

13. The Citizen's Handbook, "Episode 7: The Court System—The Citizen's Handbook," *Radio New Zealand*, April 16, 2020, https://www.rnz.co.nz/programmes/the-citizens-handbook/story/2018739434/the-citizens-handbook-episode-7-the-court-system
14. Meriana Johnsen, "Justice with a Difference: The Iwi Panels with a 92% Success Rate," *Radio New Zealand*, November 16, 2020, https://www.rnz.co.nz/news/te-manu-korihi/430754/justice-with-a-difference-the-iwi-panels-with-a-92-percent-success-rate
15. Emma S., "How is Transformative Justice Different from Restorative Justice?" *Novel Hand* (Blog), December 30, 2020, https://novelhand.com/restorative-and-transformative-justice/.

16. Margot A. Hurlbert, "Defining Justice," in *Pursuing Justice*, ed. Margot, A. Hurlbert (Winnipeg: Fernwood Publishing, 2018), 19.
17. David R. Williams, "How Racism Makes Us Sick," *TEDEd*, https://ed.ted.com/lessons/oRaEODBk.
18. Alice Snedden, "Alice Snedden's Bad News | Episode 3—Healthcare Inequity | RNZ," *RNZ*, August 16, 2020, video, 11:48, https://www.youtube.com/watch?v=4g6l5EeZfFc.
19. The Māori peoples are the majority Indigenous group in Aotearoa/New Zealand, and the experience of colonization and practices of government neglect has led to significant inequities in health.
20. Gregory Stanton, "The Eight Stages of Genocide." *Genocide Watch.* 1996. Accessed June 26, 2007, http://www.genocidewatch.org/8stages1996.htm.
21. Aotearoa/New Zealand is often termed a *bicultural* nation in reference to the presence of Indigenous and non-Indigenous peoples. However, the Islands contain multiple ethnic and cultural groups, including many Asian people who have lived here for generations. A non-Indigenous person who is yet, native to New Zealand is often referred to as a 'kiwi' after the national bird.

Bibliography

Boyer, Ernest. *Scholarship Reconsidered: Priorities for the Professoriate.* San Francisco: Jossey-Bass, 1990.

The Citizen's Handbook, "Episode 7: The Court System—The Citizen's Handbook." *Radio New Zealand*, April 16, 2020, https://www.rnz.co.nz/programmes/the-citizens-handbook/story/2018739434/the-citizen-s-handbook-episode-7-the-court-system.

de Waal, Frans. *Two Monkeys were Paid Unequally: Excerpt from Frans de Waal's TED Talk.* TED Blog Video. April 4, 2013. Video, 2:43. https://www.youtube.com/watch?v=meiU6TxysCg.

Emma, S. "How is Transformative Justice Different from Restorative Justice?" *Novel Hand (Blog).* December 30, 2020. https://novelhand.com/restorative-and-transformative-justice/.

Freire, Paulo. *The Pedagogy of the Oppressed.* New York: Continuum, 2003.

Hooks, Bell. *Teaching to Transgress.* New York: Routledge, 1994.

Hurlbert, Margot A. "Defining Justice." in *Pursuing Justice*, edited by Margot A. Hurlbert. Winnipeg: Fernwood Publishing, 2018.

Jenkins, Tony. "Transformative Peace Pedagogy: Fostering a Reflective, Critical, and Inclusive Praxis for Peace Studies." *In Factis Pax* 10, no. 1 (2016): 1–7.

Johnsen, Meriana. "Justice with a Difference: The Iwi Panels with a 92% Success Rate." *Radio New Zealand*. November 16, 2020. https://www.rnz.co.nz/news/te-manu-korihi/430754/justice-with-a-difference-the-iwi-panels-with-a-92-percent-success-rate.

Loughran, John. "Researching Teacher Education Practices: Responding to the Challenges, Demands, and Expectations of Self-Study." *Journal of Teacher Education* 58, no. 1 (2007): 12–20.

Maharaj, Nandini. "Using Field Notes to Facilitate Critical Reflection." *Reflective Practice* 17, no. 2 (2016): 114–24.

Shulman, Lee S. "Taking Learning Seriously." *Change: The Magazine of Higher Learning* 31, no. 4 (1999): 10–17. https://doi.org/10.1080/00091389909602695.

Snedden, Alice. "Alice Snedden's Bad News | Episode 3—Healthcare Inequity | RNZ." *RNZ*. August 16, 2020. Video, 11:48, https://www.youtube.com/watch?v=4g6l5EeZfFc.

Stanton, Gregory. "The Eight Stages of Genocide." *Genocide Watch*. 1996. Accessed June 26, 2007, http://www.genocidewatch.org/8stages1996.htm.

Tajfel, Henri and John Turner, "An Integrative Theory of Intergroup Conflict." in *The Social Psychology of Intergroup Relations*, edited by W. G. Austin, and S. Worchel, 33–7. Monterey, CA: Brooks/Cole, 1979.

Williams, David R. "How Racism Makes Us Sick." *TEDEd*. https://ed.ted.com/lessons/oRaEODBk.

Are Human Rights Universal?

Carlos Godoy

More than seven decades after the adoption of the Universal Declaration of Human Rights[1] (UDHR) in 1948, when 48 of the 58 members of the United Nations (UN) voted favourably to the document, and none voted against it,[2] the universality of human rights continues to be challenged. Though the majority of the countries has adhered to the main treaties established to codify the UDHR into binding law, like the covenants on civil, political, social, economic, and cultural rights, and the conventions against all forms of discrimination,[3] voices from all over the world continue to challenge the universal acceptance of human rights.[4] Despite the unquestionable civil and political rights progress across the world, notably from the second half of the twentieth century[5] onwards, many voices claim that international human rights are not universal.

Some scholars argue that universal human rights reflect Global North-Western ideas imposed over Global South states.[6] Other critics allege that the international human rights regime disregards the culture, norms, and traditions of non-Western societies.[7] Also, some critiques deem universal

C. Godoy (✉)
University of Manitoba, Winnipeg, MB, Canada
e-mail: godoyjuc@myumanitoba.ca

L. E. Reimer and K. Standish (eds.), *Perspectives on Justice, Indigeneity, Gender, and Security in Human Rights Research*,
https://doi.org/10.1007/978-981-99-1930-7_5

human rights as a manifestation of Western cultural imperialism.[8] The overemphasis on individual rights, which are essential to society's development, at the expense of collective rights,[9] is another popular argument against the acceptance of human rights as universal. By examining the concepts of human rights and universality and the main criticisms of the universal human rights argument, this chapter concludes that, because they are plurally affected worldwide by cultural aspects and diverse values and interests, human rights, as stated in the UDHR, are not universal. A minimalist system is the most feasible human rights regime that can be internationally implemented.

Unravelling Human Rights

There are multiple theories about the origins of human rights and why human beings are entitled to have rights. Although many scholars deem human rights a Western creation,[10] one cannot disregard how they were influenced by secular and religious humanistic values, which applied to all human beings.[11] Christianity and Islam advocated for human solidarity; the ancient Romans and Greeks emphasized natural laws for all humans; the Babylonians proclaimed the proportionate punishment; the Hebrews honoured the inviolability of life; Confucianism introduced universal education.[12] Also, ethical principles that emphasized the protection of individual life, children, women, aged ones, and vulnerable people were inherited from non-Western secular traditions.[13] Nevertheless, as Mende[14] articulates, human rights, as they are popularly understood, is associated with Western documents from the Medieval and Enlightenment ages, including the English Magna Carta and the French Déclaration des Droits de l'Homme et du Citoyen. In this light, human rights are primarily held by individuals and aimed to protect every human being from other individuals, organizations, society, and the own state.[15] According to Steve On,[16] human rights must be protected by and from the state to preserve metaphysical values, including equality and liberty. In turn, the Naturalist theory states that people are entitled to human rights for the only condition of belonging to the human species.[17]

Nevertheless, other respected theories do not associate human rights with ethical principles or secular doctrines. As Ignatieff[18] maintains, human rights are a minimalist set of protection from violence and abuse that all humans deserve. Human rights constitute a common language historically created to defend the free exercise of individual agency and allow human beings to be safeguarded from the state, groups, and institutions' cruelty and tyranny.[19] Hence, they aim primarily to ensure negative liberty.[20] As stated in the UDHR, human rights were brought from the Western need to prevent the repetition of its own heinous oppressive practices-like racism, antisemitism, and the holocaust against humans.[21] Hence, the rationale for the existence of human rights and their entitlement to human beings is historical, as human rights are the means available to defend individuals from abuse and oppression.[22] Samuel Moyn states that human rights only significantly came to light in the 1970s, from the beginning of Jimmy Carter's US presidential inauguration.[23] He argues that human rights, a response to previous failed socialist and post-colonial approaches, arose as a "minimalist utopia" to transcend the nation-state, providing freedom, identity, and prosperity for the people.[24] Human rights were not inspired by self-determination, anti-colonialist, and socialist ideas because they aimed to build state sovereignty instead of achieving basic individual rights for all.[25] After "failed utopias," human rights emerged as the "last utopia," to create an international framework beyond sovereign states to protect individuals' rights.[26] Yet, what do human rights aim to protect?

Human rights, as stated in the UDHR, involve civil and political rights,[27] also referred to as individual rights[28] (right to life and liberty; equality; self-determination; protection against torture, slavery, and arbitrary arrest; freedom of movement; fair trial; freedom of thought, conscience, and religion; and protection against any kind of discrimination), and economic, social, and cultural rights,[29] also known as collective rights[30] (right to work and fair working conditions; social security; family protection; appropriate living standards; education; and free enjoyment of cultural life). They refer to people's lives and society's vulnerable interests that should be preserved to ensure a worthy life in which all have their dignities protected. Le[31] maintains that universal dignity is inherent to all humans, characterizing the respect and worth that all people deserve for the only condition of being humans. As it was the paradigm that guided the elaboration of the UDHR, all the people are entitled to human rights, thus, deserving to be respectfully and equally treated. Dignity[32] is the foundation of human rights, which makes them indivisible, interdependent, and non-hierarchical.[33] Considering that all human beings share human dignity, which ensures the binding force of human rights, it brings about the "universality" topic.

The central controversy that involves the subject is defining whether human rights are universal. However, to draw into the topic is essential to understand what the universality of human rights is and encompasses. Simply put, as Arnold[34] explains, universality refers to a global predisposition to accept and adopt human rights, such as individual, women, and child protection rights, at the local, regional, and international levels. Their universality may manifest in different ways, from the interpretation of domestic norms according to international laws aimed to protect rights to states' willingness to comply with international human rights standards. Take it as an example of the latter, the ratification of international treaties, as it happened in Vienna's United Nations World Conference on human rights when most of the member-states ratified the universality of human rights.[35] Therefore, universality involves the consensual adherence to international human rights norms and the intent to defend the values that those norms protect.

Nevertheless, the consensus on international human rights in such a diverse and pluralistic world implies a political convergence of leading components of almost all states to the understanding of moral equality of every human being. The "consensus" on the rights enshrined in the UDHR is formed when most societies understand that all human beings are entitled to respect and protection from the state because holding inherent rights associated with human equality and freedom.[36] As Donnelly[37] explains, elaborating on John Rawls' (1996) Theory of Justice, the international harmony on human rights is reached through the "overlapping consensus universality,"[38] which is the political adherence to recognized international human rights by the most representative doctrines and systems across the world. Differently from a consensus on its literal sense, the overlapping harmony is grounded in moral principles that favour social unicity in pluralistic and deeply divided contexts.[39] The overlapping consensus, though universal, is partial and does not imply the uniformity of the norms adopted by states. Instead, it is characterized by the endorsement of human rights protection by national legal systems due to the common understanding that all human beings, given their intrinsic dignity, are entitled to the UDHR.[40] In such a diverse global context, the overlapping consensus is the feasible way to make human rights universal and, most importantly, to raise ordinary people's awareness of the existence of and their natural entitlement to human rights.

In a similar strand, Ignatieff asserts that a universal regime of human rights could only be achieved if it embraces a restricted array of rights to be protected.[41] The minimalist universality refers to an international human rights system compatible with minimal moral ways adopted by different civilizations, cultures, religions, and traditions to define how human life must be protected. Rather than demanding a universal agreement on the protections required by a "good life," the universality is achieved by agreeing on what human life cannot accept and so must be protected against.[42] In other words, a human rights system will succeed to be universal only if it embraces the minimum protections necessary to human existence, which the majority of states consider morally defensible and can agree with.[43]

An important question is how variable the understanding of individual and collective human rights might be to keep the consensus characterized, and so their universality. On[44] argues, agreeing with Donnelly's[45] arguments, that the universality of human rights does not encompass their interpretation and implementation. In other words, however controversial it might be, countries interpret and implement human rights according to national particularities, which Bell[46] understands as the only way to work out the overlapping consensus. In turn, elaborating on the "moderate universalism,"[47] Arnold considers that cultural particularities could be contemplated when interpreting human rights norms. That is, the overlapping consensus universality and reasonable interpretations and implementations should rest in the realms of the core concepts of a specific human right.[48] This assertion corresponds to the three-fold definition that divides human rights into conception, interpretation, and implementation levels.[49] In this sense, the UN's Covenant on Economic, Social and Cultural rights lays out that states are responsible for progressively and gradually implement the rights for education, fair labour, family protection, and cultural enjoyment,[50] and measures to adapt the national legislation to the obligations required.[51] The diversity of contextual aspects involving different countries requires that a "margin of appreciation"[52] be allowed in the domestic implementation of rights to make the universal consensus feasible.

Nevertheless, the international consensus demands a practical mechanism to ensure adherence to state activities to the UDHR. This mechanism, which Donnelly defines as "international legal universality,"[53] is characterized by the ratification of a series of treaties aimed to codify international human rights. Those treaties' importance resides in their potential to disseminate the human rights mindset into the societies, making people realize that oppression and domination are not permissible[54] and encouraging popular movements to fight for social justice and human dignity. The increasing demand for social justice improvements through the language of human rights, which Dominique Clément describes as "rights inflation,"[55] no matter how problematic it might be, evidences the social transformation potential of institutionally endorsed human rights. The impressive 91% ratification rate[56] (among 197 UN country members) of the six core international human rights treaties demonstrates the force of the international legal universality as an instrument to evidence the global consensus on human rights. Irrespective of the many criticisms addressed to human rights, the massive international adherence to the UDHR and the leading international human rights treaties are unquestionable evidence of the universality.

Challenging Human Rights: Universality at Stake

The universality of human rights, for distinct reasons, has been criticized since the advent of the UDHR. The primary challenges to human rights universality are often associated with three main assumptions. First, they claim that human rights are Western-oriented.[57] Second, critics argue that a universal system is not feasible because human rights are culturally relative.[58] Third, the international human rights system privileges individuals to the extent of collective rights, disregarding a significant parcel of states that emphasize the family and the group as the basis of society.[59] In the next sections, the universality of human rights is analysed in light of the critiques mentioned.

Are Human Rights Western-Oriented?

Critiques, based on the supposed Western bias of international human rights, contend that Western-liberal societies' values framed the UDHR. Therefore, the aspirations and views of the non-Western countries were neglected.[60] Other critics argue that the human rights system is a Western tool to interfere in the internal affairs of non-Western countries by imposing concepts that hinder their economic competitiveness.[61] Given social differences, those countries do not hold the same trading standards as those of Western countries. Also, the Western ethnocentrism that guided the drafting of the UDHR is criticized, as most states that ratified the declaration were from the West and so tended to emphasize Western values.[62] Moreover, though non-Western individuals were involved in the UDHR commission, they were cosmopolitans who often were educated in the West and had adopted Western values. Even though the Western powerful global actors have had significant participation in the development of the UDHR, the memorable contribution of non-Western counties could not balance the Western influence on the declaration.

Without denying the Western influence, it is relevant to examine the roots of the human rights ideals to determine whether they are Western. Historical documents commonly associated with human rights, which include the English Bill of Rights (1689), the United States Bill of Rights, and the French Déclaration des Droits de l'Homme et du Citoyen (1789),[63] connote the understanding that the core of human rights lays in Western civilization. However, the contemporary human rights regime, rather than a logical consequence of previous rights declarations, was an international reaction to the Second World War holocaust.[64]

Furthermore, non-Western liberation movements also played a critical role in giving rise to human rights ideals. Notably, the Haitian fight against French colonialism in the eighteenth century and the revolutionaries' demands for political engagement of people of colour were critical to influencing slavery abolishing movements across the world.[65] Equally important, individual autonomy, freedom, and tolerance values, which supposedly were born in the Western world, can be found in non-Western religious Buddhist, Confucianist, Mandarin, and Brahman thoughts and traditions.[66] As Sharma[67] illustrates, the basis for the individual entitlement of rights and the resulted state obligation to fulfil it was brought from Hinduism. The examination of the influences on the human rights ideas confirms that Western and non-Western thoughts informed the aspirations enshrined in the UDHR.

The argument of the majoritarian Western influence and participation in drafting the UDHR is also refuted. As Sikkink[68] clarifies, ex-colonial Latin-American and Asian countries played a prominent role in influencing the drafting of the UHDR. In the same sense, Tharoor[69] recalls the critical participation of China, India, Lebanon, Panama, and Chile, by giving insights into their own cultures in the UDHR works and the decisive contribution of African states-particularly Ghana and Nigeria-which had just emerged from colonialism, in encouraging other African countries to adhere to the 1960s' human rights covenants. Similarly, Mende[70] cites considerable contributions to the international human rights regime from African, Asian, Middle Eastern, and Latin-American countries in the 1950s and 1960s. International human rights enshrined in 1948's declaration reflect global values from Western and non-Western societies. It is evidenced by the ratification of the human rights covenants from 1948 to date,[71] and the adherence to 1993's Vienna Declaration and Programme of Action on human rights by a significant majority of UN member-states.[72] It also attests that international human rights are grounded in multi-regional principles.

The supposed Western bias of non-Western individuals who integrated the UDHR commissions comes from assuming that those people defended Western ideas because of their international education and cosmopolitan way of living. In contrast, Sikkink[73] cites examples of non-Western delegates who defended their regional interests rather than Western views. In this regard, Pen-Chun Chang and other delegates from Latin America pushed for the introduction of collective duties' principles in the UDHR, as opposed to the Western emphasis on individual rights. Similarly, Lebanese representative Charles Malik contributed to the inclusion of the freedom of religion right in the UDHR, not because of Western influence on his beliefs, but due to his awareness of the acceptance into his own country of refugees' suffering after escaping from religious persecution. Human rights cannot be associated only with Western nor non-Western principles and traditions because they reflect pluralistic views. Take the example of civil society movements, diplomats, and activists from all the continents and regions who address their demands through the human rights language.[74] Human rights comprise a cross-cultural set of ideas and principles. Hence, their defence cannot be confused with biased regional advocacy.

Human rights are also challenged for being considered a Western instrument to legitimize an intervention in other states' affairs, prolong colonialism, and reinforce unilateral power relations. As Sikkink[75] explains, rather than imposed by Western countries, during the UDHR works, the idea of international human rights was advocated by the less powerful countries as a protection mechanism against interventions from the global power actors. Considering this, human rights were thought of as an instrument of protection against colonialism and to minimize the impact of unequal power relations on vulnerable countries. This assertion is reinforced by the fact that human rights were institutionalized by a pluralistic process, which counted on multi-regional contributing sources rather than a Western-driven project.[76] Rather than a tool to favour inequalities, human rights came to support the unprivileged and weaker, helping to protect them from the powerful, whether it be an individual, the society, or the state.

Still, in the realm of the Western vs. non-Western dichotomy, voices, often from Asia and developing countries, contest human rights for imposing values that they argue restrain development. That is a two-fold critique. First, Asian countries argue that human rights hamper growth by imposing Western values that contradict the Confucian virtues of obedience and respect for hierarchy, facilitating state development and favouring collectivity.[77] Elaborating on the so-called "Asian values," Le[78] affirms that the suppression of rights speech in favour of development usually masks authoritarian tendencies aimed to keep the status quo and domination by suppressing agency and people's challenging of the abuse of power. Further, the significant adherence of Asian countries to the human rights covenants[79] is evidence that human rights and state actions towards development can coexist and are mutually reinforcing.

Second, critics claim that, differently from Western states, developing countries don't have the structure and resources to afford human rights and nation-building simultaneously. So authoritarianism is the most efficient solution to promote economic growth and development.[80] The historical participation of developing states in the drafting of the UHDR and, notably, ex-colonial countries from Africa to push the 1960s human rights covenants demonstrates that the human rights principles were widely adopted by countries struggling with development needs.[81] Human rights, rather than hampering development initiatives, contribute to economic growth by the evolution of civil society and the improvement of mechanisms to challenge power abuse.

Are Human Rights Culturally Relative?

Another fertile topic for criticism on the universality of human rights is culture. More precisely, critics argue that due to the multicultural diversity, it is not viable to adopt the same human rights standards across the globe. In other words, the rights enshrined in the UDHR are not equally applicable to all the countries because rights must be "relativized" to adapt to different cultures. That is to say, the thoughts, values, and behaviours of individuals are determined by standards formed according to the cultural customs of a given society.[82] Rights are culturally relative because the cultural context determines how they are enjoyed and violated.[83]

In this regard, the cultural relativist critics claim that, first, given the different ways to interpret human rights, they cannot be universal. Second, Western culture undermines traditional values and erodes social customs in non-Western societies. Third, due to cultural diversity, the UDHR is not grounded in shared moral principles and cannot be universal. Fourth, human rights stem from Western religions and so are not compatible with the traditions adopted by Islamic regimes. Fifth, some rights recognized by the UDHR, like women's rights, are not conformable with specific cultural contexts from non-Western societies. The cultural context undoubtedly influences the understanding of a right. However, before analysing the cultural relativist critiques of universal human rights, it is crucial to find if the international human rights regime admits cultural variations.

In the face of the contemporary world's cultural diversity, it would be rational to admit some level of difference in the understanding of human rights. The proclamation of the 1993 *Vienna Conference of Human Rights*[84] stated in the fifth paragraph of its programme of action that, though human rights are universal, the states should consider cultural and religious national and regional particularities in the promotion of human rights.[85] It was in line with the UDHR, which implicitly recognizes cultural differences when it refers to "all peoples and all nations" in its preamble.[86] Even before the advent of the UHDR, as Gros Espiell[87] explains, the UN had already recognized cultural diversity and its coexistence with universal human rights in Article I of the constitution of the United Nations Educational, Scientific and Cultural Organization (UNESCO).[88] After confronting different UN documents, it becomes clear that the human rights regime considers and admits that cultural particularities should coexist with universal human rights. Yet, thinking about cultural relativity and its critiques to the universality of human rights, a question arises: in practical terms, can universal human rights be applied in multicultural settings without losing its primary human dignity protection characteristic?

The first relativist critique denies universality because of the multiple interpretations of human rights that might arise from distinct cultural settings. The essence of human rights, that is, their substance, which is inherent to human dignity, is universal because based on moral principles common to different cultures, religions, and times.[89] In other words, universal human rights are not contrary to specific traditions and cultures. Yet, culture influence the way states enforce human rights. The understanding is subtle, but human rights' moral inspiration is universal because it trespasses the time, while cultural traditions might change or be forgotten.[90] The universality does not extend to the right interpretation.

Nevertheless, national legislation should absorb the essence of the protection that is sought. Thus, though attending the local cultural traditions, human rights must keep their human dignity protection characteristic.[91] Similarly, as Donnelly[92] observes, the universality of human rights rests in their concepts, their essences, and not in their interpretation, which may vary according to the cultural context, which is not immutable. Indeed, it seems logical that states have some margin of appreciation while interpreting and implementing a human right. The more adapted to the local culture, the more sociologically accepted the norm would be.[93]

Another common relativist claim poses Western and non-Western cultures in confrontation due to their clashing differences. Hence it is vital to know if both cultures, though different, can coexist and protect a standard set of human rights. As Tharoor[94] elaborates, the answer can be found in the multiple concepts shared by different societies over the world. Protection from oppressive rule, governance participation, the dignity of the individual, rightness, and justice are common principles historically cultivated in the most different civilizations, making the universality of human rights feasible. Franck,[95] in turn, maintains that Western and non-Western cultures' differences derive from contemporary world development. It created demands that were first implemented in the West and gave rise to human rights advancement. However, these advances, like the improvements in women and child protection rights, are replicable anywhere. The close comparison of both cultures shows that Western and non-Western civilizations shared comparable fundamentalist views and practices over history.[96] For instance, take the similarities between the ancient Greek civilization and Medieval Europe Christian Church's cruel practices and current Taliban methods.[97]

Another critical insight to be added to the discussion is the coercion of people to accept practices that don't reflect the culture but the political interests of those who control the state's power.[98] Suppose people are given a choice to opt-out of oppressive traditions, even if from different cultures, they will tend to walk hand to hand towards human dignity. Illustrating this point of view, Tharoor[99] cites India's case of a divorced Muslim woman who successfully demanded the Supreme Court, against the Muslim tradition, for the alimony right. At the same time, would victims of child work, limb amputation, and genital mutilation voluntarily opt to keep these "cultural traditions" rather than having their dignity protected under international human rights norms?[100] It is coercion, not culture, that is unconcealable with universal human rights. Cultural differences do not impede the adoption of universal human rights because the values to be protected are universal, though interpretation particularities might occur.

Relativists also contend that the UDHR cannot be universal because it does not reflect moral principles adopted worldwide. In 1947, UNESCO had created a committee to collect reflections on human rights from multiple sources. Ideas from different cultural, philosophical, regional, and ideological backgrounds were collected. In the end, the feedback received evidence that the moral values that inform universal human rights were present in Chinese, Hindu, Islamic, European cultures.[101] The similarities among the responses from people from such diverse cultures, who cultivated such distinct traditions and even ideologies, proved that human rights principles were shared in various cultural settings.

Religious difference is another issue that underpins the cultural relativity criticism on internationally shared human rights. Cultural traditions and religion, as Pin[102] explains, constitute one body that encompasses and expresses the fundamental rights defended by the state, which have a universal inspiration. In other words, culture and religion express, in different fashions, universal values, like freedom, tolerance, and compassion, which are common to different spiritual philosophies like Buddhism, Hinduism, and Islam.[103] According to Franck,[104] the similar methods used by different religions since ancient times, demonstrating tolerance or cruelty, evidence that Western and non-Western religions have parallel roots. What made them different was the industrialization and advances in education, transportation, urbanization, and communications that happened first in the West and gave rise to claims for equality and social change. As a result, Western religions also had to adapt first.

Most importantly, religious tradition and human rights can coexist. Take the example of Sisters of Islam, a Malaysian NGO that demands women's rights improvements. It has local credibility because its arguments are based on Islamic principles.[105] Therefore, the human rights language can be applied in diverse religious contexts. Yet, taking advantage of sectarian differences is a political way to explain authoritarian practices of dominance to keep the status quo and preserve power.

The last relativist critique addressed to universalism, which maybe is the most polemic, contends that non-Western societies cannot absorb UDHR's equal rights for women. The relevant engagement of women from different regional backgrounds, like Latin America and Asia, in defence of women's rights during the UDHR drafting work[106] indicates that different cultural contexts admit equal rights to defend common standards of human dignity. Discrimination and subjugation of women is not a cultural tradition. Instead, it is a social mindset constructed and historically disseminated by male-dominated societies. Franck[107] brings an illustrative case of an Indian woman in Canada who resourced justice because she wanted to live in her Indian community after being married to a white man. At that time, the *Indian Act*, which is currently in force,[108] denied women the right to return to the Indian community after marrying out of the tribe. In the end, the Canadian government revoked the gender-discriminatory law, giving rise to complaints from Indian leaders who claimed that granting this right to women contradicted old tribal traditions and would harm the own survival of the ethnic group. That Indigenous group "tradition," anthropological research evidenced, was copied from Victorian patriarchal societies. Hence, it seems indisputable that gender inequality is not related to culture. Women's rights are universal and can be similarly adopted in different cultural contexts.

Does the UDHR Privilege Individual Rights at the Expense of Social Rights?

The critique on the UDHR's "overemphasis" on individual rights at the expense of community values came to the international mainstream from Asian sources in defence of the so-called "Asian way" or "Asian value." The critics claim for collective-aimed human rights, which reflect the unique values of Asian countries,[109] instead of Western individualism. These complaints also echo in African societies, in which decisions are consensual and communitarian.[110] Moreover, they argue that there is the primacy of civil and political rights that privileges the individual over the family, which is the basis of the society, and rights over duties,[111] which in turn neglect society's rights, hampers development, and threatens civil obedience. The defence of collective rather than individual rights, on the one hand, benefits social growth and development, but on the other hand, it might facilitate oppressive measures of authoritarian regimes. Furthermore, as Ignatieff[112] articulates, human rights' relevance rests in their capability to empower individuals to pursue protection against institutions and the state. Even the sole purpose of collective rights is the protection of the individuals who comprise the collectivity.[113]

UDHR's civil and political [individual] rights, as well as economic, social, and cultural [collective] rights, are essential for social development and should be balanced. As stated in the UDHR, human rights are indivisible and interdependent. Hence, it is not reasonable to emphasize one or another category of rights. Civil and political rights are vital to protecting groups, while social and economic rights also protect individuals.[114] In this sense, the same protection demanded in the West, due to the modernization and advance of the market economy, will be sooner or later required to protect individuals and groups in Asia and Africa.[115] The claim for emphasis on collective rights and adaptations to specificities of the Asian culture, like informal social sanction, valuing the traditional paternalism and permanent employment, does not represent any harm to international human rights. Instead, it locally reinforces the importance and respect of the UDHR rights.[116] The risk posed by the governmental advocacy of duties over rights and collectivity over the individual is to mask authoritarian abuses through economic development myths and tyrannic measures.[117] Despite the Asian complaints, many prominent non-Western personalities had manifested support to universal human rights as defined in the UDHR.[118] "Individual" and "collective" rights are complementary and should coexist in every society, even if adapted to regional traditions.

The international human rights regime plays other relevant roles that evidence its collective approach. Indigenous rights have been advancing, even if at a slow pace, over the decades,[119] whereby protection frameworks like the *Declaration on the Rights of Indigenous Peoples* introduced collective rights as group rights and has been used by diverse Indigenous groups. It challenges centuries of discriminatory laws and helped to change national norms worldwide to improve Indigenous rights protection.[120] Moreover, the UDHR, as Le[121] highlights, emphasizes both collective and individual rights by urging, in its preamble, all to act in a "spirit of brotherhood"[122] and exploring individual and social rights in its body. All the things considered; one realizes that international human rights are not individual nor collective. Human rights are interdependent. Hence, the UDHR comprehensively establishes non-hierarchical individual and collective rights.

Conclusion

Even though the many favourable arguments, the negative impact of culture, religion, and interests on the idea of universal human rights is undeniable, in such a pluralistic world, in which the state's interpretation and implementation of international human rights are influenced by diverse values, traditions, and political interests, a universal human rights system is close to a utopia. Culture evolves and changes over time. Thus, although the increasing states' ratification of international covenants on human rights, given the significant divergencies in translating international human rights norms to national settings, human rights are not universal. However, the essence of human rights, or the minimum protection required for human existence, which human rights primarily aim to protect, remains at the core of every society, irrespective of its location and predominant belief and traditions.

In the plural Twenty-first Century world, achieving an overlapping consensus on human rights or even a moderate universality seems unrealistic. Reasonable and achievable is implementing a minimalist international human rights system, recognized by the majority of states as essential to protect humans against human wrongdoings. The acceptance of variable interpretations that do not contradict the core minimum to be protected should be deliberated, resting on the people the freedom to adopt human rights in the best ways to fit their lives. The opposition between cultural relativism and a minimalist human rights system, if not destructive, can help to strengthen the global human rights regime by stimulating the cross-cultural debate and sensitivity and creating national norms that better translate the local traditions and aspirations, without denying the substance of human rights.

Discussion Questions

1. What is the minimalist universality of human rights?
2. Why cannot human rights be considered an exclusively Western concept? How do religion and culture evidence the universality of human rights?

3. How can universal human rights coexist in the world's multiple cultural contexts? To what extent does culture influence human rights?
4. How can universal human rights contribute to minority, vulnerable, and excluded people's emancipation worldwide?

Notes

1. United Nations General Assembly, "Universal Declaration of Human Rights," 217 (III) A. Paris, 1948.
2. United Nations, "The Yearbook of the United Nations 1948–49," 1950, V; Social, Humanitarian and Cultural Questions, 535.
3. United Nations Office of the High Commissioner for Human Rights, "Status of Ratification Interactive Dashboard," 2020.
4. Janne Mende, "Are Human Rights Western—And Why Does It Matter? A Perspective from International Political Theory," *Journal of International Political Theory* 17, no. 1 (2019): 1.
5. Kathren Sikkink, *Evidence for Hope: Making Human Rights Work in the 21st Century* (Princeton: Princeton University Press, 2017), 10–11.
6. Sikkink, 63.
7. Nhina Le, "Are Human Rights Universal or Culturally Relative?" *Peace Review: Police Militarization* 28, no. 2 (2016): 204. Similarly, David A. Duquette, "Universalism and Relativism in Human Rights," in *Universal Human Rights Moral Order in a Divided World*, ed. David A. Reidy and Mortimer N.S. Sellers (Lanham: Rowman & Littlefield Publishers, 2005), 70, cites the criticism from non-Western countries to a supposed Western bias of the rights stated on the UDHR.
8. Ari Kohen, "An Overlapping Consensus on Human Rights and Human Dignity," in *Human Rights at the Crossroads*, ed. Mark Goodale (New York: Oxford University Press, 2014), 1–2.
9. Thomas M. Franck, "Are Human Rights Universal?" *Foreign Affairs* 80, no. 1 (2001): 196.
10. Mende, "Are Human Rights Western," 1.
11. Micheline Ishay, "What Are Human Rights? Six Historical Controversies," *Journal of Human Rights* 3, no. 3 (2004): 361.
12. Ishay, "What Are Human Rights?" 361.
13. Micheline Ishar, *The History of Human Rights: From Ancient Times to the Globalization Era* (Berkeley: University of California Press, 2008), 45, 47, 51, 57–60.
14. Mende, "Are Human Rights Western," 3.

15. Daniel A. Bell, "Which Rights Are Universal?" *Political Theory* 27, no. 6 (1999): 849; Shashi Tharoor, "Are Human Rights Universal?" *World Policy Journal* 16, no. 4 (1999): 5, also emphasizes the human rights role as a protection mechanism from state action.
16. Steve On, "The 'Relative Universality' of Human Rights: An Assessment," *Perspectives on Global Development and Technology* 4, no. 3/4 (2005): 579.
17. Ishay, *The History of Human Rights*, 3.
18. Michael Ignatieff, *Human Rights as Politics and Idolatry*, ed. Amy Gutmann (Princeton: Princeton University Press, 2001), 55, 83.
19. Ignatieff, 83.
20. Isaiah Berlin, *Two Concepts of Liberty* (Oxford: Clarendon Press, 1958), 7–8, explains that negative freedom defines the condition in which a human being is free of coercion, interference, or oppression from other human beings.
21. Ignatieff, *Human Rights as Politics and Idolatry*, 91–92.
22. Ignatieff, 83–84.
23. Samuel Moyn, *The Last Utopia: Human Rights in History* (Cambridge: Harvard University Press, 2010), 7, 121, 155.
24. Moyn, 121, 130, 213.
25. Moyn, 84–86, 119, 214.
26. Moyn, 122.
27. United Nations Office of the High Commissioner for Human Rights, "International Covenant on Civil and Political Rights," 1976.
28. Ishay, "What Are Human Rights?" 366.
29. United Nations Office of the High Commissioner for Human Rights, "International Covenant on Economic, Social and Cultural Rights," 1966.
30. William Felice, *Taking Suffering Seriously: The Importance of Collective Human Rights* (Albany: State University of New York Press, 1996), 20.
31. Le, "Are Human Rights Universal," 203.
32. Rainer Arnold, "Are Human Rights Universal and Binding?" in *General Reports of the XVIIIth Congress of the International Academy of Comparative Law/Rapports Généraux du XVIIIème Congrès de l'Académie Internationale de Droit Comparé*, ed. Karen B. Brown and David Snyder (Dordrecht: Springer, 2012), 587.
33. Christina M. Cerna, "Universality of Human Rights and Cultural Diversity: Implementation of Human Rights in Different Socio-Cultural Contexts," *Human Rights Quarterly* 16, no. 4 (1994): 744.
34. Arnold, "Are Human Rights Universal and Binding?" 582–583.
35. Arnold, 582.
36. On, "The 'Relative Universality' of Human Rights," 580.

37. Jack Donnelly, *Universal Human Rights in Theory and Practice. 3rd ed.* (Ithaca: Cornell University Press, 2013), 57–60.
38. Donnelly, 57–60.
39. John Rawls, "The Idea of an Overlapping Consensus," *Oxford Journal of Legal Studies* 7, no. 1 (1987): 3.
40. Kohen, "An Overlapping Consensus on Human Rights," 7.
41. Ignatieff, *Human Rights as Politics and idolatry*, xii, xix–xx, 56.
42. Ignatieff, 56–57.
43. Ignatieff, 56.
44. On, "The 'Relative Universality' of Human Rights," 581.
45. Donnelly, *Universal Human Rights*, 100–103.
46. Bell, "Which Rights Are Universal?" 851, 853.
47. Arnold, "Are Human Rights Universal and Binding?" 583.
48. On, "The 'Relative Universality' of Human Rights," 585.
49. Donnelly, *Universal Human Rights*, 99–100.
50. UN Human Rights, "International Covenant on Economic".
51. Rex Martin, "Are Human Rights Universal?" in *Human Rights: The Hard Questions*, ed. Cindy Holder and David Reidy (New York: Cambridge University Press, 2013), 67.
52. Arnold, "Are Human Rights Universal and Binding?" 583.
53. Donnelly, *Universal Human Rights*, 94, 118.
54. Le, "Are Human Rights Universal or Culturally Relative?" 206.
55. Dominique Clément, "Human Rights or Social Justice? The Problem of Rights Inflation," *International Journal of Human Rights* 22, no. 2 (2018): 155–156.
56. UN Human Rights, "Status of Ratification."
57. Bell, "Which Rights Are Universal?" 849.
58. Le, "Are Human Rights Universal or Culturally Relative?" 203.
59. Tharoor, "Are Human Rights Universal?" 1.
60. Bell, "Which Rights Are Universal?" 849.
61. Cerna, "Universality of Human Rights and Cultural Diversity," 740.
62. Duquette, "Universalism and Relativism," 62.
63. Mende, "Are Human Rights Western," 3.
64. Ignatieff, *Human Rights as Politics and idolatry*, 55–56.
65. Mende, "Are Human Rights Western," 4.
66. Mende, 4.
67. Mende, 3, quoted in Arvind Sharma, *Hinduism and Human Rights: A conceptual Approach* (New Delhi: Oxford University Press, 2004).
68. Sikkink, *Evidence for Hope*, 11, 70–72, 79.
69. Tharoor, "Are Human Rights Universal?" 3.
70. Mende, "Are Human Rights Western," 6.
71. UN Human Rights, "Status of Ratification."
72. Cerna, "Universality of Human Rights and Cultural Diversity," 742.

73. Sikkink, *Evidence for Hope*, 78, 86–87.
74. Paulo Sergio Pinheiro, "Besides Human Rights, I Don't See a Solution for Serving the Victims," interview by Maria Brant. *Sur International Journal on Human Rights* 11, no. 20 (June 1, 2014): 94.
75. Sikkink, *Evidence for Hope*, 88–89.
76. Mende, "Are Human Rights Western," 6. In the same sense, Le, "Are Human Rights Universal or Culturally Relative?" 205.
77. Tharoor, "Are Human Rights Universal?" 2.
78. Le, "Are Human Rights Universal or Culturally Relative?" 208.
79. UN Human Rights, "Status of Ratification."
80. Tharoor, "Are Human Rights Universal?" 2.
81. Tharoor, 3.
82. Duquette, "Universalism and Relativism," 63.
83. Le, "Are Human Rights Universal or Culturally Relative," 205.
84. United Nations Office of the High Commissioner for Human Rights, "Vienna Declaration and Programme of Action," 1993.
85. Hector Gros Espiell, "Universality of Human Rights and Cultural Diversity," *International Social Science Journal* 50, no. 158 (1998): 527.
86. UN General Assembly, "Universal Declaration," 1.
87. UN General Assembly, 530.
88. United Nations Educational, Scientific and Cultural Organization, "UNESCO Constitution," 1945, 6.
89. Andrea Pin, "Religions, National Identities, and the Universality of Human Rights," *Oxford Journal of Law and Religion* 3, no. 3 (2014): 433.
90. Pin, 433.
91. Arnold, "Are Human Rights Universal and Binding?" 587.
92. Donnelly, *Universal Human Rights*, 105. Elaborating on the variation levels of the substance, interpretation, and implementation of human rights, Duquette "Universalism and Relativism," 75, maintains that a "moderate universalist position" can accommodate the tensions between universalism and relativism.
93. Arnold, "Are Human Rights Universal and Binding?" 583.
94. Tharoor, "Are Human Rights Universal?" 3, 6.
95. Franck, "Are Human Rights Universal?" 198, 200.
96. Franck, 198–199.
97. Franck, 198–199.
98. Le, "Are Human Rights Universal or Culturally Relative?" 208–209.
99. Tharoor, "Are Human Rights Universal?" 4.
100. Tharoor, 4.
101. Kohen, "An Overlapping Consensus on Human Rights," 9, quoted in Mary Ann Glendon, *A World Made New: Eleanor Roosevelt and the Universal Declaration of Human Rights* (New York: Random House, 2001), 73.

102. Pin, "Religions, National Identities," 434.
103. Tharoor, "Are Human Rights Universal?" 4.
104. Franck, "Are Human Rights Universal?" 199.
105. Bell. "Which Rights Are Universal?" 854.
106. Sikkink, *Evidence for Hope*, 79–84.
107. Franck, "Are Human Rights Universal?" 197.
108. Laura Reimer, "Our Long Road," in *Our Shared Future: Windows into Canada's Reconciliation Journey*, ed. Laura E. Reimer and Robert Chrismas (New York: Lexington Books, Rowman and Littlefield, 2020): 13.
109. Le, "Are Human Rights Universal or Culturally Relative?" 207–208.
110. Tharoor, "Are Human Rights Universal?" 2.
111. Benjamin Gregg, "In Defense of Human Rights: A Non-Religious Grounding in a Pluralistic World. By Ari Kohen. New York: Routledge, 2007. 224p. $120.00," *Perspectives on Politics* 6, no. 2 (2008), 374.
112. Ignatieff, *Human Rights as Politics and Idolatry*, 66–67.
113. Ignatieff, 67.
114. Tharoor, "Are Human Rights Universal?" 3.
115. On, "The 'Relative Universality' of Human Rights," 581.
116. On, 584.
117. Le, "Are Human Rights Universal or Culturally Relative?" 208.
118. Franck, "Are Human Rights Universal?" 197.
119. Reimer, "Our Long Road," 9, 16–17, 22. The evolution of Indigenous rights might be illustrated by the creation of mechanisms, such as the *Royal Commission on Aboriginal People's*, to investigate and propose solutions to the challenges in the relationship between Indigenous peoples and the Canadian government and society. It contributed to encouraging the reflection on the need to transform the conflict with Indigenous peoples, to acknowledge the governmental responsibility in the conflict, and the need for reparation and reconciliation.
120. Mende, "Are Human Rights Western," 8.
121. Le, "Are Human Rights Universal or Culturally Relative?" 206.
122. Le, 206.

Bibliography

Arnold, Rainer. "Are Human Rights Universal and Binding?" In *General Reports of the XVIIIth Congress of the International Academy of Comparative Law/ Rapports Généraux du XVIIIème Congrès de l'Académie Internationale de Droit Comparé*, edited by Karen B. Brown and David Snyder, 581–588. Dordrecht: Springer, 2012. https://doi.org/10.1007/978-94-007-2354-2_25.

Bell, Daniel A. "Which Rights Are Universal?" *Political Theory* 27, no. 6 (December 1, 1999): 849–856. https://doi.org/10.1177/0090591799027006007.

Berlin, Isaiah. 1958. *Two Concepts of Liberty*. Oxford: Clarendon Press.

Cerna, Christina M. "Universality of Human Rights and Cultural Diversity: Implementation of Human Rights in Different Socio-Cultural Contexts." *Human Rights Quarterly* 16, no. 4 (November 1994): 740–752. https://doi.org/10.2307/762567.

Clément, Dominique. "Human Rights or Social Justice? The Problem of Rights Inflation." *International Journal of Human Rights* 22, no. 2 (February 7, 2018): 155–169. https://doi.org/10.1080/13642987.2017.1349245.

Donnelly, Jack. 2013. *Universal Human Rights in Theory and Practice*, 3rd ed. Ithaca: Cornell University Press.

Duquette, David A. "Universalism and Relativism in Human Rights." In *Universal Human Rights Moral Order in a Divided World*, edited by David A. Reidy and Mortimer N. S. Sellers, 59–77. Lanham: Rowman & Littlefield Publishers, 2005.

Felice, William. 1996. *Taking Suffering Seriously: The Importance of Collective Human Rights*. Albany: State University of New York Press.

Franck, Thomas M. "Are Human Rights Universal?" *Foreign Affairs* 80, no. 1 (January 1, 2001): 191–204. https://doi.org/10.2307/20050052.

Gregg, Benjamin. "In Defense of Human Rights: A Non-Religious Grounding in a Pluralistic World. By Ari Kohen. New York: Routledge, 2007. 224p. $120.00." *Perspectives on Politics* 6, no. 2 (June 1, 2008): 373–374.

Gros Espiell, Héctor. "Universality of Human Rights and Cultural Diversity." *International Social Science Journal* 50, no. 158 (December 1998): 525–534. https://doi.org/10.1111/1468-2451.00165.

Ignatieff, Michael. *Human Rights as Politics and Idolatry*, edited by Amy Gutmann. Princeton: Princeton University Press, 2001.

Ishay, Micheline. 2008. *The History of Human Rights: From Ancient Times to the Globalization Era*. Berkeley: University of California Press.

Kohen, Ari. "An Overlapping Consensus on Human Rights and Human Dignity." In *Human Rights at the Crossroads*, edited by Mark Goodale, 1–12. New York: Oxford University Press, 2014. https://doi.org/10.1093/acprof:osobl/9780199376414.003.0004.

Le, Nhina. "Are Human Rights Universal or Culturally Relative?" *Peace Review: Police Militarization* 28, no. 2 (April 2, 2016): 203–211. https://doi.org/10.1080/10402659.2016.1166756.
Martin, Rex. "Are Human Rights Universal?" In *Human Rights: The Hard Questions*, edited by Cindy Holder and David Reidy, 59–76. New York: Cambridge University Press, 2013. https://doi.org/10.1017/CBO9780511758553.005
Mende, Janne. "Are Human Rights Western—And Why Does It Matter? A Perspective from International Political Theory." *Journal of International Political Theory* (March 2019): 1–20. https://doi.org/10.1177/1755088219832992.
Moyn, Samuel. 2010. *The Last Utopia: Human Rights in History*. Cambridge: Harvard University Press.
On, Steve. "The 'Relative Universality' of Human Rights: An Assessment." *Perspectives on Global Development and Technology* 4, no. 3/4 (September 2005): 577–601. https://doi.org/10.1163/156915005775093241.
Pin, Andrea. "Religions, National Identities, and the Universality of Human Rights." *Oxford Journal of Law and Religion* 3, no. 3 (October 1, 2014): 419–439. https://doi.org/10.1093/ojlr/rwu038.
Pinheiro, Paulo Sérgio. "Besides Human Rights, I Don't See a Solution for Serving the Victims." Interview by Maria Brant. *Sur International Journal on Human Rights* 11, no. 20 (June 1, 2014): 90–95.
Rawls, John. "The Idea of an Overlapping Consensus." *Oxford Journal of Legal Studies* 7, no. 1 (April 1, 1987): 1–25.
Reimer, Laura. "Our Long Road." In *Our Shared Future: Windows into Canada's Reconciliation Journey*, edited by Laura E. Reimer and Robert Chrismas. New York: Lexington Books, Rowman and Littlefield, 2020.
Sikkink, Kathryn. 2017. *Evidence for Hope: Making Human Rights Work in the 21st Century*. Princeton: Princeton University Press.
Tharoor, Shashi. "Are Human Rights Universal?" *World Policy Journal* 16, no. 4 (December 1, 1999): 1–6.
United Nations. "The Yearbook of the United Nations 1948–49." 1950, V, Social, Humanitarian and Cultural Questions. Accessed January 14, 2021. https://www.unmultimedia.org/searchers/yearbook/page.jsp?bookpage=524&volume=1948-49.
United Nations Educational, Scientific and Cultural Organization. "UNESCO Constitution." 1945. Accessed January 14, 2021. https://unesdoc.unesco.org/ark:/48223/pf0000372956/PDF/372956eng.pdf.multi.page=6.
United Nations General Assembly. "Universal Declaration of Human Rights." 217 (III) A. Paris, 1948. Accessed January 14, 2021. https://www.ohchr.org/EN/UDHR/Documents/UDHR_Translations/eng.pdf.
United Nations Office of the High Commissioner for Human Rights. "International Covenant on Economic, Social and Cultural Rights." 1966. Accessed

January 14, 2021. https://www.ohchr.org/en/instruments-mechanisms/instruments/international-covenant-economic-social-and-cultural-rights.
———. "International Covenant on Civil and Political Rights." 1976. Accessed January 14, 2021. https://www.ohchr.org/Documents/ProfessionalInterest/ccpr.pdf.
———. "Vienna Declaration and Programme of Action." 1993. Accessed January 14, 2021. https://www.ohchr.org/Documents/ProfessionalInterest/vienna.pdf.
———. "Status of Ratification Interactive Dashboard." 2020. Accessed January 14, 2021. https://indicators.ohchr.org/.

Indigeneity

The United Nations Declaration on the Rights of Indigenous People: A Prototype for Reconciliation?

Rhéal Cenerini

The United Nations Declaration on the Rights of Indigenous People (UNDRIP) is an extremely significant document. Nowhere is this more the case than in Canada, where it has alternatively been a source of intense public debate, raised as a controversial election issue, and portrayed as a cornerstone of reconciliation. But what is the UNDRIP? What is its significance for a country like Canada with a long history of colonialism toward the Indigenous people who live within its borders? Most importantly, what does it have to say about where the relationship between Indigenous people and non-Indigenous Canadians is headed?

The final draft of the UNDRIP, which has now been endorsed by 148 countries, including Canada, is the result of close to 30 years of negotiations between Indigenous representatives, human rights experts, and political leaders from throughout the international community. The Declaration, as it currently reads, does not live up to the expectations of certain Indigenous leaders and scholars who wanted much more while simultaneously alarming certain political leaders who are concerned with

R. Cenerini (✉)
27 Bridgman Place, La Salle, MB, Canada
e-mail: rpcenerini@hotmail.com

L. E. Reimer and K. Standish (eds.), *Perspectives on Justice, Indigeneity, Gender, and Security in Human Rights Research*,
https://doi.org/10.1007/978-981-99-1930-7_6

the cost, economic and societal, of implementing its principles. It contains limits and what may be called, in layman's terms, *loopholes* that enable states and Indigenous people within their borders to slowly work toward accommodation, much as the process that led to the UNDRIP was itself quite protracted. It is not binding in the way a formal convention would be, but this is on purpose: it aspires to guide and not prescribe how the interests and ambitions of Indigenous peoples can be reconciled while, at the same time, allowing room for international norms and standards to be established as a framework and foundation for the collective rights of Indigenous people. In this sense, I believe that a careful examination of how the UNDRIP came to be and how this process is reflected in the articles of the Declaration itself can serve to help individual countries like Canada on its path toward reconciliation with Indigenous people. This examination will show that the UNDRIP is, first and foremost, a political document seeking to strike a balance between the collective rights of Indigenous people and the public interest of colonial nations, like Canada, that have greatly benefitted at the expense of these same people.[1]

History

Remarkably enough, one part of the UNDRIP story began almost 50 years ago, about 800 kilometers southwest of the City of Winnipeg. The Wounded Knee Reservation in South Dakota, the site of a 71-day standoff that left two Native Americans dead and over 300 arrested in 1973, is where Indigenous elders gathered to decide on a course of action to gain recognition on the international stage.[2] The Indian International Treaty Council (IITC) held its first meeting at the Standing Rock Indian Reservation in North Dakota soon thereafter. Three years later, 250 Indigenous people from the Americas made the trip to Geneva to attend the International NGO Conference on Discrimination against Indigenous Populations in the Americas that had been organized by the United Nations (UN) Subcommittee on Racial Discrimination, Apartheid, and Decolonization. This was quite a step up from the apathy that had greeted Chief Deskaheh of the Haudenosaunee when he had made the trip to Geneva some 50 years earlier in 1923 in an attempt to gain attention for the plight of Indigenous people in North America. At that time, Chief Deskaheh had been refused the opportunity to speak to the League of Nations and had been forced to return home without having been able to plead his case before the international community.[3]

This time, the results were considerably different. This first presentation before the international community eventually led to the formation of the Working Group on Indigenous Populations (WGIP) in 1982. It was established by the UN Sub-Commission on Prevention of Discrimination and Protection of Minorities (Sub-Commission), which reported, in turn, to the Commission on Human Rights (CHR).[4] The CHR itself was a subsidiary of the UN Economic and Social Council.[5] The WGIP was a five-person council of experts with a mandate to review "developments pertaining to the promotion of the human rights and fundamental freedoms of Indigenous populations" and "to give special attention to the evolution of standards concerning the rights of such populations."[6] Its relative obscurity within the UN hierarchy appears to have afforded the WGIP the opportunity to actually engage the Indigenous people who stood to benefit from its work. It should be noted that none of the WGIP experts were Indigenous themselves, but they were deemed to be open and respectful of the Indigenous representatives with whom they closely collaborated on a draft declaration.[7] The WGIP worked on a declaration for more than 10 years, meeting every summer with Indigenous representatives to add and edit the articles of a draft declaration. The final and perhaps most critical article to be added dealt with self-determination.[8] Matthew Coone Come, Grand Chief of the Grand Council of the Crees at the time, said of the draft declaration that it "began from a cry from the Indigenous people for justice, and it is drafted to confirm that the international standards which apply to the world apply to Indigenous people."[9]

By 1994, the WGIP's work was complete. Its version of the draft declaration was approved by the Sub-Commission and then sent to the CHR for its consideration and approval. At this point, and for the first time, it was turned over to government delegates. A Commission for Human Rights Working Group (CHRWG) was established to consider the draft declaration in 1995. By this time, the people who first gathered at Standing Rock were already 20 years into the process.

A year later, the Indigenous representatives walked out on the process because they felt that their voices were not being heard.[10] It was evidently very difficult for the CHRWG to continue its work without Indigenous representatives at the table. The chair of the CHRWG, Ambassador Urrutia of Peru, eventually agreed that Indigenous representatives should be part of the consensus around the draft declaration, thus opening the door for their return.

The CHRWG worked on the declaration until 2006. During this period, states pushed back on several articles but especially those related to self-determination and control over land and resources.[11] For as long as they could, Indigenous representatives refused any concessions on these important matters, using the intervening years to educate the various states in regard to the wording and content of the draft declaration. But toward the end of these protracted negotiations, it became clear that some element of compromise would be necessary to bring the process to a close. In the final two years of work on the text, as time was running out on the CHRWG's mandate, concessions were made by each side and a final draft was presented to what was then the Human Rights Council (HRC). This was in the spring of 2006. A vote was held, and the draft declaration was adopted by a vote of 30 to 2 with 12 abstentions. The only two governments to vote against it were Canada and Russia.

The declaration was then sent to the UN's General Assembly in New York for the final leg of its long journey. By the end of 2006, several African states that had not had a seat at the table during the deliberations of the CHRWG expressed concern over certain articles in the draft declaration, especially those related to self-determination and their possible use as a justification for secession.[12] They were eventually granted a deferment so that the issues of concern for them could be examined more closely. In the intervening months, a great deal of lobbying was done. By this time, the Government of Canada was working hard to get the declaration defeated on several grounds that will be examined later. Indigenous groups, on the other hand, were targeting African countries to reassure them of the sound content and wording of the draft declaration.[13] A last-minute deal was brokered by a joint Mexico-Namibia proposal, and, by the late summer of 2007, the UN General Assembly was set to vote on a revised declaration. When the actual vote took place on September 13, 2007, 144 nations endorsed the Declaration, with only four opposing it and 11 abstentions.[14] The four opposing nations were Canada, Australia, New Zealand, and the United States, four countries that Sheryl Lightfoot has labeled the four largest states in the "Anglosphere."[15] The UNDRIP had passed.

Key Provisions of the UNDRIP

A. *The right to self-determination*

From an Indigenous perspective, as well as in terms of its potential impact on the states where Indigenous peoples are found, the most important of the entitlements listed in the UNDRIP is, without a doubt, the right to self-determination. As Deer states emphatically: "This right has been key from the beginning."[16] It is listed as Article 3 in the definitive version of the UNDRIP. Many subsequent rights flow from it, including:

- The right to autonomy and self-government as it relates to their local or internal affairs (Article 4);
- The right to maintain their distinct political, legal, economic, social, and cultural institutions (Article 5);
- The right to practice and revitalize their distinct customs and traditions (Article 11);
- The right to establish and administer their own education systems (Article 14);
- The right to participate in decision-making that would affect their rights through representatives chosen according to their traditions (Article 18);
- The right to provide or to refuse their free, prior, and informed consent (FPIC) to any legislative or administrative initiative that may affect them (Article 19);
- The right to own, use, develop, and control the land that they have traditionally occupied (Article 26); and
- The right to determine their own identity and membership (Article 33).

B. *Territorial integrity and the rights of others*

These rights to self-determination are very broad in scope. They are, however, circumscribed by other important articles that were added to garner the necessary support among voting members of the UN General Assembly, which, it goes without saying, are sovereign states. First of all, Article 4 specifies that Indigenous peoples are autonomous in matters "relating to their local and internal affairs." While they retain the right to fully participate in the affairs of the state, it is clear that Article 4 puts borders around self-determination, both literally and figuratively. Article 46 goes further. Subsection 1 of this article declares that nothing in the UNDRIP can be used to justify actions or decisions that would in any way "dismember or impair, totally or in part, the territorial integrity or political unity of sovereign or independent states." Subsection 2 goes on to say that no rights found in the UNDRIP can be used to undermine others' enjoyment of their own rights (like property rights, for example, which are prominent in Article 17 of the Universal Declaration of Human Rights). In the definitive UNDRIP, the right to self-determination, therefore, does not extend to external autonomy or secession and cannot be exercised in a way that infringes upon other people's rights.

C. *Right to redress and restitution*

The UNDRIP contains several articles which call upon states to provide redress or restitution to Indigenous peoples for past harms. Some of the most noteworthy of these are the following:

- In Article 8, states are called upon to put in place "mechanisms for the prevention of, and redress for" all efforts at depriving Indigenous people of their lands, their resources, their culture, and their identity
- The right to restitution for the theft of their intellectual, cultural, spiritual, and religious property (Article 11)
- According to Article 14, states must assist Indigenous people in providing education, "when possible," that enables children to reconnect with their native language and culture
- Article 20—"Indigenous peoples deprived of their means of subsistence and development are entitled to just and fair redress"
- Indigenous people have the right to be fully compensated for the land that was "confiscated, taken, occupied, used or damaged without their free, prior and informed consent" (Article 28)
- States are called upon to ensure that no hazardous materials are stored or disposed of on Indigenous lands (Article 29); if any such activities have taken place in the past, states will provide redress (Article 32).

D. *Universal human rights*

Other important provisions of the UNDRIP focus on the same fundamental human rights that are guaranteed to all citizens by virtue of the Universal Declaration of Human Rights (UDHR). These rights are reflected in:

- Article 1—concurrence with the UDHR;
- Article 2—the right to freedom from discrimination;
- Article 7—enshrines the right "to life, physical and mental integrity, liberty and security of person;"
- Article 10—the right to not be forcibly relocated;
- Article 12—the right to complete religious freedom;
- Article 17—protects Indigenous people under the same international labor laws and standards as other workers;
- Article 22—highlights the specific needs of women, children, and the elderly, as well as Article 44, which specifies that all articles apply equally to both men and women; and
- Article 29—whereby Indigenous people have the right to protection of the environment.

Reactions to the UNDRIP

Different stakeholders hold very different views on the UNDRIP and what it means for the relationship between Indigenous people and the states where they live. For several Indigenous people, especially those who were directly involved in the process of drafting and shepherding the Declaration through the drafting and approval process, it represents a new day, a veritable turning point. Phil Fontaine, a former Grand Chief of the Assembly of First Nations originally from Sagkeeng First Nation here in Manitoba, declares "(t)he Declaration is the work of thousands of people who never gave up" (see note 16). He goes on to write:

> So what does the *Declaration* do? It sets out best practices that nation-states should implement. Consistent with principles of equality and diversity, it enshrines our right to be different as peoples. It affirms minimum standards for the survival, dignity, security, and well-being of Indigenous peoples worldwide.[17]

Several aspects of Fontaine's assessment are worthy of note. To him, the UNDRIP is both a minimum standard and an aspirational document that "sets out best practices that nation-states should implement." Indeed, the notion that fundamental human rights should equally apply to everyone, including all Indigenous people, is difficult to refute. This is the "minimum standard" part of the UNDRIP. On the other hand, the articles dealing with redress for past harms, including the confiscation of land and resources without free and informed consent, clearly represent a long-term objective to be achieved through negotiation between Indigenous peoples and their respective nation-states. Fontaine also emphasizes the recognition that the UNDRIP affords Indigenous groups as peoples. During the drafting process, when the Declaration was being developed by the WGIP, there was much debate over terminology.[18] Specifically, Indigenous advocates were adamant that they were *peoples* with an "s" and not just people (a series of individuals) or populations with no particular culture or identity and no connection to a specific territory.[19]

Fontaine's views are echoed by many Indigenous leaders throughout Canada and abroad.[20] As well, it is very significant that 16 of the 94 calls of action found in the 2015 *Final Report of the Truth and Reconciliation Commission* (TRC) refer to the need for governments and churches to endorse the UNDRIP. While supporters of the Declaration will point to different parts of the document as being particularly significant, it is often its overall thrust that is lauded. For example, James Bay Cree leader Romeo Saganash, in collaboration with Paul Joffe, a lawyer who specializes in Indigenous human rights issues, writes that "the collective rights of the world's Indigenous peoples have been elaborated in the Declaration and formally acknowledged by the international community as an integral part of international human rights standards and law."[21] It should be mentioned that Saganash was also the sponsor of Bill C-262—*An act to ensure that the laws of Canada are in harmony with the UNDRIP*. Bill C-262 received parliamentary support but failed to receive the third reading in the Senate prior to the federal election in the fall of 2019. The *United Nations Declaration on the Rights of Indigenous Peoples Act* eventually received Royal Assent in June of 2021. It builds on Saganash's bill and calls on Ottawa to ensure that Canada's laws are consistent with the UNDRIP.

Support among Indigenous political leaders and scholars for the UNDRIP is, however, far from unanimous. In an article that he entitles *A Travesty of a Mockery of a Sham—Colonialism as Self-Determination in the UN Declaration on the Rights of Indigenous People*, Cherokee scholar Ward Churchill argues that the Indigenous right to self-government was essentially sold out during the drafting process in order to secure the support of the UN General Assembly.[22] He refers, in his analysis, to a number of documents that equate self-determination with the right to secession,[23] thus refuting the notion, prevalent in the UNDRIP, that self-determination can be constrained to internal matters (Article 4) or rendered subservient to the maintenance of state sovereignty (Article 46). He cites, for example, the initial recommendation of the International Indian Treaty Council (IITC) to the WGIP in 1983 wherein it states that "Indigenous nations and peoples who so desire should be granted the full rights and obligations of external self-determination."[24] He goes on to quote a second more elaborate declaration, issued in 1985 by the IITC and several other Indigenous NGOs, which says:

> "All Indigenous nations and peoples have the right to self-determination, by virtue of which they have the right to whatever degree of autonomy or self-government they choose. This includes the right to freely determine their political status, freely pursue their own economic, social, religious and cultural development, and determine their own membership/citizenship without external influence."[25]

When the CHRWG was set up in 1995 to prepare a draft of the UNDRIP, it was thought that it could complete its work in time to inaugurate the first International Decade of the World's Indigenous Peoples that ran from 1995 to 2004.[26] It took 12 years before the Declaration was ready for the General Assembly's consideration. While self-determination was not the only bone of contention, it certainly played a large role in the delay.[27] Canada, as well as other countries of the CANZUS group (Canada, Australia, New Zealand, and the United States), led the way in registering their opposition to self-determination.[28] (Malezer; 34) This is not surprising. While many countries of Western Europe, for example, have deep colonial pasts, they are now, for the most part, nation-states with no direct claim to the far-off countries where their colonial interests have played out. It is far easier for them to commit to a declaration that will have little effect on their collective futures. The so-called CANZUS group of countries, on the other hand, are linked by a common origin story (their ties to the British Crown) and, most importantly, by the fact that Indigenous peoples with significant and legitimate claims against their governments are found within their borders. It is in the course of negotiations over the right of Indigenous peoples to self-determination that the CANZUS countries began to float the idea that self-determination could be envisaged in a new and, for them, far less threatening way. By de-linking the word "peoples" from the right to self-determination in the way that it had historically been understood, namely as the right to political sovereignty, self-determination began to emerge as a concept with an internal and an external aspect.[29] The United States, in particular, seized upon this as a way of looking at self-determination that conformed to the rights that Indigenous peoples already enjoyed on American soil. In other words, self-determination, framed in this way, was reduced to something that the United States, and ultimately the other CANZUS countries, could support. The final draft of the UNDRIP, as we have seen, does contain the language about control over internal and local affairs (Article 4) and the primacy of territorial integrity (Article 46) that was so important to the CANZUS states. But as a result, critics like Churchill see the UNDRIP as a document that is "gutted" of its core value of Indigenous self-government, and the Aboriginal Australian scholar Aileen Moreton-Robinson denounces it as an example of "patriarchal white sovereignty (…) dispossess(ing) Indigenous people from the ground of moral value."[30]

In spite of these major concessions, the four CANZUS countries voted to oppose the UNDRIP when it was brought before the UN General Assembly in September of 2007. Why? The Government of Canada and its main spokespersons, including the Honourable Chuck Strahl, the Indian Affairs Minister of the day, made several key points in explaining its opposition to the Declaration:

1. It insists on Indigenous rights at the expense of the individual rights that are central to our constitution;
2. It would prevent the military from providing assistance in the event of natural disasters and other emergencies on Indigenous territories;
3. It puts at risk the numerous treaties that the Government of Canada has signed with Indigenous peoples as well as their enforcement;
4. In terms of land claims, it "suggests that we must return to that pre-contact moment" where the entirety of the territory that is now Canada was occupied and, in this sense, belonged to First Nations;
5. It goes beyond existing rules and regulations governing control and ownership of intellectual property; and

6. It provides an effective "veto" to Indigenous peoples on all projects affecting their territory by granting them the right to "free, prior and informed consent".[31]

The legitimacy of each individual objection could be debated at length. However, it is clear from recent events surrounding the Coastal GasLink pipeline that is supposed to pass through the territory of the Wet'suwet'en people on the West Coast of Canada that the federal government is right to be concerned about the implications of FPIC, self-determination, and the right to redress for lands that were once occupied by Indigenous people. These are serious issues with very real consequences for the country as a whole.

Interestingly, all four countries of the CANZUS group did eventually withdraw their opposition to the UNDRIP. During a 20-month period from April 2009 to December 2010, they reversed their earlier positions in spite of the fact that no changes were made to the Declaration itself. The first to commit was Australia. It is the opinion of the Anishinaabe scholar Sheryl Lightfoot that the change of heart that these four nations of the Anglosphere had at this time marks the emergence of a third option alongside either opposition or support for the UNDRIP. She argues that, rather than remaining trapped in this binary, the four settler states of the Anglosphere decided to "selective(ly) endorse(...) without intent to implement."[32] In so doing, they "write down," in Lightfoot's words, the UNDRIP's articles by framing them as a mere extension of what they are already doing for the Indigenous peoples within their borders. In the case of our own country, Canada's ambassador to the UN, John McNee, had a meeting on November 12, 2010, with the president of the United Nations General Assembly to inform him that Canada was withdrawing its opposition to the UNDRIP. Later that day, a press release appeared on the federal government's Indian and Northern Affairs website stating that "Canada formally endorsed the United Nations Declaration on the Rights of Indigenous Peoples in a manner fully consistent with Canada's Constitution and laws."[33] It went on to say that "while the Declaration is non-binding, endorsing it as an important aspirational document is a significant step forward in strengthening relations with Aboriginal peoples."[34]

The implication is clear: the UNDRIP fits within what Canada is already doing to accommodate the rights of Indigenous peoples. Just like self-determination can be limited to internal and local matters so that it does not infringe upon the territorial integrity of a sovereign state, the Declaration itself can only serve to guide our interactions within the parameters of the Canadian Constitution. Lightfoot calls this a deliberate effort to "domesticate Indigenous issues."[35] It must furthermore be noted that, for Canadian officials at the time, the notion that any or all of the Declaration's articles represented "minimum standards for the survival, dignity, and well-being of Indigenous peoples of the world" (Article 43) had been cast aside: the UNDRIP was nothing more than an "aspirational document."

Appraising the UNDRIP

While there is no doubt that it took significant concessions on the issue of self-determination to get agreement from the General Assembly overall and the so-called CANZUS nations, in particular, it would be incorrect to portray the UNDRIP as a document that enshrines "in law the very structure of internal colonial domination and exploitation at the hands of state entities from which Indigenous nations have been struggling to free themselves."[36] The apprehensions concerning how self-determination is framed and limited in both Article 4 and Article 46 of the Declaration are understandable. At the same time, however, it is difficult to dismiss the voices of the many Indigenous leaders, like Kenneth Deer, Phil Fontaine, Romeo Saganash, Wilton Littlechild, and others, some of whom were heavily involved in the drafting process, who were and remain very supportive of the end result. The danger in dismissing the value of the UNDRIP is that it represents a denial of Indigenous agency in the 30-year process that led to its adoption by the UN General Assembly. The Indigenous leaders who engaged in this process on behalf of their respective peoples knew what they were doing. Davis points out that many Indigenous representatives who worked on the UNDRIP at various stages in the drafting process were "lawyers, either practicing or academic, and had undergraduate and in many cases, postgraduate law degrees and they were well aware of the law pertaining to secession."[37] If this is the case and they knew what they were doing, why did they eventually agree to circumscribe the concept of self-determination?

The answer lies in what Kirsty Gover calls "realist Indigenous strategy."[38] From a strictly political point of view, Indigenous representatives pushed as hard as they could for the right to self-determination, even going so far as to characterize their strategy as one of "no change"[39] and walking out of the deliberations of the CHRWG in 1996. Yet, according to Barelli, and contrary to the opinion of Churchill and others that were examined above, there appears to have been an understanding that "one thing has always been fairly clear, namely that sub-national groups do not have a right to independence. Indigenous people never seriously entertained secession."[40] Barelli's assertion supports the notion that, among Indigenous leaders, just as among the general population, there is no clear consensus on how to balance the fundamental right to self-determination with the public interest of states as a whole.[41] Within this context, it is altogether reasonable for Indigenous leaders to have insisted, as long as it was possible to do so, that the UNDRIP should enshrine their right to self-determination. But faced with the reality that the Declaration would not be adopted at the UN General Assembly without some of the parameters provided in Article 4 and Article 46, Indigenous representatives opted for realpolitik rather than the pursuit of an ideal that could not realistically be achieved.[42] Knowing how far they had come and having gained appreciation for the impact that such a declaration could have in the long term, they made a political decision enabling widespread support for the UNDRIP. In doing so, they did not "sell out" their people or institutionalize "internal colonial domination and exploitation." These Indigenous leaders, along with their allies among state representatives and NGOs (and against considerable odds), managed to get an overwhelming majority of the UN General Assembly's member states to vote in favor of a Declaration actively promoting Indigenous rights to self-determination, to FPIC, to preservation of their culture and language, and to redress for past injustices.

Implementing the UNDRIP

Was This the Right Approach to Take?

A declaration is not a legally binding document. In explaining its initial opposition to the UNDRIP, the Government of Canada stated that "we also underline our understanding that this Declaration is not a legally binding instrument. It has no legal effect in Canada, and its provisions do not represent customary international law."[43] In this sense, it belongs in the category of "soft international law."[44] This designation means that it is not enforceable in the way that treaties and conventions are. By the same token, however, it binds states in other ways that can be just as effective in affecting societal change and protecting the rights of Indigenous peoples.

First of all, the UNDRIP was adopted by the UN General Assembly, the foremost decision-making body within the global community of sovereign states.[45] This, in and of itself, imbues the Declaration with legitimacy and significance. Canada's initial opposition to the UNDRIP was certainly noted on the international scene. It led to our country being publicly denounced, a fact that is related by Grand Chief Edward John in reference to comments made by both Louise Arbour, the High Commissioner for Human Rights at the time, and Amnesty International that stated that Canada's "position as a global human rights champion may be slipping."[46]

Beyond whatever peer pressure may be exerted by the international community, a declaration of this nature serves to shape and mold the overall understanding of human rights and how they are perceived in international law.[47] The UNDRIP is also not a stand-alone document. As we have seen, many of its fundamental human rights provisions are closely related to the Universal Declaration of Human Rights. Self-determination, property rights, and cultural integrity are all entitlements that can be found in pre-existing treaties like the International Covenant on Civil and Political Rights and the International Convention on the Elimination of All Forms of Racial Discrimination.[48]

Lastly, and perhaps most importantly, the principles found in important declarations like the UNDRIP eventually become part of customary international law.[49] Formal treaties and covenants are hard laws: they spell out in precise terms what states can and cannot do. Customary or normative laws are no less binding, but they are based on accepted standards of behavior: they evolve over time as these standards become more widely accepted. According to S. James Anaya, a former Special Rapporteur on the Rights of Indigenous People,

> the Declaration has a significant normative weight, grounded in its high degree of legitimacy. This legitimacy is a function not only of the fact that it has been formally endorsed by an overwhelming majority of United Nations Member States but also the fact that it is the product of years of advocacy and struggle by Indigenous peoples themselves.[50]

On the other hand, Barelli believes that "viewing the Declaration or substantial parts of it as customary international law may be rather premature" and that its main strength will be the ability to inspire and inform the drafting of statutes, rights advocacy, policy decisions, and land claims negotiations far into the future.[51]

This is already beginning to happen. It figures prominently, for example, in the Final Report of the TRC that was submitted to the Government of Canada in 2015. The TRC's Final Report refers to the UNDRIP as a blueprint for the type of profound societal, judicial, and legal changes that are pre-conditions for a lasting reconciliation between Indigenous and non-Indigenous Canadians.[52] The UNDRIP also comes up repeatedly in the TRC's 94 Calls to Action. In the section entitled *Reconciliation*, for instance, Recommendation 43 states: "We call upon federal, provincial, territorial, and municipal governments to fully adopt and implement the *United Nations Declaration on the Rights of Indigenous Peoples* as the framework for reconciliation."[53] The UNDRIP is also finding its way into the settlements that continue to be negotiated between the Crown and Indigenous peoples. A case in point is the Nenqay Deni Accord between the Province of British Columbia and the Tsilhqot'in Nation.[54] The preamble to the accord refers specifically to the Declaration:

> On November 20, 2012 (sic), Canada issued a statement of support for the United Nations Declaration on the Rights of Indigenous Peoples. On November 13, 2015, the Federal Government mandated that the Minister of Indigenous and Northern Affairs support the work of reconciliation and implement the recommendations of the Truth and Reconciliation Commission, starting with the implementation of the United Nations Declaration on the Rights of Indigenous Peoples.[55]

Court cases that involve Indigenous rights are also seeing increased reference to the UNDRIP. For example, in the case of the NunatuKavut Community Council and its judicial application to the Federal Court to reverse the Government of Canada's granting of a permit to Nalcor Energy in the Churchill River watershed, it stated that the federal government had not adequately consulted before issuing its permit to Nalcor. It argued that the UNDRIP, with its support for the principle of FPIC, could be used to inform the interpretation of the government's responsibilities toward Indigenous people. The Federal Court agreed but added that the Declaration could not be used to displace Canadian laws.[56]

Lastly, it must be pointed out that Parliament itself is facing continued pressure to pass laws fully implementing the UNDRIP. Had it not been for delays in the Senate prior to the 2019 federal election, Bill C-262, *An Act to ensure that the laws of Canada are in harmony with the UNDRIP*, would have passed into law. Adopted at second reading in the House of Commons by a vote of 217 to 76, Bill C-262 called upon the Government of Canada,

> In consultation and cooperation with Indigenous peoples in Canada, (to) take all measures necessary to ensure that the laws of Canada are consistent with the United Nations Declaration on the Rights of Indigenous Peoples [as well as to] develop and implement a national action plan to achieve the objectives of the United Nations Declaration on the Rights of Indigenous Peoples.[57]

The proposed legislation was also supposed to direct the Minister of Indian and Northern Affairs to submit a report on progress toward full implementation of the UNDRIP to the House of Commons on an annual basis. While this particular private member's bill eventually died on the government order paper, the significant support that it did receive in the House of Commons and the current Liberal government's pledge to fully implement the UNDRIP led to the introduction of bill C-15, the United Nations Declaration on Indigenous Peoples Act, in December 2020. It calls on Ottawa to develop a framework for the implementation of the UNDRIP as well as to regularly report to Parliament on the progress toward aligning federal legislation with the provisions of the Declaration. As mentioned earlier, Bill C-15 was given Royal Assent in June 2021. This, of course, represents a complete about-face from the views expressed by Canada's representative to the UN when the member states of the General Assembly voted on the Declaration in September 2007. At the time, Ambassador John McNee had stated that the UNDRIP was "overly broad, unclear, and capable of a wide variety of interpretations."[58]

The level of acceptance and legitimacy that the UNDRIP has achieved here in Canada is due, I believe, to the flexibility, wisdom, and foresight of the Indigenous representatives who shepherded the Declaration through the lengthy process leading to its ratification. While the adoption of a more hardline approach may have satisfied the critics, who have accused these same leaders of "selling out" their people, it is becoming clear that Indigenous leaders have achieved something quite extraordinary with this particular document. Through their willingness to compromise and find language that affords a degree of latitude to the states upon whom the Declaration calls to implement its various articles and by opting for the kind of gradual, incremental changes that result from a "soft law" strategy, they are in the process of weaving some of their most deeply-held aspirations and ambitions into the very fabric of our country. Megan Davis says as much when she declares that "Indigenous peoples are skillfully using the tools that are available to them and it denies Indigenous peoples' agency to imply that they have somehow contributed to the limiting of self-determination and of sovereignty."[59] She goes on to argue that Indigenous leaders, fully cognizant of the nature of the societies in which they live and fully committed to delivering benefits to their own peoples in the here and now, accepted certain compromises in order to arrive at the broad-based support that the UNDRIP has been able over time to achieve. Knowing and understanding this, I believe, is a tremendous source of optimism. It means that, among Indigenous people, there is a profound commitment to working toward pragmatic solutions. Inasmuch as that commitment is met with respect and reciprocity, Indigenous people, in spite of the tragic injustices that they have had to face in the hundreds of years since the first contact, are willing to give states the opportunity to work toward a better future. But, at the same time, the message of a document like the UNDRIP is quite clear: the days of riding roughshod over Indigenous people are over.[60] Armed with the international recognition that the UNDRIP has provided and with confident, competent lawyers, leaders, and advocates, they will not be backing down from the principles, like self-determination, FPIC, and redress for past injustices, that they have managed to mainstream through years of dedication, vigilance, and sacrifice. There is no mistaking the fact that a new day is dawning in the relationship between Indigenous people and the states within whose borders they live.

Conclusion

The UNDRIP is many different things to many different people; a minimum set of standards, an aspirational document, a turning point, a sham, a sell-out, "a very weak declaratory regime,"[61] an overly broad, unclear, impractical conflation of irredentist ambitions. None of this is surprising since the Declaration is, first and foremost, a political document that tries to balance the aims and rights of Indigenous people with those of the public interest in "mostly democratic, utilitarian societies,"[62] where Indigenous peoples are not in the majority. In such societies, like Canada, not only are Indigenous peoples in the minority, but they have been subjected to hundreds of years of colonialism in the form of disease, dispossession, assimilation, and exploitation. Under the circumstances, the attainment of nearly unanimous international support for articles that declare that Indigenous peoples have the right to self-determination, to free, prior, and informed consent, to redress for past injustices is quite remarkable.

It has come at a cost, however. To critics of the UNDRIP, that cost is too high. No limits, according to them, should be placed on the right to self-determination. Self-determination is only a true right if it includes the right to secession. The Member States of the UN General Assembly were able to give their overwhelming support to the Declaration because this type of rigid adherence to principle does not characterize Indigenous people and their leadership.

The UNDRIP has a certain measure of designed flexibility, both in the wording of its articles and in the fact that it is a declaration, not a treaty or convention. It skillfully straddles the line between affirming the rights of Indigenous peoples and recognizing the political framework within which these rights must be implemented. This flexibility is not an accident: it is the result of a long process engaging Indigenous leaders, human rights experts, and state representatives. It is the same flexibility and nimbleness that will be required to make it work on Canadian soil.

It is for this reason that the UNDRIP provides hope for genuine reconciliation. Throughout the process that has led to the passage of the UNDRIP, Indigenous leaders have shown themselves to be political realists who are committed to achieving practical results for their peoples. If the Canadian state, Canadian businesses, Canadian courts, and Canadian churches are willing to engage with them as equals, in a respectful and honest manner, one entirely free of the colonialism that has characterized our nation's behavior in the past, Indigenous people will be pragmatic and constructive partners in the reconstruction, over time, of friendly relations in the service of the public good. To me, this is reconciliation, and I believe that the UNDRIP, by its very existence, proves that it is possible in the Canadian context.

Discussion Questions

1. Indigenous leader and former Liberal cabinet minister Judy Wilson-Raybould said the following in a speech to the Assembly of First Nations: "Simplistic approaches such as adopting the United Nations declaration as being Canadian law are unworkable and, respectfully, a political distraction to undertaking the hard work actually required to implement it back home in communities." Do you agree with Ms. Wilson-Raybould? Is she correct in saying that adoption of the UNDRIP is a simplistic solution? Is it a "distraction" or an asset in accomplishing the "hard work" that needs to be done to improve the lot of Indigenous peoples in Canada?
2. Rather than adopting a broad, sweeping document such as the UNDRIP, what other approaches could be taken to addressing the concerns and grievances of Indigenous peoples in Canada? What would be the advantages or disadvantages of these other potential approaches?
3. Many Indigenous leaders are saying that they are tired of the talk around reconciliation. The terms "Land Back" and "Get Real" express their frustration with symbolic gestures devoid of real impact on their lives. Is adoption of the UNDRIP more of the same from the Canadian government or does it represent a real step forward for Indigenous peoples?
4. Is it fair to designate Canada, the United States, New Zealand, and Australia as the "Anglosphere"? Do they actually have a common approach to the Indigenous peoples within their borders that is distinct from other countries? Has that approach evolved since the time of the UNDRIP's adoption by the UN General Assembly?

Notes

1. Megan Davis, "To Bind or Not to Bind: The United Nations Declaration on the Rights of Indigenous Peoples Five Years On," *Australian International Law Journal* 19 (2012): 28.
2. Kenneth Deer, "Reflections on the Development, Adoption, and Implementation of the UN Declaration on the Rights of Indigenous Peoples," in *Realizing the UN Declaration on the Rights of Indigenous Peoples: Triumph, Hope, and Action*, ed. Jackie Hartley, Paul Joffe, and Jennifer Preston (Saskatoon: Purich Publishing, 2010), 18.

3. Phil Fontaine, "A Living Instrument," in *Realizing the UN Declaration on the Rights of Indigenous Peoples: Triumph, Hope, and Action*, ed. Jackie Hartley, Paul Joffe and Jennifer Preston (Saskatoon: Purich Publishing, 2010), 9.
4. Deer, "Reflections on the Development," 19.
5. Davis, "To Bind or Not," 20.
6. Davis, 20.
7. Deer, "Reflections on the Development," 20.
8. Deer, 20.
9. Davis, "To Bind or Not," 19.
10. Deer, "Reflections on the Development," 21.
11. Deer, 20–21.
12. G. N. Barrie, "The United Nations Declaration on the Rights of Indigenous People: Implications for Land Rights and Self-Determination," *Journal of South African Law*, no. 2 (2013): 302.
13. Les Malezer, "Dreamtime Discovery: New Reality and Hope," in *Realizing the UN Declaration on the Rights of Indigenous Peoples: Triumph, Hope, and Action*, ed. Jackie Hartley, Paul Joffe, and Jennifer Preston (Saskatoon: Purich Publishing, 2010), 34.
14. Malezar, 34.
15. Deer, "Reflections on the Development," 27.
16. Fontaine, "A Living Instrument," 8.
17. Fontaine, 9.
18. Erica-Irene Daes, "The United Nations Declaration on the Rights of Indigenous People: Background and Appraisal," in *Reflections on the United Nations Declaration on the Rights of Indigenous People*, ed. Alexandra Xanthaki and Stephen Allen (Oxford and Portland: Hart Publishing, 2011), 30.
19. Deer, "Reflections on the Development," 19.
20. Wilton Littlechild, "Consistent Advocacy: Treaty Rights and the UN Declaration," in *Realizing the UN Declaration on the Rights of Indigenous Peoples: Triumph, Hope, and Action*, ed. Jackie Hartley, Paul Joffe, and Jennifer Preston (Saskatoon: Purich Publishing, 2010), 112; Ed John, "Survival, Dignity, and Well-Being: Implementing the Declaration in British Columbia," in *Realizing the UN Declaration on the Rights of Indigenous Peoples: Triumph, Hope, and Action*, ed. Jackie Hartley, Paul Joffe, and Jennifer Preston (Saskatoon: Purich Publishing, 2010), 58; Deer, "Reflections on the Development," 23; Romeo Saganash and Paul Joffe, "The Significance of the UN Declaration to a Treaty Nation: A James Bay Cree Perspective," in *Realizing the UN Declaration on the Rights of Indigenous Peoples: Triumph, Hope, and Action*, ed. Jackie Hartley, Paul Joffe, and Jennifer Preston (Saskatoon: Purich Publishing, 2010), 136; Malezer, "Dreamtime Discovery," 34.

21. Saganash and Joffe, "The Significance of," 138.
22. Ward Churchill, "A Travesty of a Mockery of a Sham: Colonialism as Self-Determination in the UN Declaration on the Rights of Indigenous Peoples," *Griffith Law Review* 20, no. 3 (2011): 526.
23. Churchill, 539.
24. Churchill, 539.
25. Churchill, 539.
26. Churchill, 544.
27. Daes, "The United Nations," 21–22.
28. Malezer, "Dreamtime Discovery," 34.
29. Churchill, "A Travesty of a Mockery," 545.
30. Davis, "To Bind or Not," 44.
31. Paul Joffe, "Canada's Opposition to the UN Declaration: Legitimate Concerns or Ideological Bias?," in *Realizing the UN Declaration on the Rights of Indigenous Peoples: Triumph, Hope, and Action*, ed. Jackie Hartley, Paul Joffe, and Jennifer Preston (Saskatoon: Purich Publishing, 2010), 76.
32. Sheryl Lightfoot, "Selective Endorsement Without Intent to Implement: Indigenous Rights and the Anglosphere," *The International Journal of Human Rights* 16, no. 1 (2012): 100.
33. Lightfoot, 113.
34. Lightfoot, 113.
35. Lightfoot, 113.
36. Churchill, "A Travesty of a Mockery," 526.
37. Davis, "To Bind or Not," 33.
38. Davis, 28.
39. Deer, "Reflections on the Development," 21.
40. Davis, "To Bind or Not," 33.
41. Davis, 28.
42. Davis, 47.
43. Lightfoot, "Selective Endorsement," 112.
44. Davis, "To Bind or Not," 36; S. James Anaya, "The Human Rights of Indigenous People: United Nations Developments," *University of Hawaii Law Review* 35, no. 2 (Spring 2013): 998.
45. Anaya, 998.
46. John, "Survival, Dignity," 48.
47. Anaya, "The Human Rights of Indigenous," 998.
48. Anaya, 999.
49. Margot Hurlbert, "Human Rights," in *Pursuing Justice: An Introduction to Justice Studies*, ed. Margot Hurlbert (Winnipeg: Fernwood Publishing, 2011), 174.
50. Davis, "To Bind or Not," 36–37.
51. Davis, 42.

52. Sheryl Lightfoot, "Using Legislation to Implant the United Nations Declaration on the Rights of Indigenous People," in *UNDRIP Implementation: More Reflections on the Braiding of International, Domestic and Indigenous Laws*, ed. Oonagh Fitzgerald and Larry Chartrand (Saskatoon and Waterloo: Centre for International Governance Innovation and Wiyasiwewin Mikiwahp Native Law Centre, 2018), 21.
53. Truth and Reconciliation Commission Final Report, "Truth and Reconciliation Commission of Canada Calls to Action," 229.
54. Larry Chartrand, "Mapping the meaning of Reconciliation in Canada: Implications for Métis-Canada Memoranda of Understanding on Reconciliation Negotiations," in *UNDRIP Implementation: More Reflections on the Braiding of International, Domestic and Indigenous Laws*, ed. Oonagh Fitzgerald and Larry Chartrand (Saskatoon and Waterloo: Centre for International Governance Innovation and Wiyasiwewin Mikiwahp Native Law Centre, 2018), 49.
55. Tsilhqot'in National Government, "Nenqay-Deni Accord," 2016.
56. vLex, "Nunatukavut Community Council Inc. v. Canada," 2015.
57. Parliament of Canada, "Bill C-262," 2016.
58. CBC News, "Canada votes 'no' as UN native rights declaration passes," *CBC News*, September 13, 2007. https://www.cbc.ca/news/canada/canada-votes-no-as-un-native-rights-declaration-passes-1.632160.
59. Davis, "To Bind or Not," 47–48.
60. Julian Burger, "The United Nations Declaration on the Rights of Indigenous People: From Advocacy to Implementation," in *Reflections on the United Nations Declaration on the Rights of Indigenous People*, ed. Alexandra Xanthaki and Stephen Allen (Oxford and Portland: Hart Publishing, 2011), 53.
61. Jack Donnelly, *Universal Human Rights in Theory and in Practice. 3rd ed.* (Ithica, New York: Cornell University Press, 2013), 190.
62. Davis, "To Bind or Not," 47.

Bibliography

Anaya, S. James. "The Human Rights of Indigenous People: United Nations Developments." *University of Hawai'i Law Review* 35, no. 2 (Spring 2013): 983–1012.

Barrie, G.N. "The United Nations Declaration on the Rights of Indigenous People: Implications for Land Rights and Self-Determination." *Journal of South African Law* 2013, no. 2 (2013): 292–305.

Burger, Julian. "The United Nations Declaration on the Rights of Indigenous People: From Advocacy to Implementation." In *Reflections on the United Nations Declaration on the Rights of Indigenous People*, edited by Alexandra

Xanthaki and Stephen Allen, 41–60. Oxford and Portland: Hart Publishing, 2011.

CBC News. "Canada Votes 'No' as UN Native Rights Declaration Passes." *CBC News*. September 13, 2007. https://www.cbc.ca/news/canada/canada-votes-no-as-un-native-rights-declaration-passes-1.632160.

Chartrand, Larry. "Mapping the Meaning of Reconciliation in Canada: Implications for Métis-Canada Memoranda of Understanding on Reconciliation Negotiations." In *UNDRIP Implementation: More Reflections on the Braiding of International, Domestic and Indigenous Laws*, edited by Oonagh Fitzgerald and Larry Chartrand, 43–52. Saskatoon and Waterloo: Centre for International Governance Innovation and Wiyasiwewin Mikiwahp Native Law Centre, 2018.

Churchill, Ward. "A Travesty of a Mockery of a Sham: Colonialism as Self-Determination in the UN Declaration on the Rights of Indigenous Peoples." *Griffith Law Review* 20, no. 3 (2011): 526–556.

Daes, Erica-Irene. "The United Nations Declaration on the Rights of Indigenous People: Background and Appraisal." In *Reflections on the United Nations Declaration on the Rights of Indigenous People*, edited by Alexandra Xanthaki and Stephen Allen, 11–40. Oxford and Portland: Hart Publishing, 2011.

Davis, Megan. "To Bind or Not to Bind: The United Nations Declaration on the Rights of Indigenous Peoples Five Years On." *Australian International Law Journal* 19 (2012): 17–48.

Deer, Kenneth. "Reflections on the Development, Adoption, and Implementation of the UN Declaration on the Rights of Indigenous Peoples." In *Realizing the UN Declaration on the Rights of Indigenous Peoples: Triumph, Hope, and Action*, edited by Jackie Hartley, Paul Joffe, and Jennifer Preston, 18–28. Saskatoon: Purich Publishing, 2010.

Donnelly, Jack. *Universal Human Rights in Theory and Practice. 3rd ed.* Ithaca: Cornell University Press, 2013.

Fontaine, Phil. "A Living Instrument." In *Realizing the UN Declaration on the Rights of Indigenous Peoples: Triumph, Hope, and Action*, edited by Jackie Hartley, Paul Joffe, and Jennifer Preston, 8–11. Saskatoon: Purich Publishing, 2010.

Hurlbert, Margot. "Human Rights." In *Pursuing Justice: An Introduction to Justice Studies*, edited by Margot Hurlbert, 174. Winnipeg: Fernwood Publishing, 2011.

Joffe, Paul. "Canada's Opposition to the UN Declaration: Legitimate Concerns or Ideological Bias?." In *Realizing the UN Declaration on the Rights of Indigenous Peoples: Triumph, Hope, and Action*, edited by Jackie Hartley, Paul Joffe, and Jennifer Preston, 70–94. Saskatoon: Purich Publishing, 2010.

John, Ed. “Survival, Dignity, and Well-Being: Implementing the Declaration in British Columbia.” In *Realizing the UN Declaration on the Rights of Indigenous Peoples: Triumph, Hope, and Action*, edited by Jackie Hartley, Paul Joffe, and Jennifer Preston, 47–59. Saskatoon: Purich Publishing, 2010.

Lightfoot, Sheryl R. “Selective Endorsement Without Intent to Implement: Indigenous Rights and the Anglosphere.” *The International Journal of Human Rights* 16, no. 1 (2012): 100–122.

Lightfoot, Sheryl R. “Using Legislation to Implant the United Nations Declaration on the Rights of Indigenous People.” In *UNDRIP Implementation: More Reflections on the Braiding of International, Domestic and Indigenous Laws*, edited by Oonagh Fitzgerald and Larry Chartrand, 17–24. Saskatoon and Waterloo: Centre for International Governance Innovation and Wiyasiwewin Mikiwahp Native Law Centre, 2018.

Littlechild, Wilton. “Consistent Advocacy: Treaty Rights and the UN Declaration.” In *Realizing the UN Declaration on the Rights of Indigenous Peoples: Triumph, Hope, and Action*, edited by Jackie Hartley, Paul Joffe, and Jennifer Preston, 112–119. Saskatoon: Purich Publishing, 2010.

Malezer, Les. “Dreamtime Discovery: New Reality and Hope.” In *Realizing the UN Declaration on the Rights of Indigenous Peoples: Triumph, Hope, and Action*, edited by Jackie Hartley, Paul Joffe, and Jennifer Preston, 29–46. Saskatoon: Purich Publishing, 2010.

Nenqay-Deni Accord. 2016. Accessed at http://www.tsilhqotin.ca/Portals/0/PDFs/Nenqay_Deni_Accord.pdf.

Nunatukavut Community Council Inc. v. Canada. 2015. Accessed at https://ca.vlex.com/vid/nunatukavut-com-council-v-681702773.

Parliament of Canada. “Bill C-262.” 2018. Accessed at https://www.parl.ca/DocumentViewer/en/42-1/bill/C-262/third-reading.

Saganash, Romeo, and Joffe, Paul. “The Significance of the UN Declaration to a Treaty Nation: A James Bay Cree Perspective.” In *Realizing the UN Declaration on the Rights of Indigenous Peoples: Triumph, Hope, and Action*, edited by Jackie Hartley, Paul Joffe, and Jennifer Preston, 135–155. Saskatoon: Purich Publishing, 2010.

Truth and Reconciliation Commission of Canada Calls to Action. 2015. Accessed at https://publications.gc.ca/collections/collection_2015/trc/IR4-8-2015-eng.pdf.

Indigenous Rights and the University

Annette Trimbee

There is a saying among Canadian University presidents that our role as leaders is to absorb chaos, portray calm, and convey hope. I heard that saying early in my term at the University of Winnipeg (UWinnipeg), around the release of the Truth and Reconciliation Commission's (TRC) Calls to Action and before COVID-19. It is even more poignant now, early in my term at MacEwan University (MacEwan), as we recoil from the news of thousands of unmarked graves of Indigenous students forced to go to residential schools, the Intergovernmental Panel on Climate Change conclusion that climate change is widespread, rapid, and intensifying,[1] and social inequities rise as we endure a global pandemic. These multiple and intersecting crises are driving universities to address societal issues with greater intention, focus, and impact. As universities, we shape the future, not just respond to it. We see first-hand on our campuses how education transforms lives and understands why Indigenous Elders refer to education as the new buffalo. We say the cause and company are like no other and take joy in being part of such a hopeful sector that builds

A. Trimbee (✉)
MacEwan University, Edmonton, AB, Canada
e-mail: annette.trimbee@macewan.ca

L. E. Reimer and K. Standish (eds.), *Perspectives on Justice, Indigeneity, Gender, and Security in Human Rights Research*,
https://doi.org/10.1007/978-981-99-1930-7_7

solutions with communities and each other to boldly create the future we envision.

When the TRC issued its Calls to Action in December 2015, it placed education at the center of reconciliation.[2] The report included calls to eliminate educational and employment gaps between Indigenous and non-Indigenous people and to build Indigenous education into existing programming.[3] Canadian universities quickly embraced the TRC and made public commitments to Indigenization, reconciliation, and decolonization without a shared view of the meaning of these terms. In this chapter I explore the motivations for making these commitments, how motivations impact one's approach, and where complexity has impacted or stalled efforts. I make the case that universities have moved beyond making these commitments for charitable, competitive, and risk-based reasons to a more hopeful mindset based on human dignity and recognition of the need to embrace Indigenous ways of knowing in teaching and research if we truly want to build back better.

I have had the honor of leading two downtown primarily undergraduate universities, the University of Winnipeg, Winnipeg, Manitoba from 2014 to 2020 and MacEwan University in Edmonton, Alberta since August 2020. Both cities are home to relatively large and rapidly growing Indigenous populations and have been traditional gathering places for Indigenous peoples for thousands of years. UWinnipeg is located on Treaty One territory in the heart of the Métis homeland. Winnipeg is home to the largest Indigenous population of any census metropolitan area in the nation[4] and is at the epicenter of an Indigenous resurgence taking place throughout Canada. MacEwan University is located on Treaty Six Territory in the Edmonton city ward now called O-day' min, a Cree word which means the heart through which the North Saskatchewan River runs. Edmonton's Indigenous population is not as large as Winnipeg's, but it is larger than other major cities such as Toronto, Calgary, Vancouver, and Montreal and represents a larger proportion of the city's population compared to the national average.[5] Although Canada's publicly funded universities see themselves as regional, national, and global institutions, their location matters. Place affects what we teach, what we research, how we serve the public good, who we attract as students, faculty and staff, our partnerships, and how we are governed and funded.

The topic of reconciliation is personal. After living in Edmonton for many years, I was drawn back to Winnipeg to take on the role of President and Vice-Chancellor of UWinnipeg for two reasons. First, I am grateful to UWinnipeg for tapping me on the shoulder, offering me a significant scholarship, providing a quality education, and giving me my start. Second, as a Métis person who left Winnipeg with two university degrees, little to no knowledge of treaties, residential schools, or my own Métis history, I jumped at the opportunity to be engaged with and positively influence the Indigenous inclusion and reconciliation efforts unfolding at UWinnipeg. After 6 years at UWinnipeg, I moved to Edmonton to lead MacEwan University during the early days of the COVID-19 pandemic and was reminded quickly that local context greatly influences the approach to, and pace, of reconciliation.

My predecessor at UWinnipeg, Dr. Lloyd Axworthy, significantly reshaped how people thought about the role of post-secondary institutions in providing opportunities for Indigenous students, and how universities should connect with their surrounding communities. Under Dr. Axworthy's leadership, UWinnipeg created pathways to university for traditionally underrepresented students, including refugees, war-affected youth, and Indigenous people, all of whom are present in high concentrations in the neighborhoods surrounding UWinnipeg. During his tenure from 2004 to 2014, Dr. Axworthy helped to shift the narrative from university as a place for the privileged, to university as a place for everyone, regardless of socio-economic or cultural background.

At the time of my installation as President and Vice-Chancellor of UWinnipeg in 2014, the TRC report and its Calls to Action were widely anticipated. In 2015, after months of consultation with the campus community, the UWinnipeg Board of Regents approved five Strategic Directions for the University, one of which is Indigenization. While the Strategic Directions framework made Indigenization an explicit institutional priority, the presence of initiatives supporting the mandate of Indigenization and the broader work of reconciliation had long preceded the framework. UWinnipeg's wide-ranging efforts related to Indigenization included incorporating Indigenous knowledge in curricula and teaching practices, hiring Indigenous academics and employees, supporting faculty to conduct research that benefits and aligns with Indigenous communities, creating community partnerships to facilitate transitions to post-secondary education for Indigenous youth, and supporting an increased number of Indigenous students to succeed in various academic programs.

Language Matters

Despite this span of work, the term "Indigenization" was not universally understood throughout the UWinnipeg campus community. Indigenization was viewed by some at UWinnipeg as an extension of the work that began in earnest in 2004 by enhancing the inclusion of Indigenous peoples and extending the role of the university beyond its core mission into the surrounding community. Others saw it as a concerted effort to adapt and change the institution—both academically and physically—to become more "Indigenous." Others understood Indigenization explicitly through the Calls to Action of the TRC's final report, which positions education as central to processes of reconciliation.

Four years into my role at UWinnipeg, as the tension between different interpretations of what Indigenization meant grew, Gaudry and Lorenz published a paper that conceptualized Indigenization visions on a continuum from "Indigenous inclusion," to "reconciliation indigenization," to "decolonization indigenization."[6] This conceptualization of Indigenization provided a useful framework to understand the growing number of approaches to Indigenization.[7]

Indigenous inclusion retains the institution's structures and "support[s] the adaption of Indigenous people to the current (often alienating) culture of the Canadian academy."[8] In this model, the "burden of change" is placed on Indigenous people while "naturaliz[ing] the status quo of academic culture."[9] Gaudry and Lorenz conclude that *Indigenous inclusion* does help in "building toward systemic indigenization," but should not be an institution's ultimate objective.[10]

The second model described is *reconciliation Indigenization, which* seeks to establish "common ground between Indigenous and Canadian ideals."[11] *Reconciliation Indigenization* supports *Indigenous inclusion* and is also "an attempt to alter the university's structure, including educating Canadian faculty, staff, and students to change how they think about, and act toward, Indigenous people."[12] *Reconciliation Indigenization* can include the creation of an Indigenous course requirement (ICR), although this has not been widely adopted by universities at this time.[13] Gaudry and Lorenz write that "power sharing, a transformation of decision-making processes, and a reintegration of Indigenous peoples, faculty, staff, and students into policymaking that affects them, and their Canadian peers" is necessary to move beyond "rhetorical shifts to aspirational reconciliation."[14]

The third model described by Gaudry and Lorenz is *decolonial Indigenization* and requires "the wholesale overhaul of the academy to fundamentally reorient knowledge production based on balancing power relations between Indigenous peoples and Canadians, transforming the academy into something dynamic and new."[15] Gaudry and Lorenz note that if "indigenization does not strengthen Indigenous communities and support the resurgence of Indigenous intellectual traditions, then it is not indigenization." *Decolonial Indigenization* is therefore achieved by supporting Indigenous methods of knowledge production, evaluation, and transmission, creation of treaty-based relationships, and perhaps in a "dual university structure" that returns control to Indigenous people and communities.[16]

Motivations Matter

Alongside language, motivations matter. I mentioned earlier that Canadian universities embraced the TRC's Calls to Action and were quick to publicly declare commitments without a shared view of terms like Indigenization, reconciliation, and decolonization. It begs the question, what motivation drove these institutions to demonstrate such a sense of urgency to act before truly understanding?

Was it a sense of guilt, a need to outshine the competition, or charitable actions done in the spirit of social justice that inspired these commitments? Given the truths exposed by the TRC report, there was ample motivation for universities to be more accessible to those who previously would not have had the opportunity to attend university. The drive to improve the social and economic disparities experienced by Indigenous people and communities as a means of social justice was also a key motivation. On the other hand, it may also have been important to be seen by others as doing the right thing, an aspect of the motivational core that was only accentuated by the competitive relationship between universities. Regardless of which source of motivation held the most sway, they all have something in common. All of these motivations stem from a base desire of "we should" and align with the vision of *Indigenous inclusion* from perspectives that I would argue are based on a deficit mindset toward Indigenous peoples.

Alternatively, the core motivation to act could stem from the notion of human dignity and a talent and hope mindset, one that recognizes that reconciliation is good for non-Indigenous and Indigenous peoples, is open to seeing the world in more than one way, and acknowledges that solving today's challenges requires all minds, hearts, and hands on deck.

Andrew Clapham suggests that concern for human dignity has at least four aspects: (1) the prohibition of all types of inhuman treatment, humiliation, or degradation by one person over another; (2) the assurance of the possibility for individual choice, self-fulfillment, and self-realization; (3) the recognition that the protection of group identity and culture may be essential for the protection of the personal dignity; and (4) the creation of the necessary conditions for each individual to have their essential needs satisfied.[17] *Indigenous inclusion* incorporates the first, second, and fourth aspects of human dignity listed above with an emphasis on supporting Indigenous students by creating safe spaces and a sense of belonging while *reconciliation Indigenization* also incorporates the third aspect. To that end, if a talent and hope-based mindset and good-for-all perspective, framed by the concept of human dignity, was the key motivation behind the commitments made by universities, we need to ensure human dignity is understood through an Indigenous lens. This means broadening the concept of human dignity to include spirituality, relations with the earth, and all orders of being, with a specific focus on collective responsibilities rather than individual rights.

If not motivated by a sense of human dignity, nor out of a guilt driven "we should" obligation, what if universities acted on the basis of human rights? Article 14 of the UN Declaration of the Rights of Indigenous Peoples states; (1) Indigenous peoples have the right to establish and control their educational systems and institutions providing education in their own languages, in a manner appropriate to their cultural methods of teaching and learning; (2) Indigenous individuals, particularly children, have the right to all levels and forms of education of the State without discrimination; and (3) States shall, in conjunction with Indigenous peoples, take effective measures, in order for Indigenous individuals, particularly children, including those living outside their communities, to have access, when possible, to an education in their own culture and provided in their own language.[18] If the motivation guiding universities toward Indigenization and reconciliation is based on human rights tied to UNDRIP, the vision in the Gaudry and Lorentz framework mostly analogous is *decolonial Indigenization*. While *decolonial Indigenization* is fundamentally about reorienting power relations, enacting this transformation through solely a debate on human rights encourages a transformation based on court decisions, with winners and losers, and all that entails. Much like human dignity, for this approach to properly reflect Indigenous people and communities, human rights must also be understood through a non-eurocentric perspective. The word for human rights in the Wikwemikon language, "Gichi dibaakonegewin tamajawich," reflects the desire to live well, have a good life, and hope for the future,[19] while "Anishinabek law does not make any mention of rights, rather roles and responsibilities to all our relations."[20] These examples show us how thinking about human rights from an Indigenous perspective requires us to consider our responsibilities to the collective as opposed to individual rights, founded on the principle of spirituality and what it means to be human. To that end, relying on human rights as the motivating impetus for universities to act toward reconciliation and Indigenization could be problematic if these conversations are limited to a traditional western interpretation of human rights. As one can imagine, regardless of the action taken, it is important to understand what motivated universities to embrace the TRC's Calls to Action and act, especially considering the lack of a shared view of terms like Indigenization, reconciliation, and decolonization. Like language, motivations matter, and moving beyond a "we should" mentality toward a hopeful one based on an Indigenous understanding of human dignity is needed if we are to embrace and act upon the spirit within the TRC's Calls to Action.

Looking Back, How Did Universities Across Canada Respond?

In 2015, Universities Canada adopted a set of Principles outlining a commitment to Indigenizing higher education and fostering reconciliation efforts in post-secondary institutions.[21] Considered in the context of Gaudry and Lorenz's framework, these Principles fall mainly into the *reconciliation Indigenization* category and align well with Clapham's four aspects of human dignity. The Principles call for increased Indigenous representation within governance structures, staff, and student bodies and enhanced consultation and collaboration with Indigenous communities to ensure Indigenous students' needs are met. Given the central distinction between *reconciliation Indigenization* and *decolonization Indigenization* is related to where power is situated in decision-making processes, the Principles do not redistribute power to Indigenous communities, nor do they align with the human rights-based approach exemplified by UNDRIP.

Similarly, the Manitoba Indigenous Education Blueprint,[22] signed by the president of each post-secondary institution in Manitoba in 2015, represents a form of *reconciliation Indigenization*. Of note, the commitments articulated in the Blueprint speak to the need for: engaging with Indigenous peoples in respectful reciprocal relationships, bringing Indigenous knowledge, languages, intellectual traditions, models and approaches into curriculum and pedagogy, increasing access to services, building cultural safety, increasing the participation rates of Indigenous students in post-secondary, and reflecting the diversity of Indigenous peoples in governance and staffing policies and practices.[23]

Together, the Universities Canada Principles and commitments outlined in the Manitoba Indigenous Education Blueprint are aspirational and speak primarily to the importance of inclusion, where most existing efforts are situated.

It has been 7 years since the TRC was released. Since then, I have observed common threads to how universities have responded as well as some commonalities in the sequence of their actions. Specifically, universities have taken action to put the spirit back in education through ceremony and inclusion of Indigenous Elders, develop pathways for youth to enter higher education supported for success, created new administrative roles for Indigenous engagement and advisory circles, and created dedicated space for Indigenous students and communities. Furthermore, universities have also taken action to add Indigenous content and pedagogical practices to teaching within the institution along with targeted efforts to increase the number of Indigenous faculty and staff. Lastly, there has continued to be an ongoing focus within post-secondary administrations to embed the spirit of Indigenization into strategic plans and partnerships with Indigenous communities, colleges, and universities.

Progress at UWinnipeg and MacEwan

University of Winnipeg

To many, Winnipeg is viewed to be a key center of Indigenous resurgence. Because of this, UWinnipeg's approach to Indigenization and reconciliation is rooted in the work done beyond the border of campus and in partnership with surrounding communities, organizations, and schools. While many other universities began this work following the TRC's Calls to Action, UWinnipeg has been actively working with

Indigenous students, faculty, Elders, traditional knowledge keepers, staff, and community members over the past decade. For instance, UWinnipeg has received counsel from an Indigenous Advisory Circle and welcomed Indigenous perspectives at the highest levels of decision-making, which have both undoubtedly had a significant impact on UWinnipeg's approach to Indigenization and reconciliation.

UWinnipeg's approach has focused on strengthening the transition to post-secondary from the elementary and secondary school system, as seen by the Build from Within—Ozhitton Onji Peenjiiie,[24] Wii Chiiwaakanak Learning Centre,[25] and UWinnipeg's Model School programs,[26] promoting Indigenous student success in undergraduate programs, developing Indigenous-focused graduate programs, and supporting transitions to work. Many of these programs found success in strengthening our community partnerships, building up Indigenous youth, and fostering a sense of belonging to the university for children, youth, and their families.[27] For Indigenous students, the Aboriginal Student Services Centre alongside UWinnipeg's Department of Urban and Inner-City Studies provide support in the form of a culturally safe, educational, and supportive environment that is paired with access to hands-on, cooperative, experiential and work-integrated learning opportunities, many of which focus on Indigenous culture and ways of knowing. For those interested in graduate programs, UWinnipeg's Pathways to Graduate Studies program[28] and Master's in Development Practice in Indigenous Development and Master of Arts in Indigenous Governance graduate programs center themselves on Indigenous ways of knowing and Indigenous research methods. Lastly, UWinnipeg approach to Indigenization and reconciliation has also reached beyond campus borders by creating partnerships, such as those represented by the Youth United inner-city work study, Walls to Bridges, and joint UWinnipeg and Canadian Museum for Human Rights Indigenous and Human Rights Executive Leadership programs, to ensure UWinnipeg's efforts are not made in isolation from community.

UWinnipeg was also one of the first post-secondary institutions in Canada to approve an Indigenous Course Requirement in 2015, making Indigenous learning a component of the undergraduate degree requirements for all new undergraduate students. In 2018, Williamson concluded that the ICR is a "vital step toward reconciliation" and that it is possible for the program to succeed by engaging in "respectful, responsive relationship building."[29] Additionally, Lepp-Friesen's survey of student and faculty experiences after the first year of the ICR provided several recommendations to improve the ICR, including "providing students with more information and intent about the ICR, more support services, pedagogical training, and debrief mechanisms for all involved."[30] While learning continues to refine the ICR, the decision to implement one exemplifies UWinnipeg's leadership toward Indigenization and reconciliation and responding to the TRC's Calls to Action.

As we reflect on Gaudry and Lorenz's framework, we can see that UWinnipeg has strived to implement initiatives that move well beyond *Indigenous Inclusion.* Alongside the various programs already mentioned above, UWinnipeg and the Manitoba Métis Federation (MMF) signed a ten-year agreement to partner in addressing policy research questions designed and developed by the MMF. This partnership has already provided new insights as UWinnipeg and the MMF co-published a research report in 2019 on the school readiness of Métis children in Manitoba.

MacEwan University

I am still in my early days at MacEwan University and arrived at a very uncertain time. MacEwan had just gone through two years of significant budget cuts and the launch of a provincial review of the entire post-secondary system fueled speculation of mergers, changing mandates, and further cuts. This was on top of a pandemic. It has been a bit harder to find my bearings both on campus and understand the community as a result. There were some very positive signs of public support for reconciliation locally, including the Indigenous naming of Edmonton city wards[31] and the opening of the Indigenous Peoples Experience at Ft. Edmonton Park.[32] At the same time, I get subtle signals that the appetite for change and pace of change here is different than in Winnipeg. Fortunately, MacEwan had already begun significant work toward Indigenization and reconciliation thanks to the previous president, Deb Saucier, and her team's leadership. Alongside a commitment to the TRC's Calls to Action, MacEwan has promoted access for Indigenous students through the Pimâcihisowin Foundation Program,[33] partnered with other institutions to provide land-based learning opportunities, and physically transformed campus space to be more inclusive and welcoming to Indigenous people. Where MacEwan's Indigenous center, kihew waciston, is one such space that acts as a home away from home for students,[34] its partnership with

Blue Quills University provides learning opportunities for students that "develops their knowledge of Indigenous teachings, customs and value systems."[35] This past year, MacEwan initiated an innovative approach to inclusive hiring. In contrast to traditional hiring methods, MacEwan has introduced hiring for joint positions, attached to departments and the kihew waciston center. I appreciate this approach as it connects new Indigenous scholars to the community. When put together, these actions certainly support and move beyond *Indigenous inclusion.*

Where It Gets Complicated—How Do Others See Progress?

A member of UWinnipeg's Indigenous Advisory circle once told me that our efforts to Indigenize needed to be uncomfortable to matter. For many Canadian universities, things did start to get uncomfortable a few years after the TRC came out. The relatively easy symbolic things had been done and celebrated. Many more indigenous scholars were hired, Indigenous spaces were created, and more Indigenous course content was added. Indigenous people and ideas were being brought into university life. After a few celebratory years, headlines started to pop up with stories about unhappy Indigenous scholars dropping out in frustration, citing a lack of support and resources and disappointment that their institutions were simply not progressing fast enough. More recently, there are growing allegations that universities are not screening candidates' claims of Indigenous identity, and this is resulting in ethnic fraud.[36] Concerns have also been quietly raised about positioning Indigenization as an aspect of institutional equity, diversity, and inclusion plans and shifting priorities and scarce resources to other equity-deserving groups.

Looking Ahead—Why It Matters

In Fall 2019, I had the opportunity to be on a panel at a round-table discussion, co-hosted by Indspire and Universities Canada, on the future of Indigenous student success. As part of the round-table, Indspire shared some preliminary results of a survey conducted with over two thousand Indigenous learners in the summer of 2018 on the barriers that hinder their ability to complete a post-secondary education.[37] While the findings discussed the financial barriers, and how it impacts student housing, food, childcare, and travel requirements, the finding I found most disturbing was that the place Indigenous students felt most uncomfortable was "in class."[38] Indigenous students are told to walk between worlds, but also clearly want to see their history and culture incorporated into their post-secondary experiences. Indigenous student services on campus help to make students feel validated and supported, but these services are often overtaxed and underfunded. Furthermore, there are few Indigenous professors, instructors, and staff, which alongside a lack of Indigenous course content, makes it hard for Indigenous students to find mentors and role models.

During the round-table discussion, I was asked "In 10 years, with proper funding, what do you envision as the ideal post-secondary education for Indigenous and non-Indigenous learners?" I liked this question for three reasons, it made me reflect on how today's decisions will influence the future, forced me to think beyond "if we had the funds" and acknowledge that financial changes are not the only path forward, and most importantly that this ideal future state needed to work for both Indigenous and non-Indigenous students. To answer this question, we need to think about who will be attending our post-secondary institutions in ten years. Ideally, virtually all students, Indigenous and non-Indigenous, will graduate from high school compared to the approximately fifty and ninety percent of Indigenous and non-Indigenous students now. These students should arrive to the post-secondary system with a full understanding of Canada's history, treaties, residential schools, and have had opportunities to learn Indigenous languages. Although I have a bias as an Indigenous university president, these future students should also be able to imagine a future for themselves that includes graduating from a post-secondary institution. So how is this ideal future structured? In my mind, it looks something akin to the New Zealand model where there is a healthy mix of universities that have Indigenous alongside fully Indigenous institutions like the Wananga, ideally built on partnerships similar to the ones held between UWinnipeg and the Manitoba Metis Federation and MacEwan with Blue Quill.

By the end of the round-table discussion, I was happy to not be asked what proper funding would look like. As a former Deputy Minister of Finance, I know that no sector ever asks for less. What I can say is that if the educational attainment gap between Indigenous and non-Indigenous students is not closed, social costs will go up, and economic competitiveness will go down. The provincial benefit in Alberta alone has been estimated to exceed a quarter of a trillion dollars.[39] These arguments are strong but intimidating because of the size of the ask. I have learned that these asks are more powerful when combined with stories about the hopes, dreams, and talents of Indigenous youth as they imagine their future. Within the context of this ideal future, my biggest fear remains that the pendulum will swing back and we will lose the forward momentum we have started to see.

It has been several years since I attended that round-table discussion in 2019, so what about today? In the words of Regional Chief Marlene Poitras of the Assembly of First Nations at the House of Commons Standing Committee on Indigenous and Northern Affairs "this pandemic has highlighted the inequities in this country and exacerbated existing challenges."[40] In October 2020, the Standing Committee on Indigenous and Northern Affairs agreed to complete a study on the challenges faced by Indigenous communities and the resources needed to support them through, at the time, a second wave of the COVID-19 pandemic.[41] Throughout this study, the committee encountered several challenges including a lack of internet access, travel restrictions, and staff shortages to complete the needed work. This is only one example of many that highlights what is at stake and why Indigenization and reconciliation matters.

Conclusion and Personal Reflection

I have been on this journey in a very personal way over the past seven years. Canadian universities are making progress. However, our efforts to embrace the truth and reconcile matter now more than ever as we emerge from the COVID-19 pandemic.

Language matters as does leadership. Looking back, I do not regret leveraging my leadership role at UWinnipeg to accelerate that institution's progress toward Indigenization, even though my understanding of what *Indigenous inclusion*, *reconciliation Indigenization*, and *decolonization Indigenization* was still evolving. In fact, it was the messiness of not having a shared view of language that led to many of the rich discussions that needed to happen on our campus, as well as other campuses, across Canada.

The day the UWinnipeg senate approved an ICR was one of the happiest days of my time there. The idea for the ICR came from students. My job as a leader was to help students and other champions gauge and gain support as they navigated our complex governance structures. Universities are systems within systems. Both UWinnipeg and MacEwan are publicly funded institutions established by provincial legislation. University mandates across the country may vary, but at our core we exist to teach, perform research, and serve the public good. If there is a tension with our primary funders, it most often relates to views on what serving the public good really means. Place matters. Universities are local, regional, and national institutions that often push the boundaries on social issues. How far you can and choose to go along the three visions of Indigenization outlined by Gaudry and Lorenz depends on the level of internal community and public support. The wholesale overhaul and redistribution of power that many Indigenous scholars are hoping for will take time and are more likely to happen through partnerships with the Indigenous Institutes now being recognized as the third pillar of education alongside universities and colleges.[42]

Motivations also matter as universities have begun to move beyond a "we should" mentality centered on a deficit mindset toward Indigenous peoples toward a hopeful one based on an Indigenous understanding of human dignity. Reconciliation is good for non-Indigenous and Indigenous peoples. Solving today's challenges requires an openness to seeing the world in more than one way and requires all minds, hearts, and hands on deck.

I remain optimistic, hopeful, and open to surprises. Indigenization and reconciliation are about cultural change. Much of the easy work has been done and the next steps will be uncomfortable for some. Universities have an important role to play but can not and should not do it alone. We need to be strategic about advancing our priorities and look for synergies and opportunities to partner with Indigenous people, organizations, and communities.[43]

Discussion Questions

1. What is your vision for reconciliation in Canada's post-secondary system? What would success look like?
2. How can universities advance reconciliation and make things better for the full range of equity-deserving groups?
3. How should individual universities prioritize efforts toward social impact issues like sustainable development and reconciliation? Are there any risks of getting too far ahead on these issues with respect

to the communities they serve? Alternatively, what are the risks of being a late mover, a follower, or lagging behind?

4. What is the role of universities in K-12 educational outcomes for Indigenous learners?

Notes

1. IPCC, 2021: *Climate Change 2021: The Physical Science Basis. Contribution of Working Group I to the Sixth Assessment Report of the Intergovernmental Panel on Climate Change*, eds. Masson-Delmotte, V., P. Zhai, A. Pirani, S.L. Connors, C. Péan, S. Berger, N. Caud, Y. Chen, L. Goldfarb, M.I. Gomis, M. Huang, K. Leitzell, E. Lonnoy, J.B.R. Matthews, T.K. Maycock, T. Waterfield, O. Yelekçi, R. Yu, and B. Zhou (Cambridge, UK: Cambridge University Press, 2021), https://doi.org/10.1017/9781009157896.
2. *Truth and Reconciliation Commission of Canada Calls to Action* (2015), accessed at https://publications.gc.ca/collections/collection_2015/trc/IR4-8-2015-eng.pdf.
3. *Truth and Reconciliation Commission*, 2.
4. Statistics Canada, *Canadian Census* 2016 Canadian Census, September, 2018. Statistics Canada. 2016 *Census of Canada Census, 2016 Census.* Catalogue number 98-316-X2016001 in Statistics Canada [database online]. Ottawa.
5. Statistics Canada, "Census Profile, 2016 Census," *Government of Canada*, last updated June 18, 2019, https://www12.statcan.gc.ca/census-recensement/2016/dp-pd/prof/index.cfm?Lang=E.
6. Adam Gaudry, and Danielle Lorenz. "Indigenization As Inclusion, Reconciliation, and Decolonization: Navigating the Different Visions for Indigenizing the Canadian Academy." *AlterNative: An International Journal of Indigenous Peoples* 14, no. 3 (2018): 218. https://doi.org/10.1177/1177180118785382.
7. Gaudry and Lorenz, 218.
8. Gaudry and Lorenz, 218.
9. Gaudry and Lorenz, 220.
10. Gaudry and Lorenz, 221.
11. Gaudry and Lorenz, 219.
12. Gaudry and Lorenz, 222.
13. Gaudry and Lorenz, 222.
14. Gaudry and Lorenz, 223.
15. Gaudry and Lorenz, 219.
16. Gaudry and Lorenz, 223.

17. Christopher McCrudden, "Human Dignity and Judicial Interpretation of Human Rights," *European Journal of International Law* 19, no. 4 (2008): 686, https://doi.org/10.1093/ejil/chn043.
18. United Nations General Assembly, "United Nations Declaration on the Rights of Indigenous Peoples," resolution/adopted by the General Assembly, 2 October 2007, A/RES/61/295, https://www.un.org/development/desa/indigenouspeoples/wp-content/uploads/sites/19/2018/11/UNDRIP_E_web.pdf.
19. Ontario Human Rights Commission, *To Dream Together: Indigenous Peoples and Human Rights Dialogue Report* (Toronto, ON: Government of Ontario, September 2018), 24, http://www.ohrc.on.ca/sites/default/files/INDIGENOUS%20POLICY%20DIALOGUE%20REPORT%20FINAL%20DESIGNED.pdf#overlay-context=en.
20. Ontario Human Rights Commission, 25.
21. Universities Canada, "Principles on Indigenous Education," June 29, 2015, https://www.univcan.ca/wp-content/uploads/2015/11/principles-on-indigenous-education-universities-canada-june-2015.pdf.
22. Manitoba Collaborative Indigenous Education Blueprint, "Resources," December 18, 2015, https://www.mcieb.ca/resources.html.
23. Manitoba Collaborative Indigenous Education.
24. Winnipeg School Division, "Build From Within—Ozhitoon Onji Peenjiiee," Winnipeg School Division, 2021, https://www.winnipegsd.ca/page/12602/build-from-within-ozhitoon-onji-peenjiiee-b.
25. University of Winnipeg, "Wii Chiiwaakanak Learning Centre," last updated September 22, 2021, https://www.uwinnipeg.ca/wiichii/.
26. University of Winnipeg, "Model School," 2021, https://www.uwinnipeg.ca/indigenous/for-community/community-learning/model-school.html.
27. Lloyd Axworthy, Linda DeRiviere, and Jennifer Rattray, "Chapter 4: Beyond Access to Inclusion: The Axworthy Years 2004–14." in *From Access to Engagement: Initiatives at the University of Winnipeg in Support of Educationally Marginalized Children and Youth*, 2018, 4–12, https://www.uwinnipeg.ca/community-engagement/Research/community-learning-initiatives.html.
28. University of Winnipeg, "Pathway to Graduate Studies (P2GS)," 2021, https://www.uwinnipeg.ca/graduate-studies/p2gs/index.html.
29. Tara Williamson, "Be a Part of History: Preliminary evaluation and assessment of the Indigenous Course Requirement (ICR), University of Winnipeg, January 7, 2018, 12.
30. Helen Lepp Friesen, "Chapter 8: 'We Are All Relations': An Indigenous Course Requirement (ICR) as Part of a Good Way to Reconciliation." in *From Access to Engagement: Initiatives at the University of Winnipeg*

in Support of Educationally Marginalized Children and Youth, 1988–2017, 2018, 8–25, https://www.uwinnipeg.ca/community-engagement/Research/indigenous-course-requirement.html.

31. Sean Amato, "Edmonton's New Indigenous Ward Names, Explained," *CTV News Edmonton*, September 24, 2021, https://edmonton.ctvnews.ca/edmonton-s-new-indigenous-ward-names-explained-1.5599364.
32. Caley Ramsey, "Indigenous Peoples Experience among New Offerings at Fort Edmonton Park Reopens after $165M Renovation," *Global News*, June 28, 2021, https://globalnews.ca/news/7986365/fort-edmonton-park-reopens-canada-day/.
33. MacEwan University, "Foundation Program Pimâcihisowin," MacEwan University, accessed November 1, 2021, https://www.macewan.ca/academics/programs/foundation-program-pimacihisowin/.
34. MacEwan University, "Kihêw Waciston Indigenous Centre," MacEwan University, accessed November 3, 2021, https://www.macewan.ca/campus-life/kihew-waciston-indigenous-centre/.
35. Deborah Saucier, "Reconciliation on University Campuses: 'Two Realities, Side by Side'," *Maclean's*, October 11, 2018, https://www.macleans.ca/education/reconciliation-on-university-campuses-two-realities-side-by-side/.
36. Douglas Quan, "Inside the 'Indigenization' of Canada's universities: Progress—but also Accusations of Tokenism, Broken Promises and 'Ethnic Fraud'," *Toronto Star*, February 27, 2021, https://www.thestar.com/news/canada/2021/02/27/inside-the-indigenization-of-canadas-universities-progress-but-also-accusations-of-tokenism-broken-promises-and-ethnic-fraud.html.
37. Indspire, "Truth and Reconciliation in Post-Secondary Settings: Student Experience," *Indspire*, November 15, 2018, 8, https://indspire.ca/wp-content/uploads/2019/10/JMGD_003_IND_TR_REPORT_FINAL_V3_NOV15_V3.pdf.
38. Indspire, 11–31.
39. Eric Howe, "Bridging the Aboriginal Gap in Alberta: The Provincial Benefit Exceeds a Quarter of a Trillion Dollars," University of Alberta, Faculty of Native Studies, March 4, 2021, https://www.ualberta.ca/native-studies/media-library/documents-and-pdfs/final-reportbridgingtheaboriginaleducationgapinalberta.pdf.
40. Canada, Parliament, House of Commons, Standing Committee on Indigenous and Northern Affairs, *Support for Indigenous Communities, Businesses, and Individuals Through a Second Wave of COVID-19*, 2nd sess., 43rd Parliament, 2020. Committee Meeting on November 3, 2020, https://www.ourcommons.ca/DocumentViewer/en/43-2/INAN/meeting-4/minutes.

41. Canada, Parliament, House of Commons, Standing Committee on Indigenous and Northern Affairs, *Support for Indigenous Communities, Businesses, and Individuals Through a Second Wave of COVID-19*, 2nd sess., 43rd Parliament, 2020. Committee Meeting on October 27, 2020, https://www.ourcommons.ca/DocumentViewer/en/43-2/INAN/meeting-4/minutes.
42. Liza Agrba, "How Indigenous institutes are reclaiming education," *Maclean's*, September 7, 2021, https://www.macleans.ca/education/how-indigenous-institutes-are-reclaiming-education/.

Bibliography

Agrba, Liza. "How Indigenous Institutes are Reclaiming Education." *Maclean's*. September 7, 2021. https://www.macleans.ca/education/how-indigenous-institutes-are-reclaiming-education/.

Amato, Sean. "Edmonton's New Indigenous Ward Names, Explained." *CTV News Edmonton*. September 24, 2021. https://edmonton.ctvnews.ca/edmonton-s-new-indigenous-ward-names-explained-1.5599364.

Axworthy, Lloyd, Linda DeRiviere, and Jennifer Rattray, "Chapter 4: Beyond Access to Inclusion: The Axworthy Years 2004–14." In *From Access to Engagement: Initiatives at the University of Winnipeg in Support of Educationally Marginalized Children and Youth*, 2018, 4–12. https://www.uwinnipeg.ca/community-engagement/Research/community-learning-initiatives.html.

Canada. Parliament. House of Commons. Standing Committee on Indigenous and Northern Affairs. *Support for Indigenous Communities, Businesses, and Individuals Through a Second Wave of COVID-19*. 2nd sess., 43rd Parliament, 2020a. Committee Meeting on October 27, 2020. https://www.ourcommons.ca/DocumentViewer/en/43-2/INAN/meeting-4/minutes.

Canada. Parliament. House of Commons. Standing Committee on Indigenous and Northern Affairs. *Support for Indigenous Communities, Businesses, and Individuals Through a Second Wave of COVID-19*. 2nd sess., 43rd Parliament, 2020b. Committee Meeting on November 3, 2020. https://www.ourcommons.ca/DocumentViewer/en/43-2/INAN/meeting-4/minutes.

Friesen, Helen Lepp. "Chapter 8: "We Are All Relations": An Indigenous Course Requirement (ICR) as Part of a Good Way to Reconciliation." in *From Access to Engagement: Initiatives at the University of Winnipeg in Support of Educationally Marginalized Children and Youth, 1988–2017*, 2018, 8–25. https://www.uwinnipeg.ca/community-engagement/Research/indigenous-course-requirement.html.

Gaudry, Adam, and Lorenz, Danielle. "Indigenization as Inclusion, Reconciliation, and Decolonization: Navigating the Different Visions for Indigenizing the Canadian Academy." *AlterNative: An International Journal of Indigenous Peoples* 14, no. 3 (2018): 218–227. https://doi.org/10.1177/1177180118785382.

Howe, Eric. "*Bridging the Aboriginal Gap in Alberta: The Provincial Benefit Exceeds a Quarter of a Trillion Dollars.*" University of Alberta, Faculty of Native Studies. March 4, 2021. https://www.ualberta.ca/native-studies/media-library/documents-and-pdfs/final-reportbridgingtheaboriginaleducationgapinalberta.pdf.

Indspire. "Truth and Reconciliation in Post-Secondary Settings: Student Experience." *Indspire*. November 15, 2018. https://indspire.ca/wp-content/uploads/2019/10/JMGD_003_IND_TR_REPORT_FINAL_V3_NOV15_V3.pdf.

IPCC, 2021. Climate Change 2021: The Physical Science Basis. Contribution of Working Group I to the Sixth Assessment Report of the Intergovernmental Panel on Climate Change, edited by Masson-Delmotte, V., P. Zhai, A. Pirani, S.L. Connors, C. Péan, S. Berger, N. Caud, Y. Chen, L. Goldfarb, M.I. Gomis, M. Huang, K. Leitzell, E. Lonnoy, J.B.R. Matthews, T.K. Maycock, T. Waterfield, O. Yelekçi, R. Yu, and B. Zhou. Cambridge, UK: Cambridge University Press, 2021. https://doi.org/10.1017/9781009157896.

MacEwan University. "*Foundation Program Pimâcihisowin.*" MacEwan University. Accessed November 1, 2021a. https://www.macewan.ca/academics/programs/foundation-program-pimacihisowin/.

MacEwan University. "*Kihêw Waciston Indigenous Centre.*" MacEwan University. Accessed November 3, 2021b. https://www.macewan.ca/campus-life/kihew-waciston-indigenous-centre/.

Manitoba Collaborative Indigenous Education Blueprint. "*Resources.*" December 18, 2015. https://www.mcieb.ca/resources.html.

McCrudden, Christopher. "Human Dignity and Judicial Interpretation of Human Rights." *European Journal of International Law* 19, no. 4 (2008): 655–724. https://doi.org/10.1093/ejil/chn043.

Ontario Human Rights Commission. *To Dream Together: Indigenous Peoples and Human Rights Dialogue Report*. Toronto, ON: Government of Ontario, September 2018. http://www.ohrc.on.ca/sites/default/files/INDIGENOUS%20POLICY%20DIALOGUE%20REPORT%20FINAL%20DESIGNED.pdf#overlay-context=en.

Quan, Douglas. "Inside the 'Indigenization' of Canada's universities: Progress—but also accusations of tokenism, broken promises and 'ethnic fraud'." *Toronto Star*. February 27, 2021. https://www.thestar.com/news/canada/2021/02/27/inside-the-indigenization-of-canadas-universities-progress-but-also-accusations-of-tokenism-broken-promises-and-ethnic-fraud.html.

Ramsey, Caley. "Indigenous Peoples Experience among New Offerings at Fort Edmonton Park Reopens after $165M Renovation." *Global News*.

June 28, 2021. https://globalnews.ca/news/7986365/fort-edmonton-park-reopens-canada-day/.

Saucier, Deborah. "Reconciliation on University Campuses: 'Two Realities, Side by Side'." *Maclean's*. October 11, 2018. https://www.macleans.ca/education/reconciliation-on-university-campuses-two-realities-side-by-side/.

Statistics Canada. "Census Profile, 2016 Census," *Statistics Canada*. Last updated June 18, 2019. https://www12.statcan.gc.ca/census-recensement/2016/dp-pd/prof/index.cfm?Lang=E.

Truth and Reconciliation Commission of Canada Calls to Action, 2015. Accessed at https://publications.gc.ca/collections/collection_2015/trc/IR4-8-2015-eng.pdf.

United Nations General Assembly. "*United Nations Declaration on the Rights of Indigenous Peoples*," Resolution/Adopted by the General Assembly, 2 October 2007, A/RES/61/295. https://www.un.org/development/desa/indigenouspeoples/wp-content/uploads/sites/19/2018/11/UNDRIP_E_web.pdf.

Universities Canada. "*Principles on Indigenous Education*," June 29, 2015. https://www.univcan.ca/wp-content/uploads/2015/11/principles-on-indigenous-education-universities-canada-june-2015.pdf.

University of Winnipeg. "*Pathway to Graduate Studies (P2GS)*." 2021. https://www.uwinnipeg.ca/graduate-studies/p2gs/index.html.

Williamson, Tara. "*Be a Part of History: Preliminary Evaluation and Assessment of the Indigenous Course Requirement (ICR)*." University of Winnipeg, January 7, 2018.

Winnipeg School Division. "*Build From Within—Ozhitoon Onji Peenjiiee*." Winnipeg School Division, 2021. https://www.winnipegsd.ca/page/12602/build-from-within-ozhitoon-onji-peenjiiee-b.

Gender

Transgender Healthcare in Canada

Sydney Laurin

Canadian society has always been ahead of the curve in terms of its acceptance of the lesbian, gay, bisexual, transgender, and queer community (LGBTQ+), leading many other nations in implementing same-sex marriage, same-sex adoption, anti-discrimination, and most recently, anti-conversion therapy legislation.[1] However, despite Canada's forward-thinking attitudes, individuals marginalized based on their gender identity and sexual orientation continue to be "excluded from mainstream health promotion research, policy and practice."[2] Although the LGBTQ+ acronym encompasses a wide range of diverse sexualities and genders, and there is acknowledgment from Canadian society and the medical community that individuals under the LGTBQ+ umbrella are unique and separate from one another, they are frequently grouped together as one homogenous entity for research and advocacy purposes.[3] Consequently, clinicians often lack pertinent skills, education, and insight into the specific health needs of the trans community and, by default, rely upon

S. Laurin (✉)
University of Manitoba, Winnipeg, MB, Canada
e-mail: sydlaurin@gmail.com

L. E. Reimer and K. Standish (eds.), *Perspectives on Justice, Indigeneity, Gender, and Security in Human Rights Research*,
https://doi.org/10.1007/978-981-99-1930-7_8

cisgender assumptions about medical treatment and care when treating transgender patients.[4]

This is no more evident than the healthcare systems response to transgender survivors of sexual assault, as our current health infrastructure remains both inaccessible and ill-equipped to care for and provide services for the trans community following instances of sexual violence. As a member of the LGBTQ+ community myself, researcher, and advocate for human rights, I wanted to explore this intersection further to better understand what is occurring, contextualize trans folks lived experiences, and highlight where improvements can be made.

For the purpose of this chapter, it should be noted that "cisgender" refers to those whose gender identity aligns with their sex at birth, while "transgender" refers to those whose gender identity, gender expression, or behavior does not match with their sex assigned at birth.[5] The term transgender therefore, is utilized as an umbrella term representing multiple different gender identities and should not be confused with the "LGB" in the LGBTQ+ acronym which refer to sexual orientations.

Literature Review

Individuals who identify as transgender experience sexual violence at much higher rates than their cisgender peers.[6] Even among the LGBTQ+ community, trans persons are twice as likely to be sexually assaulted.[7] Although statistics on trans persons in Canada remain extremely limited, a recent cross-country survey indicated that 26% of trans people reported becoming a survivor of sexual assault in the last five years.[8] Current data from the United States, places sexual victimization of trans individuals between 47 and 66%, suggesting that if more research were available, Canada's reported statistics could be much higher than indicated.[9]

In addition to high rates of sexual victimization, trans people often experience direct harassment and discrimination in "institutional and broader social contexts."[10] This is particularly relevant in regard to the healthcare system. Of the survivors who choose to access medical services, many report experiencing "fear, victim-blaming, unequal treatment, feeling unwelcome, verbal harassment, and culturally incompetent service providers."[11] In many instances, trans individuals are denied primary medical treatment outright.[12] Due to this and many other circumstances, trans folks tend to avoid the healthcare system altogether. For example, in a recent US study of transgender survivors it was found that only 9% "had received professional medical care for their physical injuries and only 14% professional emotional support within the first week of being assaulted."[13]

Currently, there has been very little effort from provinces and territories to produce qualitative or quantitative studies regarding the marginalization of transgender individuals and their experiences in Canada.[14] In fact, "analyses that have attempted to explain how such marginalization gets produced have been notably absent."[15] When data on the subject is available, sources are commonly US-based or have a tendency to be mutually exclusive, focusing on either trans individual's experience with sexual assault or health care, but rarely both. Without data on this population, it is almost impossible for "governments, service providers, and other institutions to develop programs and policies that address the concerns and needs of this community,"[16] indicating the importance of further research on the matter.

Although there are many factors to take into consideration when working with marginalized and traumatized individuals, prior research suggests "that most survivors report positive benefits of sharing their experiences in research" and that "participation does not cause additional distress"[17] in most cases. Given this knowledge, the problematic responses to trans survivors of sexual assault, high rates of sexual victimization, and obvious gap in research it is critical that the intersection between transgender individuals, sexual violence, and the healthcare system be explored much more in-depth.

The only current Canadian study with actual participation from transgender subjects who are survivors of sexual violence, was the Trans PULSE project conducted in Ontario in 2009. Despite solid research, there is only one mention of sexual violence, as the study focused almost solely on how trans person's social exclusion impacts health.[18] Another reliable Canadian study on the matter exists, however, their methods only include participation from healthcare professionals and community organizations, not trans persons themselves.[19] With that being said, there are two general overarching themes that became evident upon conducting a literature review on the subject in its entirety: first, trans persons experience disproportionate levels of sexual victimization and the impacts are severe. And second, discrimination against members of the LGBTQ+ community in health care is prevalent, severely impacting access to treatment.

The first major theme, is high rates of sexual violence among transgender individuals. As previously mentioned, several authors indicate that transgender individuals experience sexual violence, both directly and indirectly, at exponentially higher rates than their peers (between 47 and 66%).[20] When examining these figures, it is important to recognize the nature of this victimization. According to multiple studies, trans survivors frequently experience polyvictimization, with up to 23–35% of individuals reporting five or more incidences of sexual violence.[21] This suggests that trans individuals should be accessing the healthcare system far more than previously indicated. Interestingly, most victimization occurs in youth, with 78% of respondents indicating that they were assaulted by the age of 12 and another third indicating violations from age 13–40.[22] Perpetrators of this violence come from a myriad of different backgrounds, suggesting that transphobia and inequity of power exists within several hierarchal structures of society. This is especially relevant to perpetrators in institutional settings such as police (5%) and healthcare providers (6%), who participate in sexual violence at higher rates when a trans person is involved.[23]

Due to intersectional factors (ex. race, class, sexual orientation), the impact of sexual violence on transgender individuals compared to cisgender individuals is often more severe. Survivors can face significant acute and chronic physical and mental health problems including genital injuries, chronic stress, irritable bowel syndrome; mental health conditions, such as post-traumatic stress disorder, depression, anxiety, and suicidality; and social isolation.[24]

The second major theme revealed in the literature review, is rampant discrimination in health care. According to US studies, around one-third of trans individuals reported facing at least one negative experience in health care including refusal of treatment, verbal harassment, physical/ sexual assault, victim-blaming, unequal treatment, or having to educate staff in order to receive proper care.[25] This secondary victimization by healthcare professionals following experiences of violence is concerning in that it puts trans survivors at further risk of additional harm. According to a 2020 study, "29% of trans individuals had attempted suicide and 56% had seriously contemplated suicide after being sexually or physically assaulted."[26] Given this information, it is vital that healthcare providers respond appropriately and do not exacerbate survivors existing circumstances.

Overall, providers and institutions have indicated that these circumstances are created by lack of knowledge and training, inadequate resources across organizations, limited access and availability of trans-friendly services, lack of trans-positive professionals, and institutional structures (ex. oppressive policies, funding mandates, etc.), however little research or evidence exists acknowledging transphobia in health care or the power dynamics that exist between trans survivors and healthcare institutions.[27]

Do No Harm: Conducting Research with Transgender Sexual Assault Survivors

When conducting research with transgender sexual assault survivors it is suggested that the researcher take a victim-centered and trauma-informed approach. This involves placing participants at the forefront of all efforts and responses and following the principle of "do no harm"[28] including having a certified sexual assault therapist on site to recognize signs of trauma (ex. Dissociation) and deal with any other negative reactions (ex. suicidal ideation), use of transparent language in recruitment methods, providing appropriate mental health referrals, conducting a follow-up check-in, and giving participants power over how their data will be shared and de-identified.[29] This is done with the intention of empowering survivors by "enhancing their strengths and resilience, rather than pathologizing their experiences."[30]

In addition to these conceptual frameworks, queer theory and an intersectional lens should be deployed when studying this issue. Intersectionality can be described as a theoretical framework for understanding how "multiple social identities such as race, gender, sexual orientation…and disability intersect at the micro level of individual experience to reflect interlocking systems of privilege and oppression (i.e., racism, sexism, heterosexism, classism) at the macro social-structural level."[31] In the author's initial literature review, many researchers observed how sexual violence and access to health care effects members of distinct social categories differently. For example, trans individuals who are Black, Latino, and/or Asian may experience higher rates of sexual violence and have more trouble accessing medical treatment than their fellow white transgender peers.[32] This is because these individuals have multiple forms of oppression working against them (ex. racism, classism) in addition to transphobia. These insights should be considered at all stages of the research process to ensure that the voices of these participants are accessed, heard, and documented in a way that helps address their superfluous marginalization. This can be done by ensuring that the participant population reflects individuals from multiple different backgrounds, genders, classes, etc. Additionally, resource referral should consist of culturally competent providers that are low cost or sliding scale and that provide services in languages other than English.[33]

Consistent with intersectionality, it is suggested that queer theory also be used as a framework to understand how heteronormativity promotes heterosexuality as the "normal" and/or preferred sexual orientation, and how this is reinforced through institutional structures.[34] This can be helpful to understand trans individuals' interactions with healthcare professionals and how they view their personal experiences. Additionally, this theory draws from the precepts of other well-known theories such as feminism, post-structuralism, and radical movements and explores the intersection between sexuality, power, and marginalized populations,[35] all of which are relevant to research regarding sexual violence, trans folks, and their interaction with institutional structures.

Discussion

Although the Canadian healthcare system is highly regarded as universal, affordable, and easily accessible for all, it is clear from the literature review, that for some, this is not always the case. Unfortunately, healthcare discrimination toward transgender patients occurs not only in instances of sexual violence, but in most circumstances in which they attempt to access health care.[36] Informational and institutional erasure of trans culture has ultimately resulted in a lack of informed providers and knowledge on many subjects effecting the trans community, including transition care for safe hormonal therapy, gender-affirming surgeries, and appropriate mental health resourcing.[37]

While Canadian physicians are obligated by both the law and the Canadian Medical Association to abide by principles of non-discrimination, there are flaws within the system that permit clinicians to refer trans patients to specialists in trans care if they feel providing care is outside the scope of their practice.[38] In turn, this has produced long waitlists for pertinent, and often life-saving, procedures and services including mental health evaluations that are required by many provinces before trans folks can access funding and/or treatment for gender dysphoria.[39]

For example, in the province of Quebec, if a trans individual decides they would like to pursue hormone replacement therapy, they can wait anywhere from up to one to three years on a 20,000-person wait list before securing approval for treatment.[40] When put in perspective, these wait times are often double or triple the amount of time other patients wait to see a specialist and receive treatment (6 months on average).[41]

Whether these types of practices are done from a place of ill intent or not, they are harmful nonetheless. Discrimination can take many different forms, and more often than not, presents in indirect and subtle ways that appear to be neutral on the surface.[42] In fact, this is usually the case when we explore how discrimination manifests within large, institutionalized structures throughout society (ex. the legal system). But that does not mean it is not present. The goal of the above literature review is not to criticize or shame certain individuals, but rather provoke thought around the notion that we all have a role to play in the resolution of systemic discrimination against trans folks within the Canadian healthcare system. In other words, proper post-sexual assault care for trans individuals is merely one of many areas that requires our attention as researchers, as a medical community, and as a society.

As a medical community and as healthcare providers, more thought must be given to policy that is implemented (or lack thereof), and how current mandates are attributing to poorer health outcomes for trans patients. This means taking initiative to evaluate current methods of trans care, increasing trans-specific services, incentivizing trans-friendly professionals, and appropriately preparing physicians to expect, and provide care for, trans patients.[43] Despite best evidence that introducing modules on transgender health early in clinical education is valuable, and that 95% of Canadian medical students agree that training on the subject is important, there continues to be an absence of educational programming throughout Canada.[44] Currently, fewer than 10% of Canadian medical students feel sufficiently knowledgeable enough to provide transgender patients with health care specific to their needs, spending an average of 5 hours over their 4-year study period on LGBT-related content.[45] Given the notion that a majority of trans healthcare needs can indeed be delivered by primary care physicians,[46] and that there is already a willingness by medical students to learn, the system must change.

Besides our legal obligations to international human rights standards and domestic legislation, we also have a moral obligation to approach this issue from a place of compassion. In some jurisdictions throughout Canada, this is already being exemplified as Ontario and Yukon have been labeled as "gold standards" of transgender healthcare legislation, not only in Canada, but worldwide.[47] These jurisdictions have acted as beacons of hope introducing and implementing progressive policies that have led to both comprehensive care, and coverage for transgender patients, allowing them to be treated with equality, dignity, and respect. Toronto's Mount Sinai Hospital, for example, has a specific anti-discrimination policy that outlines guidelines for care of all trans patients including respecting their right to be identified and addressed by their lived gender, providing bed accommodation options to ensure confidentiality and privacy, universal single-user gender-neutral washrooms, and admittance services that provide options for preferred identification.[48] Will these types of policies be enough to eradicate trans discrimination altogether? Perhaps. Perhaps not, but they are a promising step forward. Looking to these jurisdictions as a model for appropriate care will be vital, however, there still needs to be research, transparent dialogue, and evaluations between healthcare providers, clinicians, civil society, and most importantly trans folks themselves, if Canada is truly to be regarded as a country that values health care for "all."

Discussion Questions

1. What are other jurisdictions doing internationally in terms of healthcare needs for transgender individuals?
2. What role does federal and provincial government play in addressing barriers to care for transgender individuals in Canada?
3. What are the best practices in terms of health care for transgender individuals?
4. What current policy or mandates are attributing to the oppression of transgender individuals?
5. What would a comprehensive clinical education model for transgender health entail?

Notes

1. Travis William Davidson, "A Review of Transgender Health in Canada," *University of Ottawa Journal of Medicine* 5, no. 2 (2015): 40; "Conversion Therapy Laws in Canada," No Conversion Canada, accessed November 24, 2021. https://www.noconversioncanada.com/legislation-map.
2. Dick Moore, Andrea Daley, Barry Deeprose, Loris Ross, Beth Jackson, Mulé Nick, and Anna Travers, "Promoting LGBT Health and Wellbeing Through Inclusive Policy Development," *International Journal for Equity in Health* 8, no. 1 (2009): 1.
3. Davidson, "A Review of Transgender Health," 40.
4. Institute of Medicine, Board on the Health of Select Populations, and Committee on Lesbian, Gay, Bisexual, and Transgender Health Issues and Research Gaps and Opportunities, *The Health of Lesbian, Gay, Bisexual and Transgender People: Building a Foundation for a Better Understanding* (Washington, DC: National Academies Press, 2011); Davidson, "A Review of Transgender Health in Canada," 40.
5. American Psychological Association, "Transgender People, Gender Identity and Gender Expression," (2018). Accessed April 2, 2021, https://doi.org/10.1080/15532739.2011.70087; Davidson, "A Review of Transgender Health in Canada," 41.
6. Janice Du Mont et al., "The Promise of an Intersectoral Network in Enhancing the Response to Transgender Survivors of Sexual Assault," *PLoS One* 15, no. 11 (2020): 2; Diane Santa Maria et al., "Gaps in Sexual Assault Health Care Among Homeless Young Adults," *American Journal of Preventive Medicine* 58, no. 2 (2020): 192.
7. Santa Maria, "Gaps in Sexual Assault Health Care," 192.
8. Du Mont et al., "The Promise of an Intersectoral," 2; The Trans PULSE Canada Team, "Health and Health Care Access for Trans and Non-Binary People in Canada," (2020), 8.
9. Du Mont et al., "The Promise of an Intersectoral," 2; S. E. James et al., "The Report of the 2015 US Transgender Survey" (Washington, DC: The National Center for Transgender Equality, 2016); Michael Munson and Loree Cook-Daniels, "A Guide for Facilitators of Transgender Community Groups Supporting Sexual Violence Survivors," (2016): 33.
10. Greta R. Bauer et al., "'I Don't Think This is Theoretical; This is Our Lives': How Erasure Impacts Health Care for Transgender People," *Journal of the Association of Nurses in AIDS Care* 20, no. 5 (2009): 350.
11. Du Mont et al., "The Promise of an Intersectoral," 2; Lynn C. Carson, "Transgender Women's Perceptions and Experience of Sexual Violence and Views of Rape Crisis Center Resources," (PhD diss., Indiana University of Pennsylvania, 2017), 1–14.

12. Shanna K. Kattari et al., "Intersecting Experiences of Healthcare Denials among Transgender and Nonbinary Patients," *American Journal of Preventive Medicine* 58, no. 4 (2020): 506.
13. Du Mont et al., "The Promise of an Intersectoral," 2; Munson and Cook-Daniels, "A Guide for Facilitators," 30.
14. Alex Bucik, "Canada: Discrimination and Violence against Lesbian, Bisexual, and Transgender Women and Gender Diverse and Two Spirit People on the Basis of Sexual Orientation, Gender Identity and Gender Expression" (Egale Canada Human Rights Trust, 2016), 5.
15. Bauer et al., "I Don't Think This," 350.
16. Statistics Canada, "Current Data Gaps: Technical Report on Changes for the 2021 Census" (Statistics Canada, 2020), Accessed April 5, 2021 from https://www12.statcan.gc.ca/census-recensement/2021/ref/98-20-0002/982000022020002-eng.cfm.
17. April M. Zeoli, TK Logan, Rebecca Campbell, Rachael Goodman-Williams, and McKenzie Javorka. "A Trauma-Informed Approach to Sexual Violence Research Ethics and Open Science," *Journal of Interpersonal Violence* 34, no. 23–24 (2019): 4772; Rebecca Campbell, Adrienne E. Adams, and Debra Patterson. "Methodological Challenges of Collecting Evaluation Data from Traumatized Clients/Consumers: A Comparison of Three Methods," *American Journal of Evaluation* 29, no. 3 (2008): 374.
18. Bauer et al., 350.
19. Du Mont et al., "The Promise of an Intersectoral," 1.
20. Du Mont et al., 2; Bauer et al., "I Don't Think This," 349; Munson and Cook-Daniels, "A Guide for Facilitators," 30; Chelsea Cogan et al., "Sexual Violence and Suicide Risk in the Transgender Population: The Mediating Role of Proximal Stressors," *Psychology & Sexuality* 12, no. 1–2 (2021): 129.
21. Cogan et al., 130; Du Mont et al., "The Promise of an Intersectoral," 2; Munson and Cook-Daniels, "A Guide for Facilitators," 32; Greta Bauer et al., "Suicidality among Trans People in Ontario: Implications for Social Work and Social Justice." *Service Social* 59, no. 1 (2013): 36.
22. Munson and Cook-Daniels, "A Guide for Facilitators," 30.
23. Munson and Cook-Daniels, 31.
24. Matt Kammer-Kerwick et al., "Sexual Violence among Gender and Sexual Minority College Students: The Risk and Extent of Victimization and Related Health and Educational Outcomes," *Journal of Interpersonal Violence* (2019); Munson and Cook-Daniels, "A Guide for Facilitators," 14; Du Mont et al., "The Promise of an Intersectoral," 2.
25. Justin Omar Barredo. "Room Assignments, Gender Identity, and Gender Expression: A Case Study on Caring for Transgender Patients." *Medsurg Nursing* 29, no. 4 (2020): 237; James et al., "The Report of the 2015

US Transgender," 2016; Du Mont et al., "The Promise of an Intersectoral," 2; Munson and Cook-Daniels, "A Guide for Facilitators," 62; Nicky Tettamanti, "Pulling Teeth to Get Help- Barriers Facing Transgender Survivors of Sexual Assault When Accessing Support Services and Potential Solutions," (2018): 10.

26. Du Mont et al., "The Promise of an Intersectoral," 2; Bauer et al., "Suicidality among Trans People," 36.
27. Judith Bradford et al., "Experiences of Transgender-Related Discrimination and Implications for Health: Results from the Virginia Transgender Health Initiative Study," *American Journal of Public Health* 103, no. 10 (2013): 1828; Du Mont et al., "The Promise of an Intersectoral," 1–15; Barredo, "Room Assignments," 239.
28. United Nations, *Handbook for United Nations Field Missions on Preventing and Responding to Conflict-Related Sexual Violence* (2020): 35.
29. Campbell, Goodman-Williams, and Javorka, "A Trauma-Informed Approach," 4770–76.
30. Campbell, Goodman-Williams, and Javorka, 4770–75.
31. Lisa Bowleg, "The Problem with the Phrase Women and Minorities: Intersectionality—An Important Theoretical Framework for Public Health," *American Journal of Public Health* 102, no. 7 (2012): 1267.
32. Mirella J. Flores et al., "Transgender People of Color's Experiences of Sexual Objectification: Locating Sexual Objectification Within a Matrix of Domination," *Journal of Counseling Psychology* 65, no. 3 (2018): 308; Santa Maria, "Gaps in Sexual Assault Health Care," 192; Munson and Cook-Daniels, "A Guide for Facilitators," 33.
33. Campbell, Goodman-Williams, and Javorka, "A Trauma-Informed Approach," 4777.
34. University of Illinois, "Queer Theory: Background," Last modified March 10, 2020. Available from https://guides.library.illinois.edu/queertheory/background.
35. University of Illinois, 2020.
36. Joshua D. Safer et al., "Barriers to Healthcare for Transgender Individuals," *Current Opinion in Endocrinology, Diabetes & Obesity* 23, no. 2 (2016): 168.
37. Safer et al., 169.
38. The Canadian Medical Protective Association, "Treating Transgender Individuals," October, 2019. https://www.cmpa-acpm.ca/en/advice-publications/browse-articles/2015/treating-transgendered-individuals#ref.
39. Deborah McPhail, Marina Rountree-James, and Ian Whetter, "Addressing Gaps in Physician Knowledge Regarding Transgender Health and Healthcare through Medical Education," *Canadian Medical Education Journal* 7, no. 2 (2016): 75.

40. Editorial Board, "Gender-Affirming Healthcare Must be Made Accessible," *McGill Daily*, October 25, 2021. https://www.mcgilldaily.com/2021/10/gender-affirming-healthcare-must-be-made-accessible/#close-modal.
41. "Waiting Your Turn: Wait Times for Healthcare in Canada, 2020 Report," *The Fraser Institute*, December 10, 2020. https://www.fraserinstitute.org/studies/waiting-your-turn-wait-times-for-health-care-in-canada-2020.
42. Ontario Human Rights Commission, *Policy on Preventing Discrimination Because of Gender Identity and Gender Expression* (Toronto, ON: January 31, 2014), 22. https://www3.ohrc.on.ca/sites/default/files/Policy%20on%20preventing%20discrimination%20because%20of%20gender%20identity%20and%20gender%20expression.pdf.
43. Miranda Schreiber et al., "The Case for a Canadian Standard for 2SLGBTQIA+ Medical Education." *CMAJ* 193, no. 16 (2021): 562; Mulé et al., "Promoting LGBT Health."
44. Benjamin Chan, Rachel Skocylas, and Joshua D. Safer, "Gaps in Transgender Medicine Content Identified Among Canadian Medical School Curricula," *Transgender Health* 1, no. 1 (2016): 147; Kevan Wylie et al. "Serving Transgender People: Clinical Care Considerations and Service Delivery Models in Transgender Health," *The Lancet* 388, no. 10042 (2016): 406.
45. Schreiber et al., "The Case for a Canadian Standard," 563; Juno Obedin-Maliver et al., "Lesbian, Gay, Bisexual, and Transgender–Related Content in Undergraduate Medical Education," *Jama* 306, no. 9 (2011): 976; Chan, Skocylas, and Safer, "Gaps in Transgender Medicine," 149.
46. Kevan Wylie et al., "Serving Transgender People," 401.
47. Brooke Taylor, "Trans Health Care in Canada Needs Major Improvements, Advocates Say," *CTV News*, May 22, 2021. https://www.ctvnews.ca/health/trans-health-care-in-canada-needs-major-improvements-advocates-say-1.5439295; Ontario Human Rights Commission, *Policy on Preventing Discrimination.*
48. Ontario Human Rights Commission, 43–44.

Bibliography

American Psychological Association. "Transgender People, Gender Identity and Gender Expression." 2018. Accessed April 2, 2021, https://doi.org/10.1080/15532739.2011.70087.

Barredo, Justin Omar. "Room Assignments, Gender Identity, and Gender Expression: A Case Study on Caring for Transgender Patients." *Medsurg Nursing* 29, no. 4 (2020): 239–40.

Bauer, Greta R, Jake Pyne, Matt Caron Francino, and Rebecca Hammond. "Suicidality among Trans People in Ontario: Implications for Social Work and Social Justice." *Service Social* 59, no. 1 (2013): 35–62. https://doi.org/10.7202/1017478ar.

Bauer, Greta R., Rebecca Hammond, Robb Travers, Matthias Kaay, Karin M Hohenadel, and Michelle Boyce. "'I Don't Think This Is Theoretical; This Is Our Lives': How Erasure Impacts Health Care for Transgender People." *Journal of the Association of Nurses in AIDS Care* 20, no. 5 (2009): 348–61. https://doi.org/10.1016/j.jana.2009.07.004.

Bowleg, Lisa. "The Problem with the Phrase Women and Minorities: Intersectionality—An Important Theoretical Framework for Public Health." *American Journal of Public Health* 102, no. 7 (2012): 1267–73. https://doi.org/10.2105/AJPH.2012.300750.

Bradford, Judith, Sari L. Reisner, Julie A. Honnold, and Jessica Xavier. "Experiences of Transgender-Related Discrimination and Implications for Health: Results from the Virginia Transgender Health Initiative Study." *American Journal of Public Health* 103, no. 10 (2013): 1820–29. https://doi.org/10.2105/AJPH.2012.300796.

Bucik, Alex. "Canada: Discrimination and Violence against Lesbian, Bisexual, and Transgender Women and Gender Diverse and Two Spirit People on the Basis of Sexual Orientation, Gender Identity and Gender Expression." Egale Canada Human Rights Trust, 2016. https://egale.ca/wp-content/uploads/2016/10/UN-CEDAW-Treaty-Body-Paper-2016-09-30.pdf.

Campbell, Rebecca, Adrienne E. Adams, and Debra Patterson. "Methodological Challenges of Collecting Evaluation Data from Traumatized Clients/Consumers: A Comparison of Three Methods." *American Journal of Evaluation* 29, no. 3 (2008): 369–81. https://doi.org/10.1177/1098214008320736.

The Canadian Medical Protective Association. "Treating Transgender Individuals." October, 2019. https://www.cmpa-acpm.ca/en/advice-publications/browse-articles/2015/treating-transgendered-individuals#ref.

Carson, Lynn C. "Transgender Women's Perceptions and Experience of Sexual Violence and Views of Rape Crisis Center Resources." PhD diss., Indiana University of Pennsylvania, 2017. https://www.proquest.com/docview/1889850454.

Chan, Benjamin, Rachel Skocylas, and Joshua D Safer. "Gaps in Transgender Medicine Content Identified among Canadian Medical School Curricula." *Transgender Health* 1, no. 1 (2016): 142–50. https://doi.org/10.1089/trgh.2016.0010.

Cogan, Chelsea M., James A. Scholl, Jenny Y. Lee, Hannah E. Cole, and Joanne L. Davis. "Sexual Violence and Suicide Risk in the Transgender Population:

The Mediating Role of Proximal Stressors." *Psychology & Sexuality* 12, nos. 1–2 (2021): 129–40. https://doi.org/10.1080/19419899.2020.1729847.

"Conversion Therapy Laws in Canada." No Conversion Canada, accessed November 24, 2021. https://www.noconversioncanada.com/legislation-map.

Davidson, Travis William. "A Review of Transgender Health in Canada." *University of Ottawa Journal of Medicine* 5, no. 2 (2015): 40–45. https://doi.org/10.18192/uojm.v5i2.1280.

Du Mont, Janice, Shilini Hemalal, Sarah Daisy Kosa, Lee Cameron, and Sheila Macdonald. "The Promise of an Intersectoral Network in Enhancing the Response to Transgender Survivors of Sexual Assault." *PLoS One* 15, no. 11 (2020). https://doi.org/10.1371/journal.pone.0241563.

Editorial Board. "Gender-Affirming Healthcare Must be Made Accessible." *McGill Daily*, October 25, 2021. https://www.mcgilldaily.com/2021/10/gender-affirming-healthcare-must-be-made-accessible/#close-modal.

Flores, Mirella J., L.B. Watson, L.R. Allen, M. Ford, C.R. Serpe, and P.Y. Choo. "Transgender People of Color's Experiences of Sexual Objectification: Locating Sexual Objectification Within a Matrix of Domination." *Journal of Counseling Psychology* 65, no. 3 (2018): 308–23. https://doi.org/10.1037/cou0000279.

Institute of Medicine, Board on the Health of Select Populations, and Committee on Lesbian, Gay, Bisexual, and Transgender Health Issues and Research Gaps and Opportunities. *The Health of Lesbian, Gay, Bisexual, and Transgender People: Building a Foundation for Better Understanding*. Washington, DC: National Academies Press, 2011.

James, S. E., J. L. Herman, S. Rankin, M. Keisling, L. Mottet, and M. Anafi. *The Report of the 2015 U.S. Transgender Survey*. Washington, D.C.: National Center for Transgender Equality, 2016.

Kammer-Kerwick, Matt, Alexander Wang, T'Shana McClain, Sharon Hoefer, Kevin M Swartout, Bethany Backes, and Noël Busch-Armendariz. "Sexual Violence among Gender and Sexual Minority College Students: The Risk and Extent of Victimization and Related Health and Educational Outcomes." *Journal of Interpersonal Violence* 36, no. 21–22 (2021): 10499–526. https://doi.org/10.1177/0886260519883866.

Kattari, Shanna K, Matthew Bakko, Hillary K Hecht, and M. Killian Kinney. "Intersecting Experiences of Healthcare Denials among Transgender and Nonbinary Patients." *American Journal of Preventive Medicine* 58, no. 4 (2020): 506–13. https://doi.org/10.1016/j.amepre.2019.11.014.

McPhail, Deborah, Marina Rountree-James, and Ian Whetter. "Addressing Gaps in Physician Knowledge Regarding Transgender Health and Healthcare through Medical Education." *Canadian Medical Education Journal* 7, no. 2 (2016): 78.

Munson, Michael, and Loree Cook-Daniels. "A Guide for Facilitators of Transgender Community Groups Supporting Sexual Violence Survivors."

2016. https://www.mecasatoolkit.org/uploads/4/4/3/6/44365787/facilitators-guide-trans-support-groups.pdf.

Moore, Dick, Andrea Daley, Barry Deeprose, Lori Ross, Beth Jackson, Mulé Nick, and Anna Travers. "Promoting LGBT Health and Wellbeing Through Inclusive Policy Development." *International Journal for Equity in Health* 8, no. 1 (2009): 1–11. https://doi.org/10.1186/1475-9276-8-18.

Obedin-Maliver, Juno, E.S. Goldsmith , L. Stewart, W. White, E. Tran, S. Brenman, M. Wells, D.M. Fetterman, G. Garcia, and M.R. Lunn. "Lesbian, Gay, Bisexual, and Transgender-Related Content in Undergraduate Medical Education." *Jama - Journal of the American Medical Association* 306, no. 9 (2011): 971–77. https://doi.org/10.1001/jama.2011.1255.

Ontario Human Rights Commission. *Policy on Preventing Discrimination Because of Gender Identity and Gender Expression.* Toronto, ON: Government of Ontario, 2014. https://www3.ohrc.on.ca/sites/default/files/Policy%20on%20preventing%20discrimination%20because%20of%20gender%20identity%20and%20gender%20expression.pdf.

Safer, Joshua D., Eli Coleman, Jamie Feldman, Robert Garofalo, Wylie Hembree, Asa Radix, and Jae Sevelius. "Barriers to Healthcare for Transgender Individuals." *Current Opinion in Endocrinology, Diabetes & Obesity* 23, no. 2 (2016): 168–71. https://doi.org/10.1097/MED.0000000000000227.

Santa Maria, Diane M., Khara Breeden, Stacy A. Drake, Sarah C. Narendorf, Anamika Barman-Adhikari, Robin Petering, Hsun-Ta Hsu, Jama Shelton, Kristin Ferguson-Colvin, and Kimberly Bender. "Gaps in Sexual Assault Health Care among Homeless Young Adults." *American Journal of Preventive Medicine* 58, no. 2 (2020): 191–98. https://doi.org/10.1016/j.amepre.2019.09.023.

Schreiber, Miranda, Tehmina Ahmad, Michael Scott, Kevin Imrie, and Saleem Razack. "The Case for a Canadian Standard for 2SLGBTQIA Medical Education." *CMAJ: Canadian Medical Association Journal/Journal De L'association Medicale Canadienne* 193, no. 16 (2021): E562–5. https://doi.org/10.1503/cmaj.202642.

Statistics Canada. "Current Data Gaps: Technical Report on Changes for the 2021 Census." *Statistics Canada,* 2020, accessed April 5, 2021, https://www12.statcan.gc.ca/census-recensement/2021/ref/98-20-0002/982000022020002-eng.cfm.

Taylor, Brooke. "Trans Health Care in Canada Needs Major Improvements, Advocates Say," *CTV News*, May 22, 2021. https://www.ctvnews.ca/health/trans-health-care-in-canada-needs-major-improvements-advocates-say-1.5439295.

Tettamanti, Nicky. "Pulling Teeth to Get Help- Barriers Facing Transgender Survivors of Sexual Assault When Accessing Support Services and Potential Solutions." 2018. https://doi.org/10.31235/osf.io/b5wxa.

The Trans PULSE Canada Team. "Health and Health Care Access for Trans and Non-Binary People in Canada." 2020. https://transpulsecanada.ca/research-type/reports.

United Nations. *Handbook for United Nations Field Missions on Preventing and Responding to Conflict-Related Sexual Violence*. United Nations, 2020. https://www.un.org/sexualviolenceinconflict/wp-content/uploads/2020/06/2020.08-UN-CRSV-Handbook.pdf.

University of Illinois. "Queer Theory: Background." Last modified March 10, 2020. https://guides.library.illinois.edu/queertheory/background.

"Waiting Your Turn: Wait Times for Healthcare in Canada, 2020 Report." *The Fraser Institute*, December 10, 2020. https://www.fraserinstitute.org/studies/waiting-your-turn-wait-times-for-health-care-in-canada-2020.

Wylie, Kevan, Gail Knudson, Sharful Islam Khan, Mireille Bonierbale, Suporn Watanyusakul, and Stefan Baral. "Serving Transgender People: Clinical Care Considerations and Service Delivery Models in Transgender Health." *The Lancet* 388, no. 10042 (2016): 401–11. https://doi.org/10.1016/S0140-6736(16)00682-6.

Zeoli, April M., T.K. Logan, Rebecca Campbell, Rachael Goodman-Williams, and McKenzie Javorka. "A Trauma-Informed Approach to Sexual Violence Research Ethics and Open Science." *Journal of Interpersonal Violence* 34, no. 23–24 (2019): 4765–93. https://doi.org/10.1177/0886260519871530.

Femicide in Mexico

Brandi Chartier

Violence against women and girls in Mexico is an ongoing problem, one that has been underacknowledged and unresolved for centuries. Every day in Mexico, over ten women are killed—solely because they are female.[1] In the year 2019 alone, 3825 women were killed.[2] This shameful act is known as Femicide—the intentional murder of women merely because they are women.[3] In patriarchal societies, including Mexico, domestic violence is normalized and therefore allows for women and girls to be particularly vulnerable to Femicide.[4] Social structures further the issue through cultural norms, values, traditions, and established ways of being. Femicide is preventable. Through increased government attention and widespread systematic education on the matter, Femicide can come to an end in Mexico.

B. Chartier (✉)
University of Manitoba, Winnipeg, MB, Canada

L. E. Reimer and K. Standish (eds.), *Perspectives on Justice, Indigeneity, Gender, and Security in Human Rights Research*,
https://doi.org/10.1007/978-981-99-1930-7_9

What is Femicide?

One definition of Femicide is the intentional murder of women or girls because of their gender. Femicide is gender-based and misogynistic killings, or more broadly, can include any murder of women or girls.[5] These senseless acts are often perpetrated by men, but sometimes female family members are involved.[6] In most cases, Femicide is committed by partners or ex-partners and involves ongoing abuse in the homes, threats, sexual violence, or situations where women have less power and fewer resources than their partners.[7] There are different types of recognized Femicide which include intimate Femicide, murders in the name of honor, dowry-related Femicide, and non-intimate Femicide.[8] Intimate Femicide includes murders committed by current or former male partners.[9] Honor killings are perpetrated by a family member for an actual or assumed sexual behavior transgression such as adultery or pregnancy outside of marriage.[10] Dowry-related Femicide refers to cultural practices of dowry and the woman being killed by her in-laws over dowry conflicts.[11] Lastly, non-intimate Femicide is the act of killing a woman without an intimate relationship, whether it be random or systemic.[12]

Femicide is not unique to Mexico. Aside from Latin America, where it is prevalent, Femicide persists globally. In the Middle East and South Asia, honor killings are the most common form of Femicide.[13] In India, women are often killed due to insufficient dowry.[14] There are 66,000 women violently killed every year and account for 17% of homicides worldwide.[15] Due to challenges in collecting data, this number is conservative and does not represent the true number of women murdered every year. Collecting data on Femicide is challenging because, in many countries, police and medical data collection do not have the necessary information to properly account for such crimes.[16] Often times Femicide may be reported as a homicide rather than a Femicide because police and relevant authorities do not investigate the role of gender in the crime. The issue of Femicide being underinvestigated may also be due to the lack of acknowledgment and intervention from the country's leaders. The Mexican government's response to Femicide is fairly typical to those worldwide. It has not efficiently acknowledged or taken steps to educate the population on Femicide and has likely resulted in an underrepresentation of Femicide in the country. This creates a hidden human rights issue that is in no way unique to Mexico.

Femicide in Mexico

In the past few decades, there has been significant progress internationally with respect to violence against women.[17] In 1993, the United Nations adopted the *Declaration on the Elimination of Violence against Women,* to which Mexico was a signatory.[18] Shortly after, there was the creation of the *Inter-American Convention on the Prevention, Punishment, and Eradication of Violence against Women*, the Millennium Declaration, which vowed to combat all forms of violence against women, and the *Convention on the Elimination of All Forms of Discrimination against Women.*[19] The United Nations also published a report, *Women 2000: Gender Equality, Development, and Peace for the 21st Century.* Despite these efforts and other endeavours from the international community, the problem of Femicide still exists worldwide and in Mexico. 47% of Mexican women over the age of fifteen who live with their partners suffer from some form of domestic violence.[20] The United Nations High Commissioner for Human Rights indicates that there are 10 million women who suffer from violence in Mexico.[21]

Contrary to the dire situation for women in Mexico that remains, there have been attempts to protect women in the legal system. In 1997, in addition to the conventions and treaties that were previously mentioned, the Mexican Congress approved the Civil and Penal Code. The code was in regard to violence in the home and made, for the first time in Mexico, physical and psychological violence within the family a crime.[22] Another protective system was created in 1999 called General Rule in Mexico and was designed to increase awareness of domestic violence in the public and private health sector.[23] Alongside these reforms, there have been national plans initiated such as the National Program for Equal Opportunity and Non-Discrimination against Women, the National Program for a Life without Violence, and the Institutional Table to coordinate prevention and attention to violence against women.[24] While this proves that there are, in fact, laws that protect women and girls in Mexico, the enforcement of the laws remains weak.

Governance

Mexico is representative of most of the world's smaller geographic states. It is a democratic country divided into 31 states and is considered an upper-middle-income country with a population of over 127 million people.[25] The 2021 leader is Andrés Manuel López Obrador. López Obrador is a center-left populist politician who was elected as President in July 2018 after unsuccessfully running in 2006 and 2012.[26] López Obrador's political platform was appealing to most as he focuses on social justice, reducing poverty, and believes that for the good of all people, the poor should be put first.[27] He has taken dramatic action to fulfill his campaign promises, such as selling the presidential aircraft to put the funds toward tackling poverty and opening the presidential mansion to the public, which had become a symbol of luxury in a country where there the rate of poverty is nearly 42 percent.[28] López Obrador has focused on important issues in the country, such as social justice and poverty reduction; however, he has left Femicide off his agenda. Instead, there has been an avoidance of the issue and use of the word Femicide entirely, and therefore, he is neglecting the women and girls of Mexico.[29]

Why Does Femicide Remain a Problem?

There are several reasons why Femicide remains present in Mexico. There is a lack of legal legitimacy to claims of Femicide, there are norms that further perpetuate the problem, and there is a weak response to Femicide by the government. These issues, paired with a lack of widespread systemic education and understanding about Femicide in the country, sustain the otherwise preventable, criminal acts of Femicide. To begin, the laws regarding the protection of women's rights in Mexico are more symbolic than substantive.[30] Mexico has affirmed every woman's right to life, free of violence, by signing and supporting international conventions and treaties. However, the signing of such treaties did not automatically translate into the passage of legislation and policies that protect women against violence.[31] Often initiatives regarding violence against women by leaders in the country are motivated by a desire for legitimacy at both the international and local levels, rather than for the good of their people and nation.[32] It has been found that authorities treat investigations and prosecutions of Femicide as less important than other types of violent crimes in the country.[33] Therefore, men are not persuaded against or necessarily penalized for carrying out these criminal acts.

Norms embody values, social practices, and gender roles.[34] In Mexico, cultural norms create inequality between men and women, which is a fundamental factor in domestic abuse.[35] The number of women killed is increasing because common culture is rooted in long-existing social problems such as the tendency to "romanticize intimate partner violence as an understandable by-product of love."[36] Through surveys in Mexico, the patriarchal society was revealed as women stated they believed their husbands have the right to use physical force when they do not fulfill their duties.[37] Women also believe that a wife has an obligation to have sex with her husband, even against her own will.[38] As a consequence of these norms, women are understood to be less superior to men in society and less likely to leave abusive relationships. This is especially true if the woman is reliant on her partner for financial resources.

One of the most recent victims of Femicide in Mexico was on February 9, 2020.[39] Ingrid Escamilla, a 25-year-old woman, was brutally murdered by her boyfriend. When President López Obrador was asked about the murder, he told the reporter that he "did not want to talk about gender-motivated killings of women because he did not want Femicide to distract from the raffle."[40] The raffle he was referring to is one his administration had organized around the sale of the presidential plane.[41] Other responses by President López Obrador included blaming Femicide on the "decadence of neo-liberalism" and that he was attending to the root causes of the problem by encouraging Mexicans to love their neighbors.[42] President López Obrador also responded to Femicide by publishing a list of "rules" including it is "cowardice to hit a woman" and "no to hate crimes against women."[43] The lack of appropriate response to Femicide from the government in Mexico has created an outrage in the country. Human rights activists have been pressuring governments to address Femicide and sued the government in the Inter-American Human Rights Court.[44] The court found that the Mexican government had an obligation to improve their investigations into crimes involving violence against women and to also take proactive steps to prevent the violence from occurring in the first place.[45] Due to long-existing structural inequality, cultural and patriarchal values, and strong and ingrained gender roles, there is little education on the severity of Femicide in Mexican society.

Initiatives

There are many activists and organizations that are working tirelessly to end Femicide in Mexico. The combined partnership of the European Union and the United Nations is one example. They partnered with the

Mexican government to launch a program to prevent and combat Femicide and violence against women and girls.[46] The initiative is a four-year program and is based on six pillars:

> (1) improve laws and policies to avoid discrimination and violence; (2) strengthen the institutions in charge of preventing, investigating, and eliminating violence, especially Femicide; (3) promote gender-equality norms, mentalities, and behaviors; (4) guarantee and make accessible quality health, social, legal and police services; (5) improve data collection systems that allow informed public policy decisions; and (6) strengthen women's groups and civil society organizations that promote women's rights.[47]

The European Union has allocated 500 million euros to the initiative, which will be implemented in Mexico and four additional Latin American countries.[48] It aims to reach 4,700,000 beneficiaries and 14,100,000 indirectly.[49] While this initiative works closely with the Mexican government, it will focus on intervention at the community level through a model that responds to specific local problems.[50] This program, which is supported by powerful human rights organizations, has the opportunity to create change in the lives of women and girls in Mexico.

The Mexican Institute for the Research of Family and Population (IMIFAP) is another program that strives to reduce violence against women and girls. This initiative offers training programs that build skills and knowledge through combating cultural norms that condone violence against women.[51] This has proven to be crucial because it is early in a child's life that girls learn to behave in a means that gives privilege to men and when boys grow up in a context that results in the desire to assert power over women.[52] The IMIFAP program begins with an assessment of needs for women, administrative authorities, health professionals, and men.[53] In order to identify norms and beliefs in the community around violence against women, focus groups are conducted.[54] The focus groups gather information about possible strategies for women living in abusive relationships and ways to intervene in situations of domestic violence.[55] The program also includes activities at the local community level through radio campaigns, posters, meetings with men in the community, meetings with health professionals, and creating advocacy within each community.[56]

The model that IMIFAP follows is a preventative one as the program is focused on shifting behaviours and sociocultural norms regarding men and women's views of each other's rights, despite what they may have learned from their childhood and society.[57] One of IMIFAPs main objectives is to achieve common goals among men and women and improvements in the way that they interact with each other.[58] IMIFAP also focuses on developing skills such as communication, decision-making, defining goals, self-knowledge, and learning to control one's own health and decisions to prevent violence.[59] By using IMIFAP as a preventative tool, offers important education and skills and allows for people to identify issues of domestic violence before Femicide can occur.

United Nations Recommendations

The United Nations has made a significant number of recommendations regarding strategies to reduce Femicide in Mexico. The World Health Organization created a document called Understanding and Addressing Violence Against Women in 2012, which included recommendations that should be applied in Mexico. The recommendations include strengthening surveillance and screening of Femicide and intimate partner abuse, train and sensitize health staff, police, and other authorities, increase research in prevention and intervention methods, and reduce gun ownership. The World Health Organization stressed that governmental support and action toward these suggestions is crucial in the implication process and for a successful outcome.[60]

Strengthening the investigations of Femicide and intimate partner abuse is necessary to begin the process of preventing it.[61] As earlier mentioned, there are challenges when collecting data on Femicide because investigations are limited, authorities ignore gender aspects, and women and girls are hesitant to speak up when in an abusive relationship due to norms. In order to strengthen investigations of gender-based killings, there needs to be a collection and analysis of mortality data which includes gender and the documentation of relationships between victim and perpetrator.[62] When evidence is sparse, awareness-raising and advocacy could act as encouragement to police, medical staff, and other relevant authorities to cooperate with investigations standards.[63] By increasing investigation standards of Femicide, it will result in increased attention given to the issue and lead to better widespread education on the matter. Furthermore, training and sensitizing health staff would improve the ability of healthcare providers to identify partner violence and risk of Femicide.[64] Studies have shown that many women accessed health services in the year before being killed by their partners.[65] When health staff is properly trained to detect the risk for domestic abuse, this could significantly decrease the risk of Femicide occurring.

In addition to training healthcare staff, it is important to train and sensitize police forces in Mexico. It would be beneficial for police, and other members of the criminal justice system, to receive sensitization training to identify and document cases of Femicide as well as offer means of prevention.[66] To prevent Femicide is to reduce or eliminate partner violence. To accomplish this, prevention and intervention research with a focus on perpetrators and potential perpetrators must increase.[67] As mentioned, investigations are needed in cases of near-fatal intimate partner violence to understand the needs of the victims and the characteristics of the perpetrators.[68] This allows for awareness of factors that prevent Femicide. Another prevention recommendation is to strengthen gun laws and gun control in Mexico to reduce violence and death. There are consistent studies that prove a direct correlation between the ownership of a gun and the perpetration of Femicide.[69] The studies found that women were three times more likely to be killed if there was a gun in the home.[70] The recommendation is that gun ownership is restricted to protect victims of Femicide.

Finally, there needs to be an appropriate and immediate response by the government of Mexico to support and implement these recommendations. The government needs to acknowledge the significant problem of Femicide, initiate further investigations of domestic abuse and murders, and increase education on violence against women. As a result, a shift would occur to revalue women in society and reduce the risk of women and girls being victims of Femicide. Action on Femicide is urgent because inaction will only lead to the increased death of women and girls in the country.[71]

Conclusion

Social structures in Mexico further Femicide through cultural norms, values, traditions, and established ways of being. Despite the longstanding efforts by activists and organizations, the number of Femicides in Mexico has increased by 137 percent over the past five years.[72] There is an urgent need for widespread systemic education on Femicide to change the ideology around gender roles and patriarchy in society. Femicide is preventable, and through increased government attention and support, alongside systemic education, Femicide can be diminished.

Discussion Questions

1. Despite laws, and despite its potential prevention, Femicide continues in Mexico. What other ways might this travesty be addressed to reduce and eventually eliminate Femicide?
2. How has an increased awareness of Femicide reshaped gender violence?
3. Culture plays a large role in human rights, and in human rights violations. Discuss with respect to Femicide and other forms of gender violence.
4. Explore current human rights work addressing Femicide around the globe.

Notes

1. Ella Torres, "More Than 380 Women Have Been Killed in Mexico This Year. Activists Say a Cultural Change is Needed," *ABC News*, March 14, 2020, https://abcnews.go.com/International/380-women-killed-mexico-year-activists-cultural-change/story?id=69258389.
2. Torres, "More than 380 Women."
3. World Health Organization, Pan American Health Organization, *Understanding and Addressing Violence against Women* (2012).
4. Sonia Frias, "Resisting Patriarchy Within the State: Advocacy and Family Violence in Mexico," *Women's Studies International Forum* 33, no. 6 (2010): 542–51.
5. WHO and PAHO, *Understanding and Addressing Violence Against Women.*
6. WHO and PAHO, *Understanding and Addressing Violence Against Women.*
7. WHO and PAHO, *Understanding and Addressing Violence Against Women.*
8. WHO and PAHO, *Understanding and Addressing Violence Against Women.*
9. WHO and PAHO, *Understanding and Addressing Violence Against Women.*
10. WHO and PAHO, *Understanding and Addressing Violence Against Women.*

11. WHO and PAHO, *Understanding and Addressing Violence Against Women.*
12. WHO and PAHO, *Understanding and Addressing Violence Against Women.*
13. Leah Rodriguez, "Femicide: Everything You Need to Know," *Global Citizen*, November 3, 2020, https://www.globalcitizen.org/en/content/what-is-femicide-everything-you-need-to-know/.
14. Rodriguez, "Femicide."
15. Rodriguez, "Femicide."
16. WHO and PAHO, *Understanding and Addressing Violence Against Women.*
17. Susan Pick et al., "Violence Against Women in Mexico," *Annals of the New York Academy of Sciences* 1087, no. 1 (2006). 261–78.
18. Pick et al., "Violence Against Women."
19. Pick et al., "Violence Against Women."
20. Pick et al., "Violence Against Women."
21. Pick et al., "Violence Against Women."
22. Pick et al., "Violence Against Women."
23. Pick et al., "Violence Against Women."
24. Pick et al., "Violence Against Women."
25. World Health Organization, "Country Cooperation Strategy: Mexico," May 1, 2016, https://www.who.int/publications/i/item/WHO-CCU-16.03-Mexico.
26. Encyclopaedia Britannica, "Andres Manuel Lopez Obrador," accessed January 9, 2020, https://www.britannica.com/biography/Andres-Manuel-Lopez-Obrador.
27. Rafael Romo, "Mexico's President is Just Beginning His 'Fourth Transformation' of the Country." *CNN News*, August 16, 2019, https://www.cnn.com/2019/08/16/americas/mexican-president-lopez-obrador-profile-intl/index.html.
28. Romo, "Mexico's President."
29. Estefania Camacho Jimenez, "Mexican Women Call on Government to End Violence." *Nacla*, March 3, 2020, https://nacla.org/news/2020/03/03/mexico-femicides.
30. Frias, "Resisting Patriarchy Within."
31. Frias, "Resisting Patriarchy Within."
32. Frias, "Resisting Patriarchy Within."
33. Human Rights Watch, "World Report 2020: Rights Trends in Mexico." *Human Rights Watch,* January 14, 2020, https://www.hrw.org/world-report/2020/country-chapters/mexico.
34. Pick et al., "Violence Against Women."
35. Pick et al., "Violence Against Women."
36. Human Rights Watch, "Rights Trends in Mexico."

37. Frias, "Resisting Patriarchy Within."
38. Frias, "Resisting Patriarchy Within."
39. Human Rights Watch, "Rights Trends in Mexico."
40. Human Rights Watch, "Rights Trends in Mexico."
41. Human Rights Watch, "Rights Trends in Mexico."
42. Human Rights Watch, "Rights Trends in Mexico."
43. Human Rights Watch, "Rights Trends in Mexico."
44. Human Rights Watch, "Rights Trends in Mexico."
45. Human Rights Watch, "Rights Trends in Mexico."
46. Spotlight Initiative Organization, "A Hope to Fight Femicide in Mexico," *Spotlight Initiative*, May 29, 2019, https://spotlightinitiative.org/news/spotlight-initiative-hope-fight-femicide-mexico.
47. Spotlight Initiative, "A Hope to Fight."
48. Secretaria de Relaciones Exteriores, "The Spotlight Initiative to Eliminate Violence Against Women and Girls is Presented in Mexico," *Gobierno de* Mexico, May 29, 2019, https://www.gob.mx/sre/prensa/the-spotlight-initiative-to-eliminate-violence-against-women-and-girls-is-presented-in-mexico?idiom=en.
49. United Nations Development Group, "Mexico Spotlight Country Programme," 2022. https://mptf.undp.org/project/00111639.
50. United Nations, "Mexico Spotlight."
51. Pick et al., "Violence Against Women."
52. Pick et al., "Violence Against Women."
53. Pick et al., "Violence Against Women."
54. Pick et al., "Violence Against Women."
55. Pick et al., "Violence Against Women."
56. Pick et al., "Violence Against Women."
57. Pick et al., "Violence Against Women."
58. Pick et al., "Violence Against Women."
59. Pick et al., "Violence Against Women."
60. WHO and PAHO, *Understanding and Addressing Violence Against Women.*
61. WHO and PAHO, *Understanding and Addressing Violence Against Women.*
62. WHO and PAHO, *Understanding and Addressing Violence Against Women.*
63. WHO and PAHO, *Understanding and Addressing Violence Against Women.*
64. WHO and PAHO, *Understanding and Addressing Violence Against Women.*
65. WHO and PAHO, *Understanding and Addressing Violence Against Women.*

66. WHO and PAHO, *Understanding and Addressing Violence Against Women*.
67. WHO and PAHO, *Understanding and Addressing Violence Against Women*.
68. WHO and PAHO, *Understanding and Addressing Violence Against Women*.
69. WHO and PAHO, *Understanding and Addressing Violence Against Women*.
70. WHO and PAHO, *Understanding and Addressing Violence Against Women*.
71. Jimenez, "Mexican Women Call on Government."
72. Jose Miguel Vivanco, "Mexican Government Paralyzed in the Face of a Wave of Femicides," *Human Rights Watch*, March 3, 2020, https://www.hrw.org/news/2020/03/03/mexican-government-paralyzed-face-wave-femicides.

Bibliography

Encyclopaedia Britannica. "Andres Manuel Lopez Obrador." *Britannica*. Accessed January 9, 2020. https://www.britannica.com/biography/Andres-Manuel-Lopez-Obrador.

Frias, Sonia M. "Resisting Patriarchy Within the State: Advocacy and Family Violence in Mexico." *Women's Studies International Forum* 33, no. 6 (2010): 542–51. https://doi.org/10.1016/j.wsif.2010.09.006.

Human Rights Watch. "World Report 2020: Rights Trends in Mexico." *Human Rights Watch*, January 14, 2020. https://www.hrw.org/world-report/2020/country-chapters/mexico.

Jimenez, Estefania Camacho. "Mexican Women Call on Government to End Violence." *Nacla*, March 3, 2020. https://nacla.org/news/2020/03/03/mexico-femicides.

Pick, Susan, Carmen Contreras, and Alicia Barker-Aguilar. "Violence against Women in Mexico: Conceptualization and Program Application." *Annals of the New York Academy of Sciences* 1087, no. 1 (2006): 261–78. https://doi.org/10.1196/annals.1385.014.

Rodriguez, Leah. "Femicide: Everything You Need to Know." *Global Citizen*, November 3, 2020. https://www.globalcitizen.org/en/content/what-is-femicide-everything-you-need-to-know/.

Romo, Rafael. "Mexico's President is Just Beginning His 'Fourth Transformation' of the Country." *CNN News*, August 16, 2019. https://www.cnn.com/2019/08/16/americas/mexican-president-lopez-obrador-profile-intl/index.html.

Secretaria de Relaciones Exteriores. "The Spotlight Initiative to Eliminate Violence Against Women and Girls is Presented in Mexico." *Gobierno de Mexico*, May 29, 2019. https://www.gob.mx/sre/prensa/the-spotlight-initiative-to-eliminate-violence-against-women-and-girls-is-presented-in-mexico?idiom=en.

Spotlight Initiative Organization. "A Hope to Fight Femicide in Mexico." *Spotlight Initiative*, May 29, 2019. https://spotlightinitiative.org/news/spotlight-initiative-hope-fight-femicide-mexico.

Torres, Ella. "More Than 380 Women Have Been Killed in Mexico This Year. Activists Say a Cultural Change is Needed." *ABC News*, March 14, 2020. https://abcnews.go.com/International/380-women-killed-mexico-year-activists-cultural-change/story?id=69258389.

United Nations Development Group. "Mexico Spotlight Country Programme." 2022. https://mptf.undp.org/project/00111639.

Vivanco, Jose Miguel. "Mexican Government Paralyzed in the Face of a Wave of Femicides." *Human Rights Watch*, March 3, 2020. https://www.hrw.org/news/2020/03/03/mexican-government-paralyzed-face-wave-femicides.

World Health Organization. "Country Cooperation Strategy: Mexico." May 1, 2016. https://www.who.int/publications/i/item/WHO-CCU-16.03-Mexico

World Health Organization, Pan American Health Organization. *Understanding and Addressing Violence against Women*. 2012.

Women Workers in the Ready-Made Garment Industry in Bangladesh

Korellia Schneider

It seems that a local or regional story sparks attention and captures the global audience every so often. Even if the ordeal in question has transpired for a long time, the public first hearing of it tends to react in an outpouring of disbelief, compassion, and protest. The cause of others becomes their cause, forging a sense of solidarity, however well-intentioned or misplaced in some scenarios. The controversy of sweatshops has surfaced as a topic of conversation among North Americans in past decades, through waxing and waning periods of raised awareness, inciting much debate and contempt over the "deplorable conditions" of factories in which workers must toil away. Yet, this persistent issue has faded and been re-remembered time and again. Eventually, most people lose interest and stop looking at the labels or imprints on their clothing items or purchased goods.

Even as the issue of sweatshops continues to strike the attention of "Western" consumers off and on across decades, as if it were suddenly "new" news, the reality is that many of these industries are booming.

K. Schneider (✉)
University of Manitoba, Winnipeg, MB, Canada
e-mail: korellia.schneider@gmail.com

L. E. Reimer and K. Standish (eds.), *Perspectives on Justice, Indigeneity, Gender, and Security in Human Rights Research*,
https://doi.org/10.1007/978-981-99-1930-7_10

The places that host these cheap manufacturers of exportable goods have expanded exponentially. In Bangladesh, the Ready-Made Garment (RMG) industry has developed and grown, becoming one of the largest exporters in the world. With this growth, job opportunities have opened up for women to take part, and for some, to develop a newfound sense of economic agency. While the RMG industry has carved out a new pathway of economic opportunity for women, these workers remain particularly vulnerable and constrained due to exploitation, unfair labour practices, and gender inequity.

Finding the Crossroads of Social Justice and Human Rights

Contextualizing the issues emergent in garment factories in Bangladesh, specifically those that more acutely affect women workers, requires examining how academic and theoretical understanding of social justice and human rights have taken shape. Conceptually, they have often been segmented or deemed parallel yet apart. However, cases such as labour exploitation and gender discrimination in Bangladesh's RMG industry may deepen and contribute to the discussion by demonstrating intersectionality and overlap between social justice and human rights. Identifying the connective tissue between the two establishes a more comprehensive, inclusive framework by which to evaluate the issues at hand and prioritizes holistic approaches to ameliorating the injustices women garment factory workers face.

Theorizing Human Rights

Whether viewed as a nascent ideology borne of the devastation of the Second World War, or a reincarnation of past doctrines and practices, the conception of human rights, and in turn, what constitutes as a violation, has been deliberated among scholars and academics. For this chapter, the definition laid out by Jack Donnelly in his work is utilized, in which he states,

> Human rights are a) the minimum set of goods, services, opportunities, and protections that are widely recognized today as essential prerequisites for a life of dignity, and b) a particular set of practices to realize those goods, services, opportunities, and protections.[1]

In conjunction with Donnelly's definition of human rights is his theory of the Universal Declaration Model. This model identifies articles established as internationally recognized human rights, having been iterated and enumerated in at least one or more of the following documents: the *International Bill of Human Rights; the Universal Declaration of Human Rights*; the *International Covenant on Economic, Social, and Cultural Rights*; and the *International Covenant on Civil and Political Rights*.[2] The human rights listed across these documents, some appearing more than once, are held to be inherently entitled to all individuals and as an unnegotiable foundation to human dignity.

Theorizing Social Justice

Before analysing the conflict explored in this chapter, social justice must first be defined. Margot A. Hurlbert establishes the idea of social justice in *Pursuing Justice: An Introduction to Justice Studies*. She explains:

> Social justice is a set of ideas, values, and social practices to ensure that all persons and groups enjoy economic security, can participate effectively in democratic decision-making, exercise mutual respect and caring for one another, and live their lives in ways that protect and sustain the natural environment for future generations.[3]

Thus, the pillar of social justice is theory and practice, being conceptualized, enacted upon, and typically overseen in its delivery. In Hurlbert's words, social justice occupies a space in society that functions to strive for and assure fairness for all peoples, particularly in an economic sense. While focusing on financial security, social justice is also informed by substantive or distributive justice, seeking fairness in other rivets of society to foster an environment in which, as much as possible, despite any differences, people are granted the same opportunities.[4]

Women Workers in Garment Factories in Bangladesh

With a focus on highly prominent issues such as the Rana Plaza disaster, subpar wages/excessive overtime, the gender gap, and gender-based discrimination, and the ostracism of unions, the idea is to bring depth to the matter without presuming to fully encapsulate the issue in its entirety. These are the issues that most call attention to social injustices and violations of human rights, illustrating how women's economic empowerment has been mired by the deleterious fallout of negligent and unfair labour practices. In identifying the most key and salient incidents within the brevity of this chapter, there may be other equally important and impactful aspects that go overlooked.

The Rana Plaza Disaster: A Reverberating Event

On April 24, 2013, in the Savar section of Dhaka, Bangladesh, the most fatal building collapse in the history of the garment industry occurred.[5] The eight-story building known as Rana Plaza quickly fell, killing 1129 people and injuring upwards of 2500 others who were inside.[6] Despite early warning signs discovered via cracks in the foundation on a preceding day, prompting a bank and some other shops to close, the clothing factories housed within the building were kept open for business the following day.[7] Well before the disaster, the owner of the building had reportedly authorized an expansion of the building to add three more floors, even though the building's permit allowed for only five floors.[8]

While the incident was almost certainly avoidable, it was ultimately viewed as a "sudden" and "unexpected" tragedy, bringing the entire Bangladesh Ready-Made Garment sector under a wave of intense scrutiny and backlash. In the immediate aftermath, at the behest of international criticism and major global brands with a vested interest in the Bangladeshi RMG industry, the *Accord on Fire and Building Safety* in Bangladesh was signed in commitment to address labour safety standards in garment factories.[9] However, this measure failed to directly take on the issue of the Rana Plaza survivors, many of whom were women, and the economic insecurity they have continued to grapple with due to devastating injuries.

A Story with No End: The Prolonged Suffering of Rana Plaza Survivors

For the thousands of survivors who escaped the Rana Plaza disaster with their lives, there has been no mending the permanent psychological and physical wounds sustained in the tragedy. Since the Rana Plaza collapse, some survivors, once the breadwinners of their families, now live with permanent disabilities that bar them from securing employment. As Kabir, Maple, and Fatema explain,

> As a consequence, these now disabled workers have become the burden of other family members, who already struggle with poverty, due to low social class. There are few options for these women for basic survival. One option that has been increasingly reported is becoming involved in sex work as a way of meeting basic food and housing needs.[10]

Lasting physical injuries alone do not encompass the full degree of hardship. Studies on the Rana Plaza disaster tend to elide emotional and psychological trauma. Years later, there are survivors who battle fear, depression, and suicidal ideation as they come to terms with what they have endured.[11]

Considering the tragedy, some survivors testify to having received nominal compensation in a one-time disbursement, but it is nowhere near enough to oversee, with any sense of longevity, their welfare.[12] Looking at the figures, it is evident that most of the Rana Plaza survivors remain economically insecure. In 2016, a mere 21.4% of the survivors had returned to work.[13] In the long term, being unable to return to the RMG sector, let alone find alternative forms of gainful employment, arguably deprives the women of the means to maintain a decent living and may even diminish their sense of dignity and personal fulfillment.

Moreover, some women have confronted heightened insecurity as they have had to face the odds without the assistance of family. In interviews conducted by Shamima Akhter in her field research, one survivor speaks of losing several immediate family members in the Rana Plaza collapse.[14] Another survivor tells of the abandonment she endured when her husband left her after losing both of her legs.[15] Without employment or any kind of external support, the survivors are unable to meet their basic human needs, pitching them deeper into economic insecurity, anguish, and endangering situations of sex work that may have compounding consequences upon their health.

Unfair Labour Practices: Exploitation of Women Workers

Economic Insecurity in Low Wages and Excessive Working Hours

To an undeniable extent, the RMG industry has had a significant and evolving influence over shifting societal and gender norms in Bangladesh to open avenues for women towards participation in the workforce.

Even so, the revolutionary opening up of a limited segment of the job market to women was largely undergirded by the motive to hire women as a source of cheap labour, with many eager hopefuls willing to take on the opportunity due to scarcity of options.[16]By 2013, the RMG industry was employing 4 million women as workers in more than 5000 factories, representing 80% of the industry.[17] Scholars acknowledge, in part, the successes women have reaped, namely amplified personal and economic agency, from their employment in the RMG industry. Khosla explains, "Women and adolescent girls now have better access to nutrition than before...Women also report being able to negotiate their role within families, delaying childbearing, and have a greater say in their lives."[18] Nevertheless, despite the many advantages, evidence of rampant exploitation proliferates in the form of meagre wages.

In 2013, after a thrust of protests and ignited stigma from the Rana Plaza disaster, the minimum wage for garment factory workers increased to $68 (USD) per month.[19] Analysing the sustainability of such a wage, Mark Anner explains, "Given that the normal workweek in Bangladesh is 48 hours, and with 4.3 weeks in an average month, this means that the hourly minimum wage in February 2018 stood at USD 31 cents per hour."[20] He goes on to point out that, on average, the current minimum wage only covers about 14% of living expenses, placing Bangladesh in the lowest position among major garment exporting nations.[21] Even wage increases themselves may not be viewed as purely benign when other factors fall outside oversight and regulation. In 2006, in response to a government-mandated wage increase, many factory owners raised the "individual production targets" for their employees, pressuring them to stay at work until newly enforced, exaggerated quotas were met so as to preserve their own profit margins and neutralize the effects of the wage increase.[22] In further complication of the issue, many workers report being paid late or accumulating a backlog of unpaid wages, sometimes weeks or months delayed, which threatens their ability to maintain economic stability. Wage increases remain only minimally effective when factory owners can find loopholes to continue extracting as much profit as possible.[23]

Although rapidly growing, the volatility of the garment industry can also put workers at the mercy of exorbitant work schedules with excessive hours and restrictive time-off. At one factory in Savar (in Dhaka), a typical work schedule constitutes 12 hours a day, depending on performance, with an allotment of a one-hour lunch break, six days a week, and sometimes seven days during busier seasons.[24] If workers are unable to meet their quotas, they must stay long past the scheduled time to complete the assigned work. Factory owners apply pressure to their workers, but a significant bulk of the strain is also applied from anonymous global market pressures. Corporations at the top of the global supply chain wield formidable power in demanding turnaround times for orders, trickling down to the workers on the factory floor who must put in grueling hours to meet "shorter lead times."[25] As workers go through extended periods of excessive work, they may cite physical ailments relating to exhaustion and overwork.[26] Excessive working hours have further contributed to the precarity women workers must navigate in the form of workplace injustices.

The Constraint of Gender Roles and Gender-Based Discrimination

Although much support exists for the empowerment that the Bangladeshi RMG sector has inspired in some women, in contrast, ample evidence illustrates the blockades that have persistently obstructed many women from achieving equity in the workplace. In particular, the gender pay gap forecasts the current climate for women in the RMG sector. As of 2016, across industries, women employees' earnings amounted to 76% of men's respective earnings.[27] A gender gap also exists in terms of the division of power and positions of authority in the factories. Fauzia Ahmed argues that women are often sequestered from higher-paying positions that are representative of higher authority, stating, "The spatial segregation of the sexes in the factory is an outward expression of gendered wage segregation with the few men at the top having jobs with more control and higher wages."[28] Women tend to remain on the floor while men retain ownership and managerial positions.

A high representation of women workers in each factory does not translate proportionally to the levels of opportunity or power more often enjoyed by men. Although varying from one household to another, the supposedly liberating economic agency attributed to women's participation in the garment industry rings hollow in some cases where women's earnings are collected and controlled by their spouses or family members.[29] Despite occupying a position as a breadwinner in the household, not all women retain control over their income, undercutting the celebrated "agency" that has been lauded as one of the greatest successes of and one of the main reasons for the championing of women's employment in the RMG industry.

Spanning from economic inequity to emotional plight, women workers encounter gender-based harassment and discrimination in the garment industry. Although sometimes veiled and other times more outright, verbal, physical, and sexual harassment are no less a form of workplace abuse. Such abuses are informed by patriarchal and gender norms, evoked as a power-over means to keep women workers compliant. Sexual harassment, in particular, may be exercised to threaten women who refuse to be "disciplined" or be compliant with stringent workplace demands.[30] In trying to ascertain the prevalence of sexual harassment, Khosla states, "the true incidence of sexual harassment is not known since women are reluctant to reveal personal experiences of harassment."[31] For women who do not possess the luxury of leaving their current jobs, they may compromise their personal safety, security, and dignity in order to simply take care of themselves or contribute funds to a household in dire need.

Pigeonholing and Disempowering Labour Unions

Amidst a myriad of unjust and asymmetrical labour conditions and practices, workers' abilities to mobilize and manoeuvre for change are kept in check, to a large degree, by the practices in place that make every attempt to stonewall unionizing and collective action. Trade unions are permitted by Bangladeshi law, but the global supply chain itself profits more when workers remain in lowly conditions, rendered unable to rally for the implementation of new standards, protections, and protocols.[32] Hasan Ashraf and Rebecca Prentice outline the difficulties inherent to the formation of unions, in which "legal restrictions, intimidation against organizers, and the threat of corporate flight" efforts to amass workers.[33] Moreover, unions themselves may deter membership as they "struggle to meet the complex needs of workers employed in the garment sector, such as migrant labourers and women."[34] Among the ranks of workers, unions command little appeal to combat against stigmatization, low social acceptance, and friction of contradictory visions.[35]

Many carry a repellant stigma of being male-dominated and "patronizing to female workers."[36] Others are believed to be corruptly colluding with political figures.[37] As vulnerable workers, some women eschew aligning themselves with a union for fear of singling themselves out and jeopardizing their employment status.[38] Nevertheless, if created freely and openly with equal membership and inclusion, unions present one way forward to initiating structural and paradigm shifts.

In the aftermath of the Rana Plaza disaster, hope flourished around the idea of clinching the moment as a catalyst for action. Some sanctions were lifted with the intent to soften the requirements to formally conceive of a union, yet the prohibitively high threshold, a requisite of 30% of workers, currently mandated to forge a union runs counter to international standards.[39] After the fallout of Rana Plaza, the overall number of unions saw a minuscule uptick, but in contrast, the percentage of workers belonging to a union stagnated, never exceeding 10%.[40] Whether overcome by a fear of job loss or unconvinced of a union's clout, factory workers have not flocked to form or join unions. Lacking collective bargaining power, workers are left to the limited resources at their disposal to fight the oppressive conditions of their employment in an industry that remains extensively unregulated and unstandardized.

Bangladesh's Ready-Made Garment Industry: A Human Rights or Social Justice Issue?

Considering the issues present in Bangladesh's RMG industry, particularly those that uniquely affect and constrain women, the need becomes apparent for overlap and plurality between the conception of human rights and social justice as they apply not only to the classification of the conflict but also to its amelioration. Through a human rights lens, the conflict ongoing in Bangladesh's RMG industry could be viewed as an infringement of rights guaranteed by Articles 1, 2, 20, and 23 in the *Universal Declaration of Human Rights*.[41] According to Article 1, "all human beings are born free and equal in dignity and rights," and according to Article 2, "all people are entitled to rights and freedoms without distinction based on sex."[42] The gender gap that exists within the pay scale, and even more significantly, the gender-based discrimination and harassment occurring in factories could be regarded as a human rights violation that compromises the guarantees of these two articles. Women workers are being treated unequally through monetary and social discrimination, in receiving nearly one-quarter less in pay, accessing fewer opportunities to attain promotions, and facing threats to their personal safety and dignity.

By the definition of Articles 20 and 23, current practices in Bangladeshi garment factories have impinged upon these workers' right to freedom of association and right to "just and favourable conditions of work."[43] Given the rigorous requirements deliberately being imposed upon groups to limit their ability to unionize, the right to freedom of association has arguably become compromised. Furthermore, the current working conditions, providing a non-living wage and mandating obligatory over time, either through unattainable quotas or through impossible turnaround times, violate the right to favourable conditions to which workers are entitled.

In terms of social justice, economic insecurity proves to be the most glaring form of injustice, looking at the wages that are insufficient to meet costs of living, let alone support a household. Victims of the Rana Plaza disaster, especially women, face ever-present economic insecurity as their permanent disabilities have left them unable to find compensatory work to support themselves, nor have they necessarily received "justice" for the suffering they have endured in the wake of a tragedy that could have been prevented. For women throughout the RMG industry, a limited selection of jobs, inequitable workplace conditions, and unequal access to other career tracks or promotions represent persistent social barriers that highlight major imbalances.

When determining where these two paradigms intersect, it would be difficult and less effective to conceive of them as separate branches of an issue. Rather, they are interwoven together into the complexity of the issue and must be addressed equally and simultaneously to move forward with any kind of positive, sustainable change. While some scholars would argue that economic rights factor less seamlessly into the field of human rights, there is significant support in favour of recognizing the power the two possess by working in tandem.[44] Nancy Fraser argues that most strains of inequality materialize from some confluence of economic variants and "culturally constructed distinctions."[45] Considering the multi-faceted factors that contribute to inequality, she goes on to make the case that, "The connections between status equality and distributive equality bring the egalitarianism of human rights and social justice as part of general processes protecting persons' membership status."[46] In other words, when the attributional factors driving inequality cannot be so readily isolated, nor should the approach to rectifying such asymmetries.

Further asserting the overlap between social justice and human rights, Hurlbert puts forward the argument that justice rests upon regard for people and their livelihood within communities that uphold all their rights, which includes meeting basic human needs such as access to food, water, and shelter. If the most basic of human rights go overlooked, "how can any meaning be given to the right to vote or the freedom of expression?"[47] In the way that Hurlbert juxtaposes social rights and human rights, the full picture of equality cannot be achieved without both aspects actively being present. All rights must be protected, including basic human needs, holistically in order to acknowledge human dignity and the pursuit of a good life. If basic human needs are not met, the "headier" rights do not take shape. For instance, if women workers are overcome by unstoppable and inescapable economic insecurity which encroaches upon their access to food and shelter, the others' rights they are entitled to, such as freedom of association and the right to just and favourable work conditions, remain even further afield. Therefore, social justice and human rights form part of an interconnected, multi-pronged understanding of inequalities and injustices occurring at large, as well as in the case of Bangladesh's garment factories.

Recommendations: Possible Paths Forward

Augmenting Collective Bargaining Power

First, establishing collective bargaining power on two fronts, through transnational support and through the liberation and de-stigmatization of unionization, will empower workers in negotiating with the Bangladeshi government, factory owners, subcontractors, and buyers to make necessary changes. Anner, Bair, and Blasi advocate for what they have termed "triangular collective bargaining power," based on historical evidence of "jobber agreements" formulated in the U.S. garment industry in the early twentieth century, through the formation of unions, in order to hold retailers and corporations accountable.[48] As a result, workers, factory owners, and subcontractors would establish a united front in negotiating with retailers, drafting together agreeable and mandatory stipulations to reduce the "binding power" of these powerful corporations.

Collective bargaining power has the potential to be nurtured through transnational support. With support from international consumers, activists, and NGOs, additional pressure may be directed at global brands to take responsibility to improve labour standards, as the fault does not lay solely with the Bangladeshi government. Of the merits of transnational support, Berik Gunseli insists that the very labour transnationalism that helped stoke support for the successful launch of the Accord has also culminated into an array of "international alliances among workers/unions, labour NGOs, feminists, and consumer groups in the North" that have frequently been instrumental in bolstering workers' aspirations and supporting worker organizations.[49] Without collective bargaining power, and to an extent, transnational support, it will be difficult to gain the momentum needed to take on leviathan corporations.

Strengthening Labour Standards

Overlapping somewhat with the efforts to negotiate with major retailers, the second recommendation is to strengthen, if not overhaul, further agreements to ensure Corporate Social Responsibility (CSR). The Accord on Fire and Building Safety in Bangladesh, implemented after the Rana Plaza disaster, allowed major retailers to opt into a commitment to conduct routine fire and building safety inspections.[50] Although legally binding once opted into, this initiative was never presented as an obligatory pursuit for corporations to undertake, and in the process, failed to address other priorities such as wages and working conditions.[51] Major retailers such as Walmart and Gap refused to sign the Accord.[52]

The Accord has proven to be a watershed moment, in its partial response, by enacting changes to prevent the occurrence of another disaster, yet its shortcomings are evident and many. Often driven by profit, it seems that many factory owners abuse and exploit their employees, violating their human rights, but the largest players and influencers in the global supply chain are also complicit. To date, even with the passage of the *Bangladesh Labour Law* in 2006, the RMG industry remains wildly under-regulated, with a shortage of comprehensively enforced framework in place and a dearth of oversight for policies that have been put into effect.[53] Weak regulation and governance, which both played key roles in the formula that yielded exponential growth in the industry since its inception in the 1970s, continue to prevail in contemporary times, unaltered despite the changing nature of worker's conditions, needs, and rights.[54] As such, retailers are enabled to make astronomical demands of Bangladeshi factories in order to keep their business, while employers and factory owners exert enormous pressure over their workers, devoid of bargaining power.

Increasing Representation of Women in All Facets of the RMG Sector

While the ideal, of course, is to achieve equal gender representation in all contexts of society and across different sectors, radical and sweeping transformation of gender and culture norms aside, the third feasible option to initiate change, as it pertains to the RMG sector in Bangladesh, is to increase the representation of women in managerial positions and other positions of authority, as well as in unions. With the industry consisting of nearly 80% of women, this figure is problematized by the relatively low ratio of women in positions of authority. Moreover, if trade unions continue to be connoted as male-dominated and patriarchal, women workers remain limited in their outlets and platforms, largely voiceless in addressing their concerns and needs.[55] If unions harnessed the largely untapped portion of their women colleagues in pursuit of collective action, it could help accelerate and empower the mobilization of their cause.

Firmer Governance and More Dedicated Oversight at the State Level

A ground-breaking policy brought into effect after the Rana Plaza disaster, the Accord on Fire and Building Safety in Bangladesh, was accomplished through multilateral cooperation between the Bangladeshi government, major global brands, and transnational labour support. Since its inception, substantial safety issues have been discovered in numerous garment factories across Bangladesh, and no further disasters of such scale as that of Rana Plaza have occurred.[56] However, the Accord is not a stopping point. In an industry confronted with a dearth of regulatory processes to protect workers' rights, weak governance has hindered efforts to advance workers' causes and increase workers' representation. Other measures such as CSR and labour unions remain largely rudderless in the absence of "an embeddedness within institutional frameworks, both at the national and international level."[57] As well as having enshrined social, cultural, and economic rights within its own constitution, Bangladesh is a signatory to the UDHR and to other international treaties recognizing human rights.[58] The Bangladeshi government must take a prominent leadership role in implementing firmer regulations in the garment industry and continuing to collaborate as part of multilateral efforts to protect and uphold workers' rights.

Conclusions

The various constraints and injustices levelled against women workers in the RMG industry in Bangladesh indicate several incidents of disservice to social justice and human rights. Given the overlap and complexity of social justice and human rights, it is not possible to define or reduce the issues as belonging to one category or the other. Rather, this intersectionality and overlap could be embraced and understood to be crucial in considering the approaches taken to address the imbalances and injustices currently manifesting as gender inequity and unfair working conditions in the garment industry. Through possible approaches of amassing collective bargaining power, strengthening labour standards, and advocating for equal gender representation, there may be better protections put in place to not only improve working conditions, workers' livelihoods but also adhere to social justice and human rights norms.

Discussion Questions

1. What role do individuals and groups (from consumers to corporations) play in addressing the asymmetries in labour standards and labour rights that have emerged in a globalized world?
2. What do you think about the efficacy of fair trade, Corporate Social Responsibility (CSR), and other models intended to bring fairness and sustainability to the RMG industry?
3. Does the overlap (or inversely, the division) of human rights and social justice apply universally or only in specific contexts?
4. How might the future of human rights be reconcilable with current global economic systems?

Notes

1. Jack Donnelly, *Universal Human Rights in Theory and Practice* (Ithaca: Cornell University Press, 2013), 17.
2. Donnelly, *Universal Human Rights*, 26–8.
3. Margot Hurlbert, *Pursuing Justice: An Introduction to Justice Studies* (Winnipeg, MB: Fernwood Publishing, 2011), 59.
4. Hurlbert, *Pursuing Justice*, 59.
5. Naomi Hossain, "Rana Plaza, Disaster Politics, and the Empowerment of Women Garment Workers in Bangladesh," *Contemporary South Asia:*

Contentious Empowerment: Women, Development and Power in South Asia 27, no. 4 (October 2, 2019): 521.

6. Sanchita Banerjee Saxena, *Made in Bangladesh, Cambodia, and Sri Lanka: The Labor Behind the Global Garment and Textile Industries* (Amherst, New York: Cambria Press, 2014), 199; Lamia Karim, "Disposable Bodies: Garment Factory Catastrophe and Feminist Practices in Bangladesh," *Anthropology Now* 6, no. 1 (April 1, 2014): 52–63, https://doi.org/10.5816/anthropologynow.6.1.0052.
7. Humayun Kabir, Myfanwy Maple, and Syadani Riyad Fatema, "Vulnerabilities of Women Workers in the Readymade Garment Sector of Bangladesh: A Case Study of Rana Plaza," *Journal of International Women's Studies* 19, no. 6 (August 1, 2018): 229; Humayun Kabir, Myfwany Maple, Md Shahidul Islam, and Kim Usher. "The Current Wellbeing of the Survivors of the Rana Plaza Building Collapse in Bangladesh: A Qualitative Study," *International Journal of Environmental Research and Public Health* 16, no. 13 (July 2, 2019): 1.
8. Günseli Berik, "Revisiting the Feminist Debates on International Labor Standards in the Aftermath of Rana Plaza," *Studies in Comparative International Development* 52, no. 2 (June 2017): 194, https://doi.org/10.1007/s12116-017-9246-x.
9. Saxena, *Made in Bangladesh*, 199–200.
10. Kabir, Maple, and Fatema. "Vulnerabilities of Women Workers," 227.
11. Kabir et al., "The Current Wellbeing of the Survivors," 4–5.
12. Kabir et al., "The Current Wellbeing of the Survivors," 230–1.
13. Barua and Ansary, "Workplace Safety in Bangladesh," 5, cited in Kabir et al., 232.
14. Shamima Akhter, "Endless Misery of Nimble Fingers: The Rana Plaza Disaster," *Asian Journal of Women's* Studies 20, no. 1 (January 1, 2014): 143–4, https://doi.org/10.1080/12259276.2014.11666176.
15. Akter, "Endless Misery."
16. Nidhi Khosla, "The Ready-made Garments Industry in Bangladesh: A Means to Reducing Gender-based Social Exclusion of Women?" *Journal of International Women's Studies* 11, no. 1 (2009), 292, http://search.proquest.com/docview/232112941/.
17. Afroza Anwary. "Globalization, Women Factory Workers of Bangladesh and Their Autonomy," *Géneros (Barcelona)* 6, no. 3 (October 25, 2017): 1391, https://doi.org/10.17583/generos.2017.2621; Karim, "Disposable Bodies," 54.
18. Khosla, "The Ready-made Garments Industry," 294.
19. Karim, "Disposable Bodies," 54.
20. Mark Anner, *Binding Power: The Sourcing Squeeze, Workers' Rights, and Building Safety in Bangladesh since Rana Plaza* (Research Report, Penn State: Centre for Global Workers' Rights, 2018), 7.

21. Anner, *Binding Power*.
22. Dina Siddiqi, "Do Bangladeshi Factory Workers Need Saving? Sisterhood in the Post-Sweatshop Era," *Feminist Review* 91, no. 1 (2009): 154–74, https://doi.org/10.1057/fr.2008.55.
23. Berik, "Revisiting the Feminist Debates," 199.
24. Sadika Akhter et al., "Work, Gender Roles, and Health: Neglected Mental Health Issues Among Female Workers in the Ready-made Garment Industry in Bangladesh," *International Journal of Women's Health* 9 (2017): 574, https://doi.org/10.2147/IJWH.S137250.
25. Mark Anner, Jennifer Bair, and Jeremy Blasi. "Toward Joint Liability in Global Supply Chains: Addressing the Root Causes of Labor Violations in International Subcontracting Networks." *Comparative Labor Law & Policy Journal* 35, no. 1 (September 22, 2013): 9.
26. Kabir, Maple, and Fatema, "Vulnerabilities of Women Workers," 226.
27. Jennifer Solotaroff et al., *Voices to Choices: Bangladesh's Journey in Women's Economic Empowerment* (Washington, DC: World Bank Group, 2019), 47.
28. Fauzia Erfan Ahmed, "The Rise of the Bangladesh Garment Industry: Globalization, Women Workers, and Voice: Document View," *NWSA Journal* 16, no. 2 (2004): 39, https://doi.org/10.1353/nwsa.2004.0042.
29. Salma Chaudhuri Zohir, "Household Response to Gender Issues: A Survey on Households of Female EPZ Workers in Bangladesh," In *Tracking Gender Equity Under Economic Reforms: Continuity and Change in South Asia*, ed. Swapna Mukhopadhyay and Ratna M. Sudarshan (Ottawa: International Development Research Centre, 2003), 72.
30. Siddiqi, "Do Bangladeshi Factory Workers Need Saving?" 167–8; Naila Kabeer, "Globalization, Labor Standards, and Women's Rights: Dilemmas of Collective (In)action in an Interdependent World," *Feminist Economics* 10, no. 1 (2004): 17.
31. Khosla, "The Ready-made Garments Industry," 296.
32. Saxena, *Made in Bangladesh*, 108.
33. Hasan Ashraf and Rebecca Prentice, "Beyond Factory Safety: Labor Unions, Militant Protest, and the Accelerated Ambitions of Bangladesh's Export Garment Industry," *Dialectical Anthropology* 43, no. 1 (2019): 97, https://doi.org/10.1007/s10624-018-9539-0.
34. Ashraf and Prentice, "Beyond Factory Safety."
35. Sabrina Zajak, "International Allies, Institutional Layering and Power in the Making of Labour in Bangladesh," *Development and Change* 48, no. 5 (2017): 1011, https://doi.org/10.1111/dech.12327.
36. Hossain, "Rana Plaza, Disaster Politics," 521; Saxena, *Made in Bangladesh*, 108.

37. Hossain, "Rana Plaza, Disaster Politics."; Saxena, *Made in Bangladesh*; Laura A. Carlson and Vera Bitsch. "Social Sustainability in the Ready-Made-Garment Sector in Bangladesh: An Institutional Approach to Supply Chains." *International Food and Agribusiness Management Review* 21, no. 2 (March 13, 2018): 279.
38. Hossain, "Rana Plaza, Disaster Politics," 521.
39. Ashraf and Prentice, "Beyond Factory Safety," 98.
40. Berik, "Revisiting Feminist Debates," 210.
41. United Nations General Assembly, "Universal Declaration of Human Rights," 217 (III) A. Paris, 1948.
42. United Nations, "Universal Declaration."
43. United Nations, "Universal Declaration."
44. Aryeh Neier, "Human Rights and Social Justice: Separate Causes." In *Can Human Rights Bring Social Justice? Twelve Essays*, ed. Doutje Lettinga and Lars Van Troost (Amnesty International, 2015), 49.
45. Neil Hibbert. *Are Human Rights the Rights of Social Justice?* (Saskatoon, SK: University of Saskatchewan, 2013), 7, https://www.cpsa-acsp.ca/papers-2013/Hibbert.pdf.
46. Frasier, *Social Justice*, 4, cited in Hibbert, 7.
47. Hurlbert, *Pursuing Justice*, 184.
48. Anner, Blasi, and Bair, "Toward Joint Liability," 4–5, 17.
49. Berik, "Revisiting Feminist Debates," 210.
50. Zajak, "International Allies, Institutional Layering," 1011.
51. Berik, "Revisiting Feminist Debates," 209–10.
52. Karim, "Disposable Bodies," 58.
53. Carlson and Bitsch, "Social Sustainability," 281.
54. Hossain, "Rana Plaza, Disaster Politics" 524.
55. Dilruba Shoma Chowdhury, "Women's Rights and Choice in the Ready-made Garments Sector of Bangladesh: Evidence from Theory and Practice," *Journal of International Women's Studies* 18, no. 2 (2017): 126.
56. Jimmy Donaghey and Juliane Reinecke, "When Industrial Democracy Meets Corporate Social Responsibility—A Comparison of the Bangladesh Accord and Alliance as Responses to the Rana Plaza Disaster." *British Journal of Industrial Relations* 56, no. 1 (2017): 38, https://doi.org/10.1111/bjir.12242.
57. Donaghey and Reinecke, "When Industrial Democracy," 21, 37.
58. Redwanur M. Rahman, "Human Rights, Health, and the State in Bangladesh," *BMC International Health and Human Rights* 6, no. 4 (2006): 6, https://doi.org/10.1186/1472-698X-6-4.

Bibliography

Ahmed, Fauzia Erfan. "The Rise of the Bangladesh Garment Industry: Globalization, Women Workers, and Voice: Document View." *NWSA Journal* 16, no. 2 (2004): 34–45. https://doi.org/10.1353/nwsa.2004.0042.

Akhter, Sadika, Shannon Rutherford, Feroza Akhter Kumkum, David Bromwich, Iqbal Anwar, Aminur Rahman, and Cordia Chu. "Work, Gender Roles, and Health: Neglected Mental Health Issues Among Female Workers in the Ready-Made Garment Industry in Bangladesh." *International Journal of Women's Health* 9 (2017): 571–9. https://doi.org/10.2147/IJWH.S137250

Akhter, Shamima. "Endless Misery of Nimble Fingers: The Rana Plaza Disaster." *Asian Journal of Women's Studies* 20, no. 1 (January 1, 2014): 137–47. https://doi.org/10.1080/12259276.2014.11666176.

Anner, Mark, Jennifer Bair, and Jeremy Blasi. "Toward Joint Liability in Global Supply Chains: Addressing the Root Causes of Labor Violations in International Subcontracting Networks." *Comparative Labor Law & Policy Journal* 35, no. 1 (September 22, 2013): 1–43.

Anner, Mark. *Binding Power: The Sourcing Squeeze, Workers' Rights, and Building Safety in Bangladesh since Rana Plaza.* Research Report. Penn State: Centre for Global Workers' Rights, 2018.

Anwary, Afroza. "Globalization, Women Factory Workers of Bangladesh and Their Autonomy." *Géneros (Barcelona)* 6, no. 3 (October 25, 2017): 1389–413. https://doi.org/10.17583/generos.2017.2621.

Ashraf, Hasan, and Rebecca Prentice. "Beyond Factory Safety: Labor Unions, Militant Protest, and the Accelerated Ambitions of Bangladesh's Export Garment Industry." *Dialectical Anthropology* 43, no. 1 (2019): 93–107. https://doi.org/10.1007/s10624-018-9539-0.

Berik, Günseli. "Revisiting the Feminist Debates on International Labor Standards in the Aftermath of Rana Plaza." *Studies in Comparative International Development* 52, no. 2 (June 2017): 193–216. https://doi.org/10.1007/s12116-017-9246-x.

Carlson, Laura A., and Vera Bitsch. "Social Sustainability in the Ready-Made-Garment Sector in Bangladesh: An Institutional Approach to Supply Chains." *International Food and Agribusiness Management Review* 21, no. 2 (March 13, 2018): 269–92.

Chowdhury, Dilruba Shoma. "Women's Rights and Choice in the Ready-made Garments Sector of Bangladesh: Evidence from Theory and Practice." *Journal of International Women's Studies* 18, no. 2 (2017): 118–33.

Donaghey, Jimmy, and Juliane Reinecke. "When Industrial Democracy Meets Corporate Social Responsibility—A Comparison of the Bangladesh Accord and Alliance as Responses to the Rana Plaza Disaster." *British Journal of Industrial Relations* 56, no. 1 (2017): 14–42. https://doi.org/10.1111/bjir.12242.

Donnelly, Jack. *Universal Human Rights in Theory and Practice*, 3rd ed. Ithaca: Cornell University Press, 2013.

Hibbert, Neil. *Are Human Rights the Rights of Social Justice?* University of Saskatchewan, 2013: 1–18. https://www.cpsa-acsp.ca/papers-2013/Hibbert.pdf.

Hossain, Naomi. "Rana Plaza, Disaster Politics, and the Empowerment of Women Garment Workers in Bangladesh." *Contemporary South Asia: Contentious Empowerment: Women, Development and Power in South Asia* 27, no. 4 (October 2, 2019): 516–30.

Hurlbert, Margot. *Pursuing Justice: An Introduction to Justice Studies*. Winnipeg, MB: Fernwood Publishing, 2011.

Kabir, Humayun, Myfanwy Maple, and Syadani Riyad Fatema. "Vulnerabilities of Women Workers in the Readymade Garment Sector of Bangladesh: A Case Study of Rana Plaza." *Journal of International Women's Studies* 19, no. 6 (August 1, 2018): 224–35. http://search.proquest.com/docview/2110240937/.

Kabeer, Naila. "Globalization, Labor Standards, and Women's Rights: Dilemmas of Collective (In)action in an Interdependent World." *Feminist Economics* 10, no. 1 (2004): 3–35.

Kabir, Humayun, Myfwany Maple, Md Shahidul Islam, and Kim Usher. "The Current Wellbeing of the Survivors of the Rana Plaza Building Collapse in Bangladesh: A Qualitative Study." *International Journal of Environmental Research and Public Health* 16, no. 13 (July 2, 2019): 1–21.

Karim, Lamia. "Disposable Bodies: Garment Factory Catastrophe and Feminist Practices in Bangladesh." *Anthropology Now* 6, no. 1 (April 1, 2014): 52–63. https://doi.org/10.5816/anthropologynow.6.1.0052.

Khosla, Nidhi. "The Ready-made Garments Industry in Bangladesh: A Means to Reducing Gender-based Social Exclusion of Women?" *Journal of International Women's Studies* 11, no. 1 (2009): 289–303. http://search.proquest.com/docview/232112941/

Neier, Aryeh. "Human Rights and Social Justice: Separate Causes." In *Can Human Rights Bring Social Justice? Twelve Essays*, edited by Doutje Lettinga and Lars Van Troost. Amnesty International, 2015: 47–52.

Rahman, Redwanur M. "Human Rights, Health, and the State in Bangladesh." *BMC International Health and Human Rights* 6, no. 4 (2006): 1–12. https://doi.org/10.1186/1472-698X-6-4.

Saxena, Sanchita Banerjee. *Made in Bangladesh, Cambodia, and Sri Lanka: The Labor Behind The Global Garment and Textile Industries*. Amherst, New York: Cambria Press, 2014.

Siddiqi, Dina. "Do Bangladeshi Factory Workers Need Saving? Sisterhood in the Post-Sweatshop Era." *Feminist Review* 91, no. 1 (2009): 154–74. https://doi.org/10.1057/fr.2008.55.

Solotaroff, Jennifer L., Aphichoke Kotikula, Tara Lonnberg, Snigdha Ali, Rohini Pande, and Ferdous Jahan. *Voices to Choices: Bangladesh's Journey in Women's Economic Empowerment*. Washington, DC: World Bank Group, 2019.

United Nations General Assembly, "Universal Declaration of Human Rights." 217 (III) A. Paris, 1948. Accessed January 14, 2021, https://www.ohchr.org/EN/UDHR/Documents/UDHR_Translations/eng.pdf.

Zajak, Sabrina. "International Allies, Institutional Layering and Power in the Making of Labour in Bangladesh." *Development and Change* 48, no. 5 (2017): 1007–30. https://doi.org/10.1111/dech.12327.

Zohir, Salma Chaudhuri. "Household Response to Gender Issues: A Survey on Households of Female EPZ Workers in Bangladesh." In *Tracking Gender Equity Under Economic Reforms: Continuity and Change in South Asia*. Edited by Swapna Mukhopadhyay and Ratna M. Sudarshan. Ottawa: International Development Research Centre, 2003. 64–88.

Extremism, Terrorism and Misogyny

Ashley Haller

On a December afternoon in 1989, Marc Lépine entered École Polytechnique in Montreal armed with a semi-automatic rifle disguised in a garbage bag. He walked into a classroom of aspiring engineers and ordered the men and women into separate groups—opening fire on the female group while proclaiming, "you're all a bunch of feminists, and I hate feminists."[1] Six of those women died instantly.[2] Lépine then moved through the rest of the school, killing eight more women before taking his own life. His suicide note bemoaned, "I have decided to send the feminists, who have always ruined my life, to their Maker," listing nineteen other women he hoped to kill if he had the time.[3] The violent attack, now deemed the Montreal Massacre, remains one of the deadliest shootings in Canadian history.

On a spring day in 2018, Alek Minassian barrelled a speeding van through a busy Toronto Street, killing ten people and injuring many

A. Haller (✉)
Winnipeg, MB, Canada
e-mail: ashley.haller@umanitoba.ca

L. E. Reimer and K. Standish (eds.), *Perspectives on Justice, Indigeneity, Gender, and Security in Human Rights Research*,
https://doi.org/10.1007/978-981-99-1930-7_11

others. Through this act of violence, Minassian hoped to "inspire an uprising" for fellow members of the incel community.[4] Incels (short for involuntary celibates) represent an online collective of men who promote misogynistic ideals and violence towards women in retribution for their unsuccessful romantic endeavours. The online forums where members interact often promote violence, rape, and even murder. Some incel members consider Marc Lépine a de-facto founding father of their community, heralding him as a hero.

Two of the deadliest attacks ever perpetrated on Canadian soil have one thing in common: they were motivated by misogyny. After noting this dangerous pattern, Canadian feminists have called for these crimes to be recognized for their political and ideological nature: as gender-based extremism and terrorism. This chapter explores the applicability of the labels extremism, violent extremism, and terrorism for misogynistic violence through the tragic events of the Montreal Massacre and Toronto van attack in Canada. Such designations for misogynistic violence are not only applicable but necessary, given that the language used to describe these acts substantially impacts the way they are understood—and therefore must be assessed with careful consideration. This emerging framework ultimately presents a crucial paradigm shift that more adequately addresses the gendered basis for these crimes while presenting the opportunity for more promising responses to these acts moving forward.

What Is Misogyny?

Despite Canada's reputation for being a peaceful and progressive country, misogyny has been and continues to be a prevalent issue. Misogyny is most often interpreted as "a hatred of women."[5] While hatred towards women is indeed a central aspect of the issue, it is now understood within the broader conceptions of structural violence—an important shift that recognizes misogyny as "something women face, rather than something men feel."[6] This is underscored by Kate Manne, who describes misogyny as a "system that operates within a patriarchal social order to police and enforce women's subordination and uphold male dominance."[7] This system is essential in reinforcing traditional gender stereotypes, emphasized by the fact that misogynistic behaviour is commonly exhibited towards women "who violate patriarchal norms and expectations, who aren't serving male interests in the ways they're expected to."[8] Therefore, as Berit Brogaard concisely states, "a misogynist is not simply a person who hates women. It's a person who does, or would, hate women who are not subordinate."[9]

Like many things in our modernized world, misogynistic sentiment is largely fostered online through what has been deemed the "Manosphere."[10] The Manosphere encompasses a broad collective of online groups who promote the inferiority of women and advocate for violence on account of such beliefs.[11] The collective includes Men's Rights Activists (MRA), who believe society is fundamentally based on misandry; Pickup Artists (pua), who attempt to seduce women through psychological devices; and Men Going Their Own Way, who avoid all contact with women out of the belief that they will be treated as "disposable utilities."[12] However, perhaps the most demonstrably violent group in the Manosphere is the incel community of which Alek Minassian claimed allegiance. The collective, which numbers in the tens of thousands, adheres to an ideology called "the black pill," which is underscored by a "fundamental rejection of women's sexual emancipation."[13] Incels blame women for their involuntary celibacy, as they believe women reserve their sexual prowess for "Chads," a moniker for attractive and successful men. In the aftermath of the Toronto van attack, members of the incel community celebrated Minsassian's act of violence, urging others to follow suit through rape, acid attacks, and mass shootings.[14]

Canada's position within the Manosphere is troubling—especially when noting that it is the original birthplace of the incel movement. Initially created by a young bisexual woman named Alana in the 1990s, the aim of the online community was to create an inclusive environment for people who had difficulty finding relationships due to social awkwardness, sexual orientation, rigid gender norms, and even mental illness.[15] However, over the years, both the term and its online domain were coopted by the male supremacist groups present today, with Alana likening the creation of her original forum to "a scientist who invented something that ended up being a weapon of war."[16] The proliferation of online misogynist groups in the country has indeed grown so vast that Canada tops the list for global interest in the aforementioned Manosphere group Men Going Their Own Way, according to Google Trends data.[17] While these virtual manifestations of misogyny are indeed shocking, they are not new. Emma Jane states that "while the internet did not invent sexism, it is amplifying it in unprecedented ways,"[18] providing an unregulated platform where misogynistic ideas can not only be shared but acted upon.

Despite demonstrating a propensity for dangerous rhetoric and violent acts, the Manosphere has faced little accountability for its actions from online platforms and governments. Small advancements, such as Reddit banning certain incel forums, have come only after intense public scrutiny and online petitions.[19] Concerning these markedly reactionary responses, Laura Hudson states that "online platforms have long been more concerned with free speech than the literal lives of women," calling the manner in which misogynistic groups are enabled online one of the most irresponsible things those at the helm of the internet could do.[20] Colin Clarke furthers that misogynistic forums are often dismissed as "the immature musings of young men" and continue to operate because "they are still largely considered outside the realm of terrorism"[21]—indicating a serious misunderstanding of the Manosphere's capacity for violence, and the need for a more serious designation for their acts.

Dismissing misogyny comes at a grave cost—not only to women but the entire population. Misogynistic ideas have been identified as a common trait among mass killers who have claimed men, women, and children alike as victims. Bosman et al. state that while the motivations of mass killers are often muddled and complex, the "one common thread that connects many of them—other than access to powerful firearms—is a history of hating women, assaulting wives, girlfriends, and female family members, or sharing misogynistic views online."[22] Pablo Castillo Díaz and Nahla Valji further that examples of expressed misogyny or domestic violence are found in the histories of nearly *all* the perpetrators of the worst terrorists attacks and mass killings in Western countries in recent years—a remarkable feat considering such violence is perpetually underreported.[23] While social scientists have yet to produce a concrete explanation for the correlation between misogyny and mass killers, many point to the similarities between the "intimate terrorism of domestic violence" and mass terrorism perpetuated by lone-wolf attackers as "attempts to provoke fear and assert control."[24] Therefore, negating the threat posed by expressed misogyny can have disastrous consequences, proving that silence can indeed lead to violence if these issues are ignored.

The Importance of Media Framing

In the aftermath of the Toronto van attack, many media outlets struggled to make discursive sense of the tragedy and its perpetrator, resulting in a myriad of contesting reports across Canada. Were these the actions of a madman? A misogynist? A lone wolf extremist? One journalist abandoned the notion of applying a label to Alek Minassian altogether, stating, "the very notion of fighting over these labels is exhausting, because it is all but certain it will be for naught. Few, if any, minds will be changed in the process."[25] While identifying with the exacerbated journalist is certainly understandable, the words, labels, and frameworks we use to describe these attacks *do* indeed matter and must be assessed with careful consideration—especially by those in positions of influence.

The significance of our linguistic choices can be exemplified by communications scholar Marshall McLuhan, who coined his infamous phrase "the medium is the message" in the 1960s.[26] At its most basic understanding, the phrase recognizes that the way in which we convey information (the medium) is just as important as the information itself (the message). The medium thus plays a central role in the way that the message is understood, with different methods of communication impacting the encompassing information in different ways. McLuhan identifies language as a medium "that extends our thoughts from within our minds to others."[27] Therefore, if language, as comprised of specific patterns of words, constitutes a medium in and of itself, then the rhetorical choices that constitute such language will inevitably impact the message being conveyed. At the heart of this is a very simple principle—the way we use language matters. Different words can impact our understandings of issues in different ways, and it is therefore of extreme importance that we choose such words wisely and accurately so as to convey the true meaning of the message at hand. Or, put in McLuhan's terms, we must be mindful of the messages we convey through the medium of language.

Rhetorical actions are especially salient when they reach a large audience, as they do with those in media, seeing as the "mediation of any news event is how we experience such moments of reality."[28] Therefore, the media has a great deal of control over how news events are conveyed to and understood by the general public. Crucial to this phenomenon is the concept of "media framing" which is "the way that a given story is packaged and presented to consumers of news."[29] While this involves several elements, such as the placement of stories and visual aids, language is perhaps the most crucial aspect of framing. Azadeh Aalai states that "language is critical in these presentations because it serves as a cognitive framework in which we understand the world around us and in the case of exposure to news make sense of a given event or story."[30] The language used to convey stories can thus have a drastic impact on the way they are understood. It is important to note that the prominence, or ignorance, embedded in the language of frameworks can happen advertently or inadvertently—after all, as McLuhan notes, language is a medium that conveys our inner thoughts, feelings, and beliefs which can also convey our inner biases. It is therefore imperative to be cognizant of rhetorical actions, seeing as language has the power to perpetuate harmful predispositions or inform renewed understandings of important issues.

The significance of framing can be viewed in hindsight when assessing the portrayal of the Montreal Massacre. In the wake of Lépine's murderous rampage, media coverage of the event was deemed "a second attack" that facilitated "yet another powerful assault on women."[31] This was largely due to the ways in which the Massacre was depoliticized, with many media outlets attempting to negate the gendered basis of the attack altogether. Media reports also repeatedly referred to the victims as "daughters," evoking childlike and helpless sentiments.[32] The use of this word not only made the women, who were studying in a male-dominated field at an elite institution, seem less threatening but overlooked the reason *why* they were targeted in the first place—because they represented a change to the social order.[33] In retrospect, journalists who covered the attack deplored their own stories, with Shelley Page stating, "I fear I sanitized the event of its feminist anger and then infantized and diminished the victims, turning them from elite engineering students who'd fought for a place among men into teddy-bear loving daughters, sisters, and girlfriends."[34] Coverage of the Montreal Massacre, therefore, demonstrates the powerful, albeit dangerous, nature of inaccurate media frames, which in this case, effectively diminished an "anti-feminist attack" to a "tragic event."[35]

The framing of the Montreal Massacre also demonstrates the dangerous assumption that there are two sides to every media story. Deborah Tannen underscores our adversarial debate culture by stating, "our determination to pursue truth by setting up a fight between two sides leads us to believe that every issue has two sides—no more, no less."[36] This assumption proved especially problematic when dealing with the Massacre, an event that presented an opportunity for objective truth in media. Maureen Bradley states, "assuming there are two sides to every story, reporters posed [their] questions rather than simply accepting claims by women's groups and the National Action Committee on the Status of Women."[37] Debate culture not only effectively deemphasized the gendered nature of the attack but introduced opposing frameworks to the "story" that were not applicable, relevant, or respectful.

Past Frameworks: Mental Illness

The problematic framework of mental illness has dominated media portrayals of misogynistic violence, whereby questions surrounding the mental health of perpetrators have superseded their violent acts and hateful motives. A discourse of mental illness has resulted in serious implications for the manner in which misogynistic violence is viewed and understood while simultaneously perpetuating dangerous stigmas surrounding mental health. This was evidenced in coverage surrounding the aftermath of both the Montreal Massacre *and* the Toronto van attack, which displayed striking similarities despite taking place nearly thirty years apart.

In the aftermath of the Massacre at École Polytechnique, Lépine was not deemed a violent misogynist but a "madman" fraught with mental illness. Immediately after the attack, Lépine was described as a "mad killer" by CBC radio—a broad label that negated the fact that he was indeed only a killer of *women*.[38] The narrative continued as Lépine was portrayed as someone who had succumb to his own psychosis, with a psychiatrist proclaiming he was "as innocent as his victims, and himself a victim of an increasingly merciless society."[39] Psychologist Guy Corneau further claimed that the Massacre was the consequence of Lépine having an "absent father" in childhood.[40] Finally, other commentators theorized whether the female death toll in the attack was simply an accident in his rampage, stating that women "just happened to be in the way" of his assault.[41]

Questions of mental illness also permeated the discourse surrounding Alek Minassian and the Toronto van attack. Reports described Minassian as a "disturbed, lonely man" and a "loner who never spoke to anyone."[42] A former classmate of Minassian's even stated that the attack had more to do with mental health than his views towards women, proclaiming, "no, it's not a gender thing. Focus on mental health. There's a lot of people with mental illnesses here, and they're not being helped properly."[43] Several news articles corroborated these statements with other classmates of Minassian's, contesting that his mental health problems date back to his days in high school.[44]

This framework is problematic for numerous reasons. First, focusing on mental illness deemphasizes the gendered motives of perpetrators. A preoccupation with the mental health of both Marc Lépine and Alek Minassian largely negated the fact that the perpetrators blatantly stated their misogynistic intent numerous times, providing direct explanations for their crimes. Lépine made clear that his actions were targeting feminists both *while* he was carrying out his attack and *afterward* in his suicide note, stating that his actions were explicitly for "political reasons."[45] Minassian, on the other hand, declared his allegiance to the incel movement *before* his attack through a post on Facebook and *afterward* while being interrogated by the police.[46] Despite the clear nexus between misogynistic motives and the ensuing violence, the gendered basis for these crimes is ignored in favour of uncorroborated claims of mental illness—a framework that justifies dangerous actions and absolves the attackers of agency for their crimes.

Furthermore, the use of mental illness as a justification for misogynistic actions can misrepresent our understanding of misogyny by depicting it as a mental health problem. While there is no denying that mental health issues may impact or exacerbate certain beliefs, rushing to judge actions as resulting from such can be misleading. Metzl and MacLeish acknowledge the temptation to label those who perpetrate such atrocities—particularly mass shootings—as mentally ill, as they "appear to fall outside the bounds of sanity."[47] However, when discussing extremely violent men, Lundy Bancroft states, "their *value system* is unhealthy, not their psychology," noting that many of these individuals have normal understandings of cause and effect.[48] This is supported by Kate Manne, who states that misogyny is indeed invoked purposefully, with the clear intention of "enforcing and policing social hierarchies."[49] Acts of violent misogyny are not accidental or isolated but intentional—employed with the objective of producing submission, fear, and trauma.

Additionally, this framework perpetuates dangerous stereotypes surrounding the mentally ill. While mental illness can exacerbate harmful behaviour, there is little evidence that identifies it as the *causal* factor in mass violence. According to James L. Knoll and George D. Annas, "the overall contribution of people with serious mental illness to violent crimes is only about 3%," with mass shootings specifically representing "less than 1% of all yearly gun-related homicides."[50] The Canadian Mental Health Association also notes that people with mental illness are, in fact, more likely to be *victims* rather than perpetrators of such acts.[51] The presumption of mental illness should therefore be avoided, as it misrepresents the experience of those dealing with mental health challenges and encourages harmful stereotypes.

Finally, this inaccurate framework hinders the ways in which we understand and thus act upon the issue. William C. Gay states, "when we realize the important connection between language and consciousness, we can also see how changing our language can lead to not only changed thought but also changed action."[52] If our language indeed informs and transforms our actions, it is easy to see why the issue of violent misogyny has been mishandled for so long—a reflection of inadequate language and frameworks influencing inadequate action. Frameworks that reflect the issue of violent misogyny accurately, including its ideological nature and structural basis, can inform understanding that "naturally opens the door to responses aimed at systemic reform, rather than isolated condemnation of a few bad apples."[53] After all, as Anne Thériault states, "we can't fight against violence that we can't name,"[54] and naming these acts as violent extremism and terrorism could drastically impact the way they are fought.

Extremism

Calls to address misogyny as an extremist ideology, or a mode of violent extremism, emerged as more information about mass shooters became readily available to the public. The disclosure of this information drew not one but two conclusions. First, that misogynistic views, specifically those directed towards women who challenge outdated societal archetypes, are a genuine basis for their own brand of extremism. Second, that expressed misogyny is a common thread that connects *other* forms of extremism, identifiable among all well-known extremist groups. However, despite misogyny's seemingly clear connection with extremism, there remain challenges in classifying it as such.

Extremism is a multifaceted term. It can generally be understood as "political ideologies that oppose a societies core values and principles, particularly, any ideology that advocates racial or religious supremacy, or opposes the core principles of democracy and human rights."[55] However, Daniel Kirkpatrick and Recep Onursal note that being considered an extremist "could mean anything from being a nationalist, a communist, to being an animal rights activist," so long as the ideology is extreme in relation to the dominant societal position.[56] It is important to state that holding extremist views does not constitute a crime in and of itself, even if such views are problematic, as freedom of thought, belief, opinion, and expression are protected under the Canadian Constitution through the *Charter of Rights and Freedoms*.[57] However, if violence is incited on account of extremist beliefs, such actions are indeed considered criminal.

Extremist views are most often adopted through the gradual process of radicalization. The Centre for the Prevention of Radicalization Leading to Violence states that while radicalization is a complicated process, it generally includes being influenced by a socio-political issue (either directly or indirectly) and a perceived injustice for which an individual feels entitled to redress.[58] Additionally, a myriad of "vulnerability factors" increases an individual's likelihood of identifying with extremist causes, such as disaffiliation from family and friends, difficult life events, polarizing societal debates, and easily accessible extremist propaganda, among others.[59] Alternatively, a range of "protection factors" may impede the radicalization process, including strong family connections, strong social bonds, critical thinking, empathy, and the presence of counter-extremist discourse in society.[60]

An examination of misogynistic groups, such as incels, shows that they indeed demonstrate all of the aforementioned components of radicalized extremism. Incels are motivated by the socio-political issue of women's rights and feminism, believing that these societal advancements have specifically disadvantaged men. The perceived injustice for which they feel entitled to redress is their "involuntary celibacy," a grievance they blame on feminism, claiming it has restricted their sexual access to women. Personal vulnerabilities are more difficult to discern; however, it can likely be surmised that incels are socially isolated due to the nature of their involuntary celibacy. Additionally, incel community members have acted violently on account of their beliefs—enacting seven attacks in North America—thus crossing the line from extremism into violent extremism.[61] The nature of these groups has even begun to draw comparisons to long-established extremist ideologies, with Steven Crimando stating, "in many ways the path to becoming an incel is no different from the path to other extremist groups like ISIS."[62]

However, labelling misogynistic violence as extremism and violent extremism is not without challenges. Victoria Smith, who writes under the pseudonym Glosswitch, notes that misogyny is not a minority position, as its harm is integral to the many ways in which gendered relations continue to function in our societies and perpetuate structural violence.[63] Smith states, "misogyny isn't extreme if by that we mean 'exceptional' or 'furthest from the center'; on the contrary, using those criteria, the extremist viewpoint would have to be the feminist one."[64] This presents a problem for labelling such acts as extremist, given the uncomfortable truth that misogyny is unfortunately not radical but normalized, ubiquitous, and experienced on a daily basis.

Terrorism

While discussions surrounding the label of terrorism as a framework for misogynistic violence have existed in feminist discourse for some time, it is not until recently that the idea gained traction in mainstream outlets. One of the motivating factors for this push was the Toronto van attack, an event that forced Canadians to grapple with *yet another* misogynistic assault almost thirty years after the Montreal Massacre. These incidents, accompanied by similar attacks in the United States, have fostered growing demand for a more serious designation of these crimes—one that accounts for their political and ideological motives while carrying an integral symbolic value.

A lack of consensus regarding the definition of terrorism has haunted the discipline since its conception. However, in lieu of a universal definition, the term can be broadly understood as "the unlawful use of violence and intimidation, especially against civilians, in the pursuit of political aims."[65] This definition concisely encompasses three essential facets of terrorist acts: a political aim, the use of violence, and the spread of fear. Terrorism stands apart from ordinary crimes as it poses an "existential threat to Canadian society" through acts that "challenge the shape, content, and boundaries of social order."[66] As a general framework, the term also helps us understand *why* violence happens, as "it's useful to distinguish between attacks that are related to intentionally violent social movements and those that emanate from a perpetrators' personal circumstances."[67]

The threat of misogyny-based terrorism has slowly been recognized by several actors in the public sphere. The main actors leading the charge are feminist journalists writing for outlets such as *The Globe and Mail*, *MacLean's*, *The New York Times*, *The Conversation*, and *The*

Guardian, who has brought a considerable amount of attention to the issue. Additionally, institutes such as the Southern Poverty Law Center added misogyny-based websites to its list of hate groups, categorizing "male supremacy" as "a hateful ideology advocating for the subjugation of women."[68] The International Centre for Counter-Terrorism also recognized the "terrorist intent in misogynist violence," stating that online incel communities constitute their own form of extremism.[69] Furthermore, the 2019 Canadian Security Intelligence Service (CSIS) Public Report included gender-driven violence as an example of Ideologically Motivated Violent Extremism (IMVE)[70]—adding to the growing concern of misogynistic violence.

When examining the nature of misogynistic violence, many attacks fit the parameters of the terrorism definition, including the Toronto van attack. Before the attack, Minassian posted the following to Facebook: "The incel rebellion has already begun! We will overthrow all the Chads and Staceys! All hail the supreme gentleman Elliot Rodger!"[71] This post directly states Minassian's *political aim* by referencing the aforementioned black pill ideology, an "incel rebellion," and Elliot Rodger—an incel who committed his own egregious act of violence in the United States. Minassian's post also "announces that the revolution has begun, in the form of his attack," demonstrating a nexus between his *political aim* and *an act of violence* resulting in the death of ten individuals.[72] Furthermore, his attack fulfilled the remaining facet of the terrorism definition by *instilling fear* into Canadian society through his ideologically motivated violence—with one victim stating she "is terrified there are other men like Alek Minassian."[73] However, despite these attacks meeting the conceptual qualifications of terrorist violence, they have traditionally not been recognized as such under the law.

Sara Meger facetiously states, "when is terrorism not terrorism? When the political motivations are misogyny."[74] Meger's statement speaks to the significant challenges encountered by those labelling misogynistic violence as terrorism, not only in discourse but in fact and law. Under the Criminal Code of Canada, the legal definition of terrorism has two factors. Terrorism is considered an act or omission, in or outside of Canada, "that is committed in whole or in part for a political, religious or ideological purpose, objective, or cause" with "the intention of intimidating the public, or a segment of the public, with regard to its security, including its economic security."[75] Such acts are designed to intentionally cause death or serious bodily harm, endanger a person's life, cause a risk to public health or safety, cause substantial property damage, or serious interference or disruption of essential services or facilities.[76] Under this definition, there is nothing impeding acts of violent misogyny from being treated as terrorism in Canada. However, terrorism is treated as an aggravating factor, increasing the severity of "ordinary crimes."[77] In these cases, elevated charges are also accompanied by an elevated burden of proof for the prosecution—one that has traditionally not been sought despite the legal legitimacy it would provide to victims. This is largely because "in both domestic and international law, women's experiences have been largely trivialized, overlooked, or relegated to the private sphere of concern because the law has been grounded in the experience of men."[78] The sad and understated truth is that we do not deem attacks perpetrated on account of gender as worthy of the label of terrorism, and the additional legal work associated with it, in the same manner, that we do for crimes undertaken on the basis of racial, religious, or cultural grounds. It has been continually perceived as *less important*.

Canada and Misogynistic Violence: The Bigger Picture

Despite violent misogyny fulfilling the categorical and legal requirements to be recognized as extremism and terrorism, it has rarely been acknowledged as such. This is largely because these acts are but one small aspect of an even larger issue in Canada: the casual acceptance of male violence against women. The ubiquity of the problem is exhibited through various forms of gendered violence and oppression, all of which threaten the human rights of women in the country and maintain structures of inequality.

Male violence against women in Canada poses a threat in nearly all aspects of modern life. Home continues to be the most dangerous place for women, with domestic violence being "the most common form of violence against women in Canada."[79] Sexual violence also remains prevalent, with sexual assault being the only form of violent crime that hasn't declined in the past decade.[80] Additionally, rates of femicide are alarmingly high, with one woman or girl being killed every other day in the country, along with one woman being killed by her intimate partner each week.[81] Women are also at greater risk for experiencing violence at work, with an examination of federal data stating that "women [are] at more than twice the risk of workplace violence compared to men."[82] Furthermore, women and girls are more likely to experience online hate and cyber violence, constituting "67% of the victims of police-reported intimidation on the internet."[83] Lastly, victims of human trafficking also continue to be profoundly gendered, with 95% of all victims being women and 70% of all victims being women under the age of 25.[84] Women in Canada are therefore barraged with the possibility of violence on multiple fronts, making violence both "a cause and consequence of inequality."[85]

Furthermore, violence impacts different women in different ways. For instance, disabled women in Canada are twice as likely to be victims of violence in comparison to non-disabled women.[86] Meanwhile, members of the 2SLGBTQ+ community—particularly bisexual women—are "seven times more likely to report experiencing sexual assault than their heterosexual counterparts."[87] Additionally, Indigenous women and girls face horrific and disproportionate amounts of violence, with the national homicide rate for Indigenous women in Canada being *seven* times higher than that of non-Indigenous women.[88] The issue has become so ubiquitous that the Interim Report distributed by the National Inquiry into Missing and Murdered Indigenous Girls states, "with all the information we have, we still don't know how many Indigenous women and girls are missing or have been murdered."[89] The final draft of the Inquiries' report concluded that colonial practices which have inflicted a disproportionate amount of violence against Indigenous women and girls constitute colonial genocide, highlighting the failure to protect Indigenous women and girls from human trafficking; disproportionate physical, sexual, and mental abuse; and forced sterilization, among *many* other issues.[90] Therefore, while violence against women may be ubiquitous in Canada, for some, the risk is exponentially higher.

The aforementioned statistics demonstrate that much work remains to be done in order to eradicate male violence against women in Canada. When viewed within this framework, the failure to recognize misogynistic violence as extremism, violent extremism, and terrorism is indeed far less shocking. However, with emerging understandings of these issues, a renewed sense of hope has emerged, as Canadian society is presented with a monumental opportunity for change.

Conclusion

The labels of extremism, violent extremism, and terrorism for acts of violent misogyny are not only applicable but necessary. Past frameworks have failed to convey the gendered motivations for these crimes while introducing the harmful narrative of mental illness. This emerging framework more adequately addresses the political and ideological basis for misogynistic attacks, presenting a more serious designation for this type of violence. It furthermore provides the rhetorical, factual, and legal tools necessary to combat the issue. The use of this new framework brings new possibilities, ones that bring us closer to making real change and creating true equality—and as it happens, Canada currently has the opportunity to do just that.

On a February afternoon in 2020, a 17-year-old boy walked into a Toronto massage parlour armed with a machete. His attack claimed one victim, a 24-year-old woman, and wounded one other.[91] Shortly after the incident, authorities uncovered evidence that the assault was motivated by the incel ideology.[92] In a joint press conference held by the Toronto Police and Royal Canadian Mounted Police, it was announced that the perpetrator (who cannot be named due to his status as a minor) would be charged with terrorism in connection to his crime, marking "the first time police in Canada have formally acknowledged an alleged misogynistic crime as terrorism."[93] While the outcome of the case has yet to be determined, it has the opportunity to become a "legal landmark" in the way that misogynistic violence is treated in Canada.[94]

After facing numerous attacks, Canada is presented with a monumental opportunity to change the framework of misogynistic violence. The importance of a new designation for these crimes cannot be understated. Rebeca Solnit states that "language is power. When you turn 'torture' into 'enhanced interrogation' or 'murdered children' into 'collateral damage,' you break the power of language to convey meaning, to make us see, feel, and care."[95] For too long, language has been a driving force in disguising the true nature of these crimes. We have turned "misogynist extremists" and "misogynist terrorists" into "mentally ill attackers" and "tragic incidents." However, this is the transformative power of language; as Solnit states, "you can use the power of words to bury meaning or excavate it."[96] We failed to acknowledge and label past atrocities for what they were. However, we are now presented with an opportunity to rectify the biases of the past while building a more hopeful future for women everywhere—and we must take it.

Discussion Questions

1. How are different jurisdictions responding to the threat of incel violence?
2. Which "vulnerability factors" are most likely to lead to the adoption of a gender-based extremist ideology?
3. How can incel groups be prevented from committing acts of violence?
4. What societal changes need to be enacted in order to address the broader problem of male violence against women?

Notes

1. Elizabeth Renzetti, "Violent Misogyny Is a Threat to Half Our Population. We Need to Call It What It Is: Terrorism," *The Globe and Mail*, November 30, 2019, https://www.theglobeandmail.com/opinion/article-violent-misogyny-is-a-threat-to-half-our-population-we-need-to-call/.
2. Mélissa Blais and Francis Dupuis-Déri, "The Montreal Massacre Is Finally Recognized as an Anti-Feminist Attack," *The Conversation*, December 6, 2019, https://theconversation.com/the-montreal-massacre-is-finally-recognized-as-an-anti-feminist-attack-128450.
3. Peter Langman, "Marc Lépine's Suicide Note," last modified July 29, 2014, 2, https://schoolshooters.info/sites/default/files/lepine_note_1.1.pdf.
4. Molly Hayes, "Years Before Toronto Van Attack, Alek Minassian Says He Connected Online with Misogynistic Radicals," *The Globe and Mail*, September 27, 2019, https://www.theglobeandmail.com/canada/toronto/article-years-before-toronto-van-attack-alek-minassian-says-he-connected/.
5. *Merriam-Webster*, online, May 27, 2020, s.v. "Misogyny," https://www.merriam-webster.com/dictionary/misogyny.
6. Nikila Kaushik, "Misogyny and the Limits of Language," *Women's Policy Journal of Harvard* 12 (2018): 57, https://gpj.hkspublications.org/wp-content/uploads/sites/23/2019/10/WPJ-Internal-2018-Final-pdf.pdf.
7. Kate Manne, *Down Girl: The Logic of Misogyny* (New York: Oxford University Press, 2018), 33.
8. Sean Illing, "What We Get Wrong About Misogyny," *Vox*, March 7, 2020, https://www.vox.com/identities/2017/12/5/16705284/elizabeth-warren-loss-2020-sexism-misogyny-kate-manne.

9. Berit Brogaard, "What Is Misogyny, Anyway?" *Psychology Today*, March 5, 2015, https://www.psychologytoday.com/ca/blog/the-mysteries-love/201503/what-is-misogyny-anyway.
10. Rebecca Cohen, "Welcome to the Manosphere: A Brief Guide to the Controversial Men's Rights Movement," *Mother Jones*, January 2015, https://www.motherjones.com/politics/2015/01/manosphere-mens-rights-movement-terms/.
11. Cohen, "Welcome to the Manosphere."
12. Cohen, "Welcome to the Manosphere."
13. Zach Beauchamp, "Our Incel Problem," *Vox*, April 23, 2019, https://www.vox.com/the-highlight/2019/4/16/18287446/incel-definition-reddit.
14. David Futrelle, "Incels Hail Toronto Van Driver Who Killed 10 as a New Elliot Rodger, Talk of Future Acid Attacks and Mass Rapes," *We Hunted the Mammoth* (Blog), April 24, 2018, http://www.wehuntedthemammoth.com/2018/04/24/incels-hail-toronto-van-driver-who-killed-10-as-a-new-elliot-rodger-talk-of-future-acid-attacks-and-mass-rapes/.
15. Peter Baker, "The Woman Who Accidentally Started the Incel Movement," *Elle Fashion*, March 1, 2016, https://www.elle.com/culture/news/a34512/woman-who-started-incel-movement/.
16. Baker, "The Woman Who Accidentally."
17. Caroline Orr, "Canada Occupies Unique Space in 'Manosphere' of Extremist Violence," *National Observer*, August 26, 2019, https://www.nationalobserver.com/2019/08/26/analysis/canada-occupies-unique-space-manosphere-extremist-violence.
18. Emma Jane, *Misogyny Online: A Short (and Brutish) History* (London: SAGE, 2017), 3.
19. Christine Hauser, "Reddit Bans' Incel' Group for Inciting Violence Against Women," *The New York Times*, November 9, 2017, https://www.nytimes.com/2017/11/09/technology/incels-reddit-banned.html.
20. Laura Hudson, "The Internet Is Enabling a Group of Men Who Want to Kill Women. They Need to Be Stopped," *The Verge*, April 25, 2018, https://www.theverge.com/2018/4/25/17279294/toronto-massacre-minassian-incels-internet-misogyny.
21. Stewart Bell, "Despite Crackdown on Incels, Their Discussion Forums Are Still Online," *Global News*, June 9, 2020, 1, https://globalnews.ca/news/7022100/incel-discussion-forums-still-online-crackdown/.
22. Julie Bosman, Kate Taylor, and Tim Arango, "A Common Trait Among Mass Killers: Hatred Toward Women," *The New York Times*, August 10, 2019, https://www.nytimes.com/2019/08/10/us/mass-shootings-misogyny-dayton.html?searchResultPosition=1.
23. Pablo Castillo Díaz and Nahla Valji, "Symbiosis of Misogyny and Violent Extremism: New Understandings and Policy Implications," *Journal of*

International Affairs 72, no. 2 (2019): 44, https://www.proquest.com/docview/2297100574?accountid=15067.

24. Amanda Taub, "Control and Fear: What Mass Killings and Domestic Violence Have in Common," *The New York Times*, June 15, 2016, https://www.nytimes.com/2016/06/16/world/americas/control-and-fear-what-mass-killings-and-domestic-violence-have-in-common.html.
25. Robyn Urback, "Terrorist? Misogynist? Labelling the Toronto Van Attacker a Pointless Exercise: Robyn Urback," *CBC News*, April 25, 2018, https://www.cbc.ca/news/opinion/toronto-van-attack-1.4633641.
26. Marshall McLuhan, *Understanding Media: The Extensions of Man* (Cambridge, MA: MIT Press, 1964), 1, https://web.mit.edu/allanmc/www/mcluhan.mediummessage.pdf.
27. Mark Federman, "What Is the Meaning of the Medium Is the Message?" last modified 2004, 2, http://individual.utoronto.ca/markfederman/MeaningTheMediumistheMessage.pdf.
28. Maureen Bradley, "Report: Reframing the Montreal Massacre: Strategies for Feminist Media Activism," *Canadian Journal of Communication* 31, no. 4 (2006): 930, https://www.cjc-online.ca/index.php/journal/article/viewFile/1869/1956
29. Azadeh, Aalai, "Media Framing Effects," *Psychology Today*, June 21, 2017, https://www.psychologytoday.com/ca/blog/the-first-impression/201706/media-framing-effects.
30. Azadeh Aalai, "Media Framing Effects."
31. Maureen Bradley, "Reframing the Montreal Massacre," Vimeo, October 10, 2009, video, 2:47, https://vimeo.com/6996357.
32. Bradley, "Reframing the Montreal Massacre," 15:35.
33. Bradley, "Reframing the Montreal Massacre," 16:20.
34. Shelley Page, "Page: How I Sanitized the Feminist Outrage over the Montreal Massacre," *Ottawa Citizen*, December 6, 2014, https://ottawacitizen.com/opinion/columnists/page-how-i-sanitized-the-feminist-outrage-over-the-montreal-massacre/.
35. Sidhartha Banerjee, "Polytechnique: Consensus Comes 30 Years Later That Massacre Was an Anti-Feminist Act," *CTV News Montreal*, December 6, 2019, https://montreal.ctvnews.ca/polytechnique-consensus-comes-30-years-later-that-massacre-was-an-anti-feminist-act-1.4717274.
36. Deborah Tannen, *The Argument Culture* (New York: Ballantine Books, 1998), 10.
37. Bradley, "Report: Reframing the Montreal Massacre," 934.
38. Blais and Dupuis-Déri, "The Montreal Massacre."
39. Julie Bindel, "The Montreal Massacre: Canada's Feminists Remember," *The Guardian*, December 3, 2012, https://www.theguardian.com/world/2012/dec/03/montreal-massacre-canadas-feminists-remember.

40. Blais and Dupuis-Déri, "The Montreal Massacre."
41. Bindel, "The Montreal Massacre: Canada's Feminists Remember."
42. Stewart Bell, "He Wasn't a Terrorist: Those Who Knew Alek Minassian Struggle to Explain the Toronto Van Attack," *Global News*, April 26, 2018, https://globalnews.ca/news/4168222/he-wasnt-terrorist-toronto-attack/.
43. Bell, "He Wasn't a Terrorist."
44. Jeremy Grimaldi, "Alleged Attacker Alek Minassian May Have Mental Health Issues," *York Region*, April 24, 2018, https://www.yorkregion.com/news-story/8566082-update-alleged-attacker-alek-minassian-may-have-mental-health-issues/.
45. Langman, "Marc Lépine's Suicide Note," 2.
46. Stewart Bell and Andrew Russell, "Day of Retribution: Toronto Van Attack Suspect Describes Hatred Towards Women as Motive," *Global News*, September 29, 2019, https://globalnews.ca/news/5954272/toronto-van-attack-suspect-motive-interrogation-video/.
47. Jonathan M. Metzl and Kenneth T. MacLeish, "Mental Illness, Mass Shootings, and the Politics of American Firearms," *American Journal of Public Health* 105, no. 2 (2015): 240, 10.2105/AJPH.2014.302242.
48. Lundy Bancroft, *Why Does He Do That? Inside the Minds of Angry and Controlling Men* (NY: Penguin Group, 2002), 38.
49. Regan Penaluna, "Kate Manne: The Shock Collar That Is Misogyny," *Guernica*, February 7, 2018, https://www.guernicamag.com/kate-manne-why-misogyny-isnt-really-about-hating-women/.
50. James L. Knoll and George D. Annas, "Mass Shootings and Mental Illness," in *Gun Violence and Mental Illness*, ed. Liza H. Gold and Robert I. Simon (VA: American Psychiatric Association Publishing, 2016), 81.
51. "The Myth of Violence and Mental Illness," Canadian Mental Health Association, accessed March 24, 2020, https://cmhadurham.ca/finding-help/the-myth-of-violence-and-mental-illness/.
52. William C. Gay, "Supplanting Linguistic Violence" in *Gender Violence: Interdisciplinary Perspectives*, ed. Laura L. O'Toole, Jessica R. Schiffman and Margie L. Kiter Edwards (NY: New York University Press, 2007), 441.
53. Kaushik, "Misogyny and the Limits of Language," 57.
54. Anne Thériault, "Anne Thériault: Marc Lépine Didn't Want to Kill Women, He Wanted to Kill Feminists," last modified December 6, 2018, https://www.flare.com/news/marc-lepine-feminists/.
55. Peter R. Neumann, *Prisons and Terrorism: Radicalization and De-Radicalization in 15 Countries* (London: International Centre for the Study of Radicalization and Political Violence, 2010), 12, https://www.clingendael.org/sites/default/files/pdfs/Prisons-and-terrorism-15-countries.pdf.

56. Daniel Kirkpatrick and Recep Onursal, "Not All Types of Extremism are Terrorism–Conflating the Two Is Dangerous," *The Conversation*, September 11, 2019, https://theconversation.com/not-all-types-of-extremism-are-terrorism-conflating-the-two-is-dangerous-116211.
57. Canada Centre for Community Engagement and the Prevention of Violence, *National Strategy on Countering Radicalization to Violence* (Canada Centre for Community Engagement and the Prevention of Violence, 2018), 7, https://www.publicsafety.gc.ca/cnt/rsrcs/pblctns/ntnl-strtg-cntrng-rdclztn-vlnc/ntnl-strtg-cntrng-rdclztn-vlnc-en.pdf.
58. "The Radicalization Process," Centre for the Prevention of Radicalization Leading to Violence, accessed March 26, 2020, 1, https://info-radical.org/en/the-radicalization-process/.
59. "The Radicalization Process," 1.
60. "The Radicalization Process," 1.
61. Alex DiBranco, "Male Supremacist Terrorism as a Rising Threat," *International Centre for Counter-Terrorism*, February 10, 2020, https://icct.nl/publication/male-supremacist-terrorism-as-a-rising-threat/.
62. Steven Crimando, "Alone Together and Angry: An Incel Revolution," *ASIS International*, March 1, 2019, https://www.asisonline.org/security-management-magazine/articles/2019/03/alone-together-and-angry-an-incel-revolution/.
63. Victoria Smith, "If We're Tackling All Forms of Extremism, We Need to Include Misogyny," *Independent*, June 21, 2017, https://www.independent.co.uk/voices/extremism-misogyny-need-to-tackle-it-a7800411.html.
64. Smith, "If We're Tackling All."
65. "Terrorism," *Lexico*, accessed March 25, 2020, https://www.lexico.com/en/definition/terrorism.
66. Heidi Matthews, "If Misogyny Was a Factor, Is Toronto Rampage a Terrorist Act Against Women?" *The Conversation*, April 27, 2018, https://theconversation.com/if-misogyny-was-a-factor-is-toronto-rampage-a-terrorist-act-against-women-95633.
67. J.M. Berger, "The Difference Between a Killer and a Terrorist," *The Atlantic*, April 26, 2018, https://www.theatlantic.com/politics/archive/2018/04/the-difference-between-killer-and-terrorist/558998/.
68. "Male Supremacy," Southern Poverty Law Center, accessed March 22, 2020, https://www.splcenter.org/fighting-hate/extremist-files/ideology/male-supremacy.
69. DiBranco, "Male Supremacist Terrorism."
70. Canadian Security Intelligence Service, *CSIS Public Report 2019* (Ottawa: Canadian Security Intelligence Service, 2020), 13, https://www.canada.ca/content/dam/csis-scrs/documents/publications/PubRep-2019-E.pdf

71. Patrick Cain, "What We Learned from Alek Minassian's Incel-Linked Facebook Page—And What We'd Like to Know," *Global News*, October 2, 2019, https://globalnews.ca/news/4164340/alek-minassian-facebook-page/.
72. Berger, "The Difference."
73. "Victim of Toronto Van Attack 'Very Scared' There Are Others Like Minassian," *CBC News*, November 15, 2020, https://www.cbc.ca/news/canada/toronto/ont-alek-minassian-victims-1.5802831.
74. Sara Meger, "When Is Terrorism Not Terrorism?" *Gender and War* (Blog), April 26, 2018, http://www.genderandwar.com/2018/04/26/when-is-terrorism-not-terrorism/.
75. *Criminal Code*, RSC 1985, c. C-46, s 83(1)(b).
76. *Criminal Code*, RSC 1985, c. C-46, s 83(1)(b).
77. Matthews, "If Misogyny Was a Factor."
78. Meger, "When Is Terrorism Not Terrorism?"
79. UN Human Rights Council, *Visit to Canada: Report of the Special Rapporteur on Violence Against Women, Its Causes and Consequences*, UN Doc A/HRC/41/42 (3 June 2019) at 12, https://documents-dds-ny.un.org/doc/UNDOC/GEN/G19/317/19/PDF/G1931719.pdf?OpenElement.
80. Samuel Perreault, *Criminal Victimization in Canada, 2014* (Ottawa: Statistics Canada, 2015), 5, https://www150.statcan.gc.ca/n1/pub/85-002-x/2015001/article/14241-eng.pdf.
81. "Femicide Is Preventable," Canadian Femicide Observatory for Justice and Accountability, accessed January 11, 2021, 1, https://www.femicideincanada.ca/.
82. Stephanie Lanthier, Amber Bielecky and Peter M. Smith, "Examining Risk of Workplace Violence in Canada: A Sex/Gender-Based Analysis," *Annals of Work Exposures and Health* 62, no. 8 (2018), 1012, https://doi.org/10.1093/annweh/wxy066.
83. "The Facts about Online Hate and Cyberviolence Against Women and Girls," *Canadian Women's Foundation* online, July 2019, https://canadianwomen.org/the-facts/online-hate-and-cyberviolence/.
84. Dyna Ibrahim, *Trafficking in Persons in Canada, 2016* (Ottawa: Statistics Canada, 2018), 1, https://www150.statcan.gc.ca/n1/pub/85-005-x/2018001/article/54979-eng.pdf.
85. Selim Jahan, "Violence Against Women, a Cause and Consequence of Inequality," *United Nations Development Programme*, November 19, 2018, https://www.undp.org/content/undp/en/home/blog/2018/violence-against-women-cause-consequence-inequality.html.
86. Adam Cotter, *Violent Victimization of Women with Disabilities, 2014* (Ottawa: Statistics Canada, 2018), 1, https://www150.statcan.gc.ca/n1/en/pub/85-002-x/2018001/article/54910-eng.pdf?st=JheRgYzv.

87. Laura Simpson, *Violent Victimization of Lesbians, Gays and Bisexuals in Canada, 2014* (Ottawa: Statistics Canada, 2018), 1, https://www150.statcan.gc.ca/n1/en/pub/85-002-x/2018001/article/54923-eng.pdf?st=QuvaUPTj.
88. Amnesty International, *Violence Against Indigenous Women and Girls in Canada: A Summary of Amnesty International's Concerns and Call to Action* (Ottawa: Amnesty International Canada, 2014), 2, https://www.amnesty.ca/sites/amnesty/files/iwfa_submission_amnesty_international_february_2014_-_final.pdf.
89. National Inquiry into Missing and Murdered Indigenous Women and Girls, *Interim Report: Our Women and Girls are Sacred* (Ottawa: National Inquiry into Missing and Murdered Indigenous Women and Girls, 2018), 3, https://www.mmiwg-ffada.ca/wp-content/uploads/2018/03/ni-mmiwg-interim-report.pdf.
90. National Inquiry into Missing and Murdered Indigenous Women and Girls, *Reclaiming Power and Place: The Final Report of the National Inquiry into Missing and Murdered Indigenous Women and Girls, Volume 1a* (Ottawa: National Inquiry into Missing and Murdered Indigenous Women and Girls, 2019), 53, https://www.mmiwg-ffada.ca/wp-content/uploads/2019/06/Final_Report_Vol_1a-1.pdf.
91. Molly Hayes and Colin Freeze, "Police Lay First Terrorism Charge for Toronto Case Involving Misogyny," *The Globe and Mail*, May 19, 2020, https://www.theglobeandmail.com/canada/article-police-lay-first-terrorism-charge-for-toronto-case-involving-misogyny/.
92. Hayes and Freeze, "Police Lay First Terrorism Charge," 1.
93. Hayes and Freeze, "Police Lay First Terrorism Charge," 1.
94. Hayes and Freeze, "Police Lay First Terrorism Charge," 1.
95. Rebecca Solnit, *Men Explain Things to Me* (Chicago: Haymarket Books, 2014), 129.
96. Solnit, *Men Explain Things to Me*, 129.

Bibliography

Aalai, Azadeh. "Media Framing Effects." *Psychology Today*, June 21, 2017. https://www.psychologytoday.com/ca/blog/the-first-impression/201706/media-framing-effects.

Amnesty International. *Violence Against Indigenous Women and Girls in Canada: A Summary of Amnesty International's Concerns and Calls to Action*. Ontario: Amnesty International, 2014. https://www.amnesty.ca/sites/amnesty/files/iwfa_submission_amnesty_international_february_2014_-_final.pdf.

Baker, Peter. "The Woman Who Accidentally Started the Incel Movement." *Elle Fashion*, March 1, 2016. https://www.elle.com/culture/news/a34512/woman-who-started-incel-movement/.

Bancroft, Lundy. *Why Does He Do That? Inside the Minds of Angry and Controlling Men*. New York: Penguin Group, 2002.

Banerjee, Sidhartha. "Polytechnique: Consensus Comes 30 Years Later That Massacre Was an Anti-Feminist Act." *CTV News Montreal*, December 6, 2019. https://montreal.ctvnews.ca/polytechnique-consensus-comes-30-years-later-that-massacre-was-an-anti-feminist-act-1.4717274.

Beauchamp, Zach. "Our Incel Problem." *Vox*, April 23, 2019. https://www.vox.com/the-highlight/2019/4/16/18287446/incel-definition-reddit.

Bell, Stewart. "Despite Crackdown on Incels, Their Discussion Forums Are Still Online." *Global News*, June 9, 2020. https://globalnews.ca/news/7022100/incel-discussion-forums-still-online-crackdown/.

Bell, Stewart. "He Wasn't a Terrorist: Those Who Knew Alek Minassian Struggle to Explain the Toronto Van Attack." *Global News*, April 26, 2018. https://globalnews.ca/news/4168222/he-wasnt-terrorist-toronto-attack/.

Bell, Stewart, and Andrew Russell. "Day of Retribution: Toronto Van Attack Suspect Describes Hatred Towards Women as Motive." *Global News*, September 29, 2019. https://globalnews.ca/news/5954272/toronto-van-attack-suspect-motive-interrogation-video/.

Berger, J. M. "The Difference Between a Killer and a Terrorist." *The Atlantic*, April 26, 2018. https://www.theatlantic.com/politics/archive/2018/04/the-difference-between-killer-and-terrorist/558998/.

Bindel, Julie. "The Montreal Massacre: Canada's Feminists Remember." *The Guardian*, December 3, 2012. https://www.theguardian.com/world/2012/dec/03/montreal-massacre-canadas-feminists-remember.

Blais, Mélissa, and Francis Dupuis-Deri. "The Montreal Massacre Is Finally Recognized as an Anti-Feminist Attack." *The Conversation*, December 6, 2019. https://theconversation.com/the-montreal-massacre-is-finally-recognized-as-an-anti-feminist-attack-128450.

Bosman, Julie, Kate Taylor, and Tim Arango. "A Common Trait Among Mass Killers: Hatred Toward Women." *The New York Times*, August 10, 2019. https://www.nytimes.com/2019/08/10/us/mass-shootings-misogyny-dayton.html?searchResultPosition=1.

Bradley, Maureen. "Reframing the Montreal Massacre." *Vimeo*, October 10, 2009. Video, 27:37. https://vimeo.com/6996357.

Bradley, Maureen. "Report: Reframing the Montreal Massacre: Strategies for Feminist Media Activism." *Canadian Journal of Communication* 31, no. 4 (2006): 929–936. https://www.cjc-online.ca/index.php/journal/article/viewFile/1869/1956.

Brogaard, Berit. "What Is Misogyny, Anyway?" *Psychology Today*, March 5, 2015. https://www.psychologytoday.com/ca/blog/the-mysteries-love/201503/what-is-misogyny-anyway.

Cain, Patrick. "What We Learned from Alek Minassian's Incel-Linked Facebook Page—And What We'd Like to Know." *Global News*, October 2, 2019. https://globalnews.ca/news/4164340/alek-minassian-facebook-page/.

Canada Centre for Community Engagement and Prevention of Violence. *National Strategy on Countering Radicalization to Violence*. Canada Centre for Community Engagement and Prevention of Violence, 2018. https://www.publicsafety.gc.ca/cnt/rsrcs/pblctns/ntnl-strtg-cntrng-rdclztn-vlnc/ntnl-strtg-cntrng-rdclztn-vlnc-en.pdf.

Canadian Security Intelligence Service. *CSIS Public Report 2019*. Canadian Security Intelligence Service, 2020. https://www.canada.ca/content/dam/csis-scrs/documents/publications/PubRep-2019-E.pdf.

Castillo Díaz, Pablo, and Nahla Valji. "Symbiosis of Misogyny and Violent Extremism: New Understandings and Policy Implications." *Journal of International Affairs* 72, no. 2 (2019): 37–56. http://uml.idm.oclc.org/login?url=http://search.ebscohost.com/login.aspx?direct=true&db=a9h&AN=138663343&site=ehost-live.

Cohen, Rebecca. "Welcome to the Manosphere: A Brief Guide to the Controversial Men's Rights Movement." *Mother Jones*, January 2015. https://www.motherjones.com/politics/2015/01/manosphere-mens-rights-movement-terms/.

Cotter, Adam. *Violent Victimization of Women with Disabilities, 2014*. Ottawa: Statistics Canada, 2018. https://www150.statcan.gc.ca/n1/en/pub/85-002-x/2018001/article/54910-eng.pdf?st=JheRgYzv.

Crimando, Steven. "Alone Together and Angry: An Incel Revolution." *ASIS International*, March 1, 2019. https://www.asisonline.org/security-management-magazine/articles/2019/03/alone-together-and-angry-an-incel-revolution/.

Criminal Code, R.S.A. 1985, c. C-46.

Dibranco, Alex. "Male Supremacist Terrorism as a Rising Threat." *International Centre for Counter-Terrorism*, February 10, 2020. https://icct.nl/publication/male-supremacist-terrorism-as-a-rising-threat/.

"The Facts About Online Hate and Cyberviolence Against Women and Girls in Canada." *Canadian Women's Foundation* online, July 2019. https://canadianwomen.org/the-facts/online-hate-and-cyberviolence/.

Federman, Mark. "What Is the Meaning of the Medium Is the Message?" Last modified 2004. https://webspace.ringling.edu/~dsteilin/Lit%20and%20Media%20Studies%20Resources/McLuhan/What%20is%20the%20Meaning%20of%20The%20Medium%20is%20the%20-%20Mark%20Federman.pdf.

"Femicide is Preventable." Canadian Femicide Observatory for Justice and Accountability. Accessed January 11, 2021. https://www.femicideincanada.ca/.

Gay, William C. "Supplanting Linguistic Violence." In *Gender Violence: Interdisciplinary Perspectives*, edited by Laura L. O'Toole, Jessica R. Schiffman, and Margie L. Kiter Edwards, 435–442. NY: New York University Press, 2007.

Grimaldi, Jeremy. "Alleged Attacker Alek Minassian May Have Had Mental Health Issues." *York Region*, April 24, 2018. https://www.yorkregion.com/news-story/8566082-update-alleged-attacker-alek-minassian-may-have-mental-health-issues/.

Hayes, Molly. "Years Before Toronto Van Attack, Alek Minassian Says He Connected Online with Misogynistic Radicals." *The Globe and Mail*, September 27, 2019. https://www.theglobeandmail.com/canada/toronto/article-years-before-toronto-van-attack-alek-minassian-says-he-connected/.

Hayes, Molly, and Colin Freeze. "Police Lay First Terrorism Charge for Toronto Case Involving Misogyny." *The Globe and Mail*, May 19, 2020. https://www.theglobeandmail.com/canada/article-police-lay-first-terrorism-charge-for-toronto-case-involving-misogyny/.

Hauser, Christine. "Reddit Bans 'Incel' Group for Inciting Violence Against Women." *The New York Times*, November 9, 2017. https://www.nytimes.com/2017/11/09/technology/incels-reddit-banned.html.

Hudson, Laura. "The Internet Is Enabling a Community of Men Who Want to Kill Women. They Need to Be Stopped." *The Verge*, April 25, 2018. https://www.theverge.com/2018/4/25/17279294/toronto-massacre-minassian-incels-internet-misogyny.

Ibrahim, Dyna. "Trafficking in Persons in Canada, 2016." Last modified June 27, 2018. https://www150.statcan.gc.ca/n1/pub/85-005-x/2018001/article/54979-eng.htm.

Illing, Sean. "What We Get Wrong About Misogyny." *Vox*, March 7, 2020. https://www.vox.com/identities/2017/12/5/16705284/elizabeth-warren-loss-2020-sexism-misogyny-kate-manne.

Jahan, Selim. "Violence Against Women, a Cause and Consequence of Inequality." Last modified November 19, 2018. https://www.undp.org/content/undp/en/home/blog/2018/violence-against-women-cause-consequence-inequality.html.

Jane, Emma. *Misogyny Online: A Short (and Brutish) History*. UK: Sage, 2017.

Kaushik, Nikila. "Misogyny and the Limits of Language." *Women's Policy Journal of Harvard* 12 (2018): 56–59. https://gpj.hkspublications.org/wp-content/uploads/sites/23/2019/10/WPJ-Internal-2018-Final-pdf.pdf.

Kirkpatrick, Daniel, and Recep Onursal. "Not All Types of Extremism Are Terrorism—Conflating the Two Is Dangerous." *The Conversation*, September 11, 2019. https://theconversation.com/not-all-types-of-extremism-are-terrorism-conflating-the-two-is-dangerous-116211.

Knoll, James L., and George D. Annas. "Mass Shooting and Mental Illness." In *Gun Violence and Mental Illness*, edited by Liza H. Gold and Robert I. Simon, 81–104. VA: American Psychiatric Association Publishing, 2016.

Langman, Peter. "Marc Lépine's Suicide Note." Last modified July 29, 2014. https://schoolshooters.info/sites/default/files/lepine_note_1.1.pdf.

Lanthier, Stephanie, Amber Bielecky, and Peter M. Smith. "Examining Risk of Workplace Violence in Canada: A Sex/Gender Based Analysis." *Annals of Work Exposures and Health* 62, no. 8 (2018): 1012–1020. https://academic.oup.com/annweh/article/62/8/1012/5054840?login=true.

"Male Supremacy." Southern Poverty Law Center. Accessed March 22, 2020. https://www.splcenter.org/fighting-hate/extremist-files/ideology/male-supremacy

Manne, Kate. *Down Girl: The Logic of Misogyny*. New York: Oxford University Press, 2018.

Matthews, Heidi. "If Misogyny Was a Factor, Is Toronto Rampage a Terrorist Act Against Women?" *The Conversation*, April 27, 2018. https://theconversation.com/if-misogyny-was-a-factor-is-toronto-rampage-a-terrorist-act-against-women-95633.

McLuhan, Marshall. *Understanding Media: The Extensions of Man*. Cambridge: MIT Press, 1964. https://web.mit.edu/allanmc/www/mcluhan.mediummessage.pdf.

Meger, Sara. "When Is Terrorism Not Terrorism?" *Gender and War* (Blog), April 26, 2018. http://www.genderandwar.com/2018/04/26/when-is-terrorism-not-terrorism/.

Metzl, Jonathan M., and Kenneth T. MacLeish. "Mental Illness, Mass Shooting, and the Politics of American Firearms." *American Journal of Public Health* 105, no. 2 (2015): 240–249. https://doi.org/10.2105/AJPH.2014.302242

"The Myth of Violence and Mental Illness." Canadian Mental Health Association. Accessed March 24, 2020. https://cmhadurham.ca/finding-help/the-myth-of-violence-and-mental-illness/.

National Inquiry into Missing and Murdered Indigenous Women and Girls. *Interim Report: Our Women and Girls Are Sacred*. National Inquiry into Missing and Murdered Indigenous Women and Girls, 2018. https://www.mmiwg-ffada.ca/wp-content/uploads/2018/03/ni-mmiwg-interim-report.pdf.

National Inquiry into Missing and Murdered Indigenous Women and Girls. *Reclaiming Power and Place: The Final Report of the National Inquiry into Missing and Murdered Indigenous Women and Girls, Volume 1a*. National Inquiry into Missing and Murdered Indigenous Women and Girls, 2019. https://www.mmiwg-ffada.ca/wp-content/uploads/2019/06/Final_Report_Vol_1a-1.pdf.

Neumann, Peter R. *Prisons and Terrorism: Radicalization and De-Radicalization in 15 Countries*. United Kingdom: International Centre for the Study of Radicalization and Political Violence, 2010. https://www.clingendael.org/sites/default/files/pdfs/Prisons-and-terrorism-15-countries.pdf.

Orr, Caroline. "Canada Occupies Unique Space in the 'Manosphere' of Extremist Violence." *National Observer*, August 26, 2019. https://www.nationalobserver.com/2019/08/26/analysis/canada-occupies-unique-space-manosphere-extremist-violence.

Page, Shelley. "Page: How I Sanitized the Feminist Outrage Over the Montreal Massacre." *Ottawa Citizen*. December 6, 2014. https://ottawacitizen.com/opinion/columnists/page-how-i-sanitized-the-feminist-outrage-over-the-montreal-massacre/.

Penaluna, Regan. "Kate Manne: The Shock Collar That Is Misogyny." *Guernic*, February 7, 2018. https://www.guernicamag.com/kate-manne-why-misogyny-isnt-really-about-hating-women/.

Perreault, Samuel. *Criminal Victimization in Canada, 2014*. Ottawa: Statistics Canada, 2015. https://www150.statcan.gc.ca/n1/pub/85-002-x/2015001/article/14241-eng.pdf.

"The Radicalization Process." Centre for the Prevention of Radicalization Leading to Violence. Accessed March 26, 2020. https://info-radical.org/en/the-radicalization-process/.

Renzetti, Elizabeth. "Violent Misogyny Is a Threat to Half Our Population. We Need to Call It What It Is: Terrorism." *The Globe and Mail*, November 30, 2019. https://www.theglobeandmail.com/opinion/article-violent-misogyny-is-a-threat-to-half-our-population-we-need-to-call/.

Simpson, Laura. *Violent Victimization of Lesbians, Gays and Bisexuals in Canada, 2014*. Ottawa: Statistics Canada, 2018. https://www150.statcan.gc.ca/n1/en/pub/85-002-x/2018001/article/54923-eng.pdf?st=QuvaUPTj.

Smith, Victoria. "If We're Tackling All Forms of Extremism, We Need to Include Misogyny." *Independent*. June 21, 2017. https://www.independent.co.uk/voices/extremism-misogyny-need-to-tackle-it-a7800411.html.

Solnit, Rebecca. *Men Explain Things to Me*. Illinois: Haymarket Books, 2014.

Tannen, Deborah. *The Argument Culture*. New York: Ballantine Books, 1998.

Taub, Amanda. "Control and Fear: What Mass Killings and Domestic Violence Have in Common." *The New York Times*, June 15, 2016. https://www.nytimes.com/2016/06/16/world/americas/control-and-fear-what-mass-killings-and-domestic-violence-have-in-common.html

Thériault, Anne. "Anne Thériault: Marc Lépine Didn't Want to Kill Women, He Wanted to Kill Feminists." Last modified December 6, 2018. https://www.flare.com/news/marc-lepine-feminists/.

United Nations Human Rights Council. *Visit to Canada: Report of the Special Rapporteur on Violence Against Women, Its Causes and Consequences*. HRC, 41st Sess. UN Doc A/HRC/41/42/Add.1, 2019.

Urback, Robyn. "Terrorist? Misogynist? Labelling the Toronto Van Attacker a Pointless Exercise: Robyn Urback." *CBC News*, April 25, 2018. https://www.cbc.ca/news/opinion/toronto-van-attack-1.4633641.

"Victim of Toronto Van Attack 'Very Scared' There Are Others Like Minassian." *CBC* online, November 15, 2020. https://www.cbc.ca/news/canada/toronto/ont-alek-minassian-victims-1.5802831.

Security

Hope with Charity: Human Rights, the Law, and Aging

Albert Evrard

The Book of Ecclesiastes 9:4 offers, "For everyone among the living, there is hope." The objective of this contribution is to reflect on the concept of hope in the understanding and evolution of human rights among the elderly, the older persons, the older people, the aged people, the seniors.[1] Broadly speaking, how do we think about what hope is and where and how it is present? How does the law and the legal profession, in doing justice, have as an implicit mission to preserve hope or to arouse it through the concept of dignity[2] and its inclusion in the legal context?[3]

In a narrower sense, it is a question of seeing through judgments and decisions of the European Court of Human Rights (ECtHR), how concepts of legitimate hope, interest, and (superior) well-being account for the hope of an older person. In other words, it is a question of knowing in what type of situation older people are: at home, in a nursing home, dependent or not, victims or perpetrators, alone or surrounded,

A. Evrard (✉)
Faculté Libre
de Droit (FLD), Institut Catholique de Toulouse (Catholic University of Toulouse), Toulouse, France
e-mail: albert.evard@ict-toulouse.fr

L. E. Reimer and K. Standish (eds.), *Perspectives on Justice, Indigeneity, Gender, and Security in Human Rights Research*,
https://doi.org/10.1007/978-981-99-1930-7_12

subject to a protection measure or not, for instance.[4] It is also a question of knowing which provisions from the European Convention on Human Rights and Fundamental Freedoms (ECHR) and additional protocols are invoked, and effectively lead to a declared violation or not. Although the number of decisions within the scope of this chapter is limited,[5] the reader should keep in mind that the intensity of the human situations behind these decisions is significant. This is notably witnessed by the presence of separate opinions attached to some judgments, concurring, or dissenting ones. It reflects how much the representation that judges have of old age, how the place of the older people in society varies, and how these conflicts could be the source of opposing decisions.[6]

What Kind of Hope Are We Talking About?

Let us start with the opposite of hope. Based on common sense,[7] hopelessness is defined "as one's tendency to possess a negative point of view or a set of negative expectations for the future." It is often associated with the renunciation of any project, depression, and suicidal tendencies; signs particularly observed in gerontology and geriatrics.[8] From this point on, it is certain that the whole effort of awareness (preventive-educational) regarding the rights of the elderly and the way they are to be considered will be of vital importance.[9] Some judgments clearly underline these situations without necessarily recognizing the violation of a right.

More positively, beyond the common sense, the hope of older persons, like that of any human person, refers to a "fundamental human affect," a presupposition behind the human "will to live."[10] In this sense, hope is the wager that there is some correspondence between this human will to live and the world that sustains and maintains life. Without this hope, the human will be paralyzed, for the will to live presupposes that life has some value, despite all evidence to the contrary. Hope is "the name of the human spirit as a conative openness to reality as a radiance in search of the meaning and value of life."[11]

This existential conception of hope is often associated with a spiritual and/or religious dimension[12] abundantly illustrated in evidence-based medicine, it is increasingly present in the gerontological literature.[13] Such a conception is the basis for the discussion in this chapter. It is consistent with an equally fundamental understanding of the rights inherent in every human being prior to any legal or non-legal inscription.[14]

A slow paradigm shift recently appears within the older people's human rights approach. Although still not very visible in CtEDH's case law,[15] the rights of the elderly still are insufficiently studied, especially in Europe or Africa and Asia yet for different reasons.[16]

In any case, articulated around hope, a set of questions arises in the diverse European geographical space of the 47 member countries of the Council of Europe's cooperation mechanism.[17] Especially the ECtHR: does this "world that supports and sustains life"[18] organize a safe environment (security and peace) in which the primary needs (health, housing, food, entourage, appetite for life[19]) are satisfied? How do the law and those who implement it contribute to organizing this world, in principle, naturally hoped for by everyone regardless of age or old age? Moreover, is it taken into account that an obtuse volitional and/or cognitive capacity does not mean that the "human will to live" is not present? In any case, clearly hope is a notion targeted by this level of European cooperation in which the Court is involved: Looking at hope, Older Persons Rights and potential greater impact of Aging-oriented glance at the Human Rights system as a whole, domestic and regional:

> "[could help ...] us to meet the challenges, opportunities and needs of the 21st century; to reconstruct relations between people; and leaders and to achieve the global stability, solidarity, pluralism and inclusion on which we all depend. It points to the ways in which we can transform hope into concrete action with real impact on people's lives. It must never be a pretext for power or politics; it is above both. (Council of Europe, Secretary General Report 2021, 61)[20]

This requires an older-persons-human-rights-oriented perspective,[21] which is in line with the *Our Common Agenda* roadmap, presented in October 2021 at the United Nations by the Secretary General, and which intends to breathe new hope into a community of Statesin crisis, and thus ultimately into individuals.[22]

What Kind of Older People Are We Talking About?

Without glossing over the difficulties of defining who is an older person or what is aging,[23] we will keep in mind the unique identity of every human person. However, the approach of the ECtHR case law as well as documents of a more political nature (health, social policies) defines older persons through a number of groups: Older People, Vulnerable Persons, Persons in Vulnerable Situations, Persons with Disabilities or even Grand Parents.[24]

Overall, the hypothesis is that the majority of older people whose lives are certainly marked by hardship, live on this existential hope and have the resources to nourish it as they grow older, through adequate and life-giving relationships with others and with property (whether there is little or a lot). Thus, for the majority of them, one can suppose that they do not need to resort to justice to seek to find this hope through the recognition of rights or freedoms. They cultivate it in relation to others and the *empowerment* that weaves the surest hope.

Thus, to exhaust the remedies available in the domestic courts of the country where one finds oneself, and then to file a complaint before the European Court of Human Rights would concern, beyond the potential difficulties linked to access to justice,[25] there is only a kind of minority of people. It is assumed that they are all judicially expressing "the will to live" and seeking to re-establish the "correspondence" between their individual situation and "the world that supports and sustains life" as organized in the State in which they live. In other words, because they experience injustice, they actively hope for justice.

In a coherent way from the jurisprudence of the CtEDH, appears that there are among those older people who do not want to live or no longer live this fundamental hope, those for whom this seems to be the result of a life trajectory or from an accident of life.

On one hand, a tense geopolitical context may generate violent events coming to seize older people at the risk of their lives[26]; administrative arrest for being in a demonstration in Moscow.[27] Here neither hope nor despair but the brute force that, one might say, anesthetizes the basic conditions of peace and security of everyday life, compromising the satisfaction of primary needs.

On the other hand, the decrease or loss of hope that goes hand in hand with death or the slide toward dependence can also be found in situations resulting from a life accident. This refers to the abuse or neglect experienced by older people at home or in nursing homes.[28] It appears in ECtHR case law because perpetrators have been criminally convicted[29] or because professionals denounce infamous facts,[30] or because an administrative decision results in a factual situation perceived as degrading by the person himself.[31]

In all these cases, older persons are collateral victims if they are not authors, co-authors, or proven accomplices of facts qualified as criminal offenses or degrading situations.[32] Without, however, always reaching a sufficient threshold of gravity to lead to a judgment of violation of a right or freedom guaranteed by the ECHR.[33] It could thus be said that an aspiration does not necessarily pass the threshold of a legitimate expectation, or that an interest is not deemed to be superior in particular cases illustrated by the case law of the ECtHR.

At the same time, more than any other generation, older persons have learned to live through hard events. The will to live is sometimes even stronger while the world fails to support and maintain life or seems not to want to, so that there is no longer a perceived "correspondence" between the two. In both cases, the question arises of the respect by public authorities of old age, of increased longevity, of the older human being, as a very high value that does not resist other imperatives: armed or natural, or economic, financial, budgetary, security or managerial, for example. What is the role of the law and the legal institution in such a case?

On this point, the jurisprudence of the ECtHR shows that at the heart of this "correspondence" is not the absence of existing legal texts, but rather the interpretation and implementation given to them, above all at the internal level of each State. The number and quality of concurring or dissenting separate opinions that follow some judgments or decisions highlights this very well.

If the situation is clear with regard to the "incapable adult,"[34] it is less clear when there is no judicial decision establishing protection for a "vulnerable adult."[35] For this person, more often a woman than a man, the aspiration to be treated like any other citizen and litigant in the absence of a judgment establishing protection, is however not always assimilable to a legitimate expectation or hope sufficiently established or recognized, capable of entailing the violation of a fundamental right of the ECHR. In short, there is a kind of area of aspiration that does not find its "correspondence" with the law as it is organized, which engages the responsibility of the political community, of the governments, of the rulers, and of every citizen, be it legal and/or moral?[36] In any case, a cultural change is expected from progress in the field of human rights.[37]

In such a context, could an international doctrine of RtoP (Responsibility to Protect) justifying interventions in the lives of certain States when populations are in serious danger, could similarly shape a positive obligation of State toward its own population?[38] Would it be even thinkable that it could generate a regional responsibility commensurate with the demographic transition? Would it renew the Court's understanding for an appetite for life that takes frailty into account?[39] Surely, that could renew an understanding of dignity in old and very old age[40] making one slip quickly into losing hope to preserve it?

Hope and Legitimate Expectation of Older People

Some 15 decisions mentioning or concerning older people deal with the violation of ECHR rights using this technical notion of legitimate expectation which having first appeared in Common Law, has also entered the conceptual field of civil law countries, such as France.[41] By favoring the use of the concept of legitimate expectation, the ECtHR seems to reserve the term reasonable expectation for an aspiration before it that does not meet the conditions set for access to the status of legitimate expectation.[42]

Among other examples, in the case law on a disability pension, the ECtHR states that: the "legitimate expectation [is] stemming from various sources" [51]: "an assertable right to disability benefit" [51] "continuous in its legal nature" [49]; "continued payment of contribution" [48] or "benefit" [49]."[43] In a rather recent decision M.K v. Luxemburg of May 18, 2021 the law "must be stated with sufficient precision to enable the citizen to regulate his conduct [...] [55], [58]."[44]

However, with regard to the decisions consulted, it is mainly assessed in the field of Article 1 of Protocol 1, which concerns the respect of property or a certain right to claim or a certain or sufficiently certain "asset value."[45]

In a first series of decisions, older persons are holding an aspiration to restitution of property, following a State succession or a change of political regime. In most of the cases, they die leaving the possibility for the rightful claimants to pursue the action. The ECtHR recognizes a very broad margin of maneuver for the State in determining the legal criteria opening the right to restitution: condition of eligibility, regime of proof.

So, in a judgment Berger-Krall and others v. Slovenia of June 12, 2014 the change in political regime upon Slovenia's independence and the transition from a socialist system to a market economy [16, 136, 194] degraded the protection [203–205] afforded to occupants of social housing that in practice and legally passed from generation to generation

[12, 21, 45]. This includes an 81-year-old [77, 264] and a 91-year-old whose anxiety about home led to emotional stress and the need for psychiatric help [225, 228, 230–231]. As the homes were put up for sale, their occupants were pressured and threatened with eviction and were made to assert their rights in court, while being at an advanced age without the ability to acquire them [223, 228, 232].[46] An almost similar situation where the older mother is evicted from the home she occupies with the applicant and her two children [6] without compensation [43, 88, 99], is outlined in Akhverdiyev v. Azerbaijan of January 29, 2015.[47]

Not surprisingly, financial security and the ability to plan ahead strongly modulate the possibilities that older people and their relatives have to build up a peaceful life in a safe environment. Whether by building up property assets[48] or retaining a home after paying inheritance tax[49] it will (or not) configure few options. Consequently, maintaining oneself at home, entering a nursing home, or an adapted structure when high dependency is present affect the kind of hope with which people are inhabited.

A second set of decisions deal with pension schemes. It deals with individual complaints about loss of pension rights in bankruptcy[50] exception to the scheme or non-application of a pension increase.[51] This also affects the ability to procure basic needs (housing, food, health, participation in community life-family, neighborhood, municipality).

In a third block of decisions, the legitimate aspiration to benefit from efficient health structures (physical or mental) is at stake. In case of a close relative that is raised, without however always passing the threshold of a "legitimate expectation" capable of taking precedence over the positive obligation of the State, understood by the ECtHR as limited to the establishment of a general framework and guarantees of appeal procedure.

For instance, in Volintiru v. Italy of March 19, 2013, a hospital stay reduced to a minimum by the medical profession resulted in a relapse and the rapid death of an 85-year-old woman. Her daughter filed a complaint arguing that her mother's right to life (Article 2 ECHR) was not respected in that appropriate medical treatment was not given and the deteriorated state of the hospital caused the infection that was to kill her (Article 3 ECHR, Article 8 ECHR).[52] In Lopes de Sousa Fernandez of December 19, 2017, the death in hospital of the 60-year-old husband from a hospital-acquired infection following minor surgery [10, 27], the Court rules out an extensive positive obligation relating to the provision of a health system. This is reserved only for specific situations (deprivation of liberty, vulnerable persons [162–163] (separate opinion, 72, 87), which is limited to establishing a general framework without going as far as its effectiveness in individual cases, which excludes negligence [189, 203], whereas the plaintiff argues that the systemic and structural deficiencies of the latter [192] directly caused her husband's death [201]. On the other hand, the Court took into account the considerable length of the proceedings in order to decide that there was a violation of Article 2 ECHR (right to health) from a procedural point of view [238], without therefore entering into the examination of Articles 6 §1 and 13 ECHR.[53]

In Dodov v. Bulgaria of January 17, 2008, it is on the basis of the same Article 2 ECHR on the right to life that the disappearance of her mother suffering from Alzheimer's from a public nursing home, brings the plaintiff before the Court. Eventually, this disappearance is judged by the Court as having caused a prejudice (pecuniary and non-pecuniary damages), that must be compensated. It is the direct link between the nursing home's obligations to take care of the mother and the disappearance, and not the police activity in the search for her, that constitutes a violation of Article 2 ECHR. Furthermore, the length of the proceedings before the national courts of more than 10 years and the style of treatment and response provided by the national authorities are considered contrary to Article 6 §1 ECHR (right to a timely fair trial). As in other cases, it is clear that the hope lies in a timely treatment of the litigant.[54]

Finally, in Fernandes de Oliveira v. Portugal of January 31, 2019, the Court declare a violation of Article 2 (right to life) but under the procedural aspect (procedural limb, 45) of it only. The complaint filed by a mother 63 years old (at the time of the ECtHR judgment she is 82 years old) before the administration and the domestic courts for lack of efficient hospital arrangements accommodating her son who entered in psychiatry on a voluntary basis [54] eventually committed suicide and died at age 36. Within the framework of the supervision as it exists (deficient according to the mother-[40]) it led her son (history of suicide attempt) to leave the hospital compound to end his life. The judgment shows both the multiplicity of interveners around a family that was itself fragile, the older mother appearing quite alone to surround her son. The facts also show that the son had failed his driver's license exam, which was a trigger. As for the hospital, apart from the structure [30], the fragility is also there in times of vacations with fewer and replacement staff [19]. Clearly, the judgment in the field of health shows that hope lies in the appropriate exercise of the rights of each individual within a structural framework. Even if it is deficient in the public sector [56, 65], and the classic but minimalist interpretation of the Court regarding the positive obligation of the State in the field of health (separate opinion, 46, 70) does not necessarily lead to the declaration of a violation of one or another provision of the ECHR.[55]

However, in other cases the Court may hesitate and ultimately refuse to recognize an aspiration as a legitimate expectation. For example, in Gross v. Switzerland of May 14, 2013 and of September 30, 2014, 67810/10, the plaintiff, who was 74 years old at the time of the 2013 judgment, persists in ending her life again [14 (2014), 7–8 (2013)] for fear of being in a state where she would no longer be able to do so. The complainant does not suffer at the time of her application from any limitation of her physical or mental capacities. This is supported by medical certificates [9 (2014), 15, 21 (2013)]. The Court refuses to address the situation under Article 2 ECHR (right to life) when the essential fact generating any action at the medical, administrative, or legal level, is the desire to end her life. Arguing a "right" to receive the lethal product that would achieve this result as well as the "right" to demand that a member of the nursing or medical staff administer it belongs to domestic jurisdiction. Regarding what is an aspiration, the Court considers that it is up to each State to legislate in this area (2014 final judgment), whereas in the 2013 judgment it considered that the desire to be provided with a lethal dose falls within the scope of an implementation of one's right to privacy (Article 8 ECHR) [60 (2013)]. In 2014, the Court, otherwise composed (Grand Chamber), relied solely on Article 35 ECHR (abuse of the right of individual petition) and confined itself to finding a violation of this right without addressing the question of a "right to assisted suicide."[56]

In any case, jurisprudence and doctrine show here that many people who still have much or what is needed, nevertheless lose hope—understood as the appetite for life, its "taste,"[57] when their aspirations have passed the stage of recognition in "legitimate hope." The varied European space (47 countries and blocks of countries so different in their evolution) is occupied by these contradictions. However, of what magnitude would be the question?

Hope: Interest and Well-Being of the Older

Although the notions of interest and well-being are close to the notion of legitimate expectation, they do not seem to be well distinguished in the jurisprudence of the ECtHR concerning the elderly. This justifies that they are treated together. More than often, they come into play when certain people are given the right to "choose and decide for others"[58] or to be considered by law or by a court decision as being in the best position to do so, or to act in the "interests of the adult" (33) even if this notion is criticized in favor of respecting the will of the person concerned.

Nonetheless, the The Hague International Convention of January 13, 2000, of private international law,[59] "allows the most appropriate rule of law to be applied to a person of full age with regard to his or her residence and interests." Within this specific framework, it essentially refers to relations to property or persons[60] with a direct mention to older persons "who suffer from [personal] impairment" (Article 1). Despite this convention, we are far from considerations related to the human rights of older persons.

As for the field of human rights, the notion of the interests of the older person is far from having the same robustness as that acquired in the jurisprudence of the European Court of Human Rights concerning the "best interests of the child" and to a lesser extent that of the disabled person.[61] Would this require a clear formulation, specific to the elderly[62] in national or European jurisprudence, which may be invoked before the domestic courts? It depends ultimately on the conception of law in which one is involved: a positive law requiring a specialized formulation without which it is thought that a right does not exist, or a general formulation which calls for the interpretation to unveil an existing right and its implementation.

To answer this question, it is perhaps necessary to draw inspiration from the case law of the ECtHR in the field of child protection, where the notion of "best interests" appears. This is despite the fact that this notion already existed in many domestic laws. Neulinger and Shuruk v. Switzerland of July 6, 2010 does provide a leading example [3]: relevant domestic and international law and practice [49–84]), only to be extended or reinforced in support of this international registration.[63]

The analogy could be stimulating for specific interpretations. For example, following this interest requires, according to the ECtHR, "paramount attention" [114], which is difficult to conceive of older people being deprived. In the same Neulinger and Shuruk judgment, a dissenting opinion also emphasizes the place of personal factors and "the passage of time" in the assessment of this notion by the courts and tribunals [16]. This point is particularly significant in the case of the very old or older, as is the "serious risk of psychological danger" [109]. Moreover, whereas in the case of children, their importance is linked to the establishment of personal relationships that help them to develop and to grow [123] in the family, which is considered a fundamental place in the Convention on the Rights of the Child, why should it be any different for older people, parents, and grandparents? Why is the essential place of the family recognized as an essential place of growth and development for children, not recognized in the same way for their older members?[64]

However, in the case of the elderly, it seems that the use of the interests of the person or of her/his well-being closes an argument in situations where the balance of interests and rights in presence is difficult to establish. Or it supports a teleological motivation open to multiple interests. The real danger is that the person's factual situation and intention are not adequately observed and taken into account, which then leads to despair.

In Delecolle v. France, the ECtHR decided that it was not arbitrary or disproportionate for a person aged 79 at the time of his death [7, 5, 37, 40–43] who was protected by a curatorship (French law on the protection of vulnerable adults) to have to obtain the authorization of his curator in order to marry (Article 12 ECHR) a person who had been known to him for more than 15 years and his partner for more than 8 years. The curator refuses it to him. While mentioning "the interest and the well-being of the applicant" [14, 15, 16], this seems to have little place compared to "the financial stake in the center of an important family conflict" [15]. Without regard for the personal consequences on the life of the older person and his companion, and in particular "religious motives, family traditions" (separate opinion, p. 18), the ECtHR seems to solely focus on legal and financial consequences [54]. Besides, the curator's refusal is motivated by the applicant's "inability to control the consequences of his consent at the level of his property and finances" [60–61], and therefore this marriage project is judged to be "contrary to his interests" [61]. In so doing, it is the interests of the future beneficiaries that are protected, that is to say the unborn interests of persons other than the interested party: "the authorities have completely neglected the social and personal aspects of marriage. However, these were the ones that mattered to the applicant".[65] What hope did the applicant have had for the rest of his life?

In M.K v. Luxembourg of May 18, 2021, the first thing that strikes one is the solitude in which Mrs. M.K. lives. In this context, the concern raised by the ECHR relates to the possibility of a good or bad acquaintance In this case, meeting a young man of 28 by chance at the store and entering into relations similar to "those of a grandmother with her grandson" [6]. And from there, assuming (unproven) that he would take advantage of her in a way that is considered undue. Here again, the social or personal aspects (manifested in particular by the desire to adopt the young man [32]) are ignored while at the same time the Court says that it does not ignore "the complications, even the suffering, that inevitably go hand in hand with the steps and measures imposed" [67]. Behind this decision acting in the "interest of vulnerable adults" [49] to protect her and ensure "her well-being in the broad sense" [67] by making her appear to be prodigal (which dispenses with the need to provide a medical certificate to support the decision [21, 24, 26, 38, 63], inspired by a former French law [37, 47, 50]), there is a question raised: whether, in the absence of heirs, the State is not seeking to protect the mass of assets that inevitably would revert to it by disinheritance, upon the future death of the person.[66]

In W.A v. Switzerland, November 2, 2021, W.A is 61 years old and has just served a 20-year prison sentence for two homicides. This prisoner presents severe mental disorders that are difficult to treat. Thus, an internment is ordered in a non-psychiatric institution for the offenses initially charged and which gave rise to the imprisonment which is coming to an end. The domestic court has the interest of society in mind here: to ensure that this person is not free. This was based on the fact that it had been established by an expert that his discernment was impaired at the time of the facts, and thus the interest of the person himself to see his well-being. The Court considers that the ordered internment is comparable to a second and more severe punishment than the first, and condemns Switzerland for violation of Articles 5 §1, 7 §1, 4 of Protocol 7 to the Convention.[67]

In H.L. v. United Kingdom of October 5, 2004, a man aged 55 at the time of the judgment, autistic, mute, and unable to consent or not to medical treatment [9], after a placement with a couple of people paid to take care of him and who are presumably older, finds himself informally detained in a psychiatric institution [116, 125] because of an English jurisprudential principle of necessity and of the "best interest" of the person who in this case is alone and disabled. The ECtHR decided that this constituted a violation of Article 5 ECHR, due to the absence of sufficient procedural guarantees and the lack of protection against the possibility of arbitrary detention [139].[68]

Finally, in H.M v. Switzerland of February 22, 2002, it is more the well-being that is finally retained by the ECtHR and the internal decision-making bodies. A 90-year-old woman at the time of the decision complained of the arbitrary deprivation of her liberty due to a nursing home placement decided by social services [16, 31] in the interest of the person (and her cohabiting son), insofar as the living conditions at home (state of abandonment [3, 18, 23]) were deemed to be degraded and the cooperation of the persons in search of an improvement, non-existent [24, 44]. However, at one point, the placement measure was lifted because H.M. the person concerned had "consented to reside in the home of her own free will" [27, 47]. What could have caused a person, otherwise described as senile demented [23, 33] while being contradicted, to consent is a mystery. Certainly, the improvement of her living conditions and a peaceful and safe place to live must have weighed, but what about hope after abandoning her home? She who always refused to enter a home where "it was no longer possible for her to freely make decisions about her place of residence or her daily life" [32]. The situation of the son who did not wish to leave his mother is also mentioned [46]. However, the Court considers that a "responsible" decision was taken by the authorities in "the applicant's own interest" [48] and that there is therefore no violation of Article 5 §1, which is not applicable in this case [48–49]. In a separate opinion, a judge noted the difficulties of such a decision, particularly when a person is declared to be suffering from senile dementia without a medical certificate, or when the de facto imperative of placement seems to be necessary without having to be analyzed as a deprivation of liberty contrary to Article 5 §1 ECHR.[69]

Conclusion

Of the rights thus examined by the ECtHR, it is clear that the "hard core" of "unconditional rights"[70] is regularly invoked in relation to the elderly. This makes it all the more necessary to examine them. It is equally clear that there is a blind spot: missing is an examination of the lived reality of older people who have received a court decision. Did this decision give or stifle hope? How can it be said that hope is more a part of society because its system of promoting or protecting basic rights has advanced, judicial or otherwise?

The fact remains that hope in this context of the human rights of the elderly through the prism of the jurisprudence of the ECHR offers this opportunity to return to the fundamental dimensions of every human being and to think or rethink human rights. How can human rights, under these conditions, constitute a means of giving hope, of increasing it, of maintaining it? How does the positive law of human rights and its interpretation take hope understood in this way?

To lose sight of this teleological aim and to focus only on a positivist vision centered on human rights focused exclusively on material needs would again lead to reforms that, it is to be feared, will not bear the expected fruits.[71] [Clearly], innovations are extremely useful in bridging the gap between the legitimate expectations of citizens and the decisions taken on their behalf.[72]

In this respect, since these are values to be revisited, in a globalized world where the place of religious factors would be more recognized, such a reflection could involve a revisited reference to the origin of living together with the elderly shared by the monotheistic religions.[73]

In addition, from the examination of the jurisprudence of the CtEDH, hope is not just an individual requirement (aspiration or claim) or a legitimate aspiration (admissible by the Court without it makes right). It is especially shaped in a relational situation where the legitimate hope, the well-being, or the interest, find important grounds of application in the field of material resources but little opened to personal and social, emotional and affective aspirations.

In terms of proposals, why would the Council of Europe Parliamentary Assembly not adopt a resolution focused on this balance between a best interest of the elderly and the need to keep the family together, similarly, like Resolution 2232 "Balancing the Best Interests of the Child and the Need to Keep Families Together" of June 28, 2018?

Nonetheless, despite such a case-law aging-rooted approach, the fear is always there that policy documents or court decisions only convey words of hope that never convert into filled hope. On the other hand, filled hope gives way, most of the time, to other hopes. In other words, hope follows the meanders of life, so it is necessary to be attentive to it all the time. Therefore, as Pope Francis says in the Encyclical letter *Fratelli Tutti*: "it is truly noble to place our hope in the hidden power of the seeds of goodness we sow […]" (no. 196).

Notes

1. Reference is made in an undifferentiated way to the same reality to which it is referred by different terms more or less accepted according to the circumstances of time or place. For instance, the United Nations recently recommended to use the term Older Persons, Older People and to banish the term elderly. Nonetheless, this latter continues to be used in an Asian environment or even in the jurisprudence of the European Court of Human Rights, for instance.
2. G. N. Thompson, J. McArthur, and M. Doupe, "Identifying Markers of Dignity-Conserving Care in Long-Term Care: A Modified Delphi Study," *PLoS ONE* 11, no. 6 (2016): 2, 4; Š. Šaňáková, and J. Čáp, "Dignity of Elderly Adults from the Perspective of Nurses: A Qualitative Descriptive Study," *Central European Journal of Nursing and Midwifery* 9, no. 4 (2018): 906–907.
3. Pretty v. United Kingdom, 29 April 2002, [65].
4. Benny Spanier, Israel Doron, and Faina Milman-Sivan, "Older Persons' use of the European Court of Human, Rights," *Journal of Cross-Cultural Gerontology* 28 (2013): 560.
5. A future article "L'espoir dans la jurisprudence de la Cour européenne des droits de l'homme (CtEDH): Que suggère une perspective centrée sur les personnes âgées?" (to be published in 2022–2023) considers the concept of hope in a more systematic study of the human rights of older persons.
6. Khamtokhu and Aksenchik v. Russia, 24 January 2017, separate opinions, 27, 32, 36, 38, 40, 47–54; Kopecký v. Slovakia, 28 September 2004, 21–27; Delecolle v. France, 25 October 2018, 16.
7. *Merriam-Webster*, online, s.v. "Despair," https://www.merriam-webster.com/dictionary/despair. The notion refers to: "utter loss of hope".
8. Ertuğrul Şahin, Nursel Topkaya, Cem Gençoğlu, and Ercümend Ersanlı. "Prevalence and Correlates of Hopelessness among Turkish Elderly People Living with Family or in Nursing Homes," *Societies* 8, no. 2 (2018): 2, 8.
9. This is in line with one of the 10 key findings of the WHO: "Fact 7: Comprehensive public health action will require fundamental shifts in how we think about ageing and health: Health in older age shouldn't be defined by the absence of disease. Healthy Ageing is achievable by every older person. It is a process that enables older people to continue to do the things that are important to them. While health and social care expenditures for older people are often viewed as costs to society they should be understood as investments in realising opportunities and enabling older people to continue to make their many positive contributions".

10. *Cambridge Dictionary*, online, s.v. "Hope," https://dictionary.cambridge.org/dictionary/english/hope. Usually refers to a verb: "to want something to happen or to be true, and to have generally good reason to think that it might happen;" *Merriam-Webster*, online, s.v. "Hope," https://www.merriam-webster.com/dictionary/hope. Is also a noun referring to: "a desire accompanied by an expectation or belief in its fulfillment [...]: an expectation of fulfillment or success [...]; someone or something on which hopes are centered [...]; something desired or hoped for [...]".
11. Michael Scanlon, V° "Hope". In Joseph A. Komonchak, Mary Collins, and Dermot A. Lane, *The New Dictionary of Theology* (Collegeville, MN: Liturgical Press, 1990), 493.
12. Pope Francis, *Encyclical Letter Fratelli Tutti on Fraternity and Social Friendship* of 3 October 2020. https://www.vatican.va/content/francesco/en/encyclicals/documents/papa-francesco_20201003_enciclica-fratelli-tutti.html. No. 55 "I invite everyone to a renewed hope, because hope" speaks to us of something deeply rooted in every human heart, regardless of our circumstances and historical conditioning. Hope speaks to us of a thirst, a longing, a yearning for a fulfilled life, a desire to achieve great things, things that fill our hearts and lift our spirits to such lofty realities as truth, goodness and beauty, justice and love... Hope is bold; it can look beyond the personal conveniences, securities, and petty compensations that limit our horizon and it can open us to great ideals that make life more beautiful and worthwhile. "Let us continue, then, to advance along the paths of hope"; Cara Kiernan Fallon and Jason Karlawish, "Is the WHO Definition of Health Aging Well? Framework for "Health" after Three Sore and Ten," *AJPH* 109, no. 8 (2019): 1105.
13. Neda Abdolahrezaee, Arsalan Khanmohammadi, Mahboubeh Dadfar, Vahid Rashedi, and Liela Behnam "Prediction of Hope, Physical Health, and Mental Health by Mediating Variable of Religious Spiritual Well-Being in Elderly," *Mental Health, Religion & Culture* 23, no. 10 (2020): 929–930, 935, https://doi.org/10.1080/13674676.2020.1819220; Şahin, "Prevalence and Correlates of Hopelessness" 2; Sara Carmel, Leeat Granek, Alon Zamir, "Influences of Nationalism and Historical Traumatic Events on the Will-to-Live of Elderly Israelis," *The Gerontologist* 56, no. 4 (2016): 753–754, https://doi.org/10.1093/geront/gnv031.
14. John Trent, "Promoting and Protecting Human Rights," in *A United Nation Renaissance. What the UN Is and What It Could Be*, ed. John Trent and Laura Shnurr (Opladen/Berlin/Toronto: Barbara Budrich Publishers, 2018), 98–99, which is even more important in the context of the Covid-19 pandemic; Gerard McCann and Féilim Ó'hAdhmaill,

eds, *International Human Rights, Social Policy and Global Development: Critical Perspectives* (Bristol: Bristol University Press, 2020), 36, https://www.researchgate.net/publication/342039515_International_Human_Rights_Social_Policy_and_Global_Development_Critical_Perspectives.
15. Lopes de Sousa Fernandes v. Portugal, 19 December 2017, separate opinion, 107.
16. European Agency for Fundamental Rights, *Fundamental Rights Report 2018* (Parliamentary Assembly, Res. 2168, 2017), 17–24; Israel Doron, Israel Doron, "25 Years of Elder Law: An Integrative and Historical Account of the Field of Law and Aging," in *Theoretical Inquiries in Law* 21, no. 1 (2019): 10–14. https://www.researchgate.net/publication/338856340.
17. The problems raised in the European space are "rich country" problems (WEIRD—Western, Educated, Industrialized, Rich, Democratic), compared to the non-satisfaction of the basic needs of entire populations on other continents, and yet the relegation, the despair up to the desire to hasten the death of the older in increased longevity are very present.
18. Scanlon, *The New Dictionary of Theology*, 493.
19. For the author, this appetite for life, which is maintained, necessarily passes by the existence of an interior, spiritual life. Relegated in the silent domain of the private sphere by many public authorities, this existential instance has however an essential role in old age. It is the aggregator of the integration and the efficiency of the other dimensions proper to any dignified human life. This hypothesis will be the subject of separate work on "well-being" and its definition by the WHO. A shared hypothesis is that such a definition should be changed in its Constitution (July 22, 1946) to include the spiritual dimension, as it already exists in the definition of health for specific groups.
20. Pre-pandemic documents express little expectations, aspirations or hope (Committee of Ministers, Recommendation CM/Rec(2014)2; CDDH(2018)R90 Addendum, 07/01/2019).
21. Andrew Byrnes, "Human Rights Unbound: An Unrepentant Call for a More Complete Application of Human Rights in Relation to Older Persons—And Beyond," *Australasian Journal on Ageing* 39, (2020): 92–96. https://doi-org.uml.idm.oclc.org/10.1111/ajag.12800.
22. UN Secretary General, *Our Common Agenda—Report of the Secretary General* (New York: United Nations, 2021), https://www.un.org/en/content/common-agenda-report/assets/pdf/Common_Agenda_Report_English.pdf. Our common agenda is there: "to recover this positive spirit" (p. 5) and to fight "disenchantment with institutions and political leaders" (no. 3, p. 12) as well as individual disenchantment. It is stated at the international level that: "the time has come to take stock, to rejuvenate our common values and to update our thinking on human rights as well

as individual disenchantment; UN Secretary-General, *The Highest Aspiration. A Call to Action for Human Rights* (New York: United Nations, 2020), https://www.un.org/sg/sites/www.un.org.sg/files/atoms/files/The_Highest_Asperation_A_Call_To_Action_For_Human_Right_English.pdf. It is acknowledged at the international level that: "the time has come to take stock, to rejuvenate our shared values and to update our thinking on human rights" "We must give people hope and a vision of what the future can be" (no. 35, p. 33).

23. Sudre, *Les grands Arrêts*..., 145–147, 164, 186–187; Trakhel v Switzerland, 4 November 2014, [97]. ECHR case law does not attempt to define the older person or the vulnerable group or persons in a vulnerable situation, while using these terms. Nor does any European policy document (EU or Council of Europe) impose a definition (understanding and extension) of what Ageing is or what older people are (Recommendation CM/Rec (2014)..., 2; Explanatory Memorandum..., 32). In this context, the reference to the numerical age (the number of years alive since birth) of 65 years is maintained as a technical and practical way of identifying people belonging to the group of the older (Tonolo, "International Human Rights and"..., 108). This, while at the same time it is declared outdated as "social policy has come to recognize this reality of 'regional differences, of healthy life expectancy, by fragmenting the categories of aging into young older (65–74), older (75–84), and older or older (85 plus)" (British Columbia Law Institute, 2011).
24. Terna v. Italy, 14 January 2021; Amanalachioai v. Romania, 26 May 2009; AFR, *Fundamental Rights Report 2018*, 10–11; Phyllis Talley, "The Elderly Disabled: The Applicability of Disability Rights for Age-Related Disability," *Journal of Legal Medicine* 40, no. 1 (2020): 119–123, https://doi.org/10.1080/01947648.2020.1731330.
25. INPEA, "World Elder Abuse Awareness Day, Access to Justice," Virtual Event, Concept Note, 21 June 2021, https://www.un.org/development/desa/ageing/wp-content/uploads/sites/24/2021/06/2021.05.31-Concept-note-WEAAD-2021-Access-to-Justice.pdf; American Bar Association, *Human Rights and Access to Justice. ABA ROLI Programme.* No date. https://www.americanbar.org/advocacy/rule_of_law/what-we-do/human-rights-access-to-justice/.
26. It refers, for instance, to a number of situations: Hostage taking (Tagayeva and others v. Russia, 13 April 2017); Anti-terrorist operation (Denizci and others v. Cyprus); Finogenov and others v. Russia, 04 June 2012.
27. Frumkin v. Russia, 5 January 2016.
28. For a very recent study that incudes some pandemic-related aspects, see Manitoba Law Reform Commission, *Elder Abuse and Neglect in Manitoba. Consultation Paper* (Winnipeg, June 2021), 10–17, http://www.manitobalawreform.ca/pubs/pdf/elder_abuse_consultation.pdf

29. Cabbia and others v. Italy, 5 March 1990, 1–3; x. Federal Republic of Germany, 14 December 1961; Niess v. France, 17 January 1996.
30. Heinish v. Germany, 21 July 2011.
31. McDonnald v. United Kingdom, 20 May 2014: being forced to wear diapers at night yet not being incontinent.
32. Dufour-Gompers, Dictionnaire de la violence et du crime, Toulouse, Erès, v° Personnes-Âgées, 255–256; v° Older people (violence against), 403.
33. Sawoniuk v. United Kingdom, 29 May 2001; Haidn v. Germany, 13 January 2011—a case where the threshold is reached: Bancsók and László Magyar v. Hungary, 28 October 2021.
34. Shtukaturov v. Russia, 27 March 2008.
35. A-M.V. v. Finland, 23 March 2017.
36. Ursula von der Leyen, President of the EU Commission, "Speech on the State of the European Union" (speech, EU Commission, Strausberg, Germany, September 15, 2021), https://ec.europa.eu/commission/presscorner/detail/en/SPEECH_21_4701. It might be a source of inspiration and hope for all EU Members that are all members of the Council of Europe and part to the mechanism of the ECtHR; Secretary General of the Council of Europe, 2021st edition of the state of democracy, human rights and the rule of law. Older persons are not mentioned, although on many points they should be associated with the expectations of citizens: legitimate needs, aspirations to be met, the need for effective public institutions (7, 61, 66, 137), the fight against growing poverty generating personal and collective insecurity (7, 82), the duty of the public authority to improve "their justice systems and meet the expectations of the users of these systems" (15). Moreover, since 2014 but certainly accelerated with the pandemic, the shift to a more digitalized administration and public services such as social and health create "expectations" (69) in every citizen and employee not to be left behind. Finally, the fight against domestic violence and the mistreatment of vulnerable people, especially children (sexual abuse and trafficking) should meet the high "expectations" of the public and civil society (86).
37. Claudia Mahler, *Report of the Independent Expert on the Enjoyment of all Human Rights by Older Persons* (New York: United Nations Human Rights Council, 2021), 18–19, A/HRC/48/53, https://ngocoa-ny.org/recent-documents-of-interes/a_hrc_48_53_ie-report-on.pdf.
38. Global Citizenship Commission, *The Universal Declaration of Human Rights in the 21st Century: A Living Document in a Changing World*, ed. Gordon Brown, 1st ed., Vol. 2 (Open Book Publishers, 2016), 102–104, http://www.jstor.org/stable/j.ctt1bpmb7v.

39. Andrew Clegg, John Young, Steve Iliffe, Marcel Olde Rikkert, and Kenneth Rockwood, "Frailty in Elderly People," *The Lancet* 381, no. 9868 (2013): 752–759, https://doi.org/10.1016/S0140-6736(12)62167-9.
40. Khamtokhu and Aksenchik v. Russia, 24 January 2017, separate opinion, 65, 67.
41. Sudre, *Les grands arrêts*, 825–828.
42. Zubac v. Croatia, 5 April 2018, [120].
43. Béláné Nagy v. Hungary, 13 December 2013.
44. M.K v. Luxembourg of 18 May 2021.
45. Marta Nunes Vicente, "Property Rights and Legitimate Expectations Under United States Constitutional Law and the European Convention on Human Rights: Some Comparative Remarks," *Comparative Law Review* 26, no. 1 (2021), 52, 70–73, 75–78, https://apcz.umk.pl/CLR/article/view/CLR.2020.002; Mel Cousins, "Legitimate Expectation and Social Security Law Under the European Convention of Human Rights," *European Journal of Social Security* 23, no. 1 (2021): 25–37, https://journals-sagepub-com.uml.idm.oclc.org/doi/full/10.1177/1388262720961792.
46. Berger-Krall and others v. Slovenia of 12 June 2014.
47. Akhverdiyev v. Azerbaijan, 29 January 2015.
48. Ivanova and Cherkezov v. Bulgaria, 21 April 2016 [65].
49. Burden v. United Kingdom, 29 April 2008.
50. Zadonik v. Slovenia, 21 May 2015; Vicente, "Property Rights and Legitimate Expectation," 78–81.
51. Carson v. others v. United Kingdom, 16 March 2012; Stefanetti and others v. Italy, 15 April 2014.
52. Volintiru v. Italy of 19 March 2013.
53. Lopes de Sousa Fernandez, 19 December 2017.
54. Dodov v. Bulgaria, 17 January 2008.
55. Fernandes de Oliveira v. Portugal, 31 January 2019.
56. Gross v. Switzerland of 14 May 2013 and of 30 September 2014, 67810/10.
57. This is described in the religious sphere as acedia. *Merriam-Webster*, online, s.v. "Acedia," https://www.merriam-webster.com/dictionary/acedia. "Acedia now tends to be used more generally to simply imply a lack of interest or caring, although it sometimes still carries overtones of laziness"; Anupama Datta, "Socio-ethical Issues in the Existing Paradigm of Care of the Older Persons: Emerging Challenges and Possible Responses," in *Discourses on Aging and Dying*, ed. Suhita Chopra Chatterjee, Priyadarshi Patnaik, and Vijayaraghavan M. Chariar (New Dehli:

Sages India, 2008), 150–151, 157, https://dx.doi.org/10.4135/9788132111894.

58. Peterka, Protection de la personne vulnérable..., 299.
59. The older person is among other beneficiaries of this protection of national law, which the Convention only helps to find the criterion of connection and choice in the field of legal capacity to support.
60. Peterka, Protection de la personne vulnérable..., 32.
61. On one side, article 12 of the International Convention on the Rights of Persons with Disabilities (ICRPD) of 30 March 2007 does mention: "the rights and interests of the person concerned". On the other side, similar terms of which are taken up in the International Convention for the Protection of the Rights of the Child of 20 November 1989 are originated in Declaration of the Rights of the Child of 20 November 1959.
62. Tourrette, "Can we apply the 'best interests'?" 5.
63. Neulinger and Shuruk v. Switzerland of 6 July 2010.
64. Parliamentary Assembly of the Council of Europe, Resolution 2232 June 28, 2018.
65. Delecolle v. France, separate opinion, 19–20.
66. M.K v. Luxembourg of 18 May 2021.
67. W.A v. Switzerland, 2 November 2021.
68. H.L. v. United Kingdom of 5 October 2004.
69. H.M v. Switzerland of 22 February 2002.
70. Renucci, Droit européen..., 69.
71. Marie-Bénédicte Dembour, "Critiques," in *International Human Rights*, ed. Daniel Moeckli (Oxford: Oxford University Press, 2018), 50–58; Trent, "Promoting and Protecting Human Rights," 120–123.
72. Council of Europe, Report of the Secretary General 2021, 61.
73. Religious Leaders in Canada, *Hope, Gratitude and Solidarity: A Message to Canadians in Response to the COVID-19 Pandemic*. https://www.councilofchurches.ca/news/hope-gratitude-and-solidarity/?xdomain_data=w0XBJS8jmzftBNDi8BROiWL98LLL1UwDKqw89D1jctNTDXxGPMJE1kbRPrM%2BbSmj, 2, 4; The "Honor your father and mother" principle is in Charlotte K. Goldberg, "The Normative Influence of the Fifth Commandment on Filial Responsibility," *Marquette Elder's Advisor* 10, no. 2 (2009): 221, 224–225, http://scholarship.law.marquette.edu/elders/vol10/iss2/3; in The Catechism of the Catholic Church, the Fourth commandment. It also surfaces in Confucianism (Bu, Qingxiu, "To Legislate Filial Piety," 220, 228), in Hinduism (Swami, "Life and Immortality in Indian Though," 91, 95) or Islam (Ahaddour, "What Goes Around Comes Around," 993).

Bibliography

Journal Articles and Monographs

Ahaddour, C., S. Van den Branden, and B. Broeckaert. "'What Goes Around Comes Around': Attitudes and Practices Regarding Ageing and Care for the Elderly Among Moroccan Muslim Women Living in Antwerp (Belgium)." *Journal of Religion and Health* 59 (2020): 986–1012. https://pubmed.ncbi.nlm.nih.gov/29362969/.

American Bar Association. *Human Rights and Access to Justice. ABA ROLI Programme*. No date. https://www.americanbar.org/advocacy/rule_of_law/what-we-do/human-rights-access-to-justice/.

British Columbia Law Institute. "Older Adult, Older Person, Senior, Elderly or Elder: A Few Thoughts on the Language We Use to Reference Aging" (2011). https://www.bcli.org/older-adult-older-person.

Bu, Qingxiu, "To Legislate Filial Piety: Is the Elderly Rights Law a Panacea?" *Statute Law Review* 42, no. 2 (2021): 219–240. https://doi-org.uml.idm.oclc.org/10.1093/slr/hmz010.

Byrnes, Andrew. "Human Rights Unbound: An Unrepentant Call for a More Complete Application of Human Rights in Relation to Older Persons—And Beyond." *Australasian Journal on Ageing* 39 (2020): 91–98. https://doi-org.uml.idm.oclc.org/10.1111/ajag.12800.

Cambridge Dictionary Online. https://dictionary.cambridge.org/dictionary/english/hope; https://dictionary.cambridge.org/fr/dictionnaire/anglais/elderly.

Carmel, Sara, Leeat Granek, and B. A. Alon Zamir. "Influences of Nationalism and Historical Traumatic Events on the Will-to-Live of Elderly Israelis." *The Gerontologist* 56, no. 4 (2016): 753–761. https://doi.org/10.1093/geront/gnv031.

Catechism of the Catholic Church, the Fourth Commandment. https://www.vatican.va/archive/ENG0015/_INDEX.HTM.

Clegg, Andrew, Young John, Iliffe Steve, and Marcel Olde Rikkert. "Frailty in Elderly People." *The Lancet* 381, no. 9868 (2013): 752–762. https://doi.org/10.1016/S0140-6736(12)62167-9.

Cousins, Mel. "Legitimate Expectation and Social Security Law Under the European Convention of Human Rights." *European Journal of Social Security* 23, no. 1 (2021): 24–43. https://journals-sagepub-com.uml.idm.oclc.org/doi/full/10.1177/1388262720961792.

Datta, Anupama. "Socio-ethical Issues in the Existing Paradigm of Care of the Older Persons: Emerging Challenges and Possible Responses." In *Discourses on Aging and Dying*, edited by Suhita C. Chatterjee, Priyadarshi Patnaik, and Vijayaraghavan M. Chariar. New Delhi: SAGE Publications India Pvt Ltd., 2008. https://doi.org/10.4135/9788132111894.

Dembour, Marie-Bénédicte. "Critiques". In *International Human Rights*, edited by Daniel Moeckli, 41–59. Oxford: Oxford University Press, 2018.

Doron, Israel, "25 Years of Elder Law: An Integrative and Historical Account of the Field of Law and Aging." *Theoretical Inquiries in Law* 21, no. 1 (2019): 1–24. https://www.researchgate.net/publication/338856340.

Dufour-Gompers, Roger. *Dictionnaire de la violence et du crime*, Toulouse, Erès, v° Personnes-Âgées, 255–256; v° Older people (violence against), 403.

Global Citizenship Commission. *The Universal Declaration of Human Rights in the 21st Century: A Living Document in a Changing World*. Edited by Gordon Brown. 1st ed., Vol. 2. Open Book Publishers, 2016. http://www.jstor.org/stable/j.ctt1bpmb7v.

Goldberg, Charlotte K. "The Normative Influence of the Fifth Commandment on Filial Responsibility." *Marquette Elder's Advisor* 10, no. 2 (2009): 221–244. http://scholarship.law.marquette.edu/elders/vol10/iss2/3.

INPEA, "World Elder Abuse Awareness Day, Access to Justice," Virtual Event. Concept Note, 21 June 2021. https://www.un.org/development/desa/ageing/wp-content/uploads/sites/24/2021/06/2021.05.31-Concept-note-WEAAD-2021-Access-to-Justice.pdf.

Jitatmananda, Swami. "Life and Immortality in Indian Thought." In *Discourses on Aging and Dying*, 83–96. New Delhi: SAGE Publications India Pvt Ltd, 2008. https://ebookcentral.proquest.com/lib/umanitoba/detail.action?docID=409005.

Kiernan Fallon, Cara, and Jason Karlawish. "Is the WHO Definition of Health Aging Well? Framework for "Health" after Three Sore and Ten." *AJPH* 109, no. 8 (2019): 1104–1105. Manitoba Law Reform Commission, *Elder Abuse and Neglect in Manitoba. Consultation Paper*, Winnipeg, June 2021, 68 p. http://www.manitobalawreform.ca/pubs/pdf/elder_abuse_consultation.pdf.

McCann, Gerard, and Féilim Ó'hAdhmaill, eds. *International Human Rights, Social Policy and Global Development: Critical Perspectives*. Bristol: Bristol University Press, 2020. https://www.researchgate.net/publication/342039515_International_Human_Rights_Social_Policy_and_Global_Development_Critical_Perspectives.

Mulley, Graham P. "European Courts and Old People." *Age Ageing* 42, no. 5 (2013): 559–560. https://pubmed.ncbi.nlm.nih.gov/23694841/.

Neda, Abdolahrezaee, Arsalan Khanmohammadi, Mahboubeh Dadfar, Vahid Rashedi, and Liela Behnam. "Prediction of Hope, Physical Health, and Mental Health by Mediating Variable of Religious Spiritual Well-Being in Elderly." *Mental Health, Religion & Culture* 23, no. 10 (2020): 928–940. https://doi.org/10.1080/13674676.2020.1819220.

Nunes Vicente, Marta. "Property Rights and Legitimate Expectations Under United States Constitutional Law and the European Convention on Human Rights: Some Comparative Remarks." *Comparative Law Review* [online] 26, no. 1 (2021): 51–96. https://apcz.umk.pl/CLR/article/view/CLR.2020.002.

Peterka, Nathalie, Anne Caron-Deglise, and Frédéric Arbellot. *Protection de la personne vulnérable. Protection judicaire et juridique des mineurs et des majeurs*. Paris, Dalloz, 2021–2022, coll. Dalloz Action.

Pope Francis. *Encyclical Letter Fratelli Tutti on Fraternity and Social Friendship* of 3 October 2020. https://www.vatican.va/content/francesco/en/encyclicals/documents/papa-francesco_20201003_enciclica-fratelli-tutti.html.

Religious Leaders in Canada. *Hope, Gratitude and Solidarity: A Message to Canadians in Response to the COVID-19 Pandemic.* https://www.councilofchurches.ca/news/hope-gratitude-and-solidarity/?xdomain_data=w0XBJS8jmzftBNDi8BROiWL98LLL1UwDKqw89D1jctNTDXxGPMJE1kbRPrM%2BbSmj.

Renucci, Jean-François, *Droit européen des droits de l'homme. Droits et Libertés fondamentaux garantis par la CEDH*. Paris, LGDJ, 2021.

Šaňáková, Š., and J. Čáp. Dignity of Elderly Adults from the Perspective of Nurses: A Qualitative Descriptive Study. *Central European Journal of Nursing and Midwifery* 9, no. 4 (2018): 906–914. http://cejnm.osu.cz/artkey/cjn-201804-0002_dignity-of-elderly-adults-from-the-perspective-of-nurses-a-qualitative-descriptive-study.php.

Şahin, Ertuğrul, Nursel Topkaya, Cem Gençoğlu, and Ercümend Ersanlı. "Prevalence and Correlates of Hopelessness among Turkish Elderly People Living with Family or in Nursing Homes." *Societies* 8, no. 2 (2018): 39. https://doi.org/10.3390/soc8020039.

Scanlon, Michael, V° "Hope". In Komonchak, Joseph A., Mary Collins, and Dermot A. Lane. *The New Dictionary of Theology*. Collegeville, MN: Liturgical Press, 1990.

Spanier, Benny, Israel Doron, and Faina Milman-Sivan. "Older Persons' Use of the European Court of Human, Rights." *Journal of Cross-Cultural Gerontology* 28 (2013): 407–420. https://pubmed.ncbi.nlm.nih.gov/24142028/.

Sudre, Frédéric, Joël Andriantsimbazovina, and Gérard Gonzalez, e.o. *Les grands arrêts de la Cour Européenne des Droits de l'Homme*, Paris, P.U.F., 2019 (9e éd.), coll. Thémis Droit.

Talley, Phyllis. "The Elderly Disabled: The Applicability of Disability Rights for Age-Related Disability." *Journal of Legal Medicine* 40, no. 1 (2020): 115–129. https://doi.org/10.1080/01947648.2020.1731330.

Thompson, G. N., J. McArthur, and M. Doupe. "Identifying Markers of Dignity-Conserving Care in Long-Term Care: A Modified Delphi Study." In *PLoS ONE* 11, no. 6 (2016): 14. https://journals.plos.org/plosone/article/file?id=10.1371/journal.pone.0156816&type=printable.

Tonolo, Sarah. "International Human Rights Law and the Protection of the Elderly in Europe." *Medicine, Law & Society* 11, no. 2 (2018): 107–120. https://doi.org/10.18690/ml&s.11.2.107-120.2018.

Tourrette, Catherine. «Peut-on appliquer le principe "d'intérêt supérieur" aux personnes dites vulnérables?». *Revue de Bioéthique de Nouvelle-Aquitaine* (Espace de Réflexion Ethique Nouvelle-Aquitaine) 4 (2019): 57–66. https://hal.archives-ouvertes.fr/hal-03257011/document.

Trent, John. "Promoting and Protecting Human Rights." In *A United Nation Renaissance. What the UN Is and What It Could Be*, edited by John Trent and Laura Shnurr, 98–123. Opladen/Berlin/Toronto: Barbara Budrich Publishers, 2018.

UN-Council of Europe and EU Documents

UN

Declaration of the Rights of the Child of 20 November 1959 (GA Resolution 1386(XIV) of 20 November 1959). https://archive.crin.org/en/library/legal-database/un-declaration-rights-child-1959.html#:~:text=The%20child%20shall%20enjoy%20special,conditions%20of%20freedom%20and%20dignity.

International Convention on the Rights of Persons with Disabilities (ICRPD) of 30 March 2007 (entry into force May 3, 2008). https://www.un.org/development/desa/disabilities/convention-on-the-rights-of-persons-with-disabilities.html.

Mahler, Claudia, Report of the Independent Expert on the Enjoyment of all Human Rights by Older Persons, A/HRC/48/53, August 2021. https://ngocoa-ny.org/recent-documents-of-interes/a_hrc_48_53_ie-report-on.pdf.

UN Convention on the Rights of the Child of 20 November 1989 (entry into force September 2, 1990). https://www.ohchr.org/en/professionalinterest/pages/crc.aspx.

UN Secretary General, *Our Common Agenda- Report of the Secretary General*, UN, New York, 2021, 86 p. https://www.un.org/en/content/common-agenda-report/assets/pdf/Common_Agenda_Report_English.pdf.

UN Secretary-General, *The Highest Aspiration. A Call to Action for Human Rights*. UN, New York, 2020, 14 p. https://www.un.org/sg/sites/www.un.org.sg/files/atoms/files/The_Highest_Asperation_A_Call_To_Action_For_Human_Right_English.pdf.

World Health Organization (WHO). *10 Facts on Ageing and Health*, 1 May 2017. https://www.who.int/news-room/fact-sheets/detail/10-facts-on-ageing-and-health.

Council of Europe

Council of Europe, *The Human Rights of Older Persons, Strasburg*, 2019, compilation. https://rm.coe.int/promotion-of-human-rights-of-older-persons/16809fb9bf

– Recommendation CM/Rec (2014)2 of the Committee of Ministers to member states adopted on 19 February 2014 on the promotion of the Human Rights of Older Persons.

– Recommendation CM/Rec (2014)2. Explanatory Memorandum.

– Parliamentary Assembly, Human Rights of Older Persons and their comprehensive care, Res. 2168 (2017).

– CDDH Report on the implementation of the Committee of Ministers' Recommendation CM/Rec(2014) 2 on the promotion of the Human Rights of Older Persons, CDDH(2018)R90 Addendum, 07/01/2019.

European Court of Human Rights (ECtHR). *Elderly People and the European Convention on Human Rights*, Factsheet February 2019. https://www.echr.coe.int/Documents/FS_Elderly_ENG.pdf.

Parliamentary Assembly of the Council of Europe adopted Resolution June 28, 2018, 2232: Resolution 2232 (2018) "Striking a Balance Between the Best Interest of the Child and the Need to Keep Families Together." https://assembly.coe.int/nw/xml/XRef/Xref-XML2HTML-en.asp?fileid=25014&lang=en.

Pejčinović Burić, Marija. Secretary General of the Council of Europe. *State of Democracy, Human Rights and the Rule of Law. A democratic renewal for Europe*, 2021 report, Strasburg. https://rm.coe.int/annual-report-sg-2021/1680a264a2.

EU

European Agency for Fundamental Rights (AFR): Fundamental Rights Report 2018, Part 1: "Shifting perceptions: towards a rights-based approach to Ageing," 9–30. http://fra.europa.eu/en/publication/2018/fundamental-rights-report-2018.

von der Leyen, Ursula. President of the EU Commission. *Speech on the state of the European Union* delivered on September 15, 2021. https://ec.europa.eu/commission/presscorner/detail/en/SPEECH_21_4701.

ECtHR Case Law

Akhverdiyev v. Azerbaijan, 29 January 2015, 76254/11.

Amanalachioai v. Romania, 26 May 2009, 4023/04.

Bancsók and László Magyar v. Hungary, 28 October 2021, 52374/15 and 53364/15.

Béláné Nagy v. Hungary, 13 December 2013, 53080/13.
Berger-Krall and others v. Slovenia of 12 June 2014, 14717/04.
Burden v. United Kingdom, 29 April 2008, 13378/05.
Cabbia and others v. Italy, 5 March 1990, 11975/86.
Carson v. others v. United Kingdom, 16 March 2012, 42184/05.
Delecolle v. France, 25 October 2018, 37646/13.
Denizci and others v. Cyprus, 25316–25321/94 and 27207/95.
Dodov v. Bulgaria, 17 January 2008, 59548/00.
Fernandes de Oliveira v. Portugal, 31 January 2019, 78103/14.
Finogenov and others v. Russia, 04 June 2012, 18299/03 and 27311/03.
Frumkin v. Russia 5 January 2016, 74568/12.
Haidn v. Germany, 13 January 2011, 6587/04.
Heinish v. Germany, 21 July 2011, 28274/08.
H.L. v. United Kingdom of 5 October 2004, 45508/99.
H.M v. Switzerland of 22 February 2002, 39187/98.
Ivanova and Cherkezov v. Bulgaria, 21 April 2016, 46577/15.
Khamtokhu and Aksenchik v. Russia, 24 January 2017, 60367/08, 961/11.
Kopecký v. Slovakia, 28 September 2004, 44912/98.
Lopes de Sousa Fernandes v. Portugal, 19 December 2017, 56080/13.
McDonnald v. United Kingdom, 20 May 2014, 4241/12.
M.K v. Luxembourg of 18 May 2021, 51746/18.
M.V v. Finland, 23 March 2017, 53251/13.
Neulinger and Shuruk v. Switzerland of 6 July 2010, 41615/07.
Niess v. France, 17 January 1996, 26202.
Pretty v. United Kingdom, 29 April 2002, 2346/02.
Sawoniuk v. United Kingdom, 29 May 2001, 63716/00.
Shtukaturov v. Russia, 27 March 2008, 44009/05.
Stefanetti and others v. Italy, 15 April 2014, 21838/10, 21849/10, 21855/10, 21860/10, 21863/10, 21869/10, 21870/10.
Tagayeva and others v. Russia, 13 April 2017, 26562/07.
Terna v. Italy, 14 January 2021, 21052/18.
Trakhel v Switzerland, 4 November 2014, 29217/12.
Volintiru v. Italy of 19 March 2013 No. 8530/08.
W.A v. Switzerland, 2 November 2021, 38958/16.
x. Federal Republic of Germany, 14 December 1961, 599/59.
Zadonik v. Slovenia, 21 May 2015, 53723/13.
Zubac v. Croatia, 5 April 2018, 40160/12.

Human Security and the Digital Threat: Russia and Ukraine

Stephen Lunn

In 2014 Russia engaged in hybrid warfare against Ukraine to undermine the Ukrainian government's authority and autonomy over the Crimea and Donbas regions. The ongoing conflict between Russia and Ukraine illustrates both the physical and psychological effects of cyber operations on states and their people. Since 2013, Ukraine has been the target of numerous cyber operations at the hands of Russia. These operations have persisted both in peacetime and during armed conflict. Cyber operations were actively used in 2014 in the buildup to and in the annexation of Crimea and during the conflict in the Donbas region. Following Crimea's annexation, Ukraine was subjected to the first attack on its critical infrastructure in December of 2015. In the last two months of 2016 alone, Ukraine was subject to 6500 cyber-attacks.[1] In 2017, Ukraine was again subject to attacks on its critical infrastructure. The Ministry of Infrastructure, Central Bank, postal service, major telecommunications companies, and metro services in Kyiv were all affected.[2] Understanding the human

S. Lunn (✉)
University of Manitoba, Winnipeg, MB, Canada
e-mail: slunn11@gmail.com

L. E. Reimer and K. Standish (eds.), *Perspectives on Justice, Indigeneity, Gender, and Security in Human Rights Research*,
https://doi.org/10.1007/978-981-99-1930-7_13

costs and impacts needs to be understood in terms of how the perpetrator intends it. Cyber operations have two distinct uses, kinetic and non-kinetic, and states need to address the inadequacies in Law as they apply to non-kinetic, non-destructive cyber operations. Cyber operations penetrate the state at a much deeper capacity than a territorial breach of sovereignty, and it is the far-reaching influence campaigns through cyber operations that need to be better addressed under International Law and protect citizens from.

What Is a Cyber Operation, and How Does It Fit into Conflict?

For this paper, a cyber operation refers to both computer network attacks (CNA) and computer network espionage (CNE). A CNA is an operation that targets and incapacitates a computer system, whereas a CNE is associated more with illicit information gathering. In a report specifically on the use of cyber operations in the Ukraine conflict, James Lewis argued that a cyber operation could include the manipulation of software, data, knowledge, and opinion to degrade computer performance and produce political and/or psychological disruption.[3] A cyber-attack can have the capacity to manipulate public opinion to damage a state's authority and legitimacy among both domestic and international audiences.[4] Ultimately, civilians are the target of cyber operations. Cyber operations have evolved past the conventional view of computer system disruption and illicit information gathering and instead provide a larger context of how a cyber operation is a disruptor for a perpetrating state. Cyber operations create public confusion, shape opinion, and inflict damage to data and services.[5] Cyber operations manipulate public opinion, and the human rights of civilians are indirectly put at risk by means of these operations.

Cyber operations are rarely used as the primary method to conduct state-on-state conflict and often belong to a larger strategic picture. Cyber operations fit very well both in hybrid warfare and information warfare. Hybrid warfare is a collection of tactics designed to circumvent deterrence and avoid retaliation by operating under the threshold of what would be considered state use of armed force recognized under the United Nations (UN) Charter.[6] Hybrid warfare tactics also include the use of unmarked troops and include irregular forces, covert actions, and political manipulation to achieve strategic goals.[7] A hybrid threat can be a multimodal, low intensity, kinetic, or non-kinetic threat to international peace.[8] Conventional warfare is now only part of the larger picture in terms of coercive actions available to states.[9] Cyber operations create a space in which a state can conduct offensive actions against another state with low political risk because there is a lack of consensus as to how International Law applies.[10] Cyber operations are able to create similar effects in a kinetic attack without directly attributing the perpetrating state.[11]

The Silent Battle for the Internet

Protecting individuals from cyber operations requires an understanding of how different states conceptualize and use the Internet. The Internet is the main means of conducting cyber and information operations. Different states want to regulate the Internet and the laws surrounding them to defend their own interests. There are two main arguments on how the Internet should be governed. The first is the open Internet, supported by the United States (US) and most Western democracies. This is the most common form of Internet governance. The Internet is largely a non-state domain and relies on stakeholders working together instead of one group trying to promote its role and power.[12] Russia and China subscribe to the idea of Internet sovereignty. This concept of cyber sovereignty argues that a state should be sovereign within its borders and free from foreign state intervention in its national interest and will.[13] It implies that the state has complete control of all the information its citizens consume and that it controls any physical infrastructure related to the Internet.[14] It is a stark contrast to the open Internet faction and speaks to how these different factions conceptualize and deploy their cyber operations.

Russia, along with the US and the other UN States, created an international norm in the United Nations that generally condemns attacks on critical infrastructure, but more importantly, keeps the cyber/information tactics Russia commonly uses in a legal grey zone.[15] This presents a very difficult and broader issue regarding the Internet. The First Committee of the UN spent nearly two decades discussing how to limit cyber operations and the use of ICTs.[16] Russia outright rejects the term cybersecurity and instead has pushed for the term information security.[17] Framing the discussion around information security, as opposed to cybersecurity, encompasses state sovereignty and the control of and dissemination of information by the Internet.[18] In a global effort to decide how we define violence and force in relation to cyber, this rejection of cyber language in favor of information arguably creates more ambiguity and difficulty creating new norms and laws.[19] This ambiguity creates a legal grey area where there are no certain grounds for what actions constitute retaliation.[20]

Russia is involved in the creation of new norms, such as through the process of the UN Group of Governmental Experts (UN GGE) and UN Open-Ended Working Group process. It appears they continue to support positions and norms that contribute to the legal grey zones and ambiguity that allow them to maintain their current practices. At a UN GGE meeting in 2015, all participating states, including Russia and the United States, agreed to adopt the norm not to target critical infrastructure with cyber operations.[21] However, the norm also failed to address any potential concerns regarding the use of cyber as a tool for political coercion.[22] Russia's norm-setting history and patterns [LR3] clearly creates a situation that allows for the use of non-kinetic cyber operations without directly violating any norms that they themselves agreed to at the UN.

The Current State of International Law as It Applies to Cyber Attacks

International Law has proved to be problematic in addressing cyber operations used both in peacetime and in armed conflict. There is no clear consensus on how International Law applies, and when consensus has been reached, states have been known to change their position. In the 2015 UN GGE report, Russia agreed to the norm that states will not attack another state's critical infrastructure.[23] Shortly after the 2013 GGE report, Russia shifted its position that the UN Charter and International Law applies to the cyber conflict in full.[24] Along with China, it has distanced itself from this position, arguing instead against the entire application of the UN Charter.[25]

Cyber operations present a particularly interesting problem for International Humanitarian Law that stems back well before the Great War. Cyber harms objects and people in a fundamentally different way than a gun or bomb. As Michael Schmitt argues, it is not the fact that an object is physically damaged but the fact it is no longer used for its intended purpose that invokes the harm verdict.[26] Consider how this applies to cyber. That would have significant impacts on how we treat data, software, and hardware. Malware can exist in software or data and cause minimal damage but changes the object's intent. This was a tactic used on December 23, 2015, when a cyber operation on a Ukrainian power grid caused a blackout in the capital region for nearly six hours.[27] In a *postmortem* of the 2015 Ukrainian blackout, officials determined that the malware responsible for the attack had infected the system six months prior to the event. The intended use of the software had then arguably changed without it physically being destroyed. This again speaks to how states can exploit the grey areas in the law to use cyber operations without violating any International Laws or norms. States are the primary decision-makers in International Law. If they want to regulate this, they certainly have the option to better apply laws to cyber.[28] However, Schmitt argues that states will not want to extend the notion of damage on the civilian objects intent to cyber.[29]

The term "attack" in International Law requires the qualification of significant destruction or death. In terms of International Law, we have not yet seen a proper "cyber-attack."[30] This qualification fails to consider the manipulation of a population that does not demonstrate a tangible physical result but still has significant consequences. This legal qualification evidently suits the position of cyber sovereignty supporting states such as Russia and China.[31] Operations that generate consequences significant to the targeted state but fall below the threshold of an "attack" are therefore not in violation of International Law. This is perfect for cyber operations that do not overtly cause significant destruction or death because they fall into a legal grey area where the law does not indicate if the victim state would be allowed to retaliate.[32] The term attack under IHL provides a more inclusive definition than the UN Charter. Any operation that disables the function of an object is considered an attack.[33] This wider definition is useful; however, IHL applies only in the certain context of armed conflict.

Laws that exist to protect states and their citizens from cyber operations of interference have been outpaced by their growing capacities of cyber operations to disrupt civilian life. Russia's use of hybrid warfare, with cyber operations as a prominent tool, has made it easier to bypass the legal norms of violating a state's territorial sovereignty and regulations on the use of force.[34] This is problematic for Western liberal democracies. It limits their ability to respond to these events as they have built their decision-making structures on existing international norms and laws founded in the UN Charter. The responses they have available are confined by International Law and their commitment to these principles, inherently limiting their responses to hybrid threats and cyber operations.[35]

Dr. Michael Schmitt, Professor of International Law at the University of Reading, Senior Fellow at NATO CCDCOE, and Project lead for the Tallinn Manual on the application of International Law to cyberspace is a leading scholar in the Cyber Law field. He reached the initial conclusion that cyber operations directed at civilians and civilian objects do not violate International Humanitarian Law (IHL) in terms of an "attack" unless they result in the death, injury, physical damage, or destruction of civilian life or property.[36] While Schmitt concluded that human physical or mental suffering was included in the concept of injury, acts that are deemed an inconvenience, harassment, and diminishment in quality of life due to a cyber operation do not suffice as human suffering.[37] In this context, human suffering must be an injury and/or loss of property, including monetary items that could be used toward physical property.[38] This reasoning leaves much to be desired in the application of laws to protect against human harm and suffering. Dr. Schmitt accurately notes in his still relevant 2002 paper that "the advent of [Computer Network Attack] reveals a normative lacuna that, unless filled, will inevitably result in an expansion of war's impact on the civilian population."[39] In other words, left untouched by International Laws and state regulation, cyber operations will increasingly impact the civilian population. There is a massive gap in protection. While there is no consensus that International Law, such as the UN Charter, and IHL may not be invoked in the use of cyber operations, there could be opportunities to apply International Human Rights Law in the future.

What is not considered is whether operations below the threshold of attack over a sustained period can amount to injury under IHL. The most common cyber operation, the Distributed Denial of Service (DDOS) attack, can have detrimental consequences for a civilian population and can interfere with the use of a system without affecting the system itself.[40] Experts have determined that the activity of a DDoS could eventually rise to an attack under IHL, but the laws of armed conflict do not presently extend this far.[41] Equally problematic in the history of IHL is the emphasis on the nature of the harm as opposed to its severity. The emphasis has traditionally been on harm conceptualized as death, injury, and damage. In the history of warfare, the nature of the attack was more critical than the inconveniences or disruption caused.[42]

In a proper analysis of cyber operations in the Ukraine–Russia conflict, Russian cyber operations must be conceptualized as a tool for information warfare. There are four dimensions to information warfare, which were all present during the 2014 annexation of Crimea from Ukraine.[43] These four dimensions are electronic warfare, intelligence gathering and manipulation, hacker warfare, and psychological warfare. All four dimensions used computer systems in some capacity. The most important of these is psychological warfare, used to drive wedges in Western alliances like NATO and to prepare the target area in case a conventional conflict starts.[44] To understand the actual human impact of psychological warfare, it is necessary to understand how cyber operations fit into Russian strategic doctrine.

Through the Eyes of the Perpetrator—Russian Cyber Operations

Russia has a different understanding of war from Western countries, which also complicates the address of cyber operations. The common phrase by Clausewitz in *On War* is that war is the continuation of politics by other means.[45] In Russian strategic doctrine, politics is the continuation of war by other means.[46] Wars conducted by Russia are invisible and drawn out.[47] There is no difference between wartime and peacetime in Russian strategic doctrine. There is only conflict, which stems from classic Marxist-Leninist thought that war is permanent and ongoing.[48] Cyber operations are an extension of this framework. The Russian system of warfare engages the idea of total warfare. All aspects of society are involved. The actors are not purely military, and the aim of warfare is to reduce citizen's access to their basic needs as well as the revenues required for the impacted state to function.[49]

The first steps in Russian warfare doctrine is economic and diplomatic maneuvering in combination with disinformation campaigns against the targeted civilian population.[50] Before any shots are fired or boots touch the ground, cyber operations have been deployed specifically to disrupt civil society subtly or directly. In 2007, Russia launched one of the first major cyber operations in history against Estonia. That country was targeted with DDoS attacks that forced various government websites and financial institutions off the Internet.[51] A DDoS attack means that the computer system is overwhelmed with requests and shuts down. The outcome of the Estonia attack was the loss of access to the Internet for a country considered to be one of the most online countries in the world. Government websites were forced offline, the efficiency of the media was slowed, and Estonian officials were confronted with the difficult tasks of considering how essential services could be delivered while the banking system and payment methods remained offline.[52] The level of disruption and uncertainty was crucial; the fear that Russia would soon follow with an armed attack on Estonia was significant.

This event pushed cyber operations into the minds of international and state policymakers for the first time. Estonia was already relying heavily on the Internet and networking for many of its government functions and public services.[53] The attacks demonstrated how devastating a cyber operation could be. Responding to DDoS attacks is now a top training exercise for both the United States and the European Union.[54] In 2008, Russia used cyber operations in tandem with its armed conflict with Georgia.

In the case of Ukraine, prior to the annexation of Crimea, Russia used DDoS during its presidential election. Russian operators used DDoS attacks to freeze the political operations of certain Ukrainian presidential candidates. Its goal was to make funds and other campaign tools unavailable to the candidate.[55]

Russia is not interested in cyber operations to physically damage critical civilian infrastructure.[56] Instead, its overall goal is to influence and direct the overall political discourse within civilian space. That is, cyber operations serve to control and influence the thinking of the target population.[57] As an information warfare tool, cyber operations achieve a political objective without the direct use of military force.[58] Cyber operations are thus not a conventional military tool in the way that Western military thinkers believe it to be. The Russian concept of cyber warfare blends elements of what would be considered information warfare in the West with its military doctrine.[59] The Russian regime does not recognize the term "cyber" to begin with. It prefers to use the term "information operation," with cyber serving as a sub-category, and this is reflected in how these tools are deployed against its enemies.[60] Russians do not measure the success of their cyber operations by what a hacker has accomplished, but instead, by the reach and influence of its propaganda.[61] This means of conducting warfare is one of the most dangerous challenges facing democratic societies as a whole, making everything from freedom of speech to basic human rights a battleground.[62] The overall Russian tactic is to defeat the enemy by first using information warfare that fundamentally weakens a state's democratic institutions well before a kinetic conflict begins or is needed.[63]

As we progress through the twenty-first century, Western states are concerned with the potential impact a cyber operation may have on critical infrastructure. In fact, it is one of the key concerns of the ICRC.[64] Its current commentary focuses on the consequences of a cyber operation on a hospital. The United States is similarly concerned with the physical outcomes of a cyber operation, and this is reflected in its strategic thought. The United States and its Western allies show no desire in allowing psychological warfare to become a key component of cyber operations.[65] The United States continually tries to argue that cyber operations and information warfare are mutually exclusive from each other instead of being interconnected. However, this is a very dangerous way of thinking. While the United States has sound strategic and legal reasoning for arguing the separation of cyber warfare and information warfare, accepting that information warfare and cyber operations are interconnected could help states understand the intended purpose of a non-kinetic cyber-attack. As noted by Alexander Klimburg, the most effective hackers were not ones that could hack by code but ones able to manipulate the person behind the technology.[66]

The use of cyber operations by Russia against Ukraine demonstrates how information-style cyber operations, along with kinetic cyber operations, pose a significant danger to innocent civilians. These information-styled cyber operations allowed Russia to create a condition where Human Rights laws and treaty violations could be weaponized. For example, Russia deployed misinformation, spreading rumors that Ukrainian forces were torturing Russian-speaking children in Crimea.[67] The danger to civilians needs to be understood in the context of Russian information warfare doctrine, with cyber as a subsection to fully comprehend and circumvent these actions. Failure to do so could run the risk of leaving civilians and states without adequate and agreed-upon protection under International Laws.

The Case of Ukraine 2014 to Present

The current situation in Ukraine and Russia stems back to November 2013 when the pro-Russian President of Ukraine, Viktor Yanukovych, did not sign an association agreement with the European Union and opted to pursue closer ties with Russia.[68] This led to mass public protests in the Western regions of Ukraine and the occupation of the Kyiv Independence Square by pro-EU supporters.[69] In February 2014, Yanukovych fled to Russia, and a few days later, unmarked military personnel, believed to be Russian troops, were found in the Crimea region.[70] These events marked the start of the ongoing conflict that Ukraine currently faces with Russia. Ukrainian Security Services have identified at least 6500 cyber incidents in the last two months of 2016.[71]

In February 2014, Russia successfully annexed the Crimean Peninsula from Ukraine using hybrid warfare tactics, including cyber operations via social media, deployment of Russian special and naval forces without insignias and manipulating the local population and outside world views as to what was happening. Since the annexation, Ukraine has been subject to continued cyber operations, manifested in different ways compared to what was experienced in 2014. A disinformation campaign was used to confuse Ukrainian decision-makers as to who these forces were. A St. Petersburg-based company spent ten million dollars on misinformation campaigns in Ukraine to spread disinformation in 2014.[72] Other Russian assets were used to confuse and slow the response of Western governments. This included the use of battlefield cyber techniques to slow communications within the Ukrainian government.[73]

In the annexation of Crimea, Russia also made use of cyber operations-based information warfare tactics. In an edited collection on Russian Information warfare in Ukraine, published by NATO CCDCOE, Marie Jaitner noted that Ukrainian government officials' mobile devices were disabled and that Ukrainian government websites and news portals were defaced and subject to DDoS attacks.[74] This cyber-based information warfare tactic slowed the Ukrainian government's response and led to an information blackout.[75] Jaitner concluded that while the success of these cyber-based information warfare tactics is unclear, the information warfare campaign made it more difficult for the Ukrainian government to get an accurate picture of the situation in Crimea.[76]

This information warfare campaign in Crimea entailed manipulating the population through social media and slowing government responses through DDoS attacks.[77] Other strategic cyber-attacks during the 2014 Ukraine conflict targeted the Ukrainian government as a whole as well as the media services.[78] However, the psychological warfare aspect of Russia's information warfare campaign was its most powerful tool in

Ukraine. The Crimea region has a large minority of Russian-speaking citizens.[79] By targeting this minority, Russia was able to create a picture of Ukraine that did not reflect reality. Examples of this include claiming that the Ukrainian government was fascist, and its armed forces were committing human rights abuses in the region.[80] Russia also used information-cyber operations against the people of Ukraine.[81] Information operations were used to transmit to the outside world that the conflict did not exist in Ukraine, denied Russian involvement and that the annexation of Crimea was an internal matter.[82]

On December 23rd of 2015, Ukraine was hit by what is regarded as the first cyber-attack on critical infrastructure.[83] The attack on the power grid caused a blackout in the capital region of Ukraine for approximately six hours. Experts determined that this attack could have been much more intense with a more significant outcome had the perpetrators desired. The conclusion drawn from this is that similar-style cyber operations can be conducted on infrastructure, like power grids, anywhere around the world.[84] The 2015 attack on the power grid was not designed for the physical effect that it had on the critical infrastructure but rather the psychological impact it had on the citizens of Ukraine.[85] For all key Russian cyber operations, the emphasis is on how to interfere with the decision-making process of the target.[86] The conflict in Ukraine illustrates the many facets of the Russian concept of "Cyber Power."[87]

The incident on December 23, 2015 is critical to this analysis. Earlier in the day, pro-Ukrainian activists physically attacked a substation that feeds power to a large section of the Crimea region, causing widespread power outages.[88] Russia was able to respond in kind in a matter of hours, causing a major blackout in the city of Kyiv, on the other side of the country. It is impossible to attribute Russia to the incident for certain, but the common belief is that it was responsible. The perpetrators disabled the backup systems, sabotaged digital workstations, and made it practically impossible to restore power to the region.[89] In tandem, call centers were flooded with fake calls originating from Moscow, preventing real customers from contacting the proper authorities.[90] More than 225,000 Ukrainians were suddenly without power and heating.[91] The operation was a DDoS attack that was not considered especially devastating.[92] However, this could have been particularly devastating if power was unable to be restored. The malware used in the attack on the 23rd of December wiped out essential service files causing the computers to crash. The malware in the power grid was found in other Ukrainian utilities and infrastructure. Blackouts have transpired since 2015. One of the most recent occurrences being December 17th of 2016.

In 2017 Ukraine was also subject to an attack that damaged the government's computers.[93] Institutions such as the Central Bank, state postal service, and ATMs were all taken offline.[94] This attack also spread internationally, affecting companies in Denmark, the United Kingdom, the United States, and Australia, and was believed to be a political message by Russia.[95] One of the most recent attacks on Ukraine was in December 2019. Russian government hackers targeted various diplomats, military officers, journalists, law enforcement personnel, and NGOs.[96] What happened was specific emails were sent to different individuals in the listed industries; once opened, their device was infected with malware. The desired outcome is to either receive money or information from the victim of the attack.[97]

The Human Security Issue in Cyber

The case of the Ukraine–Russian conflict presents two very different applications of cyber operations. We see events such as blackouts, which are tangible physical outcomes. We also see the use of information warfare. The blackouts caused by the cyber operations of December 2015 and December 2016 had an immediate tangible effect on the average citizen. Cyber operations may have physical effects on human security, but it should also be assessed in terms of the psychological effect it has on human security as well. If the argument that the main goal of the Crimean annexation was to keep Ukraine in the Russian sphere of influence and to destabilize its political, social, and economic situation, then the human impact is one that is primarily psychological.[98] Looking at the 2015 attack on the power grid, Randolph Kent argues that the shutdown was not about causing human damage and spilling blood but impacting noncombatants in their daily lives and eroding existing infrastructure.[99] It is reasonable to believe that the attack could have been physically dangerous if it had been really cold that day or if it had adversely impacted the healthcare system. While the events had very different outcomes, one being an outright shutdown of Kyiv's power grid and the other shutting down of banking institutions, government offices, and ATMs, assuming Kent's argument is correct, all had the desired psychological effect of impeding civilians' daily life and eroding existing infrastructure for a later purpose.

The real damage caused was psychological, with the intent to undermine the credibility of the state.

The human impact in cyber operations should not be solely interpreted on the basis of the physical effect.[100] The psychological impact by manipulation of opinion and decision-making is equally, if not more important than the physical consequences.[101] Although cyber operations have the potential to cause devastating physical consequences, they have not been used in the past for this purpose.[102] Cyber operations that aim to influence and manipulate are used much more frequently and, therefore, more consideration should be given to information warfare type of attack, even though the human and financial impacts are not immediately seen. The primary effect is to manipulate data, knowledge, and opinions to produce political and psychological effects rather than physical damage.[103] More attention should be paid by Western states to cyber operations that are used for political coercion. The experience from Ukraine and other case studies such as Estonia in 2007 and Georgia in 2008 suggests that NATO-allied countries may need to rethink how their opponents use and deploy cyber operations.[104]

Despite the case of Ukraine, Western states, and organizations International Committee of the Red Cross (ICRC) continue to focus on physical damage caused by cyber operations. The ICRC is focused on the physical damage to the economy and the abilities of governments and businesses to provide essential services to civilians. The ICRC placed emphasis on protecting civilian infrastructure from being disabled and protecting civilian and state data.[105] The ICRC has concluded that the tangible cost of cyber operations for humans is a substantial economic loss.[106] Cyber operations pose a particular threat to critical infrastructure and the daily functions of society.[107] This reflects the status as to how Western states approach cyber operations and the laws that apply. An attack on critical infrastructure may not individually amount to much physical damage. An isolated attack like that in 2015 may not lead to substantial economic loss and prevent the delivery of essential services. The psychological effect, however, may be more pertinent, ongoing, and do more long-term damage.

The Russian strategic use of cyber operations sheds light on their desired outcome and the potential adverse effects it has on human security and rights. The blackouts caused by the cyber operations of December 23, 2015, and December 17, 2016, need to consider the greater Russian strategic use of information warfare. For example, one ordinary citizen interviewed after the December 2016 attack stated that she had similar feelings to the ones she had during the mandatory power outages from 1997 to 1998. During that year, power was regularly shut off from 5 to 7 p.m. to maintain the capacity of the power system. This individual noted feelings of depression and hopelessness. The consistent loss of power had a negative psychological impact on citizens affected and shifted their day-to-day actions. Cyber operations that consistently disable civilian infrastructure, which affects day-to-day life, like power grids, could achieve similar circumstances to the event described above. Sustained cyber operations of this nature could easily move from the level of significant inconvenience to one of major civilian disruption. Indeed, there is some belief that a cyber operation that produces intangible effects of such scope, intensity, gravity, and duration could also be considered an armed attack.[108] Returning to the application of International Law, this may still not reach the level of armed attack because diminishment in quality of life does not meet the definition of human suffering.[109] While it is at this point unclear if a cyber operation akin to 2015 overtime could reach the definition of armed attack under the UN Charter, it is clear that there would be significant disruption to civilian life that needs to be addressed.

The cyber operations of Ukraine in 2014 were used for political coercion, opinion-shaping, and intelligence gathering.[110] They were not the type of cyber operation that would allow NATO to invoke Article V of the Washington Treaty if Ukraine was an ally or be in violation of the UN Charter Article 51.[111] A cyber operation of that level currently needs to cause damage physically equivalent to what a conventional weapon is capable of.[112] The overall purpose of cyber operations by Russia was to use and disrupt civil society using a strategic objective that navigated the grey areas of international laws. The physical effects of cyber operations, such as creating economic distress and lowering government and business capacity, should be understood as well for the psychological and manipulation impact it has.

Conclusion

Cyber operations penetrate the state at a much deeper capacity than a territorial breach of sovereignty, and it is the far-reaching influence campaigns through cyber operations that need to be better addressed under International Law and protect citizens from. As policymakers navigate the grey areas of International Law applicable to cyberspace, great consideration must be paid to the intended effects of the operation and the strategic doctrine of the perpetrating state. The ideological differences between states and uncertainty in the application of international law are likely to continue in the years to come. Future research and scholarship should aim to address how the law of *jus ad bellum* should grow to include cyber operations and information operations that coerce and psychologically harm civilians. Equally, it is becoming clear that attention must be given to how International Human Rights Law applies to these situations.

Just prior to the annexation of Crimea from Ukraine by the Russian Federation in 2014, an onslaught of cyber operations targeted various aspects of the Ukrainian state and civil society. Its civilian infrastructure was subject to repeated attacks causing blackouts and major disruptions to daily life. As well, citizens were subjected to information campaigns geared at manipulating their belief in government and its institutions. Western democracies believe that the most serious consequences of cyber operations to civilians are the economic impact, destruction of infrastructure, and the ability of the government to deliver services. Russia uses its cyber operations to achieve political coercion, undermine the credibility of the target state, and exploit the legal grey areas of International Law. This paper has demonstrated that while both kinds of cyber operations pose risks and consequences to civilians, more attention needs to be paid by Western nations to Russia's intended use of their cyber operations.

Discussion Questions

Potential discussion question could include:

- Is there an avenue for human rights laws and/or norms to address the use of cyber operations as presented in this article?
- Can human rights laws and/or norms address the issues presented in this article? why, or why not?
- Is there a "grey area" in international law as described in this chapter? Or can international law appropriately cover the use of cyber operations.

- Should elements such as the "Psychological effect" of cyber operations be considered when considering the legality of an operation?

Notes

1. Julia E. Sullivan, and Dmitriy Kamensky, "How Cyber-Attacks in Ukraine Show the Vulnerability of the US Power Grid," *The Electricity Journal* 30, no. 3 (2017): 31.
2. Nicole Perlroth, Marki Scott, and Sheera Frenkel, "Cyber Attack Hits Ukraine then Spreads Internationally," *The New York Times*, June 27, 2017, https://www.nytimes.com/2017/06/27/technology/ransomware-hackers.html#:~:text=Computer%20systems%20from%20Ukraine%20to,of%20Ukraine%2C%20A.T.M.s%20stopped%20working.
3. James Lewis, "'Compelling Opponents to Our Will': The Role of Cyber Warfare in Ukraine," in *Cyber War in Perspective: Russian Aggression against Ukraine*, ed. Kenneth Geers (Tallinn: NATO Cooperative Cyber Defence Centre of Excellence, 2015), 39.
4. Lewis, 39.
5. Lewis, 39.
6. Lewis, 40.
7. Lewis, 40.
8. Sascha Bachmann and Hakan Gunneriusson, "Russia's Hybrid Warfare in the East: The Integral Nature of the Information Sphere," *Georgetown Journal of International Affairs* 16, no. special issue (2015): 198.
9. Lewis, "Compelling Opponents," 40.
10. Lewis, 40.
11. Lewis, 40.
12. Alexander Klimburg, *The Darkening Web: The War for Cyberspace* (New York: Penguin Books, 2017), 109.
13. Klimburg, 109.
14. Klimburg, 109.
15. Lewis, "Compelling Opponents," 43.
16. Lewis, 43.
17. Klimburg, *The Darkening Web*, 119.
18. Anders Henriksen, "The End of the Road for the UN GGE Process: The Future Regulation of Cyberspace," *Journal of Cybersecurity* 5, no. 1 (2019): 5.
19. Lewis, "Compelling Opponents," 42.
20. Lewis, 42.
21. Lewis, 43.

22. Lewis, 43.
23. Klimburg, *The Darkening Web*, 121.
24. Klimburg, 121.
25. Klimburg, 121.
26. Michael Schmitt, "Rewired Warfare: Rethinking the Law of Cyber-Attack," *International Review of the Red Cross* 96, no. 893 (2014): 203.
27. Sullivan, "How Cyber-Attacks in Ukraine," 30.
28. Schmitt, "Rewired Warfare," 203.
29. Schmitt, 203.
30. Klimburg, *The Darkening Web*, 122.
31. Klimburg, 122.
32. Lewis, "Compelling Opponents," 41.
33. Klimburg, *The Darkening Web*, 125.
34. Bachmann, "Russia's Hybrid Warfare," 205.
35. Bachmann, 205.
36. Schmitt, "Rewired Warfare," 196.
37. Schmitt, 195.
38. Schmitt, 195.
39. Schmitt, 196.
40. Schmitt, 199–200.
41. Schmitt, 199–200.
42. Schmitt, 204.
43. Klimburg, *The Darkening Web*, 223.
44. Klimburg, 218.
45. Carl von Clausewitz, *On War* (Oxford: Oxford University Press, 2007), 71.
46. Klimburg, *The Darkening Web*, 223.
47. Klimburg, 223.
48. Klimburg, 223.
49. Randolph Kent, "The Future of Warfare: Are We Ready?" *International Review of the Red Cross* 97, no. 900 (2015): 1357.
50. Bachmann, "Russia's Hybrid Warfare," 205.
51. Bachmann, 198.
52. Klimburg, *The Darkening Web*, 59.
53. Michael Schmitt, "Cyber Operations and the Jus Ad Bellum Revisited," *Villanova Law Review* 56, no. 3 (2011): 570.
54. Klimburg, *The Darkening Web*, 59.
55. Bachmann, "Russia's Hybrid Warfare," 205.
56. Klimburg, *The Darkening Web*, 126.
57. Klimburg, 126.
58. Bachmann, "Russia's Hybrid Warfare," 205.
59. Lewis, "Compelling Opponents," 43.

60. Lewis, 43.
61. Klimburg, *The Darkening Web*, 126.
62. Klimburg, 129.
63. Klimburg, 129.
64. United States of America, "Cyber Attacks Are a Known Threat: Now Is the Time for Preventive Action—Statement to Arria Formula Meeting on Cyber Attacks Against Critical Infrastructure." *International Committee of the Red Cross*, August 26, 2020, https://www.icrc.org/en/document/cyber-attacks-are-known-threat-preventive-action.
65. Klimburg, *The Darkening Web*, 139.
66. Klimburg, 54–55.
67. Elina Lange-Ionatamishvili and Sandra Svetoka, "Strategic Communications and Social Media in the Russia Ukraine Conflict," in *Cyber War in Perspective: Russian Aggression against Ukraine*, ed. Kenneth Geers (Tallin: NATO Cooperative Cyber Defence Centre of Excellence, 2015), 109.
68. Sullivan, 30.
69. Sullivan, 30.
70. Sullivan, 31.
71. Sullivan, 31.
72. Klimburg, *The Darkening Web*, 217.
73. Klimburg, 219.
74. Margarita Jaintner, "Russian Information Warfare: Lessons from Ukraine," in *Cyber War in Perspective: Russian Aggression against Ukraine*, ed. Kenneth Geers (Tallinn: NATO Cooperative Cyber Defence Centre of Excellence, 2015), 91.
75. Jaintner, 91.
76. Jaintner, 91.
77. Jaintner, 91.
78. Klimburg, *The Darkening Web*, 220.
79. "Crimea Profile" *BBC News*, January 17, 2018, https://www.bbc.com/news/world-europe-18287223.
80. Klimburg, *The Darkening Web*, 220.
81. Bachmann, "Russia's Hybrid Warfare," 198.
82. Bachmann, 201.
83. Sullivan, 30.
84. Sullivan, 30.
85. Klimburg, *The Darkening Web*, 220.
86. Klimburg, 220.
87. Klimburg, 221.
88. Sullivan, 31.
89. Sullivan, 31.
90. Sullivan, 31.

91. Klimburg, *The Darkening Web*, 205.
92. Klimburg, 205.
93. Perlroth, "Cyber Attack Hits Ukraine."
94. Perlroth.
95. Perlroth.
96. "Significant Cyber Incidents," *Centre for Strategic and International Studies*, accessed April 6, 2020, https://www.csis.org/programs/strategic-technologies-program/significant-cyber-incidents.
97. Dan Swinhoe, "What Is Spear Phishing? Why Targeted Email Attacks Are so Difficult to Stop," *CSO USA*, January 21, 2019. https://www.csoonline.com/article/3334617/what-is-spear-phishing-examples-tactics-and-techniques.html.
98. Kazimierz Pierzchala, "Information Warfare between Russia and Ukraine," *Polish Political Science Yearbook* 48, no. 1 (2019): 105.
99. Kent, "The Future of Warfare," 1357.
100. Lewis, "Compelling Opponents," 40.
101. Lewis, 40.
102. Lewis, 40.
103. Lewis, 40.
104. Lewis, 41.
105. Helen Durham, "Cyber Operations during Armed Conflict: 7 Essential Law and Policy Questions," *Humanitarian Law & Policy* (Blog), International Committee of the Red Cross, March 26, 2020, https://blogs.icrc.org/law-and-policy/2020/03/26/cyber-armed-conflict-7-law-policy-questions/.
106. Laurent Gisel, "The Potential Human Cost of Cyber Operations," *International Committee of the Red Cross*, November 2018.
107. Durham, "Cyber Operations."
108. Lewis, "Compelling Opponents," 40.
109. Schmitt, "Rewired Warfare," 196.
110. Lewis, "Compelling Opponents," 41.
111. Lewis, 41.
112. Lewis, 41.

Bibliography

Bachmann, Sascha, and Hakan Gunneriusson. "Russia's Hybrid Warfare in the East: The Integral Nature of the Information Sphere." *Georgetown Journal of International Affairs* 16, no. special issue (2015): 198–211.

"Crimea Profile." *BBC News*, January 17, 2018. https://www.bbc.com/news/world-europe-18287223.

Durham, Helen. "Cyber Operations During Armed Conflict: 7 Essential Law and Policy Questions." Humanitarian Law and Policy Blog. *International Committee of the Red Cross*, March 26, 2020. https://blogs.icrc.org/law-and-policy/2020/03/26/cyber-armed-conflict-7-law-policy-questions/.

Gisel, Laurent. "The Potential Human Cost of Cyber Operations." *International Committee of the Red Cross*, November 2018.

Henriksen, Anders. "The End of the Road for the UN GGE Process: The Future Regulation of Cyberspace." *Journal of Cybersecurity* 5, no. 1 (2019): 1–9.

Jaintner, M. "Russian Information Warfare: Lessons from Ukraine." In *Cyber War in Perspective: Russian Aggression against Ukraine*, edited by Kenneth Geers. Tallinn: NATO Cooperative Cyber Defence Centre of Excellence, 2015.

Kent, Randolph. "The Future of Warfare: Are We Ready?" *International Review of the Red Cross* 97, no. 900 (2015): 1341–1378.

Klimburg, A. *The Darkening Web: The War for Cyberspace*. New York: Penguin Books, 2017.

Lange-Ionatamishvili, E. Svetoka, S. "Strategic Communications and Social Media in the Russia Ukraine Conflict." In *Cyber War in Perspective: Russian Aggression against Ukraine*, edited by Kenneth Geers. Tallin: NATO Cooperative Cyber Defence Centre of Excellence, 2015.

Lewis, James. "Compelling Opponents to Our Will': The Role of Cyber Warfare in Ukraine." In *Cyber War in Perspective: Russian Aggression against Ukraine*, edited by Kenneth Geers. Tallinn: NATO Cooperative Cyber Defence Centre of Excellence, 2015.

Perlroth, N., M. Scott, and S. Frenkel. "Cyber Attack Hits Ukraine Then Spreads Internationally." *The New York Times*, June 27, 2017. https://www.nytimes.com/2017/06/27/technology/ransomware-hackers.html#:~:text=Computer%20systems%20from%20Ukraine%20to,of%20Ukraine%2C%20A.T.M.s%20stopped%20working.

Pierzchala, Kazimierz. "Information Warfare between Russia and Ukraine." *Polish Political Science Yearbook* 48, no. 1 (2019): 103–111.

Schmitt, Michael. "Cyber Operations and the Jus Ad Bellum Revisited." *Villanova Law Review* 56, no. 3 (2011): 569–606

Schmitt, Michael. "Rewired Warfare: Rethinking the Law of Cyber-Attack." *International Review of the Red Cross* 96, no. 893 (2014): 189–206.

"Significant Cyber Incidents" CSIS.org. *Center for Strategic and International Studies*. Accessed April 6, 2020. https://www.csis.org/programs/strategic-technologies-program/significant-cyber-incidents.

Sullivan, Julia E., and Dmitriy Kamensky. "How Cyber-Attacks in Ukraine Show the Vulnerability of the U.S Power Grid." *The Electricity Journal* 30, no. 3 (2017): 30–35.

Swinhoe, D. "What Is Spear Phishing? Why Targeted Email Attacks Are so Difficult to Stop." csoonline.com, *CSO USA*, January 21, 2019. https://www.csoonline.com/article/3334617/what-is-spear-phishing-examples-tactics-and-techniques.html.

Von Clausewitz, Carl. *On War*. Oxford: Oxford University Press, 2007.

Protecting Students: Bullying and School

Ha Bich Dong

In Canada, the promotion and protection of human rights begin in the school system. Rooted in the democratic purposes of education, the Canadian school system transmits the core values of the nation, such as diversity, equity, inclusion, safety, and democracy.[1] In the 150 years since the establishment of public schools under Canada's provinces—the second level of Constitutional government, schools have become more than a place for students to learn to read, write, and count. Schools provide a safe and caring environment that promotes common values, encourages multiculturalism, and engenders a culture of peace, equity, and justice for all students. As the human rights movement emerges in Canada, schools and school divisions that govern them have become important actors to promote and protect the human rights of students. But how do human rights in education play out in practice? Should all human rights receive equal concern and protection at schools?

This chapter explores how two school divisions in one of the world's leading school systems respond to legislation that focuses on protecting

H. B. Dong (✉)
Winnipeg, MB, Canada
e-mail: habichdong@gmail.com

L. E. Reimer and K. Standish (eds.), *Perspectives on Justice, Indigeneity, Gender, and Security in Human Rights Research*,
https://doi.org/10.1007/978-981-99-1930-7_14

the human rights of LGBTQ+ students under the banner of anti-bullying. Analysing these responses offers an opportunity to explore the larger contexts in which these school divisions are operating—how provincial policies support or hinder school divisions' efforts to protect students and the role of local governance when provincial policies are ineffective. This chapter briefly describes how schools are governed in Canada and then focuses especially on Manitoba. Next, the chapter explores the provincial anti-bullying legislation and its controversies, critically examining the quality of the policy and its impact on the two school divisions. Based on Jack Donnelly's thesis on the Universal Declaration of Human Rights model, the chapter addresses challenges that emerge in efforts to balance the promotion of various rights, especially when these efforts are premised on the promise of equal respect and inclusion of all students. This chapter does not offer a comprehensive review of all Manitoba school divisions' responses to the provincial legislation but rather highlights the issues around protecting student rights. The ultimate goal is to explore schools as sites for human rights protection and links public education with human rights.

Context

Canada is geographically the second-largest country in the world and occupies the northern half of North America.[2] Canada does not have a federal department or national system of education; rather, the responsibility for education is decentralized in each of the eleven provinces and territories. Under *The Constitution Act* of 1867, provincial and territorial governments are responsible for developing their own autonomous education systems and making all decisions regarding schools, teachers, and curricula.[3] To govern the delivery of education, Canadian provinces have created a fourth-level government—the school board, which is elected by voters of a school division to serve the educational needs of their community's children and become "the public's most immediate form of democracy and the protection of liberties."[4] When school boards govern properly, they allow school divisions to develop purposeful visions that reflect the common values of their communities.[5] Interestingly, school boards have no Constitutional protection and must comply with the will of the elected provincial government. Therefore, school divisions' efforts to protect students' human rights are largely influenced by provincial legislation and political agendas.

Located in the centre of Canada and bordered by the United States to the south, the province of Manitoba encompasses a vast landmass, resulting in a population density of only 2.2 persons per square kilometre.[6] With most of the total population concentrated in the southwestern corner of the province, this population dispersal has implications for schools and their efforts to teach and protect students in terms of fiscal and human resources. Regarding the governance of schools, *The Public Schools Act* and *The Education Administration Act* regulate the Manitoba school system.[7] Within the last decade, Manitoba has seen more newcomers reside in the province, creating both opportunities and challenges for the school system. About 5.7% of total immigration to Canada settled in Manitoba as of 2016.[8] This demographic change provides Manitoba with opportunities to strengthen its economic and cultural ties around the world. In 2016, a total of 14,298 international students studied in the province, contributing to approximately CAD $374.8 million in total annual expenditures.[9] On the other hand, there are new challenges for school divisions in terms of effectively integrating diverse students into the Manitoba school system. Many immigrants and refugee students and international students come from countries whose legal systems and human rights performances are drastically different from those of Canada. This urges school divisions to re-examine their policies and programmes to ensure that schools provide a safe, inclusive, and respectful environment where all students can learn and grow.

One of the most recent and significant pieces of legislation in Manitoba to protect students' human rights is *The Public Schools Amendment Act (Safe and Inclusive School)*, or *Bill 18*.[10] As a part of the provincial government's Anti-bullying Plan, this bill amends *The Public Schools Act* in the areas of bullying and respect for human diversity. When Education Minister Nancy Allan introduced *Bill 18* on December 4, 2012, she stated that her focus was to protect students from bullying, including cyberbullying. She informed the public that this bill was influenced by the breaking news of Amanda Todd, a Grade 10 student in British Columbia who was cyberbullied until she committed suicide in October of that year.[11] *Bill 18* offers Manitoba school divisions a definition of bullying, including cyberbullying. According to section 1.2, bullying is defined as a "behaviour that (a) is intended to cause or should be known to cause, fear, intimidation, humiliation, distress or other forms of harm to another person's body, feelings, self-esteem, reputation or property; or (b) is intended to create, or should be known to create, a negative school environment for another person."[12]

The introduction of this bill demonstrates Manitoba's commitment to fighting against bullying, a prominent human rights violation at schools. The inclusion of "cyberbullying" in the legal definition of bullying is of a timely manner, particularly as the nation was still in shock from the story and death of Amanda Todd. A 2018 report from Ipsos Group found that about one in five parents in Canada claimed their child has experienced cyberbullying.[13] Nonetheless, for legislation on such an important human rights issue, this bill was rammed through the legislation rather quickly. It went to the second reading in the legislative process just two days after being introduced. Even after the bill raised public debates and opposition from the Progressive Conservatives around its definition of bullying and a concern for the rights to religious freedom, it still managed to go into effect by September 2013.[14]

There have been critics about how this bill defines bullying insufficiently.[15] According to the Manitoba government, bullying includes one-time incidents to cause hurt feelings, whether other provinces see bullying as repetitive behaviours.[16] The legislation does not offer any insight to distinguish between serious incidents of bullying from oversensitive feelings of students. This is problematic because schools and the public tend to mistake any kind of aggression with bullying, which makes anti-bullying policy often become a general anti-violence effort that fails to address the nature and root causes of bullying.[17] In addition, research finds that "over-scrupulous anti-bullying measures run the risk of undermining and consequently devaluing the importance of free expression in the classroom."[18] It is important to note that, during the third reading of *Bill 18*, the Progressive Conservatives put forward nine amendments to address various areas, such as defining what is not bullying to protect staff and students from unreasonable bullying claims or adding "ethnicity" and "religion or creed, or religious belief" to the list of groups to be protected.[19] All amendments were vetoed by the New Democratic Party (NDP), which held the majority and, as the government, initiated this bill. Some commentators suggested the NDP government was concerned about favourable political posturing instead of creating good public policy.[20]

What makes *Bill 18* controversial, however, is not its insufficient definition of bullying but the fact that the Manitoba government chose to focus its anti-bullying effort on LGBTQ+ rights and overrode the rights and legal responsibilities of local school divisions. *Bill 18* faced opposition from various religious communities and schools who were concerned that it infringed with the freedom of religion of stakeholders in religiously affiliated funded independent schools that have school boards.[21] In general, provisions of *The Public Schools Act* only applies to public schools, but this bill requires all school boards, including all private and all religious schools (Christian, Islam, Montessori), to establish a policy to respect human diversity in gender equity, race, (dis)ability, sexual orientation, and gender identity.[22] It includes a clause requiring schools to accommodate students who want to start student organizations, specifically a Gay-Straight Alliances. While the first clause provides an overarching framework and expectations for school divisions to ensure an inclusive learning environment, the second clause implies a specific mandate emphasizing the rights of one student group. Two years after the establishment of *Bill 18*, the provincial government established a support document titled *Respect for Human Diversity Policies* to "assist school divisions and funded independent schools to comply with new legislation."[23] This support document emphasizes LGBTQ+ rights and the formation of a Gay-Straight Alliances student organization.

Framework for Analysis and Method

This chapter provides an exploratory case study using a human rights-based approach, which analyses public policy through a lens that provides further understanding of how inequality under the law denies some individuals their recognized human rights.[24] According to Jack Donnelly, a renowned human rights theorist, "every human being has certain equal and inalienable rights and is thus entitled to equal concern and respect from the state—and that what holds this otherwise disparate group together is a fundamental commitment to human equality and autonomy."[25] This conceptual framework is fundamental to the chapter's comparative analysis of public documents that stem from *Bill 18* from a large urban and a small rural school division in Manitoba. Identifying information was removed: the large urban school division is referred to as "Big City School Division" and the small rural one as "Prairie Grass School Division."

The different sizes, capacities, and largely different communities provide a rich landscape to demonstrate how local governance of education influences the outcomes of provincial policy. Big City School

Division, which is in Winnipeg—the capital and largest city of Manitoba, has over 16,000 students and almost 3000 staff. It has a high number of refugee students and over 150 international students from more than 20 countries. Within the school division's local communities, over 26% of residents speak a non-official language (non-English or Canadian French) as their first language—reflecting the multicultural characteristic of any big city in Canada. On the other hand, Prairie Grass School Division, which is located across farmlands outside of Winnipeg, has half the number of total schools compared to Big City. Prairie Grass has less than 5000 students and 800 staff, and only about 13% of residents from its local communities speak a non-official language as their first language. Both school divisions have schools offering different language programmes—English, French immersion, and English–Ukrainian bilingual. Big City School Division has several English–German bilingual schools, while Prairie Grass has several Hutterian colony schools, which are designed to preserve the cultural values and religious beliefs of the Hutterian community, an ethnoreligious group that belongs to a communal branch of Anabaptists.

Responses to Anti-Bullying Policy

Overall, the responses of the two school divisions position themselves in one of two ways. Prairie Grass School Division follows provincial legislation and focuses its anti-bullying efforts on protecting LGBTQ+ rights. Meanwhile, Big City School Division follows the provincial legislation but also develops other policies to protect other rights. Both school divisions repeatedly claim that their mission is to provide a safe, caring, and respectful environment for all students.

To comply with *Bill 18*, they established two anti-bullying documents to guide their schools: one document conveys their commitment to fighting against bullying, and the other document defines bullying and outlines actions of bullying. Big City and Prairie Grass also have a document that follows the provincial guideline in the 2015 support document *Respect for Human Diversity Policies*. While these documents are mostly similar, there are differences that show the larger contexts in which these school divisions are operating.

In terms of the first anti-bullying document, Big City and Prairie Grass share the exact word-for-word statement. More than a claim about their respect for the rights to freedom from discrimination and to the security of persons, this statement illustrates a firm belief that schools are not only sites for learning to read, write, and count but also for developing healthy and positive personal and social development for all. As a result, schools must promote and protect the human rights of all students to ensure a safe, caring, inclusive environment where everyone can learn, grow, and live together for the greater good. The only difference between the two statements is that Prairie Grass School Division adds the term "harassment" to the title of its document. While this difference seems minor, a bigger implication can be seen in the support document that defines bullying and bullying behaviours.

In the support document, Big City and Prairie Grass apply the definition of bullying from section 1.2a of *Bill 18*. Prairie Grass also includes section 1.2b, which lists out natural characteristics and patterns of bullying, highlighting the imbalance of power or strength in bullying incidents. This additional section aligns with Prairie Grass' decision to include the term "harassment" in its anti-bullying statement because harassment is a bullying behaviour reinforced by inequalities and discrimination. What makes these two school divisions' responses interesting is that in comparison to *Bill 18's* short and limited list on potential places where cyberbullying may occur, both Big City and Prairie Grass provide a more detailed description. Prairie Grass has two extra sections to further explain cyberbullying and cyberstalking, which are not included in *Bill 18*.

These differences are likely to be the result of the influence of local governance. Again, the Manitoba government has been criticized for its narrow definition of bullying.[26] The school divisions' decision to be more informative about defining bullying provides clearer guidance for schools to better recognize bullying behaviours and develop appropriate proactive and intervention strategies. On the other hand, even though *Bill 18* mentions "social media" as a potential place where bullying can occur, Big City and Prairie Grass leave that term out of their documents. Bullying as traditionally known may be within a school setting, but with new Internet technology developments, cyberbullying can take place anywhere and anytime.[27] The two school divisions may find it difficult and, perhaps, out of their capacity to protect students from bullying on social media when schools are not in session. Nonetheless, excluding social media from the list makes their anti-bullying effort vulnerable. According to Ipsos Group's (2018) report, out of one in five parents in Canada who claimed their child was cyberbullied, 68% of them said the bullying was done by a classmate—a shocking rate that was 17% higher than the worldwide rate.[28] School divisions cannot claim a commitment to protect students from bullying if they pick and choose which bullying behaviours and which bullying environments to tackle.

Responses to the Provincial Emphasis on LGBTQ+ Rights

How did these two school divisions understand and apply *Bill 18* and the provincial support document? To comply with *Bill 18's* mandate for school boards to create policies respecting human diversity, both school divisions provide a document with a comprehensive description and guideline to recognize, promote, and protect the human rights of LGBTQ+ students at schools. At first glance, Big City and Prairie Grass share the exact word-for-word document. Big City's document went into effect in October 2015. The school division revised the document in 2016 to better protect transgender students and staff after a human rights complaint to the Manitoba Human Rights Commission on the issue of transgender students' rights. Prairie Grass' document was adopted in April 2018—much later compared to Big City School Division. There was no further information to explain why there was a delay in issuing this policy document. It is important to point out that the provincial support document emphasizes LGBTQ+ rights but also mentions other areas of human diversity that are subjected to bullying. However, Big City and Prairie Grass title their policy document "Respect for Human Diversity: Gender Identity Guidelines for Students" and solely focus on LGBTQ+ rights. How does a bill that the Manitoba government claims to protect all students from bullying be translated into a bill that focuses on protecting LGBTQ+ students from bullying?

The Manitoba government did not address bullying from a holistic view. The provincial legislation and guidance have been interpreted by at least these two school divisions as anti-bullying legislation specifically for LGBTQ+ students. *Bill 18* illustrates an interest in one potential bullied group by going as far as including a clause that requires schools to accommodate students who want to start a Gay-Straight Alliances. The language of this clause indicates that although this bill is supposed to be an apparently marginal effort to protect various rights under the banner of anti-bullying, it is specifically for LGBTQ+ students. This clause is a distraction from the overarching purpose of this bill, which according to Education Minister Nancy Allan, was to protect all students from the increasingly diverse forms of bullying in Canadian schools.[29] It seemed that this bill was introduced largely to attract LGBTQ+ voters. The emphasis of this bill on LGBTQ+ rights was amplified by the provincial 2015 support document, which was designed to guide school divisions in complying *with Bill 18*. During the 2016 general election, the New Democratic Party promised to appoint a minister to address LGBTQ+ issues if they were re-elected. Meanwhile, Conservative Leader Brian Pallister, who once called same-sex marriage "a social experiment," expressed his desire to participate in pride celebrations if he was elected Manitoba premier.[30] To put it simply, *Bill 18* is not a good policy that concerns equal rights of students but rather a strategic move to support political interests.

If *Bill 18* is a vulnerable policy that fails to address the problem of bullying that needs to be fixed, do any school divisions have policies to protect other areas of human diversity that are not mentioned in the provincial legislation? Does local governance make a difference in protecting students' rights? The Big City School Division has two documents on the rights to religious freedom that went into effect in 2011, but Prairie Grass School Division does not, which is interesting in a school division with a large Christian/Huttarian population. The first document is a public statement about the division's recognition of and respect for the religious diversity within its communities, as well as its commitment to protecting students from discrimination or harassment based on religion. The second document clarifies the process to accommodate students' religious practices and the levels of authorities involved. *Bill 18* does not list religious beliefs as a group to be protected by the legislation; therefore, the decision to develop policies on freedom from bullying based on religion belongs to the school divisions.

The language of the first document points out that Big City's policy on religious accommodation comes out of the needs of its local communities. Big City is a large school division in a diverse urban area. In Winnipeg, it has one of the highest numbers of refugee students from predominantly Muslim countries, as well as over 150 international students from over 20 countries. The decision to have a legally enforceable policy document to protect students from being bullied based on religion is an appropriate response of the school board, showing a commitment to represent the local voices. Unlike Big City, Prairie Grass does not have any similar documents. This school division locates in a rural area and has a significantly smaller and less diverse student population. Prairie Grass also has several Hutterian colony schools which have their own religious authorities. Perhaps, Prairie Grass has not seen a need from its local communities to accommodate different religious practices. Nonetheless, in recent years, Manitoba has been welcoming more immigrants and refugees; many reside in rural areas where the cost of living and housing prices are more affordable, and agricultural-related jobs are abundant.[31] School divisions in smaller cities and rural areas in Manitoba have been facing increasing pressure to create programmes that enhance school staff and administrators' cultural competency to serve their increasingly diverse student population.[32] In essence, rural school divisions like Prairie Grass must have proactive strategies instead of taking actions only after a human rights violation occurs.

Overall, Prairie Grass' lack of policy to protect diverse areas of human rights further illustrates the downside of *Bill 18*—this bill does not serve its purpose, which is to protect all students from bullying. Clearly, because the protection of students' rights to religious freedom is not specified in the anti-bullying legislation or the human diversity support document, not all school divisions have a policy guide on religious accommodation for students. After reviewing policy documents of all school divisions in Manitoba, the result is only six out of 37 school divisions have such documents. Furthermore, four out of those six school divisions focus on fulfilling parents' requests and do not mention concerns for human rights or equity.

Equal Concern and Respect

According to Donnelly, "a system of equal and inalienable rights cannot be sustained in the face of social practices that deny the possibility of each enjoying his or her rights equally."[33] The Manitoba government has not developed a framework that can effectively guide school divisions to pay equal concern and respect to all students. LGBTQ+ students deserve support, equal protection, and access to safe and caring school environments. As an underrepresented and marginalized group, these students endure higher levels of bullying and harassment compared to heterosexual students.[34] At the same time, if the provincial legislation's goal is to guide school divisions in protecting all students from diverse forms of bullying, it should not highlight one aspect of human diversity and omit others. The impact of this vulnerable policy is clear: two school divisions largely focus their human diversity policies on sexual orientation and gender identity.

Jurisdictionally, the provincial government does not have the authority to demand schools support the formation of a specific student-run organization. The emphasis on supporting Gay-Straight Alliances distracts the overall purpose of the bill, which is to protect all students. By micromanaging the school divisions and the schools they administer, the provincial government is potentially violating other rights and freedoms of local governments. It may also imply a low level of trust, in which the provincial government does not have faith in the school boards' capability to effectively govern and serve as a pivotal link between the provincial government and the local schools and communities, which is another discussion beyond the scope of this paper.

Conclusion

Education is the cornerstone of democracy, liberty, and safe, inclusive, and equitable communities. Thus, schools are not only places for learning but also for possibilities and hope, for the promotion of common values and the protection of human rights. The government of Manitoba fell short of their stated goals and of the greater purposes of dignity and human rights as outlined by Jack Donnelly, that is, all human beings must be given equal concern and respect to ensure a sustainable system where everyone can enjoy his or her fundamental human rights. Since the Manitoba government acknowledges bullying as an important human rights issue, it should include all potential bullied student groups. Instead of micromanaging to the point of endorsing one student-led organization, it would be more appropriate and beneficial for the provincial government to provide a holistic and inclusive framework that can guide school divisions to protect diverse student groups from bullying.

School divisions should be more proactive in establishing human rights instruments necessary to protect various areas of students' rights, even when they are not being specified in the provincial legislation. As representatives of local voices, school divisions need to become active protectors of students' human rights by identifying which policies are vulnerable, irrelevant, or not inclusive. More than ever, the provincial government and school divisions must work together to become beacons of hope for the communities they serve and develop dignity-promoting, rights-based policies that protect all students in a rapidly changing, complex, diverse, and interdependent world.

Discussion Questions

1. Some people criticize the province of Manitoba for its insufficient definition of bullying, which includes one-time incidents and leaves out many aspects of human diversity. How would a narrow definition of bullying affect how human rights are protected at school?
2. Some people believe *Bill 18* creates a conflict between the rights to freedom of religion and the rights to freedom from discrimination for individuals of the LGBTQ+ community. Is that the case? Are all human rights equal?
3. Should human rights policies at school respond to the specific context of the school? If so, would it be considered a conflict between universal human rights and schools?
4. What is the link between public education and human rights? Who should be responsible for protecting students at schools?

Notes

1. "Reflecting Canadian values," *Canadian Index of Wellbeing, University of Waterloo*. Accessed September 05, 2020, https://www.uwaterloo.ca/canadian-index-wellbeing/about-canadian-index-wellbeing/reflecting-canadian-values.
2. Ralph R. Krueger, "Canada." *Britannica*. Last updated September 1, 2020. Accessed September 5, 2020, https://www.britannica.com/place/Canada.
3. Government of Canada, "Education in Canada." *Government of Canada*. Last modified June 24, 2020. Accessed February 10, 2020. https://www.canada.ca/en/immigration-refugees-citizenship/services/new-immigrants/new-life-canada/enrol-school.html.
4. Laura Reimer, *Leadership and School Boards*. Maryland: Rowman & Littlefield Publishers, Inc., 2008.
5. Reimer, *Leadership and School Boards*, 10.

6. Statistics Canada, "Focus on Geography Series, 2011 Census." *Statistics Canada.* Last updated October 24, 2012, accessed September 5, 2020, https://www12.statcan.gc.ca/census-recensement/2011/as-sa/fogs-spg/Facts-pr-eng.cfm?Lang=Eng&GK=PR&GC=46.
7. Zhachary Kinahan, Stacy Senkbell, and Matthew Carvell, "Wedge Issues Politics in Manitoba: Bill 18-The Public Schools Amendment Act (Safe and Inclusive School)." *Manitoba Law Journal*, 37, no. 2 (2014): 177–205. http://www.canlii.org/t/2c2h.
8. Government of Manitoba, "Manitoba Immigration Facts Report 2016." *Immigration Manitoba.* Accessed February 15, 2020. http://www.immigratemanitoba.com/data-portal/facts-report-2016/.
9. Government of Canada, "Economic Impact of International Education in Canada – 2017 Update." *Government of Canada.* Last modified February 7, 2018. Accessed February 24, 2020. https://www.international.gc.ca/education/report-rapport/impact-2017/sec-3.aspx?lang=eng.
10. Government of Manitoba, "The Public Schools Amendment Act (Safe and Inclusive Schools)." *Government of Manitoba.* Accessed February 23, 2020. https://web2.gov.mb.ca/bills/40-2/b018e.php#:~:text=This%20Bill%20amends%20The%20Public,and%20respect%20for%20human%20diversity.&text=The%20Bill%20also%20requires%20each,caring%20and%20inclusive%20school%20environment.
11. Bruce Owen, 2013. "Bill 18: The Anatomy of a Controversy." *Winnipeg Free Press.* November 03, 2013. https://www.winnipegfreepress.com/local/the-anatomy-of-a-controversy-196810921.html.
12. Government of Manitoba, "The Public Schools Amendment Act".
13. IPSOS Group, "Public Perspectives: Cyberbullying." *IPSOS Group.* July 2018. Accessed March 1, 2020. https://www.ipsos.com/sites/default/files/ct/publication/documents/2018-07/public-perspectives-cyberbullying-2018-07-v1.pdf.
14. IPSOS Group, "Public Perspectives."
15. Manitoba School Boards Association, "Bill 18, The Public Schools Amendment Act (Safe and Inclusive Schools). 2018. https://www.mbschoolboards.ca/documents/Bill%2018%20Presentation.pdf.
16. Steve Lambert, "Provinces Differ on How Broadly to Define 'Bullying'." *The Globe and Mail.* March 24, 2013. https://www.theglobeandmail.com/news/national/provinces-differ-on-how-broadly-to-define-bullying/article10275006/.
17. Kathy Bickmore, "Policies and Programming for Safer Schools: Are 'Anti-Bullying' Approaches Impeding Education for Peacebuilding?" *Educational Policy* 25, no. 4 (2011): 648–687. https://doi.org/10.1177/0895904810374849.
18. Kinahan, Senkbell, and Carvell, "Wedge Issues Politics in Manitoba," 184.
19. Kinahan, Senkbell, and Carvell, "Wedge Issues Politics in Manitoba," 184.

20. Kinahan, Senkbell, and Carvell, "Wedge Issues Politics in Manitoba," 197.
21. Joshua D. M. Shaw, "The Queer Child Deserves Protection: Bill 18 and the Justifiable Infringement of Denominational Schools' Freedom of Religion." *Manitoba Law Journal* 38, no. 1 (2014): 331–357. https://heinonline.org/HOL/P?h=hein.journals/manitob38&i=343.
22. Government of Manitoba, "The Public Schools Amendment Act".
23. Government of Manitoba, "Respect for Human Diversity Policies." *Government of Manitoba*. Accessed February 23, 2020, https://www.edu.gov.mb.ca/k12/docs/support/human_diversity/index.html.
24. Government of Canada, "Human Rights-Based Approaches." *Government of Canada*. Last modified May 26, 2017. Accessed March 10, 2020. https://www.international.gc.ca/world-monde/issues_development-enjeux_developpement/priorities-priorites/human_rights-droits_personne.aspx?lang=eng.
25. Jack Donnelly, *Universal Human Rights in Theory and Practice*. 3rd ed. Ithaca: Cornell University Press, 2013.
26. Lambert, "Provinces Differ on How Broadly to Define 'Bullying'".
27. Matthew B. Stanbrook, "Stopping Cyberbullying Requires a Combined Societal Effort." *CMAJ: Canadian Medical Association journal / journal de l'Association medicale canadienne* 186, no. 7 (2014): 483–483. https://doi.org/10.1503/cmaj.140299.
28. IPSOS Group, "Public perspectives: Cyberbullying."
29. Owen, "Bill 18: The Anatomy of a Controversy".
30. The Canadian Press, "Manitoba minister for LGBTQ 'not helpful:' Tories." *Global News*. April 6, 2016. Accessed March 15, 2020. https://globalnews.ca/news/2622436/manitoba-minister-for-lgbtq-not-helpful-tories/.
31. Tom Carter, Margot Morrish, and Benjamin Amoyaw, "Attracting Immigrants to Smaller Urban and Rural Communities: Lessons Learned from the Manitoba Provincial Nominee Program." *Journal of International Migration and Integration / Revue de l'integration et de la migration internationale* 9, no. 2 (June 2008): 161–183, http://dx.doi.org.uml.idm.oclc.org/10.1007/s12134-008-0051-2.
32. Val Schellenberg, "The Impact of Immigration on Southern Manitoba Schools: A Case Study of a Rural School Division." *Diaspora, Indigenous, and Minority Education: Professional Development in a Time of Mass Migration* 5, no. 4 (2011): 277–284. https://doi-org.uml.idm.oclc.org/10.1080/15595692.2011.606013.
33. Donnelly, *Universal Human Rights*, 71.
34. Kinahan, Senkbell, and Carvell, "Wedge Issues Politics in Manitoba," 183.

Bibliography

Bickmore, Kathy. Policies and Programming for Safer Schools: Are 'Anti-Bullying' Approaches Impeding Education for Peacebuilding? *Educational Policy* 25, no. 4 (2011): 648–687. https://doi.org/10.1177/0895904810374849.

Carter, Tom, Morrish, Margot, and Amoyaw, Benjamin. "Attracting Immigrants to Smaller Urban and Rural Communities: Lessons Learned from the Manitoba Provincial Nominee Program." *Journal of International Migration and Integration/Revue de l'integration et de la migration internationale* 9, no. 2 (2008): 161–183. https://doi.org/10.1007/s12134-008-0051-2.

The Canadian Press. "Manitoba Minister for LGBTQ 'Not Helpful:' Tories." *Global News*. April 6. Accessed March 15, 2020. https://globalnews.ca/news/2622436/manitoba-minister-for-lgbtq-not-helpful-tories/.

Donnelly, Jack. *Universal Human Rights In Theory and Practice*, 3rd ed. Ithaca: Cornell University Press, 2013.

Government of Canada. "Economic Impact of International Education in Canada—2017 Update." *Government of Canada*. Last modified February 7, 2018. Accessed February 24, 2020. https://www.international.gc.ca/education/report-rapport/impact-2017a/sec-3.aspx?lang=eng.

Government of Canada. "Education in Canada." *Government of Canada*. Last modified June 24, 2020. Accessed February 10, 2020. https://www.canada.ca/en/immigration-refugees-citizenship/services/new-immigrants/new-life-canada/enrol-school.html.

Government of Canada. "Human Rights-Based Approaches." *Government of Canada*. Last modified May 26, 2017. Accessed March 10, 2020. https://www.international.gc.ca/world-monde/issues_development-enjeux_developpement/priorities-priorites/human_rights-droits_personne.aspx?lang=eng.

Government of Manitoba. "Manitoba Immigration Facts Report 2016." *Immigration Manitoba*. Accessed February 15, 2020. http://www.immigratemanitoba.com/data-portal/facts-report-2016/.

Government of Manitoba. "Respect for Human Diversity Policies." *Government of Manitoba*. Accessed February 23, 2020. https://www.edu.gov.mb.ca/k12/docs/support/human_diversity/index.html.

Government of Manitoba. "The Public Schools Amendment Act (Safe and Inclusive Schools)." *Government of Manitoba*. Accessed February 23, 2020. https://web2.gov.mb.ca/bills/40-2/b018e.php#:~:text=This%20Bill%20amends%20The%20Public,and%20respect%20for%20human%20diversity.&text=The%20Bill%20also%20requires%20each,caring%20and%20inclusive%20school%20environment.

IPSOS Group. "Public Perspectives: Cyberbullying." *IPSOS Group*. July 2018. Accessed March 1, 2020. https://www.ipsos.com/sites/default/files/ct/publication/documents/2018-07/public-perspectives-cyberbullying-2018-07-v1.pdf.

Kinahan, Zhachary, Senkbell, Stacy, and Carvell, Matthew. "Wedge Issues Politics in Manitoba: Bill 18: The Public Schools Amendment Act (Safe and Inclusive School)." *Manitoba Law Journal* 37, no. 2 (2014): 177–205. http://www.canlii.org/t/2c2h.

Krueger, Ralph R. "Canada." *Britannica*. Last updated September 1, 2020. Accessed September 5, 2020. https://www.britannica.com/place/Canada.

Lambert, Steve. "Provinces Differ on How Broadly to Define 'Bullying'." *The Globe and Mail*. March 24, 2013. https://www.theglobeandmail.com/news/national/provinces-differ-on-how-broadly-to-define-bullying/article10275006/.

Manitoba School Boards Association. "Bill 18, The Public Schools Amendment Act (Safe and Inclusive Schools). 2018. https://www.mbschoolboards.ca/documents/Bill%2018%20Presentation.pdf.

Owen, Bruce. "Bill 18: The Anatomy of a Controversy." *Winnipeg Free Press*. November 03, 2013. https://www.winnipegfreepress.com/local/the-anatomy-of-a-controversy-196810921.html.

"Reflecting Canadian values." *Canadian Index of Wellbeing, University of Waterloo*. Accessed September 05, 2020. https://www.uwaterloo.ca/canadian-index-wellbeing/about-canadian-index-wellbeing/reflecting-canadian-values.

Reimer, Laura. *Leadership and School Boards*. Maryland: Rowman & Littlefield Publishers Inc, 2008.

Schellenberg, Val. "The Impact of Immigration on Southern Manitoba Schools: A Case Study of a Rural School Division." *Diaspora, Indigenous, and Minority Education: Professional Development in a Time of Mass Migration* 5, no. 4 (2011): 277–284. https://doi.org/10.1080/15595692.2011.606013.

Shaw, Joshua D. M. "The Queer Child Deserves Protection: Bill 18 and the Justifiable Infringement of Denominational Schools' Freedom of Religion." *Manitoba Law Journal* 38, no. 1 (2014): 331–357. https://heinonline.org/HOL/P?h=hein.journals/manitob38&i=343.

Stanbrook, Matthew B. "Stopping Cyberbullying Requires a Combined Societal Effort." *CMAJ: Canadian Medical Association journal/journal de l'Association medicale canadienne* 186, no. 7 (2014): 483–483. https://doi.org/10.1503/cmaj.140299.

Statistics Canada. "Focus on Geography Series, 2011 Census." *Statistics Canada*. Last updated October 24, 2012. Accessed September 5, 2020. https://www12.statcan.gc.ca/census-recensement/2011/as-sa/fogs-spg/Facts-pr-eng.cfm?Lang=Eng&GK=PR&GC=46.

Climate Change: Environmental Justice, Human Rights, and Peaceful Practices

Christa C. Gilliam, Lacey Sloan, and Cathryne L. Schmitz

Environmental justice, human rights, and peace are inextricably linked. Peace and sustainable development are not possible without equity and justice.[1] Millions are being forced from their homes by rising shorelines, increase in drylands, loss of biodiversity, rising food insecurity, degradation of the air and water, and increasing violent conflict.[2] To achieve human rights, environmental justice and peace, all humans must have equitable access to a healthy environment with none suffering

C. C. Gilliam (✉)
Department of Social Work, Coppin State University, Baltimore, MD, USA
e-mail: chrgilliam@coppin.edu

L. Sloan
Department of Sociology, Anthropology & Social Work, Auburn University, Montgomery, AL, USA
e-mail: lacey.sloan@uvm.edu

Present Address:
C. L. Schmitz
Department of Social Work, University of North Carolina Greensboro (UNCG), Greensboro, NC, USA
e-mail: clschmit@uncg.edu

L. E. Reimer and K. Standish (eds.), *Perspectives on Justice, Indigeneity, Gender, and Security in Human Rights Research*,
https://doi.org/10.1007/978-981-99-1930-7_15

from environmental degradation. Environmental justice is intertwined with ecological and climate justice which "links human rights and ecological sustainability."[3] To successfully address climate change, we must recognize the interconnected relationships between climate change; human-caused environmental degradation; and racial, social, economic, and environmental injustice.[4]

Escalating environmental threats are a human rights concern: social, economic, and environmental inequities are deeply intertwined. The average temperature of the earth has increased 1.1 degrees Celsius since the pre-industrial age (1880–1900), negatively impacting weather, sea levels, migration, and conflict across the globe.[5] The rising temperatures are destabilizing the earth's poles, creating *peril* for the planet.[6] The average global temperature has risen twice as fast since 1981 than in the previous 100 years.[7] At this rate, with no changes, the temperature on earth will increase as much as five to ten degrees Celsius by the end of the twenty-first century.[8]

"The climate crisis is an existential threat to life on Earth."[9] As temperatures rise quickly, the rhythms of nature are disrupted.[10] Due to rising global temperatures, ocean currents are *speeding up*[11] causing Atlantic hurricanes to become stronger and more frequent.[12] In northeast Brazil, droughts are transitioning the once fertile land to the desert.[13] Other nations, including parts of the world's youngest, South Sudan, are trapped by waters that are rising to new levels.[14] In the United States, hotter summers have led to increasing fire risk in the western United States,[15] with lower snowfall threatening the water supply.[16] In Alaska, the state farthest north in the United States, temperatures are soaring,[17] while in the middle of the continent, the prairies are shrinking.[18]

The trends in the increase of extreme weather will continue as long as we continue to emit greenhouse gasses; this means an increasing pace of disasters and environmental degradation bringing too much and too little water.[19] Repeat natural disasters (e.g., massive wildfires, tornadoes, floods, hurricanes) combined with the global COVID pandemic have contributed to the awareness of the impact of environmental degradation on humans, particularly our most vulnerable communities.[20] According to Environmental Health News,

> The common denominator of these disasters is their role in exacerbating social and health inequities, from negative health outcomes to increasing

> wealth gaps. Many communities, particularly Indigenous communities, have been dealing with similar challenges for decades now.[21]

As environmental injustice is recognized as a human rights violation, individuals, communities, nations, and international organizations must work to mitigate and heal the effects of environmental degradation and inequality.

The Glasgow Climate Pact, adopted at the 26th United Nations Climate Change Conference (COP26) seeks to prevent global temperatures from rising beyond 1.5 Celsius.[22] It also urges nations in the global north to fulfill their financial promises to developing countries to support both adaptation to, and mitigation of, climate change.[23] We have learned that when human destruction can be mitigated/tempered, nature has the potential for healing. For example, there is evidence that tropical forests have the potential to heal from deforestation.[24] Likewise, after a reprieve from human activity due to Covid-19 lockdowns, the River Thames in London showed life again with the reappearances of seals and sharks.[25]

In this chapter, we examine the connection between environmental degradation, climate change, and White patriarchal supremacy, colonization, racism, and conflict. We then offer examples of sustainable environmental practices that can help secure the human and environmental rights of food, health, clean air and water, security, and justice. We also highlight the rights of nature and the leadership of women for environmental justice. The intersection of human rights, environmental justice, and peace is emphasized throughout.

White Patriarchal Supremacy and Climate Change

To understand the roots of climate change and inequality, we first consider colonization as a source of human-caused environmental degradation. White patriarchal supremacy informed colonization and resulted in disparate impacts of environmental degradation on people of color, women, and other historically marginalized communities. We discuss the connection between environmental injustice and racism, and the growth of the environmental justice movement from the civil rights movement. Finally, we examine the impact of conflict on environmental degradation and the impact of environmental degradation.

Colonization: Roots of White Patriarchal Supremacy and Climate Change

No conversation on climate change—especially on climate adaptation and resilience—can be candid without an acknowledgment of the violent history of colonialism. Colonization of Africa, Australia, and the Americas by Europeans began a process of ecological and environmental degradation and genocide that continue to impact the world today.[26] Colonizers extracted minerals and resources from the lands they invaded, often with enslaved labor, leaving behind poisons and pollution that still scar the earth.[27] Arsenic and other materials left behind from mining continue to contaminate parts of what is now the Diné (Navajo) reservation in New Mexico and Arizona. Today, local communities are still trying to clean the contamination of water and land along the Yukon River that began with fur traders, followed by mining, followed by the United States military.[28] Across the globe, colonization also resulted in the loss of many cultural practices that once balanced and protected the ecosystem.

Due to colonization and the transport of foreign species around the globe, local flora and fauna have sometimes been decimated, the ecology degraded, and resources depleted.[29] European expansionism resulted in the occupation and colonization of the Americas. Europeans sought to extract resources from the land and, in many parts of the world, to also establish European dominance of the region and the original inhabitants. In North America, contact with Europeans devastated the Indigenous and Tribal Peoples, resulting in extensive loss of crop production and reforestation that caused cooling and drying of the global climate.[30] In the Americas, heavily armed Europeans decimated the Indigenous and Tribal Peoples with their cannons, guns, and diseases. With the Indigenous population depleted, they violently kidnapped and enslaved peoples from Africa to provide labor for the colonial project. Colonizers exploited mineral resources (e.g., gold, silver, copper) and unique plants (e.g., indigo dyes, cacao, vanilla, sugar, cotton, tobacco). Today, the negative impact of colonization is still found in environmental racism, displacement, and land degradation caused by centuries of deforestation, pollution from agriculture and mining, destruction of natural habitats that support local flora and fauna, and more recently, tourism.

White patriarchy supremacy continues to exert global power, with countries in the global north—White men—accumulating resources and wealth to the detriment of our planet and all of life. Around the world, many people still live under colonial occupation (e.g., Indigenous and Tribal Peoples of North America by the United States and Canada; Indigenous Peoples of Turks and Caicos by Great Britain) and many more people in now-independent nations still live with the impact. Archeologists have examined the climate in the islands of the Caribbean and southwestern Indian Ocean and found changes have been magnified by histories of colonization and injustice. For many Indigenous communities, the need to adapt to the changing climate is particularly pressing.[31] "Including Indigenous communities in the development of equitable climate adaptation policies is critical as some strategies, such as the relocation of entire communities, may amount to environmental genocide."[32] However, "climate policy has historically excluded Indigenous populations, even though Indigenous communities across the globe have been some of the most impacted by global warming."[33]

Environmental Degradation and Racism

Environmental justice, as defined in 1979 by Dr. Robert Bullard, recognized as the father of the environmental justice movement, established that environmental injustice is rooted in systemic racism.[34] The relationship between poor environmental conditions and racially marginalized communities is well documented.[35] Ecological destruction "exacerbate[s] growing inequality and... increase[s]...the 'othering' of vulnerable populations."[36] Growing out of the United States Civil Rights Movement in the 1960s, environmental justice acknowledges the disproportionate impact of environmental degradation on communities of color.[37] As people of color pressed for equal rights, they also sounded the alarm about the public health dangers of pollution and environmental toxins in their communities.[38] During the 1968 Memphis Sanitation Strike, organizers explicitly opposed environmental injustice. This was followed up in 1969 with Houston homeowners using the Civil Rights Act to stop a waste management facility.[39] Then, in 1982, Black activists organized against a landfill in North Carolina, in what is often considered the spark that started the environmental justice movement.[40]

Where people live, work, and play has an impact on their health. "Whether by conscious design or institutional neglect, communities of color in urban ghettos, in rural 'poverty pockets', or on economically impoverished Native-American reservations face some of the worst environmental devastation in the nation."[41] Once vibrant Black communities have been placed in harm's way due to redlining and other zoning decisions that allowed transportation infrastructure and toxic waste facilities to be built in these neighborhoods. Recent research on urban areas in the United States found that formerly redlined communities were up to 13 degrees hotter than those that were not subjected to redlining.[42] And, although air pollution has decreased from 1990 to 2010, Black communities continue to experience higher levels of exposure compared to all other ethnic/racial groups.[43] "Air pollution and extreme heat are killing inner-city residents at a higher rate than almost all other causes."[44]

Community redevelopment efforts to address environmental dangers too often result in gentrification, a process that changes and transforms neighborhoods as the value of real estate increases in historically lower-income areas. Gentrification results in displacement, which has negative health consequences as people lose social support, access to health care, and other protective resources.[45] Urbanization, gentrification, and the legacy of displacement that residents of urban cities have endured after years of economic disinvestment and abandonment have left the poorest citizens particularly vulnerable to the impacts of climate change. The uneven distribution of green space and exposure to environmental hazards has resulted in health problems and contributed to health inequity.[46] Unfortunately, people of color and people with lower incomes "are increasingly excluded, either physically or culturally, from benefiting from new or improved environmental amenities…and from the clean-up of long-lasting environmental hazards" even as environmental justice is demanded.[47]

Climate Change, Conflict, and Transformation

Climate change is recognized as a cause of conflict.[48] Environmental scarcities contribute to civil violence in urban and rural contexts, interacting with political, social, and economic factors.[49] As temperatures reach unprecedented levels, there is a likelihood of increased societal instability and violent conflict.[50] Researchers have learned that warmer temperatures and reduced rainfall are linked to increases in conflict, including interpersonal violence and war.[51] The United Nations describes climate change as a *threat multiplier* and identifies ways climate change affects security and peace, including increasing food insecurity, health problems, and extreme weather events for the most vulnerable people.[52]

Current petro and oil capitalism and ecological practices are not sustainable; if we are to survive, a shift to eco-centered politics and economics is necessary.[53]

Conflicts related to environmental degradation and climate change "are numerous and complex."[54] Competition over resources such as food, water, and energy has long been the source of violence and conflict. However, as temperatures rise and humans overuse and misuse natural resources, resulting in scarcity of renewable (i.e., fertile soil, forests, ozone layer, water) and nonrenewable resources (i.e., oil, gas, minerals), violent conflict often ensues.[55] "Because about half of the people on the planet depend on local renewable resources for some aspect of their day-to-day livelihood, these worsening scarcities have an immediate and intimate impact on the well-being of a substantial fraction of humankind."[56] Conflict is escalated when renewable resources are degraded and interact with population increases, encouraging groups with the power to shift resources in their favor resulting in ecological marginalization.[57]

Climate change can slow or reverse development threatening the stability of countries.[58] Failure to mitigate or adapt to climate change can result in forced migration, conflict over resources, and/or other coping strategies resulting in domestic and/or international conflict.[59] This includes the potential loss of entire island nations due to rising sea levels which could bring about statelessness and/or displaced populations.[60] We have already seen increased migration in the southern hemisphere because of higher temperatures and the subsequent climate change impacts.[61] Climate change will likely result in more terrorism that negatively impacts the developed world.[62]

The ecological and environmental justice challenges we are facing create opportunities for transformative change.[63] Restoring balance and engaging in peacebuilding requires social, economic, and institutional change.[64] "Social justice and environmental justice are inseparable. As climate change transforms ecosystems around the globe, local communities, nation states and the global coalitions need to work together to develop and implement solutions to environmental degradation."[65] This process is an ongoing one that requires relationship building, cultural/historical self-reflection and honesty, and structural and systemic change.[66]

Environmental Justice Is a Human Right

The United Nations Human Rights Council (UNHRC) recently passed a resolution that "recognizes the right to a safe, clean, healthy and sustainable environment as a human right that is important for the enjoyment of human rights."[67] Many human rights are particularly vulnerable to climate change and environmental degradation, such as the right to water, food, health, housing, education, nationality, and security.[68] Over the last decade, the number and scope of United Nations resolutions and reports, international and domestic laws, and judicial decisions acknowledging the relationship between human rights and environmental justice have grown rapidly. Since 2012, the United Nations has adopted seven resolutions recognizing the human right to a safe and clean environment; 155 nations have also recognized the right to a healthy environment.[69] It is now "firmly established…that environmental degradation can and does adversely affect the enjoyment of a broad range of human rights, including rights to life, health, food and water."[70]

In 1991, at the multinational People of Color Environmental Leadership Summit which included more than 1000 delegates from the United States, Chile, Mexico, Nigeria, and the Marshall Islands, the first Principles of Environmental Justice were adopted.[71] Seventeen principles for environmental justice were laid out, including a call for political, economic, and cultural liberation which has been denied by ongoing colonization and oppression.[72] The human rights frame was asserted in Principle 10, "Environmental Justice considers governmental acts of environmental injustice a violation of international law, the Universal Declaration on Human Rights, and the United Nations Convention on Genocide."[73]

The United Nations Environmental Programme has mapped the connection between human rights obligations and environmental protection policies (2016). For example, article 19 of the Universal Declaration of Human Rights and the International Covenant on Civil and Political Rights "state that the right to freedom of expression includes the freedom 'to seek, receive and impart information'."[74] This right impacts other rights and is necessary for the enjoyment of the right to participate in one's government.[75] These human rights obligations can thus be used to insist that governments conduct environmental impact assessments, make environmental information available to the public, and encourage public participation in environmental decision-making.[76]

Below, we offer practices that protect both human rights and the environment, specifically the human rights to food, health, clean water, security, and a healthy ecology. We also discuss the rights of nature, a newer strategy that could balance our relationship with the environment. Although discussed separately, these rights and mitigation and adaptation strategies are interdependent. For instance, strategies that mitigate water and air pollution not only impact the right to clean water and air but also the rights to food, health, education, and more. Eco-centered strategies that result in successful mitigation and adaptation to climate change can also lead us to peace.

Right to Safety and Peace

The peacebuilding process and environmental justice are closely linked.[77] Too often, the environmental/ecological dimensions of conflict are overlooked leading to a narrow focus on politics; expanding to include a focus on the environmental and ecological dimensions opens a window for addressing ongoing injustice.[78] The United States Pentagon focuses on responding to the effects of climate change on several fronts, including security, disaster response, growing conflicts, and food shortages.[79] Environmental approaches can "abate the manifold environmental injustices that are jeopardizing the lives and livelihoods of millions."[80] Petro or oil capitalism is often a source of volatile conflicts as it enriches those in power while providing little compensation to those most impacted by its negative consequences.[81]

A sustainable peace is not possible without attaining justice.[82] The injustices of pollution and resource misuse along with the oppression of local farmers who are exposed to degrading conditions and removed from their land, contributes to the domination by those who are stealing the resources which can lead to violence and lasting instability.[83] Responses to climate change can strain the availability of key nonrenewable resources resulting in international conflict over increasing scarcity and competition for "shared or undemarcated resources."[84] Analyzing the links between conflict and ecological and environmental justice opens the window to more effectively address conflict by engaging ecological dimensions and encouraging local participation and cooperation.[85]

The movement to peace and security does not occur immediately but evolves over time.[86] It requires the observer to see the system as a whole; the picture includes envisioning the entirety of the interactions between and across system components and movement forward interspersed with bumps along the way.[87] Mack's analysis of peace research by comprehensive peace research centers indicated that while peaceful coexistence emerged over the decades, it was not perceived in the moment.[88] Instead, people tended to focus on the immediate disaster or conflict. "Not one of the peacebuilding and conflict prevention programs on its own had much of an impact on global security … Taken together, however, their effect has been profound."[89] For success, peacebuilding must address the rights to health, clean water and air, and food.

Right to Health

The global crisis of climate change is considered the greatest threat to public health[90] and a contributing factor to the growing food crisis across the globe.[91] Women and children, poor communities, and communities of color disproportionately bear the consequences.[92] WHO director general, Dr. Tedros Adhanom Ghebreyesus, makes clear the link between climate change, inequality, and health,

> Climate change impacts health in all countries, but it hits people in low- and middle-income countries the hardest, especially small island developing states, whose very existence is under threat from rising sea levels. Any delay in acting on this global health threat will disproportionately affect the most disadvantaged around the world.[93]

Human-caused environmental degradation has already negatively impacted health, including death and illness from extreme weather, such as "heatwaves, storms and floods, the disruption of food systems, increases in zoonoses and food-, water- and vector-borne diseases, and mental health issues."[94] It is considered a threat multiplier, increasing existing health disparities. Social and environmental determinants of health, such as clean air, clean water, sufficient food, and secure shelter, are impacted by climate change.[95] These threats are expected to increase as the planet warms. As noted previously, the impacts are disproportionately experienced by our most vulnerable people and communities.[96] For example, people of color living in segregated urban neighborhoods are disproportionately living without adequate tree canopy, and thus living in urban heat islands that can be as much as 20 degrees hotter than similar White neighborhoods.[97] People of color, who are more likely to have cardiovascular disease, living in these urban heat islands are more vulnerable to heat illness.[98]

At this point, international efforts to address the health consequences of climate change focus on both mitigating damage and adapting to change.[99] Mitigation is primary prevention that focuses on "efforts to slow, stabilize, or reverse climate change by reducing greenhouse gas emissions."[100] Actions to mitigate climate change, such as reducing greenhouse gas emissions, often have direct and indirect health benefits, such as improving air quality and reducing respiratory and heart disease.[101] Adaptation focuses on secondary and tertiary prevention, anticipating and preparing for the impacts of climate change; it requires the identification of health risks with plans made to respond to those risks.[102] Actions to adapt to climate change include disaster response plans that include evacuation of people who are elderly and/or disabled, building homes high above potential sea rise levels; and, identifying alternative sources of fresh water as oceans contaminate island aquifers.[103]

Climate change is also contributing to worsening mental health.[104] Experiencing disasters as a result of extreme weather events and climate change can contribute to serious mental health issues.[105] The enormity of the climate emergency can feel overwhelming, causing eco-grief.[106] Although climate change has been identified as the greatest threat to public health,[107] climate change has not yet been declared a public health emergency despite evidence that climate change contributes to chronic and severe mental and behavioral health issues, such as anxiety, depression, substance misuse, and post-traumatic stress.[108] Proactive approaches to wellness such as disaster preparedness, creating social networks with neighbors, and taking steps to prevent and mitigate the adverse effects of climate change help with mental health have been helpful.[109]

Climate Change and Health in Fiji

Small island developing states (SIDS) are particularly vulnerable to climate change and the related health problems, with limited capacity to prepare or respond.[110] Fiji, one such SIDS, has been, and will continue to be, negatively impacted by climate change.[111] The islands of Fiji have experienced increases in temperature that affect many aspects of health, including strong cyclones that cause flooding and increase the risk of drowning, injuries, and water borne diseases.[112] Climate change also results in "increased...respiratory illnesses...; increased mental health problems…; [and] compromised food security."[113] Actions taken to mitigate and adapt to climate change and protect health overlap actions that are necessary for protecting the rights to food, clean water, clean air, and safety.

Fiji has been at the forefront of responding to climate change with both mitigation and adaptive strategies. Fiji developed a national climate change policy that is explicitly human rights-based, gender-responsive, and evidence-based.[114] To help mitigate the impact of climate change, the policy includes a commitment for 100% of the electricity to come from renewable energy sources by 2030, and for the country to be at net zero greenhouse gas emissions by 2050.[115] In addition to mitigating the effects of carbon emissions on climate change, renewable energy will allow the country to be less reliant on energy imports, which can be important during times of disaster when infrastructure (e.g., ports, electricity) may be damaged.[116]

Fiji's national adaptation plan uses an ecosystems-based adaptation (EBA) approach that centers ecosystems, biodiversity, and natural resources.[117] Adaptive strategies to reduce some of the negative health consequences of climate change (e.g., injuries, drownings, disease) include reducing disaster risks, enhancing food security, and expanding resilient housing.[118] To accomplish this, many people and communities will have to be relocated in response to rising oceans. The government of Fiji has already relocated several coastal villages and identified over 600 more communities that will need to be relocated as oceans rise.[119] As Fijian people are forced to move—temporarily or permanently—because of climate change, there are Indigenous and local practices that enhance the ability to adapt.

Right to Clean Air

Climate change and air pollution are closely linked—climate change mitigation can reduce air pollution, and reducing air pollution can reduce climate change.[120] Air pollution and climate change interact to create a variety of environmental hazards, including warmer air and water temperatures, acid rain, extreme weather events, flooding, and drought.[121] Air pollution includes outdoor/ambient air pollution—the primary source being the burning of fossil fuels—and indoor air pollution—primarily from burning biomass and coal.[122] Although there are natural causes of air pollution, such as methane emitted from rotting vegetation, human sources account for the majority of contamination.[123] Fortunately, countries that have adopted strong green policies have seen success in reducing air pollution (e.g., Denmark, Malta, Iceland).[124]

Worldwide, air pollution is the fourth leading cause of death.[125] Almost all people—99%–breathe air that exceeds air quality limits, increasing the risk of "heart disease, lung cancer, chronic obstructive pulmonary disease (COPD), lower-respiratory infections…stroke, type 2 diabetes, and…low birth weight and preterm birth."[126] Each year, air pollution costs billions in additional healthcare costs and lost wages.[127] Air pollution not only negatively affects the air we breathe but also contaminates the water and land; contributes to the destruction of plants, forests, and habitats; and disrupts ecosystems.[128]

As with other forms of environmental degradation, people in low income and developing countries bear a higher burden from air pollution.[129] Newborn babies (birth to six days) and elders experience much higher rates of pollution-related death from indoor/household air pollution than all other age groups.[130] In the United States, people of color, people experiencing poverty, children, and elders are "more likely to live in a county with a failing grade for at least one [air] pollutant."[131] Poorer people, people of color, and people with less education are more likely to live or work closer to sources of air pollution and thus experience higher rates of exposure to vehicle emissions, resulting in disproportionate negative health impacts.[132]

Just Transitions in Jharkhand, India

Coal is considered the dirtiest of all fuels used for energy—not only does it release more carbon dioxide than oil and gas but when burned it produces mercury, arsenic, and soot.[133] In India, over half the energy is generated from coal.[134] In Jharkhand, India, coal mining has caused significant degradation to the land, water, and air.[135] "Despite its coal resources, Jharkhand is one of the poorest states in India, with **around half** its population living **in poverty**."[136] Dhanbad, Jharkhand, is considered the coal capital of India and is critically polluted.[137] Once 65% of the region was covered in forests, now only 0.05% of the forests remain.[138] In another Jharkhand town, Jharia, "the ground has been on fire" since last century, burning for more than 100 years.[139] The fire burns "through the town's underground coal reserves, releasing toxic fumes and destroying homes."[140] Despite attempts, efforts to put out the fire have been unsuccessful.

At COP26, India's Prime Minister Modi agreed to "phase down coal" to reach net zero carbon emissions by 2070.[141] To achieve this goal, Prime Minister Modi agreed to increase India's use of non-fossil energy; increase the use of renewable energy to 50%; reduce carbon emissions; and reduce the "carbon intensity of the economy" by 2030.[142] This means the country must reduce its reliance on coal. Yet, coal jobs comprise 10% of the Indian economy, a significant source of income for the government.[143] Therefore, the idea of phasing down coal is not to delay ending the use of coal, but to provide adequate time for economic and social transitions from coal to green energy to occur.

Just transitions is a global framework to ensure that actions taken to protect the climate, such as the move from fossil fuels to renewable energies, do not result in "stranded workers" or "stranded communities."[144] While meeting international climate goals could create 18 million jobs by 2030, it could also result in the loss of six million jobs by that time.[145] A study done by the Center for Strategic and International Studies (CSIS) and Climate Investment Funds (CIF) on coal in India, encourages a just transition from coal, recognizing the importance of coal to the economy of India.[146] To ensure a just transition, CSIS and CIF recommend diversifying India's economy by expanding agriculture, tourism, non-coal mining, and non-timber forest production; they also acknowledge the necessity of environmental rehabilitation.[147] It is noted that all the coal sites in Jharkhand have adequate sun to support a transition to solar energy.[148]

California Controls Emissions

Burning of fossil fuels is the major source of pollutants that degrade the quality of the air.[149] Globally, one in five people die from the pollution created by burning fossil fuels.[150] While emissions from vehicles are the leading cause of outdoor air pollution, the global variations range from 12 to 70%.[151] According to the World Health Organization, Africa, Asia, and parts of the Middle East suffer the highest rates of air pollution from vehicle emissions, primarily because of old diesel vehicles and lack of public transportation.[152] In the United States, emissions from transportation remain a leading source of greenhouse gas from burning fossil fuels (29%).[153]

As early as 1903, Los Angeles was struggling with what would eventually be labeled as *smog*.[154] At times, the smog reduced visibility enough to threaten aviation safety and caused people to suffer from "burning eyes and lungs, and nausea."[155] The Los Angeles City Council tried to regulate what they thought were causes of the smog (e.g., backyard trash burning), but with limited success.[156] Recognizing the need to unify all the towns in Los Angeles County if efforts to combat air pollution were to succeed, in 1947 the first-in-the-nation county Air Pollution Control District was established.[157] Since that time, and the discovery of the role vehicle emissions play in air pollution, California passed the country's first tailpipe emissions standards, requirements for catalytic converters on vehicles (1970), zero-emission vehicle mandates (1990), and greenhouse gas emission standards (2002).[158] California recently passed legislation requiring that 50% of all energy come from renewable sources by 2030.[159] California continues to enforce stricter vehicle emissions standards than required by the Federal Air Quality Act, a stance that former President Trump sought, unsuccessfully, to stop.

Over the past five decades, California has experienced some success in reducing emissions through the adoption and enforcement of strict emissions controls. Since 1967, California has successfully reduced carbon emissions by 90%.[160] Smog alerts have dropped from 186 days in 1967 to zero days in 2019.[161] Reductions in air pollution in Los Angeles over the past 20 years have improved health outcomes, with 20% fewer new cases of asthma in children.[162] Despite concerns to the contrary, California's economy has continued to grow, even with increased regulations that limit emissions from burning fossil fuels.[163] Unfortunately, even with these improvements, Los Angeles continues to have one of highest levels of ozone pollution in the country.[164]

Right to Clean Water

Water is essential to life on the planet and critical to public health.[165] The right to water includes the right to safe accessible water for drinking, sanitation, and hygiene along with the right to healthy ecosystems including rivers, lakes, and groundwater.[166] Global climate change is making water more unpredictable, with flooding contaminating fresh water sources in some areas and droughts making water scarce in other areas.[167]

Despite recent improvements, over two billion people lack access to "safely managed drinking water services."[168] Safely managed drinking water services means "drinking water from an improved water source that is located on premises, available when needed, and free from fecal and priority chemical contamination."[169] Over 1.2 million people die each year because of contaminated water and another 1.4 million die from unsafe sanitation and lack of access to handwashing facilities.[170] Death rates from unsafe water are highest in sub-Saharan Africa and Southeast Asia; up to 14% of deaths in Chad are attributed to unsafe water.[171] The lack of access to safe water disproportionately impacts women and children, who are responsible for collecting water in most parts of the world. In some places, collecting water can take up to four hours a day, exposing women and children to water-borne diseases, violence, and the prevention of engagement in other activities, such as attending school.[172]

Yukon River Intertribal Watershed Council

For most Indigenous and Tribal Peoples, water is recognized as the source of life, even sacred, and central to culture and traditions.[173] Following centuries of colonization, the waters of the Yukon River, the largest free-flowing river in the world, no longer sustained healthy life. Arsenic, mercury, cyanide, heavy metals, acids, hydrocarbons, toxic waste, and rotting metal from abandoned gold mines and United States military sites contaminated the river, killing fish and migratory birds and causing diseases in humans and animals.[174] This contamination also negatively impacted the many Indigenous and Tribal Peoples who not only relied on the river for clean water and food, but for whom it served as a spiritual connection important to culture and traditions.[175]

In 1997, Indigenous chiefs and elders from across the Yukon River Watershed gathered to address the contamination and health problems caused by the toxins and waste in the river.[176] Grounded in Indigenous spirituality and culture, they formed the Yukon River Inter-Tribal Watershed Council (YRITWC).[177] The YRITWC agreed to use nonviolent strategies to restore the health of the river, with a 50-year vision of being able to drink from the Yukon once again.[178]

Recognizing that Indigenous Peoples have been collecting data for thousands of years, and disseminating that knowledge through stories shared across the generations, the YRITWC combined Indigenous wisdom with modern science to understand the health of the river and communities.[179] They recognized that the quality of the water is directly connected to the health of the people, communities, and environment.[180] They began an annual healing journey—a 2000 mile canoe trip up the Yukon River—to "take the pulse of the river."[181] Along the journey, they learned from people in villages about the health of the river while using scientific equipment to measure water quality.[182] Since that time, they have removed over "6 million pounds of hazardous waste and recyclable materials" from the area.[183] The healing journey now occurs annually to promote Indigenous stewardship of the environment.

Water, Sewage, and Infrastructure

The water crisis in Flint, Michigan occurred at the intersections of increasing poverty, water quality, wastewater management, disintegrating pipes, health impact, political corruption, and environmental injustice. Between 1970 and 1980, Flint lost industry and population from "white flight" that eventually resulted in Flint becoming a city with a majority Black population.[184] By the beginning of the twenty-first century, Flint lost over 30% of its property and income tax revenues.[185] In response, in April 2014, state and local government entities switched from Detroit's regulated pretreated water system and began piping water directly from the Flint River to an old water treatment facility that needed major updates.[186] An aging infrastructure of lead pipes, failure to use corrosion prevention, and inadequate water quality monitoring, resulted in widespread lead poisoning.[187]

For 18 months, until the city switched back to Detroit water in October 2015, residents of Flint complained about, and were forced to endure, "foul-smelling, discolored, and off-tasting water ... causing skin rashes, hair loss, and itchy skin."[188] However, the problems with lead pipes continue. Despite water experts and public health officials sounding the alarm about high levels of contaminants, including lead,[189] state and local officials and the EPA failed to take necessary action until local and international pressure came to bear; these failures eventually led to civil and criminal charges. Many of those in power continue to sidestep the consequences of their actions and the community is still encountering health and economic risk. Local residents united to petition the EPA to take action and when EPA failed to act, they sued.[190]

To obtain corrective action took strong and persistent organizing, advocacy, and political and legal action.[191] In Flint, transformative action is expanding through the work of Environmental Transformation of Flint[192] with its focus on developing a collective strategy for building a healthy and sustainable community. They bring together organizations and groups that have been developing environmental solutions and value the voice of residents in framing direction. They provide mentoring, education, and training on restorative practices, local planning, and policy-action. They focus on providing the "tools to heal and strengthen relationships, creating rich social environments that promote a strong and active community."[193]

Unfortunately, these issues are not confined to Flint or Michigan and are not confined to clean drinking water. Inadequate and contaminated water systems have been found in low-income and majority of minority communities across the United States.[194] In many of the cities plagued by the violence of inadequate and aging systems, it is low-income residents facing racial discrimination who pay the cost.[195] The Biden Infrastructure Investment and Jobs Act passed in 2021, calls attention to aging and inadequate water, wastewater, and stormwater projects.[196] Fifty-five billion dollars are allocated to ensure clean drinking water is accessible in rural and urban areas, Tribal communities, and in our most vulnerable communities.[197] These funds are also targeted toward getting rid of all lead water pipes and improving water system infrastructure.[198]

Right to Food

Climate change and environmental degradation are already impacting the human right to food. Worldwide, farms are refocusing to use sustainable methods.[199] Crop diversity, rotation of crops, use of no-till methods, and agroforestry are among the methods used to increase ecosystem production and health.[200] There are examples of the transition to sustainable farming including *The Biggest Little Farm*[201] and the Shepard farm in Viola, Wisconsin.[202] They exemplify the process and methods for restoring the depleted soil of colonized farmland to land with rich soil and multi-faceted productivity. Other sustainable strategies include "organic farming, alternative agriculture, biodynamic farming, community supported agriculture, local food systems," and Indigenous practices.[203] These practices are being reclaimed and taught to restore the health of the land.

Industrialization of farming during the twentieth century enabled increased food production in the name of feeding the world's growing population, although unequal distribution and access still results in hunger.[204] Further, agriculture today is highly dependent upon fossil fuels for all aspects of farming and distribution, including manufacture of fertilizers and pesticides.[205] Unfortunately, many of the innovations that enabled farmers to increase yields have also resulted in environmental degradation. For example, plowing with heavy machinery, rather than lighter oxen-pulled plows, causes the land to become compacted, making it more susceptible to erosion. Erosion results not only in the loss of nutrient-rich topsoil but also washes fertilizers and pesticides into rivers and streams, polluting the water. The use of pesticides also negatively impacts the biodiversity of the impacted area, resulting in the collapse of bee colonies and other pollinators.

Urban Farming

Low-income, urban areas in the United States are often devoid of affordable, healthy food options. These *food deserts* are typically found in areas with residents who have "lower levels of education, lower incomes, and higher rates of unemployment."[206] Over 6% of the United States population has limited access to supermarkets.[207] People who live in food deserts are often forced to turn to inexpensive but highly processed fast food or convenience stores that typically lack fresh fruits and vegetables.[208] Lack of access to quality food results in poor nutrition and malnutrition that "plays a key role in the development of chronic diseases" such as "heart disease, stroke, Type 2 diabetes, high blood pressure, and cancer. ... This results in lower mortality rates for those living in *food deserts*."[209] For women who are pregnant, malnutrition is particularly problematic because it contributes to a weaker immune system that makes the women "more prone to miscarriages and birth defects."[210]

Urban farming is one response to food deserts and food insecurity that can transform a community.[211] Examples of urban farming include community gardens in vacant lots; rooftop and patio gardens; warehouse farming; and indoor hydroponic farming.[212] It can also include using open spaces for animals to graze. Urban farming provides "access to healthy, locally grown, and culturally appropriate food sources."[213] In addition to increasing access to healthy, fresh food, "growing that food also boosts physical and mental health....putting our hands in the dirt...induces relaxation, and reduces stress, anxiety, blood pressure, and muscle tension."[214]

While urban farming can enhance access to healthy food, it also "reconnects communities to the practice of growing food, and engages the community on a variety of levels."[215] Urban farming locations often become a hub of community interactions and activities. Urban farming has environmental, health, social, and economic benefits for communities, improving the quality of life in poor disenfranchised areas.[216] Urban farming initiatives improve air and land quality and increase local residents involvement in cleaning up neighborhoods as they reclaim vacant lots, reduce community violence, and attract greater investment in neighborhoods, resulting in overall improved neighborhood health.[217] These activities also enhance the aesthetics of the community with food-bearing plants and trees.

Indigenous Agricultural Practices

Across the globe, many Indigenous and Tribal Peoples continue the use of traditional practices that protect the environment, people, and culture. The farming practices of Indigenous and Tribal Peoples may help feed a warming world.[218] Prior to contact by Europeans in territories now called the United States and Mexico, Indigenous and Tribal Peoples had developed sophisticated agricultural systems, including irrigation and manipulation of plants to enhance yields.[219] For several thousand years, Mexico supported large-scale agriculture, making it central to the Green Revolution.[220]

One sustainable agricultural practice used traditionally by Indigenous and Tribal Peoples of North America is intercropping, or companion planting, to enhance yields and protect the environment. In the United States, the three sisters–corn, beans, and squash—are planted together to create a polyculture that feeds and protects the soil and controls pests. Once the corn is about four inches tall, beans are planted near the stalk of the corn; the stalk of corn provides a structure for the beans to grow.[221] Squash is also planted nearby, providing shade that reduces the loss of moisture from the soil.[222] Beans produce nitrogen that enriches the soil for both corn and squash.[223] After harvest, the plant waste is worked back into the soil, providing important nutrients.[224] This practice is re-emerging around the globe as a means to reduce the use of water and synthetic fertilizers.

In Mexico, the cafetal system of shade growing is a type of intercropping used in coffee production.[225] In a cafetale, tall fruit trees provide protection for the coffee from the wind and cold; leaves provide "a natural mulch that inhibits weed growth, adds fertility, and retains soil humidity."[226] Smaller plants are grown beneath the coffee. Like the three sisters, the combination of plants provides shade and nutrients that enhance the growth and production of coffee and other plants.

Rights of Nature

Whether one sees nature as natural resources to be exploited for the sole benefit of humans or as an entity with which humans are "inextricably linked by reciprocal ties of mutual care and obligation," all would agree that nature is essential to human life and well-being.[227] The entire ecosystem (i.e., nature) relies on a rich biodiversity to pollinate crops, purify water, improve soil, protect the coastlines, and reduce flooding.[228] The Rights of Nature movement goes beyond seeing nature in relation to benefits for humans and acknowledges that "ecosystems and species have the right to exist, thrive, flourish, and regenerate."[229] Unfortunately, many scientists believe the earth is currently experiencing the sixth great extinction of species—a mass extinction caused by human activity.[230]

Scientists have indicated that we must protect 30% of earth's land and oceans by 2030 if we are going to prevent the collapse of our ecosystems.[231] Current research suggests that lands managed by local and Indigenous Peoples—approximately 22% of the land with 80% of global biodiversity[232]—are healthier than those managed by governments or conservation groups.[233] On lands managed by Indigenous Peoples, biodiversity is maintained by living in harmony with nature, rather than exploiting it.[234] Rather than pushing Indigenous Peoples off lands for formal government-managed conservation, expanding Indigenous management and authority over lands is critical to protecting the global ecology.[235]

Natural climate solutions, such as allowing forests to age longer before harvesting, can benefit biodiversity without impacting food security.[236] Natural climate solutions could provide 37% of the climate mitigation needed to reach global climate goals.[237] Rewilding is a natural climate solution for restoring balance to ecosystems through the reintroduction of indigenous plants and animals, including natural predators.[238] Rewilding allows nature to return to natural processes.[239] For example, the reintroduction of wolves in Yellowstone National Park in the United States changed the balance among wildlife allowing the regrowth of natural vegetation.[240] In Slovenia, Parliament supported the building of bear bridges over highways allowing brown bears to migrate.[241] In New Zealand, Tiritiri Mantungi Island was depleted from colonization. Through a process of rewilding, invasive species were removed, and indigenous wildlife and vegetation were reintroduced to become a wildlife sanctuary.[242]

Sacred Forests

Around the world, forests provide immense biodiversity and are often central to human culture and religion. European colonizers sought to claim forest resources from the original peoples of India, Africa, Australia, and the Americas. Colonization resulted in Europeans clearing forests for timber and denying the original inhabitants access to the forests. These actions weakened local peoples' bond with nature, "distancing them from environmental stewardship."[243] After extracting and depleting valuable resources, Europeans left behind environmental and human devastation.[244]

In some places, forests are protected through religious beliefs (sacred forests) or local taboos and norms (taboo forests).[245] Sacred forests are forests protected because they are inhabited by spirits, gods, goddesses, and/or royal ancestors.[246] Research has shown that sacred forests are successful in protecting the forests, local culture, and resources.[247] Sacred forests still exist in India and parts of Asia, Africa, and South America.[248] In India, there are over 13,000 sacred groves—patches of fertile, lush green land—reserved for deities.[249] In Ethiopia, where deforestation has devastated the country, sacred forests have remained protected.[250] In Benin and Togo, sacred forests are some of the only forests that remain.[251]

Madagascar has some of the most biodiverse areas on earth and is prioritized globally for conservation and protection.[252] In Madagascar, there are *taboo forests*, a type of sacred forests, that are protected by traditional rules that govern the use of natural resources.[253] Some of these forests are burial sites where people are not allowed (except for burials), nor can resources be removed, without penalty.[254] Local taboos dictate that forests with spirits must be avoided; failure to do so could result in bad luck or even death.[255] Other forests are designated as places for harvesting honey and dead wood, with penalties for cutting live trees.[256] Taboos also protect forests used for ceremonies by restricting access to healers only.[257] Unfortunately, poverty, population growth, climate change, and erosion of religious beliefs that protected sacred forests are making these forests more vulnerable and rare.[258]

Legal Rights of Nature

The global rights of the nature movement take a concept long practiced by Indigenous and Tribal Peoples and codifies it in today's legal language and culture: "ecosystems and species have the right to exist, thrive, flourish, and regenerate."[259] This requires a shift away from current thinking which considers nature as property with environmental protection laws allowing certain levels of damage to the environment.[260] Tribes, cities, nations, and communities around the globe are adopting laws that recognize various ecosystems as legal entities with rights to be protected. Although the means of securing the rights of nature may vary (e.g., ordinances, constitutional amendments, court decisions), there are some general principles common across strategies. First, ecosystems are recognized as entities with rights, not just property belonging to individuals or organizations.[261] Second, individuals or organizations are able to sue in court on behalf of nature, although specific guardians may be designated.[262] And third, such laws prioritize the rights of nature over the property rights of individuals and corporations.[263] Although principles promoted by CELDF in the United States specifically do *not* grant personhood to ecosystems,[264] New Zealand has granted personhood status to the Whanganui River and the Te Urewera National Park.[265]

The Atrato River in the Choco region of Columbia is fundamental to life for the predominantly African-descent and Indigenous Peoples who live along its shores.[266] Indigenous Peoples of the region long practiced artisanal mining (i.e., mining done with handmade tools); this is unlike the mechanized and industrial mining that poisons the land and water with cyanide and mercury.[267] These activities have resulted in

> deforestation, sedimentation and the discharge of oils, fuel residues, mercury and cyanide into soils and water, which have resulted in significant alterations of the river course, loss of biodiversity and contamination, causing grave risks to human health, water supply and food security.[268]

As in colonial times, the resources extracted from the region today rarely benefit the local communities who nonetheless live with the damage done by such activities.[269]

To combat this environmental degradation, ethnic communities along the Atrato River filed suit with the Constitutional Court of Columbia on behalf of the ecosystems.[270] The Constitutional Court of Columbia recognized "the Atrato River, its basin and tributaries as an entity subject to rights of protection, conservation, maintenance and restoration by the State and ethnic communities."[271] They based this decision on

> the recognition of the deep and intrinsic connection that exists between nature, its resources, and the culture of the ethnic and Indigenous communities that inhabit them, all of which are interdependent with each other and cannot be understood in isolation.[272]

The court ordered the Colombian government to designate a guardian for the river comprised of one representative of the state and one from Indigenous communities.[273] Recognizing the Atara River as a rights-holder significantly shifts the public policy discourse, at least symbolically, if not materially.[274]

Women at the Forefront

"Women exist at the juncture of gender, race, class, and the natural world."[275] Ecofeminism recognizes the way women's existence at the intersection of gender and the environment broadens the lens they/we bring for analysis and action.[276] Across the globe, women have been engaged in fighting for sustainability and ecological integrity, exhibiting a commitment across the environmental justice movement.[277] As women provide leadership across the globe and across cultures and ecological vulnerabilities, they form alliances, build relationships, and mentor others.[278] Wisdom/knowledge can be found as we turn to those who have been impacted the most by environmental degradation—women, elders, Indigenous and Tribal peoples, and people of color.[279] Indigenous women and women of color are in the forefront of the climate crisis struggling to save homes.[280] Indigenous cultures, including Native Hawaiians and Pacific Islanders, voice respect for the land that involves taking responsibility for its care.[281] Weaving multiple strands of knowing together—Indigenous knowledge, scientific knowledge, and the wisdom of nature—is our best way forward to protect the environment.[282]

"In the work to protect and rehabilitate the planet, women have shown leadership and entrepreneurship."[283] Women recognize the need to work within communities, identifying and addressing local needs and vulnerabilities. Vandana Shiva is a leader who challenges us to link justice, peace, and sustainability,[284] genders, ecology, and development,[285] and sustainable agriculture.[286] Jane Goodall, recognizing the debilitating effects of poverty on local communities, addressed poverty before working collaboratively with communities to protect gorillas and chimpanzees.[287] In spite of their leadership, women's voices are often not acknowledged, silencing their work.[288] Women make up 60–90% of those in environmental justice work but they are often left out of funding, negotiations, and policy and economic decisions.[289]

Wangari Maathai worked in community with women to address ecological destruction, linking it to environmental justice, gender oppression, and political oppression.[290] When Wangari Maathai returned to her childhood village in Kenya after her pursuing undergraduate and first graduate degree abroad, she discovered the ecological destruction of her village and recognized the oppressive conditions women faced within the political conditions of the times.[291] As she mobilized the women to germinate and grow trees, they claimed their voice and agency in developing a path forward, restoring the ecosystem.[292] What started at the local moved to the national, and now the global, becoming the Greenbelt Movement.[293] The women became organizers, trainers, consultants, mentors, and entrepreneurs who worked in the community to reclaim government control and topple violent systems through the use of nonviolence, involving indigenous practices.[294]

In 2018, Kenyan women organized to restore the mangroves.[295] A partnership formed with the Nature Conservancy and their partners came together to preserve the mangroves which are key to preserving the ecosystem. The county of focus, Lamu County, is home to 60% of Kenya's mangroves and is already home to community-based conservation projects.[296] Mangroves protect communities from coastal erosion while blunting storm surges and absorbing more carbon than other plants/trees. They provide vital habitats for land and water animals. The ecosystem had been exploited, degrading 40% of the area.[297] The partnership of organizations approached the women of Mtangawanda Village asking them to join. When the women learned the value and vulnerability of the mangroves, they came together to form the Mtangawanda Women's Association with the leadership of Zulfa Hassan, known as "Mama Mikoko" (or "Mother Mangrove").[298] They, along with The Nature Conservancy and their research partners, are now responsible for restoration activities, raising seedlings then planting and replanting in degraded areas. Alongside other women's groups, they have planted more than 61,000 mangroves covering 30 acres. They also monitor exploitation of the mangroves and make the ecology friendlier to healthy mangrove growth. They already see an increase in crabs, important in local fishing.[299]

Their success with mangrove restoration has led the Mtangawanda Mangrove Restoration Women Group into other ventures.[300] Two Community Forest Associations (CFAs) have formed in Lamu County that help improve connections with other community-led conservation initiatives. In connection with additional CFAs, they are involved with multiple community-led conservation initiatives. They are planning for agreements with the Kenya Forest Service and the possibility to co-manage the forest and partner with community players for sustainable harvesting.[301] Because of their work, the women who are active in the association are eligible to join a microfinance group allowing them to apply for loans to support sustainable enterprises. For members of the Mtangawanda Women's Association, the projects bring hope for a future with opportunities for them and their children.[302]

Implications and Conclusion

Addressing environmental justice, climate justice, human rights, and the rights of nature through peaceful means requires respecting and exploring many ways of knowing, including Western science, Indigenous knowledge, and learning from and with the land and all of life.

We cannot achieve human rights or peace without environmental justice. Environmental degradation is a source of conflict and war, so to reduce this violence, we must protect and rehabilitate the environment. While climate change has impacts that are global, the loss of resources such as forests, cropland, and water has dramatic local and regional impacts and lends themselves to the local response. There are many ways to mitigate and/or adapt to climate change; the examples in this chapter were intended to offer strategies at the intersection of human rights, environmental justice, and peace. Although we included examples of strategies implemented by governments, much of the work is done at the intersection of local and Indigenous knowledge, women's leadership, and racial justice.

Hope is vital to supporting the insight and imagination that is necessary to create environmental justice and sustainability.[303] Jane Goodall maintains hope that we can tackle the extreme and looming danger of climate change. Her optimism rests on her observations of and belief in the human intellect, nature's resilience, the power and passion of youth, and the human spirit.[304] An increasing number of young people are coming together to fight despair and direct their energy toward solutions.[305] They feel frustration with those who decide it is hopeless and use that as an excuse to do nothing.[306] Goodall points out that if young people lose hope, it hampers the ability to empower change.

Environmental justice comes together at the intersection of race, class, indigeneity, gender, geography, and nature. The core of environmental justice is ensuring that vulnerable groups (e.g., people of color, Indigenous Peoples, children, women, elders, people experiencing poverty, people in developing countries) no longer bear the burden of environmental degradation and climate change. It fundamentally involves human rights and is organized around expanding economic and racial justice at the juncture of the ecology and environment—land, pollution, and health.[307] We must reduce inequities in exposure to environmental risks and in access to needed resources. Because those who contribute the least to environmental degradation experience the greatest impacts (e.g., small island nations, south Asia), there have been continued calls for climate reparations from the global north to compensate the global south for the damage caused by "extractive capitalism."[308]

Many countries have adopted laws that make clear the right to a healthy environment.[309] A healthy environment is essential to achieve human rights, such as the right to security and the right to a "standard of living adequate for health and well-being."[310] For example, strategies that help mitigate the impact of air pollution will directly impact people's right to health. There are also human rights that can be leveraged to advocate for a healthy environment. For example, the right to non-discrimination and the right to effective remedies can be asserted to address environmental racism; the right to receive information may be used to obtain information on pollutants.

Climate change is a threat multiplier that increases the risk of conflict, although conflict can also cause environmental degradation and contribute to climate change.[311] Researchers have shown that violence and war increase as the temperatures rise and rainfall is diminished.[312] As climate change reduces access to clean water, air, land, and food, violence and conflict over these resources escalate.[313] Thoughtful and just climate change mitigation and adaptation can reduce these sources of conflict.

Women continue to be at the forefront of the environmental justice movement. The well-being of their communities and families depends on their constant advocacy and leadership. The global crisis intersecting the environment, gender discrimination, and two pandemics (COVID-19 and racism) emphasized the threats to the well-being of women.[314] As women have organized to protect the environment, they have also organized to protect human rights and work for peace. As noted by Tulika Srivastava of the South Asia Women's Fund, "Donors investing in women to create their own solutions to the daily challenges they identify will support both positive environmental outcomes and women's rights."[315] Yet, 80% of funding goes to organizations led by men; less than 0.02% is explicitly for women.[316]

One of the concepts that is important to support the human rights of communities on the frontline of environmental degradation is that of *just transitions*. While time is critical, if we are to avert more serious consequences of climate change, we must replace extractive jobs with green jobs in communities where fossil fuels and other resources are extracted; it is imperative that these communities are not left as ghost towns.[317] As noted by the International Labor Organization,[318] even though millions of jobs will be lost to meet international climate goals, three times as many jobs will be created. Just transitions attempt to balance the urgency to mitigate and adapt to climate change with protecting local and Indigenous communities which have few employment options if extractive jobs disappear.

Across the globe, cities, tribes, and nations are beginning to protect the rights of nature. This shift replaces the current environmental protection paradigms that still see nature as the property of humans, typically identifying acceptable levels of contamination and degradation. When we consider the rights of nature, we change our interactions with nature from one of power-over to a more balanced relationship. This chapter gave a broad overview of some of the serious environmental conditions that are linked to human consumption and disregard for practices that are instrumental to ecological survival. Yet, we have learned that when human destruction can be mitigated/tempered, nature has the potential for healing.

Unfortunately, climate change is already occurring.[319] We are lagging behind in the goal of keeping temperatures from increasing less than two degrees Celsius—and ideally less than 1.5 Celsius—above pre-industrial levels. While some progress has been made, it is not sufficient, requiring us to adapt to the changing climate while we attempt to mitigate the damage.[320]

Discussion Questions

1. What evidence is there in your community of environmental racism? Who is most impacted? (Hint: look at https://www.epa.gov/tri nationalanalysis/where-you-live [US] or www.pollution.org [global] for location of toxins and overlay with demographic data).
2. What can be done in your community to reduce/correct the inequitable exposure to environmental toxins or climate change?
3. Where/how in your community are the rights of nature being protected? Who is leading the effort (locally, nationally, and/or globally)? What are the larger implications (economic, social, political, justice, and equity)? If there is no effort to protect nature, what is one action you would propose?
4. What types of adaptive actions are needed in your community to respond to threats anticipated from climate change? (Hint: https://coast.noaa.gov/slr/#/layer/slr [US coastlines] or https://impact lab.org maps [global]).

Notes

1. Jürg Staudenmann, Karolina Eklow, and Caspar Trimmer, "No sustainable development without an environment of peace," *The International Institute for Sustainable Development (IISD)* (July 2021), https://sdg.iisd.org/commentary/guest-articles/no-sustainable-development-without-an-environment-of-peace/.
2. Intergovernmental Science-Policy Platform on Biodiversity and Ecosystem Services (IPBES), *Summary for policymakers of the assessment report on land degradation and restoration of the intergovernmental science-policy platform on biodiversity and ecosystem services* (Bonn, Germany: IPBES, 2018), https://www.ipbes.net/event/ipbes-6-ple nary; Lacey M. Sloan and Cathryne L. Schmitz, "The global environmental crisis: Human systems embedded in the natural environment," in *Integrated social work practice: Bridging micro, mezzo, and macro level practice*, Bronwyn Cross-Denny (San Diego, CA: Cognella, In press).
3. Robert D. Bullard, Glenn S. Johnson, and Angel O. Torres, in *The quest for environmental justice: Human rights and the politics of pollution*, Robert D. Bullard (San Francisco, CA: Sierra Club Books, 2005), 292.

4. Ande Nesmith et al., *The intersection of environmental justice, climate change, community, and the ecology of life* (New York: Springer International, 2021); Julie Sze, *Environmental justice in a moment of danger* (Oakland, CA: University of California Press, 2020).
5. IPBES, *Summary for policymakers*; Intergovernmental Panel on Climate Change (IPCC), *Global warming of 1.5 C* (2018), http://www.ipcc.ch/pdf/special-reports/sr15/sr15ts.pdf; Paul C. Stern, Oran R. Young, and Daniel Druckman, eds., *Global environmental change: Understanding human dimensions* (Washington, DC: National Academy Press, 1992).
6. Sarah Kaplan, "Climate change has destabilized Earth's poles, putting the rest of the planet in peril," *Washington Post* (December 2021), https://www.washingtonpost.com/climate-environment/2021/12/14/climate-change-arctic-antarctic-poles/.
7. Rebecca Lindsey and LuAnn Dahlman, *Climate change: Global temperature* (2021), https://www.climate.gov/news-features/understanding-climate/climate-change-global-temperature; United Nations Framework Convention on Climate Change (UNFCCC), *Glasgow climate pact–Advance unedited version (2021)*, https://unfccc.int/sites/default/files/resource/cop26_auv_2f_cover_decision.pdf.
8. Lindsey and Dahlman, *Climate change: Global temperature*.
9. Deniss Martinez and Ans Irfan, "Colonialism, the climate crisis, and the need to center Indigenous voices," *Environmental Health News* (2021), par. 3, https://www.ehn.org/indigenous-people-and-climate-change-2655479728.html.
10. Kasha Patel, "Enter winter, the fastest-warming season," *Washington Post* (December 2021), https://www.washingtonpost.com/weather/2021/12/21/winter-warm-us-climate/.
11. Michael Birnbaum, Brady Dennis, and Jason Samenow, "A warming world could add more fuel to tornadoes, scientists say," *Washington Post* (December 2021), https://www.washingtonpost.com/climate-environment/2021/12/11/tornadoes-climate-change/; Erin Blakemore, "World's strongest ocean current is speeding up—and humans are to blame," *Washington Post* (December 2021), https://www.washingtonpost.com/science/ocean-currents-speeding-humans-warming/2021/12/03/7123d38c-52d4-11ec-8927-c396fa861a71_story.html.
12. Matthew Cappucci and Jason Samenow, "Study finds Atlantic hurricanes becoming more frequent, destructive," *Washington Post* (December 2021), https://www.washingtonpost.com/weather/2021/12/02/atlantic-hurricanes-increasing-frequency-climate/.
13. Jack Nicas, "A slow-motion climate disaster: The spread of barren land," *New York Times* (December 2021), https://www.nytimes.com/2021/12/03/world/americas/brazil-climate-change-barren-land.html.

14. Rachel Chason and Adrienne Surprenant, "Trapped by rising water: Record floods linked to climate change have left the people of South Sudan in crisis," *Washington Post* (December 2021), https://www.washingtonpost.com/world/interactive/2021/south-sudan-flooding/.
15. Henry Fountain, "Hotter summer days mean more Sierra Nevada wildfires, study finds," *New York Times* (November 2021), https://www.nytimes.com/2021/11/17/climate/climate-change-wildfire-risk.html?action=click&module=Well&pgtype=Homepage&section=Climate%20and%20Environment.
16. Diana Leonard, "Snowfall may be nearly zero for years at a time in Mountain West because of climate change, study finds," *Washington Post* (December 2021), https://www.washingtonpost.com/weather/2021/12/03/snow-water-resources-california/.
17. Matthew Cappucci and Emily Schwing, "Alaska experiences record-high temperature for December, freezing rain," *Washington Post* (December 2021), https://www.washingtonpost.com/weather/2021/12/28/alaska-record-temperatures-climate/.
18. Sarah Spicer, "Kansas's prairie is rapidly shrinking. Its future depends on private landowners like Lorna Harder," *Washington Post* (November 2021), https://www.washingtonpost.com/magazine/2021/11/30/kansas-shrinking-prairie/.
19. Sarah Kaplan and Brady Dennis, "2021 had wave of extreme weather disasters: Scientists say worse lies ahead," *Washington Post* (December 2021), https://www.washingtonpost.com/climate-environment/2021/12/17/climate-change-extreme-weather-future/.
20. Nesmith et al., *The intersection of environmental justice.*
21. Martinez and Irfan, *Colonialism, the climate crisis, and the need to center Indigenous voices*, par. 4.
22. United Nations Framework Convention on Climate Change (UNFCCC), *Glasgow climate pact.*
23. UNFCCC, *Glasgow climate pact.*
24. Tik Root, "Tropical forests can recover quickly from deforestation on their own, new study finds," *Washington Post* (December 2021), https://www.washingtonpost.com/climate-solutions/2021/12/09/climate-change-forest-recovery-deforestation/.
25. Amy Cheng, "London's River Thames, now home to sharks, seals and sea horses, is no longer 'biologically dead'," *New York Times* (November 2021), https://www.washingtonpost.com/world/2021/11/11/sharks-thames-river-london/.
26. Alexander Koch et al., "Earth system impacts of the European arrival and Great Dying in the Americas after 1492," *Quaternary Science Review* 207, 13–36 (2018), https://doi.org/10.1016/j.quascirev.2018.12.004;

Simon L. Lewis and Mark A. Maslin, *The human planet: How we created the Anthropocene* (New Haven, CT: Yale University Press, 2018).

27. Lacey M. Sloan and Cathryne L. Schmitz, "Resilience and the claiming of voice by marginalized communities" in *The Palgrave handbook of positive peace*, Katerina Standish et al., eds. (Palgrave Macmillan, Singapore, 2021), https://doi.org/10.1007/978-981-15-3877-3_6-1.
28. Sloan and Schmitz, "Resilience and the claiming of voice by marginalized communities".
29. Randall Robinson, *The debt: What America owes to Blacks* (New York: Penguin, 2001).
30. Robert L. Brooks, "Precontact agriculture," *The Encyclopedia of Oklahoma History and Culture* (n.d.), https://www.okhistory.org/publications/enc/entry.php?entry=PR005; Sloan and Schmitz, "Resilience and the claiming of voice by marginalized communities".
31. Martinez and Irfan, *Colonialism, the climate crisis, and the need to center Indigenous voices.*
32. Martinez and Irfan, par. 5.
33. Martinez and Irfan, par. 5.
34. Amal Ahmed, "The father of environmental justice is not done yet," *The Nation* (May 2021), https://www.thenation.com/article/politics/robert-bullard-isnt-done/.
35. Helen V. Cole et al., "Adapting the environmental risk transition theory for urban health inequities: An observational study examining complex environmental riskscapes in seven neighborhoods in Global North cities," *Social Science & Medicine* 277 (2021), https://doi.org/10.1016/j.socscimed.2021.113907.
36. Lacey M. Sloan et al., *Critical multiculturalism and intersectionality in a complex world* (New York: Oxford University Press, 2018), 133.
37. Environmental Protection Agency (EPA), *Environmental justice* (2022), https://www.epa.gov/environmentaljustice.
38. Environmental Protection Agency (EPA), *Environmental justice* (2022).
39. EPA, *Environmental justice* (2022).
40. EPA, *Environmental justice.*
41. Environmental Protection Agency (EPA), *Learn about environmental justice* (2021), par. 5, https://www.epa.gov/environmentaljustice/learn-about-environmental-justice.
42. Jeremy S. Hoffman, Vivek Shandas, and Nicholas Pendelton, "The effects of historical housing policies on resident exposure to intra-urban heat: A study of 108 US urban areas," *Climate* 8, no. 1 (2020): 1–15. https://doi.org/10.3390/cli8010012.
43. Jiawen Liu et al., "Disparities in air pollution exposure in the United States by race/ethnicity and income, 1990–2010," *Environmental*

Health Perspectives 129, no. 12 (December 2021), https://doi.org/10.1289/EHP8584.

44. Daniel Cusick, "Past racist "redlining" practices increased climate burden on minority neighborhoods," *E&E News* (2020), par. 4, https://www.scientificamerican.com/article/past-racist-redlining-practices-increased-climate-burden-on-minority-neighborhoods/.
45. Center for Disease Control (CDC), *Healthy places: Health effects of gentrification* (2009), https://www.cdc.gov/healthyplaces/healthtopics/gentrification.htm.
46. Isabelle Anguelovski et al., "Opinion: Why green "climate gentrification" threatens poor and vulnerable populations," *Proceedings of the National Academy of Sciences* 116, no. 52 (2019), https://doi.org/10.1073/pnas.1920490117; Helen V. Cole et al., "Adapting the environmental risk transition theory".
47. Helen V. Cole et al., "Adapting the environmental risk transition theory," 2.
48. Lacey M. Sloan and Cathryne L. Schmitz, "Environmental degradation: Communities forging a path forward," *Journal of Transdisciplinary Peace Praxis* 1, no. 1 (2019): 17–46; Stern, Young, and Druckman, eds., *Global environmental change: Understanding human dimensions*; United Nations General Assembly (UNGA), *Climate change and its possible security implications* A/64/20 (2009), https://www.un.org/ga/search/view_doc.asp?symbol=A/64/350.
49. Thomas F. Homer-Dixon, *Environment, scarcity, and violence* (Princeton, NJ: Princeton University Press, 1999).
50. Jürgen Scheffran et al., "Climate change and violent conflict," *Science, New Series* 336, no. 6083 (2012): 869–871.
51. Richard Akresh, "Climate change, conflict and children," *The Future of Children* 26, no. 1 (2016): 51–71.
52. United Nations General Assembly (UNGA), *Climate change and its possible security implications*.
53. Vandana Shiva, *Making peace with the earth* (Halifax, Canada: Fernwood Publishing, 2012).
54. Laura E. Reimer et al., *Transformative change: An introduction to peace and conflict studies* (Lanham, MD: Lexington Books, 2015), 5.
55. Homer-Dixon, *Environment, scarcity, and violence*; Michael T. Klare, *Resource wars: The new landscape of global* conflict (New York: Henry Holt and Company, 2002).
56. Homer-Dixon, *Environment, scarcity, and violence*, 53.
57. Homer-Dixon, *Environment, scarcity, and violence*.
58. United Nations General Assembly (UNGA), *Climate change and its possible security implications* A/64/20 (2009).
59. UNGA, *Climate change and its possible security implications*.

60. UNGA, *Climate change*.
61. Meredith C. F. Powers et al., "Environmental migration: Social work at the nexus of climate change and global migration," *Advances in Social Work* 18, no. 3 (2018): 1023–1040.
62. Nils Petter Gleditsch and Ragnhild Nordås, "Climate change and conflict: a critical overview," *Die Friedens-Warte* 84, no. 2 (2009): 11–28.
63. Sloan and Schmitz, "Environmental degradation".
64. Hanne Fjelde and Kristine Hoglund, "Building peace, creating conflict?" in *Building peace, creating conflict? Conflictual dimensions of local and international peace-building*, Hanne Fjelde and Kristine Hoglund, eds. (Sweden: Nordic eAcademic Press, 2011): 11–24; Sloan and Schmitz, "Environmental degradation".
65. Sloan and Schmitz, "Environmental degradation," 38.
66. Fjelde and Hoglund, "Building peace, creating conflict?"; Sloan and Schmitz, "Environmental degradation"; Carolyn Yoder, *The little book of trauma healing: When violence strikes and community security is threatened* (revised and updated) (New York: Good Books, 2022).
67. United Nations Human Rights Council (UNHRC), *The human right to a clean, healthy and sustainable environment* A/HRC/48/L.23/Rev.1 (2021), par. 20, https://documents-dds-ny.un.org/doc/UNDOC/GEN/G21/289/50/PDF/G2128950.pdf?OpenElement.
68. United Nations Human Rights Council (UNHRC), *Report of the Independent Expert on the issue of human rights obligations relating to the enjoyment of a safe, clean, healthy and sustainable environment*, *John H. Knox, A/HRC/22/43* (2012), https://www.ohchr.org/sites/default/files/Documents/HRBodies/HRCouncil/RegularSession/Session22/A-HRC-22-43_en.pdf.
69. United Nations Environmental Programme (UNEP), *New UN resolution reinforces link between human rights and the environment* (April 2021), https://www.unep.org/news-and-stories/story/new-un-resolution-reinforces-link-between-human-rights-and-environment.
70. United Nations Human Rights Council (UNHRC), *Report of the Independent Expert on the issue of human rights*, 12.
71. Amelia Annen, "On the intersection of environmental and racial justice," *HoneySuckle Magazine* (June 2020), https://honeysucklemag.com/on-the-intersection-of-environmental-and-racial-justicenbsp/.
72. Annen, "On the intersection of environmental and racial justice".
73. Environmental Justice Platform, *Environmental justice/environmental racism* (1991), 1, http://www.ejnet.org/ej/index.html.
74. United Nations Human Rights Council (UNHRC), *Report of the Independent Expert on the issue of human rights obligations relating*

to the enjoyment of a safe, clean, healthy and sustainable environment, John H. Knox: Mapping report, A/HRC/25/53 (2013), 9, https://documents-dds-ny.un.org/doc/UNDOC/GEN/G13/192/11/PDF/G1319211.pdf?OpenElement.

75. United Nations (UN), *Universal declaration of human rights* (1948), art. 21, https://www.un.org/en/about-us/universal-declaration-of-human-rights.
76. United Nations Environmental Programme (UNEP), *Compendium of good practices for human rights and the environment* (2016), https://www.ajne.org/sites/default/files/resource/publications/7224/compendium-of-good-practices-human-rights-and-the-environment.pdf.
77. Mengistu A. Dibaba, "Environmental justice and peacebuilding practices in Ethiopia," *International Journal of Ecosystem* 10, no. 1 (2020): 23–29, https://doi.org/10.5923/j.ije.20201001.02; Reimer et al., *Transformative change.*
78. Dibaba, "Environmental justice and peacebuilding practices in Ethiopia".
79. Michael T. Klare, *All hell breaking loose: The Pentagon's perspective on climate change* (New York: Henry Holt and Company, 2019).
80. Dibaba, "Environmental justice and peacebuilding practices in Ethiopia," 28.
81. Femi Aborisade, "Petro-capitalism, neoliberalism, labour and community mobilization in Nigeria," *Labour, Capital and Society/Travail, Capital et Société* (2010): 31–62, https://www.jstor.org/stable/43158363.
82. Dibaba, "Environmental justice and peacebuilding practices in Ethiopia".
83. Dibaba, "Environmental justice and peacebuilding practices in Ethiopia".
84. UNGA, *Climate change*, 7.
85. Dibaba, "Environmental justice and peacebuilding practices in Ethiopia".
86. John Paul Lederach and Angela Jill Lederach, *When blood and bones cry out: Journeys through the soundscape of healing and reconciliation* (New York: Oxford University Press, 2010).
87. Lederach and Lederach, *When blood and bones cry out.*
88. Andrew Mack, ed., *Human security report 2005: War and peace in the twenty-first century* (New York: Oxford University Press, 2005), http://www.humansecurityreport.info/.
89. Mack, ed., *Human security report 2005: War and peace in the twenty-first century*, 9.
90. World Health Organization (WHO), *Climate change and health* (2021), https://www.who.int/news-room/fact-sheets/detail/climate-change-and-health.
91. Anthony Faiola, "Amid drought, conflict and skyrocketing prices, a global food crisis could be nearing, expert warns," *Washington Post* (2021), https://www.washingtonpost.com/world/2021/12/15/global-food-crisis-pandemic/; Rachel Pannett, "The U.N. blames climate

change for Madagascar's food crisis: Scientists say it's not the main cause," *Washington Post* (2021), https://www.washingtonpost.com/world/2021/12/02/madagascar-famine-climate-change/; John Roy Porter, "The world's food supply is made insecure by climate change," *Academic Impact* (n.d.), https://www.un.org/en/academic-impact/worlds-food-supply-made-insecure-climate-change; United Nations News, *Madagascar: Severe drought could spur world's first climate change famine* (October 2021), https://news.un.org/en/story/2021/10/1103712.

92. Ahmed, "The father of environmental justice is not done yet".
93. WHO, *Climate change and health*, IV.
94. WHO, *Climate change and health*, par. 5.
95. WHO, *Climate change.*
96. Kristie L. Ebi et al., "Human health," in *Impacts, risks, and adaptation in the United States: Fourth national climate assessment, volume II*, David R. Reidmiller et al., eds. (U.S. Global Change Research Program, Washington, DC, USA, 2018): 572–603. https://doi.org/10.7930/NCA4.2018.CH14; WHO, *Climate change.*
97. Hoffman, Shandas, and Pendelton, "The effects of historical housing policies"; Dongying Li et al., "Modeling the relationships between historical redlining, urban heat, and heat-related emergency department visits: An examination of 11 Texas cities," *Environment and Planning B: Urban Analytics and City Science* 49, no. 3 (2021): 933–952.
98. Linda Rudolph and Solange Gould, "Climate change and health inequities: A Framework for action," *Annals of Global Health* 81, no. 3 (2015): 432–444, http://dx.doi.org/10.1016/j.aogh.2015.06.003.
99. Adelle Thomas et al., "Climate change and small island developing states," *Annual Review of Environment and Resources* 45 (2020): 1–27, https://doi.org/10.1146/annurev-environ-012320-083355; Victoria State Government, *Climate change and health* (2021), https://www.betterhealth.vic.gov.au/health/healthyliving/climate-change-and-health#bhc-content; World Health Organization (WHO), *Climate change and health in Small Island Developing States: A WHO special initiative* (Geneva, 2018); World Health Organization (WHO), *COP26 special report on climate change and health: The health argument for climate action* (2021), https://www.who.int/publications/i/item/9789240036727.
100. Howard Frumkin et al., "Climate change: The public health response," *American Journal of Public Health* 98, no. 3 (2008), par. 7. https://doi.org/10.2105/AJPH.2007.119362.
101. Luis Cifuentes et al., "Climate change: Hidden health benefits of greenhouse gas mitigation," *Science* 293 (2001): 1257–1259; Frumkin et al., "Climate change: The public health response"; J. Jason West et al.,

"Global health benefits of mitigating ozone pollution with methane emission controls," *Proceedings of the National Academy of Science* 103 (2006): 3988–3993.
102. Frumkin et al., "Climate change: The public health response".
103. Frumkin et al., "Climate change: The public health response"; Thomas et al., "Climate change and small island developing states"; World Health Organization (WHO), *Climate change and adaptation to protect human health* (2010), https://www.who.int/news/item/01-10-2010-climate-change-adaptation-to-protect-human-health; WHO, *COP26 special report on climate change and health.*
104. Climate Psychiatry Alliance, *IPCC report urges climate action* (2022), https://www.climatepsychiatry.org/featured-articles/2022/3/14/ipcc-report-urges-climate-action.
105. American Psychiatric Association (APA), *Climate change and mental health connections* (2022), https://www.psychiatry.org/patients-families/climate-change-and-mental-health-connections.
106. Anna Turns, *Eco-Grief: Why climate change anxiety is keeping us awake at night* (2019), https://welldoing.org/article/eco-grief-why-climate-change-anxiety-keeping-us-awake-night.
107. National Public Radio (NPR), *Climate change is the greatest threat to public health, top medical journals warn* (September 2021), https://www.npr.org/2021/09/07/1034670549/climate-change-is-the-greatest-threat-to-public-health-top-medical-journals-warn.
108. APA, *Climate change and mental health connections*; Climate Psychiatry Alliance, *IPCC report urges climate action.*
109. APA, *Climate change and mental health connections.*
110. WHO, *Climate change and adaptation to protect human health.*
111. WHO, *Climate change.*
112. Lachlan McIver et al., "Climate change & health in Fiji: Environmental epidemiology of infectious diseases & potential for climate-based early warning systems," *Fiji Journal of Public Health* 1, no. 1 (2012): 7–13, https://www.health.gov.fj/PDFs/Fiji%20Journal%20of%20Public%20Health%20Vol1Issue1.pdf.
113. McIver et al., "Climate change & health in Fiji," 7.
114. Republic of Fiji, *Republic of Fiji national climate change policy: 2018–2030* (2019), https://www.economy.gov.fj/images/CCIC/uploads/General/FIJI-National-Climate-Change-Policy-2018-2030-FINAL.pdf.
115. Republic of Fiji, *Republic of Fiji national climate change policy: 2018–2030*; Thomas et al., "Climate change and small island developing states".

116. Thomas et al., "Climate change and small island developing states".
117. Republic of Fiji, *Republic of Fiji national climate change policy.*
118. Republic of Fiji, *Republic of Fiji.*
119. Scott Leckie, "Using human rights to resolve the climate replacement problem: The promise of the Peninsula principles," in *Repairing domestic climate displacement: The peninsula principles*, Scott Leckie and Chris Huggins, eds. (New York: Routledge, 2016), 1–14; Andreas Neef et al., "Climate adaptation strategies in Fiji: The role of social norms and cultural values," *World Development* 107 (2018): 125–137, https://doi.org/10.1016/j.worlddev.2018.02.029.
120. Kathy Law, "Editorial: Combined policies for better tackling of climate change and air pollution," *Science for Environmental Policy* 24 (November 2010): 1–3, https://ec.europa.eu/environment/integration/research/newsalert/pdf/24si_en.pdf.
121. Environmental Protection Agency (EPA), *What is acid rain?* (2021), https://www.epa.gov/acidrain/what-acid-rain; WHO, *Climate change and health.*
122. World Health Organization (WHO), *Air pollution* (2022), https://www.who.int/health-topics/air-pollution#tab=tab_1.
123. Environmental Protection Agency (EPA), *Pollutants and sources* (2018), https://www3.epa.gov/airtoxics/pollsour.html.
124. Sonali Singh, "Top 10 countries that have the least pollution," *Steam-Daily* (2021), https://steamdaily.com/top-10-countries-that-have-the-least-pollution/.
125. State of Global Air, *Global health impacts of air pollution* (2020), https://www.stateofglobalair.org/health/global#Millions-deaths.
126. State of Global Air, *Global health impacts of air pollution*, par. 4.
127. Jane V. Hall, Victor Brajer, and Frederick W. Lurmann, "Measuring the gains from improved air quality in the San Joaquin Valley," *Journal of Environmental Management* 88, no. 4 (2008): 1003–1015. https://doi.org/10.1016/j.jenvman.2007.05.002.
128. Andrzej Bytnerowicz, Mark Fenn, and Chuck Sams, "Air pollution and climate change," *U.S. Department of Agriculture, Forest Service, Climate Change Resource Center* (January 2014). www.fs.usda.gov/ccrc/topics/air-pollution; World Health Organization (WHO), *Air pollution.*
129. WHO, *Air pollution.*
130. State of Global Air, *Global health impacts of air pollution.*
131. American Lung Association, *Key findings* (2022), par. 5, https://www.lung.org/research/sota/key-findings.
132. Marie Lynn Miranda et al., "Making the environmental justice grade: The relative burden of air pollution exposure in the United States," *International Journal of Environmental Research and Public Health*

8, no. 6 (2011): 1755–1771, https://www.ncbi.nlm.nih.gov/pmc/articles/PMC3137995/; Anthony Nardone, et al., "Associations between historical residential redlining and current age-adjusted rates of emergency department visits due to asthma across eight cities in California: an ecological study," *Lancet Planet Health* 4, no. 1 (2020): e24–e31; Marie S. O'Neill et al., "Health, wealth, and air pollution: Advancing theory and methods," *Environment Health Perspectives* 111, no. 16 (2003): 1861–1870. https://doi.org/10.1289/ehp.6334.

133. Greenpeace, *Coal* (n.d.), https://www.greenpeace.org.uk/challenges/coal/.
134. Ministry of Coal, "Coal: Indian energy choice," *Government of India* (2022), https://coal.nic.in/en/major-statistics/coal-indian-energy-choice.
135. Sandeep Pai et al., "Understanding just transitions in coal-dependent communities: Case studies from Mpumalanga, South Africa, and Jharkhand, India," *Center for Strategic and International Studies (CSIS) and Climate Investment Funds (CIF)* (2021), https://justtransitioninitiative.org/wp-content/uploads/2021/10/CoalDependentCommunities_Report.pdf.
136. Akshay Deschmane, "How a just transition can make India's coal history," *BBC* (November 2021), par. 2, https://www.bbc.com/future/article/20211103-india-how-a-just-transition-can-make-coal-history.
137. Pai et al., "Understanding just transitions in coal-dependent communities".
138. Nitish Priyadarshi, "Effects of mining on environment in the state of Jharkhand, India," *Environment and Geology* (May 2012), https://nitishpriyadarshi.blogspot.com/2012/05/effects-of-mining-on-environment-in.html.
139. Deschmane, "How a just transition can make India's coal history," par. 1.
140. Deschmane, "How a just transition can make India's coal history," par. 1.
141. Madhura Joshi, "Coal in 2022: India's climate and energy evolution," *E3G* (2022), par. 1, https://www.e3g.org/news/coal-in-2022-india-s-climate-and-energy-evolution/.
142. Joshi, "Coal in 2022: India's climate and energy evolution," par. 8; Bhupender Yadav, *COP26 Diary 01-11-2021* (January 2021), https://bhupenderyadav.in/blog/cop26-diary-01-11-2021.
143. Pai et al., "Understanding just transitions in coal-dependent communities".
144. Nick Robins, Vonda Brunsting, and David Wood, "Climate change and the just transition: A guide for investor action," *Grantham Research Institute on Climate Change and the Environment* (2018),

6, https://sustainabledevelopment.un.org/content/documents/22101ijtguidanceforinvestors23november1118_541095.pdf.
145. International Labor Organization, *Greening jobs: World employment and social outlook 2018* (2018), https://www.ilo.org/weso-greening/#Intro-2.
146. Pai et al., "Understanding just transitions".
147. Pai et al., "Understanding".
148. Pai et al., "Understanding".
149. Environmental Protection Agency (EPA), *Greenhouse gas emissions* (2017), https://www3.epa.gov/climatechange/ghgemissions; Jamey Keaten, "Nearly everyone in the world is breathing polluted air, says WHO," *Time* (April 2022), https://time.com/6164235/world-breathing-air-pollution/?utm_medium.
150. Karn Vohra et al., "Global mortality from outdoor fine particle pollution generated by fossil fuel combustion: Results from GEOS-Chem," *Environmental Research* 195 (2021), https://doi.org/10.1016/j.envres.2021.110754.
151. WHO, *Air pollution*.
152. WHO, *Air pollution*.
153. Environmental Protection Agency (EPA), *Carbon pollution from transportation* (2021), https://www.epa.gov/transportation-air-pollution-and-climate-change/carbon-pollution-transportation.
154. South Coast Air Quality Management District, *The Southland's war on smog: Fifty years of progress toward clean air (through May 1997)* (2022), https://www.aqmd.gov/home/research/publications/50-years-of-progress#The%20Arrival%20of%20Air%20Pollution.
155. California Air Resources Board, *History* (2022), par. 3, https://ww2.arb.ca.gov/about/history.
156. California Air Resources Board, *History*; South Coast Air Quality Management District, *The Southland's war on smog*.
157. South Coast Air Quality Management District, *The Southland's war on smog*.
158. California Air Resources Board, *History*.
159. Clean Energy and Pollution Reduction Act (2015), chap. 547, https://leginfo.legislature.ca.gov/faces/billTextClient.xhtml?bill_id=201520160SB350.
160. California Air Resources Board, *Homepage* (2022), https://ww2.arb.ca.gov.
161. California Air Resources Board, *Homepage*.
162. University of Southern California, *Children's health study* (2022), https://healthstudy.usc.edu/study-findings/.
163. California Climate Leadership, "Myths and facts," *S.B. 350* (n.d.), https://focus.senate.ca.gov/climate/sb350-facts.

164. American Lung Association, *Most polluted cities* (2022), https://www.lung.org/research/sota/city-rankings/most-polluted-cities.
165. World Health Organization (WHO), *Drinking water* (2022), https://www.who.int/news-room/fact-sheets/detail/drinking-water.
166. United Nations Water, *Summary progress update 2021: SDG 6–Water and sanitation for all* (2021), https://www.unwater.org/app/uploads/2021/12/SDG-6-Summary-Progress-Update-2021_Version-July-2021a.pdf.
167. United Nations Water, *Summary progress update.*
168. United Nations Water, *Summary progress update.*
169. WHO, *Drinking water*, par. 3.
170. Global Burden of Disease, "Global, regional, and national comparative risk assessment of 84 behavioural, environmental and occupational, and metabolic risks or clusters of risks for 195 countries and territories, 1990–2017: A systematic analysis for the Global Burden of Disease Study 2017," *The Lancet* 392, no. 10159, 1923–1994 (2018), https://doi.org/10.1016/S0140-6736(18)32225-6.
171. Global Burden of Disease, "Global, regional, and national comparative risk assessment".
172. United Nations Office of the High Commissioner for Human Rights (OHCHR), *Fact sheet no. 35: The right to water* (2010), https://www.ohchr.org/sites/default/files/Documents/Publications/FactSheet35en.pdf.
173. Human Rights Watch, *The human right to water: A guide for First Nations communities and advocates* (2019), https://www.hrw.org/report/2019/10/23/human-right-water/guide-first-nations-communities-and-advocates#; Jane Goodall Institute, *Supporting First Nations, Métis and Inuit Youth to make positive changes in their communities: A guide for educators and youth program facilitators* (n.d.), https://janegoodall.ca/wp-content/uploads/2017/02/ProtectingOurSacredWater-FNMIResource.pdf.
174. Monique G. Dubé et al., "Accumulated state of the Yukon River watershed: Part I critical review of literature," *Integrated Environmental Assessment and Management* 9, no. 3 (2013): 426–438, https://doi-org.ezproxy.uvm.edu/10.1002/ieam.1360; Sloan and Schmitz, "Resilience and the claiming of voice by marginalized communities".
175. Sloan and Schmitz, "Resilience and the claiming of voice".
176. Office of Indian Energy Policy and Programs, *The Yukon River Inter-Tribal Watershed Council project-2011* (2011), https://www.energy.gov/indianenergy/yukon-river-inter-tribal-watershedcouncil-2011-project; Rob Rosenfeld, "Celebrating an important anniversary," *Currents (YRITWC)* (2003), https://docs.wixstatic.com/ugd/dcbdaf_cccf0fbf6de94d6987cca5e598766bda.pdf.

177. Harvard Project on American Indian Economic Development, *Honoring nations 2005 honoree* (2005), http://nnigovernance.arizona.edu/sites/default/files/attachments/text/honoring_nations/2005_HN_Yukon_River_Inter-Tribal_Watershed_Council.pdf; Rosenfeld, "Celebrating an important anniversary"; Yukon River Inter-Tribal Watershed Council (YRITWC), *Homepage* (2022), https://www.yritwc.org.
178. Harvard Project on American Indian Economic Development, *Honoring nations 2005 honoree*; Rosenfeld, "Celebrating an important anniversary"; Sloan and Schmitz, "Resilience and the claiming of voice"; YRITWC, *Homepage*.
179. Yukon River Inter-Tribal Watershed Council (YRITWC), *Science: Indigenous Observation Network* (2022), https://www.yritwc.org/science.
180. Yukon River Inter-Tribal Watershed Council (YRITWC), *Talking points to accompany draft watershed/water quality plan* (2017), https://www.yritwc.org/yr-watershed-plan/.
181. Zachary Michel, *Environmental steward: Jon Waterhouse* (2011), par. 8, https://www.nationalgeographic.org/article/real-world-geography-jon-waterhouse/.
182. Michel, *Environmental steward: Jon Waterhouse*.
183. Environmental Protection Agency (EPA), *Yukon river solid waste backhaul and recycling program* (2016), par. 5, https://archive.epa.gov/publicinvolvement/web/html/yukonriversolidwastebackhaulandrecyclingprogram.html.
184. Andrew R. Highsmith, "Demolition means progress: Urban renewal, local politics, and state-sanctioned ghetto formation in Flint, Michigan," *Journal of Urban History* 35, no. 3 (2009): 348–368, https://doi.org/10.1177/0096144208330403.
185. Alan Mallach and Eric Scorsone, *Long-Term stress and systemic failure: Taking seriously the fiscal crisis of America's older cities* (2011), https://community-wealth.org/sites/clone.community-wealth.org/files/downloads/paper-mallach-scorsone.pdf.
186. City of Flint, *Progress report of Flint water FAQs* (2021), https://www.cityofflint.com/progress-report-of-flint-water-faqs/.
187. Merrit Kennedy, "Lead-laced water in Flint: A step-by-step look at the makings of a crisis," *npr* (April 2016), https://www.npr.org/sections/thetwo-way/2016/04/20/465545378/lead-laced-water-in-flint-a-step-by-step-look-at-the-makings-of-a-crisis.
188. Melissa Denchak, "Flint water crisis: Everything you need to know," *NRDC* (November 2018), par. 1, https://www.nrdc.org/stories/flint-water-crisis-everything-you-need-know.
189. Denchak, "Flint water crisis"; Mona Hannah-Attisha, *What the eyes don't see: A story of crisis, resistance, and hope in an American city* (New York: One World, 2019).

190. Denchak, "Flint water crisis".
191. Nesmith et al., *The intersection of environmental justice.*
192. Environmental Transformation Movement of Flint (n.d.), https://www.etmflint.org/.
193. Environmental Transformation Movement of Flint, par. 4.
194. Lindsey J. Butler, Madeleine K. Scammell, and Eugene B. Benson, "The Flint, Michigan, water crisis: A case study in regulatory failure and environmental injustice," *Environmental Justice* 9, no. 4 (2016). https://doi.org/10.1089/env.2016.0014.
195. Butler, Scammell, and Benson, "The Flint, Michigan, water crisis".
196. Glenn Thrush, "An Alabama town's sewage woes test Biden's infrastructure ambitions," *The New York Times* (January 2022), https://www.nytimes.com/2022/01/12/us/politics/infrastructure-environmental-racism-alabama-black-belt.html.
197. The White House, *President Biden's bipartisan infrastructure law* (n.d.), https://www.whitehouse.gov/bipartisan-infrastructure-law/.
198. The White House, *President Biden's bipartisan infrastructure law.*
199. Washington State University, "Environmentally friendly farming practices used by nearly one third of world's farms: Less developed countries tend to see the largest improvements in productivity," *ScienceDaily* (August 2018), www.sciencedaily.com/releases/2018/08/180827180741.htm.
200. Washington State University, "Environmentally friendly farming practices used by nearly one third of world's farms".
201. John Chester and Sandra Keats, producers, *The biggest little farm*, directed by John Chester (United States: Erica Messer Productions, 2019), motion picture.
202. Kristen Dirksen, "Homestead paradise: Got barren land, boosted it at a profit," *YouTube* (March 2021), video, https://www.youtube.com/watch?v=sRPP4Ilpxso.
203. John Ikerd, *Sustainable agriculture: An alternative to industrial agriculture* (1996), par. 27, http://web.missouri.edu/ikerdj/papers/Ks-hrtld.htm.
204. Johns Hopkins, *History of agriculture* (n.d.), https://www.foodsystemprimer.org/food-production/history-of-agriculture/.
205. Roni A. Neff et al., "Peak oil, food systems, and public health," *American Journal of Public Health* 101, no. 9 (2010): 1587–1597; Jeremy Woods et al., "Energy and the food system," *Philosophical Transactions of the Royal Society of London* 365, no. 1554 (2010): 2991–3006.
206. Annie E. Casey Foundation, *Food deserts in the United States* (February 2021), par. 2, https://www.aecf.org/blog/exploring-americas-food-deserts.
207. Annie E. Casey Foundation, *Food deserts in the United States.*

208. Esperanca, *Food deserts and their impact on community health* (July 2021), https://esperanca.org/food-deserts-and-their-impact-on-community-health/.
209. Esperanca, *Food deserts and their impact on community health*, par. 12.
210. Esperanca, *Food deserts and their impact on community health.*
211. Sara Dewey, "Urban agriculture in our communities," *Conservation Law Foundation* (December 2021), https://www.clf.org/blog/the-power-of-urban-agriculture-in-transforming-a-community/.
212. United States Department of Agriculture (USDA), *Urban agriculture* (n.d.), https://www.usda.gov/topics/urban.
213. Dewey, "Urban agriculture in our communities," par. 6.
214. Dewey, "Urban agriculture in our communities," par. 7.
215. United States Department of Agriculture (USDA), *Urban agriculture*, par. 1.
216. Susanne A. Heckler, "A right to farm in the city: Providing a legal framework for legitimizing urban farming in American Cities," *Val. U. L. Rev.* 47, no. 217 (2012), https://scholar.valpo.edu/vulr/vol47/iss1/6; Alana Bowen Siegner, Charisma Acey, and Jennifer Sowerwine, "Producing urban agroecology in the East Bay: from soil health to community empowerment," *Agroecology and Sustainable Food Systems* 44, no. 5 (2020): 566–593, https://doi.org/10.1080/21683565.2019.1690615.
217. Environmental Protection Agency (EPA), *Smart growth and equitable development* (2021), https://www.epa.gov/smartgrowth/smart-growth-and-equitable-development10.1089/env.2016.0014; Heckler, "A Right to Farm in the City".
218. Samuel Gilbert, "Native Americans' farming practices may help feed a warming world," *Washington Post* (December 2021), https://www.washingtonpost.com/climate-solutions/interactive/2021/native-americans-farming-practices-may-help-feed-warming-world/.
219. Brooks, "Precontact agriculture".
220. Paul Robertson, "Sustainable agriculture in Mexico: Exporting practices worldwide," *The Borgen Project* (January 2018), https://borgenproject.org/sustainable-agriculture-in-mexico/.
221. Katie Pace, *The three sisters* (2015), https://sustainablefoodcenter.org/latest/gardening/the-three-sisters.
222. Pace, *The three sisters.*
223. Pace, *The three sisters.*
224. Pace, *The three sisters.*
225. Robertson, "Sustainable agriculture in Mexico".
226. Katie Pace, *Indigenous agriculture and sustainable food* (2015), par. 5, https://sustainablefoodcenter.org/latest/gardening/indigenous-agriculture-and-sustainable-food.

227. Intergovernmental Science-Policy Platform on Biodiversity and Ecosystem Services (IPBES), *Global assessment report on biodiversity and ecosystem services of the Intergovernmental Science-Policy Platform on Biodiversity and Ecosystem Services* (2019), 16, https://doi.org/10.5281/zenodo.3831673.
228. Gerardo Ceballos et al., "Accelerated modern human–induced species losses: Entering the sixth mass extinction," *Science Advances* 1, no. 5 (2015). https://doi.org/10.1126/sciadv.1400253; The Royal Society, *Reversing biodiversity loss: Why is biodiversity so important?* (2022), https://royalsociety.org/topics-policy/projects/biodiversity/why-is-biodiversity-important/.
229. Wankaam: People for the Estuary, *Rights of nature* (n.d.), par. 1, https://peoplefortheestuary.org/rights-of-nature/.
230. Ceballos et al., "Accelerated modern human–induced species losses"; Robert H. Cowie, Philippe Bouchet, and Benoît Fontaine, "The sixth mass extinction: Fact, fiction or speculation?" *Biological Reviews* 97, no. 2 (2022): 640–663, https://doi.org/10.1111/brv.12816; IPBES, *Global assessment report on biodiversity and ecosystem services*; Elizabeth Kolbert, *The sixth extinction. An unnatural history* (New York: Henry Holt & Company, 2014).
231. Anthony Waldron et al., *Protecting 30% of the planet for nature: Costs, benefits and economic implications* (n.d.), https://www.conservation.cam.ac.uk/files/waldron_report_30_by_30_publish.pdf.
232. United Nations Department of Economic and Social Affairs (UNDESA), *State of the world's Indigenous Peoples* 5 (2021), https://www.un.org/en/desa/state-world's-indigenous-peoples.
233. Eduardo Brondizio et al., eds., *Global assessment report on biodiversity and ecosystem services of the Intergovernmental Science-Policy Platform on Biodiversity and Ecosystem Services* (Bonn, Germany: IPBES, 2019), https://doi.org/10.5281/zenodo.3831673; IPBES, Global assessment report on biodiversity and ecosystem services.
234. Benji Jones, *Indigenous people are the world's biggest conservationists, but they rarely get credit for it* (June 2021), https://www.vox.com/22518592/indigenous-people-conserve-nature-icca.
235. Food and Agricultural Organization of the United Nations (FAO), *Forest governance by indigenous and tribal peoples. An opportunity for climate action in Latin America and the Caribbean* (2021), https://www.fao.org/3/cb2953en/cb2953en.pdf; Jones, *Indigenous people are the world's biggest conservationists.*
236. Kai M. A. Chan et al., eds., "Pathways towards a sustainable future," in *Global assessment on biodiversity and ecosystem services*,

IPBES, ed. (2019), https://zenodo.org/record/5519483#.YmSNqiB2Td; Bronson W. Griscom et al., "Natural climate solutions," *Proceedings of the National Academy of Sciences* 114, no. 44 (2017): 11645–11650, https://doi.org/10.1073/pnas.1710465114; Beverly E. Law et al., "Land use strategies to mitigate climate change in carbon dense temperate forests," *Proceedings of the National Academy of Sciences* 115, no. 14 (2018): 3663–3668, https://doi.org/10.1073/pnas.1720064115.

237. Griscom et al., "Natural climate solutions"; Law et al., "Land use strategies to mitigate climate change".
238. Jaxx Artz, *What is 'rewilding' and how can it help restore our planet's biodiversity?* (July 2021), https://www.globalcitizen.org/en/content/rewilding-biodiversity-defend-the-planet/; Caroline Fraser, *Rewilding the world: Dispatches from the conservation revolution* (New York: Metropolitan Books, 2009).
239. Artz, *What is 'rewilding' and how can it help restore our planet's biodiversity?*
240. JoAnna Klein, "'Rewilding' missing carnivores can help restore some landscapes," *The New York Times* (March 2018), https://www.nytimes.com/2018/03/16/science/rewilding-carnivores-wolves.html.
241. Andrej Kobler and Miha Adamic, "Brown bears in Slovenia: Identifying locations for construction of wildlife bridges across highways," in *Proceedings of International Conference on Ecology and Transportation*, Gary Evink, Paul Garrett, and David Zeigler, eds. (1999), http://www.icoet.net/ICOWET/99proceedings.asp.
242. 100% Pure New Zealand, *Tiritiri Matangi Island* (n.d.), https://www.newzealand.com/us/tiritiri-matangi/?cid=p:sem:US:FY19:Pure_H2:Google:DSA_Destinations:Text:auckland&kwid=dsa-425930918066&gclid=EAIaIQobChMIhL_Xvabz4gIVD7azCh3ZUw4SEAAYASAAEgJqOPDBwE&gclsrc=aw.ds.
243. Claudia Randrup, *Evaluating the effects of colonialism on deforestation in Madagascar: A social and environmental history* (2010), 4. https://etd.ohiolink.edu/apexprod/rws_etd/send_file/send?accession=oberlin1277525774&disposition=inline.
244. Sloan and Schmitz, "Resilience and the claiming of voice by marginalized communities".
245. Yoseph Maru, Aster Gebrekirstos, and Getahun Haile, "Indigenous sacred forests as a tool for climate Change mitigation: Lessons from Gedeo community, southern Ethiopia," *Journal of Sustainable Forestry* (2022), https://doi.org/10.1080/10549811.2021.2007490; Maria Tengö et al., *Local protection of tropical dry forest: Taboos and ecosystem*

services in southern Madagascar (2015), https://www.iccaconsortium.org/wp-content/uploads/2015/08/example-sacred-forests-madagascar-tengo-2004-en.pdf; World Wildlife Fund (WWF), *Sacred forests help conserve Madagascar's biodiversity* (June 2003), https://wwf.panda.org/wwf_news/?7603/Sacred-forests-help-conserve-Madagascars-biodiversity.

246. World Wildlife Fund (WWF), *Sacred forests help conserve Madagascar's biodiversity.*
247. Maru, Gebrekirstos, and Haile, "Indigenous sacred forests as a tool for climate Change mitigation"; Tengö et al., *Local protection of tropical dry forest*; United Nations Educational, Scientific and Cultural Organization (UNESCO), *Linking indigenous and scientific knowledge to counter biodiversity erosion* (2019), https://en.unesco.org/news/linking-indigenous-and-scientific-knowledge-counter-biodiversity-erosion.
248. Madhav Gadgil, *Sacred groves: An ancient tradition of nature conservation* (December 2018), https://www.scientificamerican.com/article/sacred-groves-an-ancient-tradition-of-nature-conservation/.
249. K.P. Sivakumar, "Indigenous reverence for environment: A review of sacred groves in India," *Technical Proceedings of the International Conference on Indigenous Initiatives for Environment and Development* (2014), https://www.academia.edu/7703027/INDIGENOUS_REVERENCE_FOR_ENVIRONMENT_A_REVIEW_ON_SACRED_GROVES_IN_INDIA_INTRODUCTION.
250. Rajendra K. Joshi and Shalini Dhyani, "Biomass, carbon density and diversity of tree species in tropical dry deciduous forests in Central India," *Acta Ecologica Sinica* (2018), https://doi.org/10.1016/j.chnaes.2018.09.009; Maru, Gebrekirstos, and Haile, "Indigenous sacred forests as a tool for climate Change mitigation"; Alemayehu Wassie, Frank J. Sterck, and Frans Bongers, "Species and structural diversity of church forests in a fragmented Ethiopian highland landscape," *Journal of Vegetarian Science* 21, no. 7 (2010): 938–948, https://doi.org/10.1111/j.1654-1103.2010.01202.x.
251. Hafeez U. Rehman et al., "A carbon-sink in a sacred forest: Biologically-driven calcite formation in highly weathered soils in Northern Togo (West Africa)," *CATENA* 198 (2021), https://doi.org/10.1016/j.catena.2020.105027.
252. WWF, *Sacred forests help conserve Madagascar's biodiversity.*
253. Tengö et al., *Local protection of tropical dry forest.*
254. Tengö et al., *Local protection.*
255. Tengö et al., *Local protection.*
256. Tengö et al., *Local protection.*
257. Tengö et al., *Local protection.*
258. Rehman et al., "A carbon-sink in a sacred forest".

259. Wankaam: People for the Estuary, *Rights of nature*, par. 1.
260. Wankaam: People for the Estuary, *Rights of nature*.
261. Community Environmental Legal Defense Fund (CELDF), *Rights of nature principles* (2021), https://celdf.org/2021/08/rights-of-nature-principles/.
262. David R. Boyd, "Recognizing the rights of nature," *Natural Resources & Environment* 32, no. 4 (2018): 13–17, https://www.jstor.org/stable/26418846.
263. CELDF, *Rights of nature principles*; National Lawyers Guild, *Proposed amendment to the preamble of the constitution* (2019), https://www.nlg.org/wp-content/uploads/2018/11/Proposed-Amendment-to-the-Preamble-of-the-Constitution.pdf.
264. The Guardian, *Guardian weekly letters: Personhood will not protect the environment* (November 2019), https://www.theguardian.com/global/2019/nov/19/weekly-letters-failure-of-democracy.
265. Boyd, "Recognizing the rights of nature".
266. Constitutional Court of Columbia, "Center for Social Justice Studies et al. v. Presidency of the Republic et al.," *Judgment T-622/16* (Delaware Law School, Dignity Rights Project. Trans., 2019), Original decision November 10, 2016; Philipp Wesche, "Rights of nature in practice: A case study on the impacts of the Colombian Atrato River decision," *Journal of Environmental Law* 33, no. 3 (2021): 531–556, https://doi.org/10.1093/jel/eqab021.
267. Constitutional Court of Columbia, "Center for Social Justice Studies et al. v. Presidency of the Republic et al."; Wesche, "Rights of nature in practice".
268. Wesche, "Rights of nature in practice," 538.
269. Constitutional Court of Columbia, "Center for Social Justice Studies et al. v. Presidency of the Republic et al."; Wesche, "Rights of nature in practice".
270. Constitutional Court of Columbia, "Center for Social Justice Studies et al. v. Presidency of the Republic et al."; Wesche, "Rights of nature in practice".
271. Constitutional Court of Columbia, "Center for Social Justice Studies et al. v. Presidency of the Republic et al.," 114.
272. Constitutional Court of Columbia, "Center for Social Justice Studies et al. v. Presidency of the Republic et al.," 3.
273. Constitutional Court of Columbia, "Center for Social Justice Studies et al. v. Presidency of the Republic et al.".
274. Wesche, "Rights of nature in practice".
275. Nesmith et al., *The intersection of environmental justice*, 51.
276. Greta Gaard, *Critical ecofeminism* (Lanham, MD: Lexington Books, 2017); Greta Gaard, "Feminism and environmental justice," in *The*

Routledge handbook of environmental justice, Ryan Holifield, Jayajit Chakraborty, and Gordon Walker, eds. (New York: Routledge, 2018): 74–88.

277. Susan Buckingham and Rakibe Kulcur, "Gender geographies of environmental injustices," *ANTIPODE* 41, no. 4 (2009): 659–683, https://doi.org/10.1111/j.1467-8330.2009.00693.x.
278. Saundra H. Starks et al., *Mentoring women for leadership: Empowering the next generation* (Alexandria, VA: NASW Press, 2021).
279. Grace Lynch, "For climate solutions, listen to Indigenous women," *YES!* (October 2021), https://www.yesmagazine.org/opinion/2021/10/05/climate-solutions-listen-to-indigenous-women.
280. Lynch, "For climate solutions, listen to Indigenous women".
281. Shanondora Billiot and Jessica Parfait, "Reclaiming land: Adaptation activities and global environmental change challenges within Indigenous communities," in *People and climate change: Vulnerability, adaptation, and social justice*, Lisa Reyes Mason and Jonathan Rigg, eds. (New York: Oxford University Press, 2019), 108–121; Dina Gilio-Whitaker, *As long as grass grows: The Indigenous fight for environmental justice, from colonization to Standing Rock* (Boston, MA: Beacon, 2019); Tammy Kaho'olemana Martin, Lynette K. Paglinawan, and Richard Paglinawan, "Pathways to healing the Native Hawaiian spirit through culturally competent practice," in *Transnational Pacific Islander American and social work: Dancing to the beat of a different drum*, Halaevalu F. Ofahengaue Vakalahi and Meripa Taiai Godinet, eds. (Washington, DC: NASW Press, 2014), 55–90.
282. Robin Wall Kimmerer, *Braiding sweetgrass* (Minneapolis, MN: Milkweed, 2013).
283. Sloan and Schmitz, "Environmental degradation," 38.
284. Vandana Shiva, *Earth democracy: Justice, sustainability, and peace* (Berkeley, CA: North Atlantic Books, 2015).
285. Vandana Shiva, *Staying alive: Women, ecology and development* (Brooklyn, NY: South End Press, 2010).
286. Vandana Shiva, *Who really feeds the world? The failures of agribusiness and the promise of agroecology* (Berkeley, CA: North Atlantic Books, 2016).
287. Jane Goodall and Gail Hudson, *The book of hope: A survival guide for trying times* (New York: Celadon Books, 2021).
288. Starks et al., *Mentoring women for leadership: Empowering the next generation.*
289. Gaard, "Feminism and environmental justice".
290. Sloan et al., *Critical multiculturalism and intersectionality in a complex world.*
291. Lisa Merton and Alan Dater, producers and directors, *Taking root: The vision of Wangari Maathai* (United States: Marlboro Productions,

2008), DVD, https://m.youtube.com/watch?v=BQU7JoxkGvo; Strides in Development, *Wangari Maathai & the Green Belt Movement* (2010), (Original video file: Syme & Eaton, 1989).
292. The Greenbelt Movement, *Gender livelihood and advocacy* (2018), http://www.greenbeltmovement.org/what-we-do/community-empowerment; The Greenbelt Movement, *Wangari Maathai: Biography* (2018), http://www.greenbeltmovement.org/wangari-maathai/biography; Merton and Dater, *Taking root: The vision of Wangari Maathai.*
293. The Greenbelt Movement, *Gender livelihood and advocacy*; The Greenbelt Movement, *Wangari Maathai: Biography;* Wangari Maathai, *The Greenbelt movement: Sharing the approach and the experience* (New York: Lantern Books, 2003); Merton and Dater, *Taking root: The vision of Wangari Maathai.*
294. Wangari Maathai, *Unbowed: A memoir* (New York: Knopf, 2006).
295. Geoffrey Kamadi, "Green growth: The save-the-mangroves scheme reaping rewards for women in Kenya," *The Guardian* (May 2021), https://www.theguardian.com/global-development/2021/may/24/green-growth-the-save-the-mangrove-scheme-reaping-rewards-for-women-in-kenya; The Nature Conservancy, "Mother Mangrove: The women behind Kenya's mangrove restoration," *Stories in Africa* (November 2021), https://www.nature.org/en-us/about-us/where-we-work/africa/stories-in-africa/women-kenya-mangrove-forest/?en_txn8=NewSch.WJEMSA2201NPNZNZZE01Z00-ZZZZZ-ST00&lu=9b9bb89c-82b1-41e7-825-1906a258198a&en_txn1=e.ch_nc.eg.x.gpn.0105.n.sas.unv.
296. The Nature Conservancy, "Mother Mangrove: The women behind Kenya's mangrove restoration".
297. Kamadi, "Green growth: The save-the-mangroves scheme reaping rewards for women in Kenya"; The Nature Conservancy, "Mother Mangrove".
298. Kamadi, "Green growth"; The Nature Conservancy, "Mother Mangrove".
299. The Nature Conservancy, "Mother Mangrove".
300. Kamadi, "Green growth".
301. The Nature Conservancy, "Mother Mangrove".
302. The Nature Conservancy, "Mother Mangrove".
303. David W. Orr, *Hope is an imperative* (Washington: Island Press, 2011).
304. Goodall and Hudson, *The book of hope: A survival guide for trying times.*
305. Cara Buckley, "'OK Doomer' and the climate advocates who say it's not too late," *New York Times* (March 2022), https://www.nytimes.com/2022/03/22/climate/climate-change-ok-doomer.html.
306. Buckley, "'OK Doomer' and the climate advocates who say it's not too late".

307. Sze, *Environmental justice in a moment of danger.*
308. Daniel Willis, "Climate reparations need to happen. Now," *openDemocracy* (March 2022), par. 13, https://www.opendemocracy.net/en/oureconomy/the-case-for-climate-reparations-is-now-irrefutable/.
309. United Nations Office of the High Commissioner for Human Rights (OHCHR), *About human rights and the environment: Special Rapporteur on human rights and the environment* (n.d.), https://www.ohchr.org/en/special-procedures/sr-environment/about-human-rights-and-environment.
310. United Nations (UN), *Universal declaration of human rights* (1948), art. 25.
311. Sloan et al., *Critical multiculturalism and intersectionality in a complex world;* György Széll, "Environmental conflicts as a new dimension of peace research," *158th Seminar of the Institute for Peace Science* (Hiroshima University, 2005): 21–31, https://heiwa.hiroshima-u.ac.jp/Pub/35/Part4.pdf; UNGA, *Climate change and its possible security implications.*
312. Akresh, "Climate change, conflict and children".
313. UNGA, *Climate change.*
314. Starks et al., *Mentoring women for leadership: Empowering the next generation.*
315. Eva Rehse and Ursula Miniszewski, "The state of funding for women's environmental action," *Environmental Funders Network* (March 2018), par. 1, https://www.greenfunders.org/2018/03/08/the-state-of-funding-for-womens-environmental-action/.
316. Dimitri Selibas, *Funding for women-led conservation remains tiny, but that's changing fast* (April 2022), https://news.mongabay.com/2022/04/funding-for-women-led-conservation-remains-tiny-but-thats-changing-fast/.
317. Robins, Brunsting, and Wood, "Climate change and the just transition".
318. International Labor Organization, *Greening jobs: World employment and social outlook 2018.*
319. Intergovernmental Panel on Climate Change (IPCC), *Climate change 2022 impacts, adaptation and vulnerability: Summary for policymakers* (2022), https://report.ipcc.ch/ar6wg2/pdf/IPCC_AR6_WGII_FinalDraft_FullReport.pdf.
320. Brad Plumer and Nadja Popovich, "Yes, There has been progress on climate. No, It's not nearly enough," *New York Times* (October 2021), https://www.nytimes.com/interactive/2021/10/25/climate/world-climate-pledges-cop26.html.

Conclusion: Finding Hope in Human Rights Research

Katerina Standish

Hope is a desire for something different, something better, and something attainable. It is not a wish. Hope is something planned for, manifested, and ultimately possible. This collection of writing originating from the University of Manitoba is evidence of forward-thinking, future planning, and critical reflection on emergent issues related to Human Rights and Justice. There is no lack of important issues for the scholar-practitioners attention in 2023. Indeed, it can be said that a significant concern for forward-thinking authors is the ability to stay in one lane, focus their attention, and not be distracted from the myriad and monstrous needs that surround us. As has been reflected by hope scholars and those working at the nexus of social reality and societal change, 'a critical middle step between identifying spaces in need of transformation and working for change is the capacity to move from the perceived to the possible—the ability to imagine *other than what is*.'[1] In this collection, scholars

K. Standish (✉)
Canadian Peace Research Association (CPRA), Winnipeg, Manitoba, Canada
e-mail: Katerina.standish@umanitoba.ca

L. E. Reimer and K. Standish (eds.), *Perspectives on Justice, Indigeneity, Gender, and Security in Human Rights Research*,
https://doi.org/10.1007/978-981-99-1930-7_16

have immersed, illuminated, communicated, and proposed vital considerations in the address of essential concerns related to human rights, justice, indigeneity, gender, and security.

Human Rights and Justice

The international values of human rights and justice exist in manifold cultural and structural contexts. For this collection, four authors have presented considerations regarding the vital fulcrum of *access*; access is crucial to the experience and availability of rights and justice and depends upon multiple social, cultural, political, and economic factors.

In *Access to Justice*, Will Jordan offered an examination of restorative justice in the Canadian legal framework including the *Criminal Code*, the *Youth Criminal Justice Act* (YCJA), and the *Canadian Victims Bill of Rights* (CVBR). This study examined the importance of restorative justice (RJ) when accessing justice in Canada, and, critically, identified numerous impediments to access including 'co-option of restorative programmes through government policy and the institutionalization of restorative practices which results in the "sanitization" of restorative values through penal policy.' Jordan averred that the expansion of RJ access in Canada requires enlarging understandings of justice to include alternative practices and philosophies of justice, such as RJ, and the cognition of barriers such as the co-optation of alternative forms of justice by both provincial and federal governments.

In *Allyship and Equality in Youth Organizations: A Case Study of HOBY Canada*, Abby Myles investigated the role of allyship to support social inequality and injustice. Myles expounded a case study of allyship at HOBY Canada to investigate individuals who engage with social movements that support equality. To locate empirical findings of actions that combat injustice, Myles examined the role of allies, individuals external to marginalization, to determine HOBY Canada, a company that forefronts inequality and discrimination in their business operations to support and implement values and policies that directly tackle accessibility, diversity, and inclusion.

In my own contribution in this collection entitled *Teaching Human Rights and Social Justice*, I conducted a self-study of teaching transformative values to medical students. Those who engage with this work can find valuable illumination of practice through dedicated reflective work such as auto-inquiry. Teacher 'self-study' is a methodology for probing expert practice and has a real impact on how and what we teach. Educators working at the interdisciplinary locus of human rights and social justice can benefit from sharing educative praxis (theory and action) and in this chapter, I shared an ethnographic inquiry of the work of transformative education utilizing class curriculum and field notes such as post-class reflections.

In the final entry in this section, Carlos Godoy asked *Are Human Rights Universal?* In this chapter challenges to the universality of human rights were examined to query the hegemonic discourse of individual human rights which disregards cultural norms and traditions in the Global South. Godoy avers that the cultural specificity from which the human rights regime emerged is unsuitable for all nations, can be considered an act of cultural imperialism in non-Western cultures and concludes that 'given the significant divergencies in translating international human rights norms to national settings, human rights are not universal,' and that only a 'minimalist' human rights regime' can be internationally implemented.

Indigeneity

Indigeneity refers to consciousness of the historical, social, and political acts of violence experienced by First Peoples under global colonization and the work aimed at recognition, reconciliation, and preserving ethnic distinctiveness and ancestral territories. As a topic of international importance, work that focuses on indigeneity brings to the forefront the realities of past, present, and enduring discriminations against First Peoples and efforts to decolonize and unfetter indigenous peoples.

In *The United Nations Declaration on the Rights of Indigenous People: A Prototype for Reconciliation?* Rhéal Cenerini examined the significance of the United Nations Declaration on the Rights of Indigenous People (UNDRIP). Cenerini explored the role of UNDRIP in post-colonial reconciliation in Canada to determine that it is 'a political document seeking to strike a balance between the collective rights of Indigenous people and the public interest of colonial nations, like Canada.' Cenerini concluded that UNDRIP is not binding so much as aspirations and therefore enables 'states and Indigenous people within their borders to slowly work towards accommodation.'

In *Indigenous Rights and the University,* Annette Trimbee explores the effort called for by the *Truth and Reconciliation Commission (TRC)* placing education at the core of the reconciliation. Trimbee's chapter explores how Canadian universities publicly committed to forward the work of 'Indigenization, reconciliation, and decolonization' but that they held no common understanding of what these three terms meant or required. Trimbee's chapter examined why Canadian universities adopted the TRC calls to action, how university motives influence their educative approaches, and the impact and obstacles of complex situations in higher education.

Gender

Gender is a social and cultural construct that defines and determines characteristics associated with being women, men, girls, or boys. Gender is a facet of the social world that is hierarchal and discriminatory and it can chang over time. It creates inequalities that intersect with other aspects of identity to delimit the full humanity of people. When gender is investigated, it is essential to unravel the hidden social norms, societal responsibilities, transgressive penalties, and cultural constructs that seek to corral gender roles. Gender relates to biological sex because material reality (biology) is often a facet of gendered expectations and discrimination. In the current global patriarchy, a system of male supremacy that impacts gender expectations for women, men, girls, and boys, human rights and justice remain contingent on sex and gender.

In *Transgender Healthcare in Canada*, Sydney Laurin illuminated the challenges for gender-diverse individuals to receive targeted health care in Canada with a focus on the medical response to sexual violence in the trans community. Laurin maintained that due to current 'responses to trans survivors of sexual assault, high rates of sexual victimization, and obvious gap in research it is critical that the intersection between transgender individuals, sexual violence and the healthcare system be explored much more in-depth.' Laurin's chapter promoted greater inquiry into experiences of sexualized violence against gender-diverse individuals in Canada via evidence-based research.

In *Femicide in Mexico*, Brandi Chartier examined the subordination of women in Mexico and the normalization of violence against women (VAW) that can culminate in deadly femicide. Chartier illustrates the phenomenon of femicide-deliberate killing of women, because they are women-in global and national contexts, and as a major site of femicidal violence, Mexico, and their 'response' to lethal violence against women, is examined. After examining the state of femicide in Mexico, Chartier goes on to declare a resistance to call femicide, *femicide* in Mexico, enmeshed as it is with cultural inequality between males and females, a disinclination to target VAW nationally, as well as the limited official address of this form of violence. Chartier then illuminates organizations and operations to combat femicide in Mexico including aspects of prevention and redress but also norm change. The chapter, sadly, reports an increase in femicidal violence despite years of activism and advocacy.

In *Women Workers in the Ready-made Garment Industry in Bangladesh*, Korellia Schneider examined the Ready-Made Garment (RMG) industry in Bangladesh, and the injustices that accompany the creation of 'cheap exportable goods.' As a major exporter, RMG sweatshops remain an often-hidden aspect of the violence of globalization. In this chapter, Schneider ruminated upon obstacles to human dignity and rights in the RMG industry for women workers and articulated circumstances of disenfranchisement with both poverty and degradation. The exploitation of women garment workers is then examined in a case study of the Rana Plaza collapse to conclude that infringement of labour rights is a part of the gender-based violence women experience in the RMG industry but that collective bargaining could aid workers to make vital changes to the fates of women workers.

In *Extremism, Terrorism and Misogyny*, Ashley Haller uses a multi-case study of misogynistic murder in Canada from two recent incel attacks against women. Through an examination of the École Polytechnique and Minassian killing (in Montreal and Toronto respectively), Haller deconstructed the two deadliest attacks in recent Canadian history as acts of violent misogyny. Misogyny emerges as a reinforcement of gender hierarchies in patriarchy. The hatred of things not male, acts to target and dehumanize females and gender-non-conforming males and in these instances, comprise a form of gender terror that elevates these crimes as identity-based. Haller's exploration includes the online aspect of misogyny and the lamentable roots of online misogyny in Canada. The work goes on to alert us to the dangers of misogyny, the role of the media in amplifying violence against women, and the importance of language and framing, in understanding extremism.

Security

Security can be conceived of as shelter, protection, freedom from danger, risk, and fear, but also a state of safety that includes well-being and care. To be 'safe' has both a material and intangible quality. Past definitions of security as state-based have been challenged in the past century to include human security, or security of people, rather than governments. Security in this collection relates to examining how people are constrained from being or feeling secure in the external social environment, a domain of institutions, policies, protocols, and practices.

In *Hope with Charity: Human Rights, the Law, and Aging*, Albert Evrard looks at the circumstances related to the rights of the aged, how individual rights are imagined, and what rights erode for older people, that remain fulsome for the younger. In the European context, Evrard examined how older people were conceptualized, and how this acts to define and constrain their experience, both materially and existentially—their rights. As 'Vulnerable Persons, Persons in Vulnerable Situations, Persons with Disabilities or even Grand Parents' aged people are categorized as less-fully human than younger counterparts and Evrard looks at the realities of what life, a good life, a quality of living, and right to life mean.

In *Human Security and the Digital Threat: Russia and Ukraine*, Stephen Lunn looks at the realities of cyber operations (computer network attacks and espionage) in Ukraine. As a portent of the crisis between Russia and Ukraine, Lunn examines how the digital landscape poses as a front or silent attack in the conflict. By looking through the lens of Internet sovereignty, and International Law, Lunn elevated cyber harms such as electrical attacks (blackouts), and the limits, conceptually, of these new online violence. Through looking at the limits of International Law, rooted in twentieth-century warfare, the notion of the cyber-attack, is anomalous, and like other forms of emergent violence, requires terminological clarity for address. As the main targets of Russian cyber-attacks are the civilian populations, Lunn alerted us to a new reality in warfare and urged us to create routes to combat cyber violence in the future.

In *Protecting Students: Bullying and School*, Ha Bich Dong looked at the role of education in both instilling the values of human rights and democracy in schooling, but also how aspects of student bullying are addressed in relation to sex and gender-diverse students. Dong examines how human rights in education 'play out in practice' via case studies in Manitoba to investigate tensions between competing human rights, and education. As bullying (and cyberbullying) is harassment and aggression of victims from student peers, it represents a deviance common in schools and one that seriously harms children. With the advent of online bullying, victims are often targeted anonymously, a reality that Manitoba has sought to address through *The Public Schools Amendment Act (Safe and Inclusive School)*. Analysis of the act shows definitional incongruence with other provinces and some barriers to implementation.

In *Climate Change: Environmental Justice, Human Rights, & Peaceful Practices*, Christa C. Gilliam, Lacey Sloan, and Cathryne L. Schmitz look at the links between the environment and human rights to intone that environmental justice, 'equitable access to a healthy environment' free from 'environmental degradation' is necessary for the experience of full human rights. In their chapter, Gilliam, Sloan, and Schmitz examine the current and escalating climate incidences worldwide resulting from global warming and climate change. They maintain that this is a crisis for the living systems of all life on Earth but with unequal consequences due to geography, wealth, culture, and ecological stewardship. In their chapter they trace the cultural roots of the current extreme conditions to colonization, linking white supremacy and racism with environmental degradation and they call for environmental justice in the facilitation of unequal rights.

As mentioned in the opening paragraph of this CODA, a significant concern for forward-thinking authors is the ability to stay in one lane, focus their attention, and not be distracted from the myriad and monstrous needs surrounding us. This book is a collection of different routes that comprise an enormous and interconnected super-highway leading us into the future. It will remain for readers, scholars, practitioners, and laypeople to choose what direction we go in, what destination that necessitates, and who gets left behind on the ride. That said, the direction of hope, a new future that seeks to remain focused on human rights and justice, is not only possible but also the only way out of the current realities of our globe. No other road is open to us—we cannot, not hope, and we have much ground to cover.

Note

1. Standish, Katerina, "Learning How to Hope: A Hope Curriculum." *Humanity & Society* 43, no. 4 (2019): 48–504.

Winnipeg—The New Geneva: *The Pursuit of Social Justice*

Delivered by Dr. Arthur Mauro
at the Jewish Foundation of Manitoba's 35th Annual Luncheon,
November 12, 2009

I want to thank the Jewish Foundation for the opportunity to participate in this annual event. When I was contacted a number of months ago I said I would gladly accept, but I indicated that my age made making long-term commitments risky. I was told that the committee had considered that possibility and was prepared to take a chance. I can only assume that the frequent phone calls during the intervening period, inquiring as to my health, were a sign of deepening friendship and not a reassessment of risk.

One of the diminishing benefits of advancing age is the ability to give perspective to the past, purpose to the present, and hope for the future. I concluded that my remarks should, in part, relate to the Jewish Foundation within the context of the major changes and developments of this community. And the topic that I have chosen is deliberate.

After the First World War, Geneva, a small city in Switzerland, became the location for the League of Nations, the International Court of Justice, and the Red Cross and now is the headquarters for agencies of the United Nations. It is a city associated with freedom, and where the Geneva Conventions were signed, dealing with the treatment of non-combatants and prisoners of war. I believe that Winnipeg, both because of its history,

L. E. Reimer and K. Standish (eds.), *Perspectives on Justice, Indigeneity, Gender, and Security in Human Rights Research*,
https://doi.org/10.1007/978-981-99-1930-7

existing institutions, and those under development, can become a new Geneva. And therefore I chose as my topic, "Winnipeg—the New Geneva: The pursuit of social justice."

In 2012, the Museum of Human Rights will be completed and will become an international symbol projecting the past from the continuing global struggle and the pursuit of human dignity. For me, it will represent the achievement of this community that has confronted the challenges of discrimination and has chosen respect for diversity and reconciliation over intolerance and conflict. And this is reflected in institutions such as the Jewish Foundation, the Winnipeg Foundation, the United Way, and a myriad of other agencies, all in pursuit of social justice.

Next year, Manitoba will celebrate a hundred and forty years since its entry into confederation in 1870. But in the first fifty years of that entry into confederation, the period from 1870 to 1920, three issues would test the resolve of this community and resonate for the next half century, both provincially and nationally.

The first event was the treatment of Louis Riel. As head of the provisional government, Riel had negotiated the terms of the Manitoba Act and the entry into confederation. Riel had been elected to parliament on three occasions but was never allowed to take his seat. And fifteen years after entering confederation, in 1885, he was hanged for treason. Four years later, in breach of the Manitoba Act, the legislature of the Province stopped publications of legislation and proceedings in French.

The second event was termed the "Catholic School question." It was caused by the withdrawal of public support for Catholic schools which had been provided support since the entry into confederation. This conflict went up to the Imperial Privy Council on two occasions, led to the defeat of a national government, and was temporarily settled by an agreement between the Prime Minister of Canada and the Premier of Manitoba.

The third event was the General Strike of 1919, considered the most influential labour action in Canadian history. Some of the leaders of that strike were charged with seditious conspiracy and jailed.

So in simplistic terms, the Riel issue was a conflict between French, Metis, and English; the second issue was a conflict between Catholics and Protestants; and the third was a conflict between labour, capital, and immigrants. In each case, confrontation was chosen rather than conciliation, and it was resolved by the majority exercising political power, without regard to the minority.

Now I reference these events not to relive history, but rather as benchmarks against which we can judge how far this community has developed since those dark days. It was as if Winnipeg had been predestined to test whether a community so ethnically, economically, and religiously diverse, could survive. And it is this struggle that explains in part the development of the Centre for Peace and Justice, the Museum for Human Rights, and the existence of such institutions as the Jewish Foundation of Manitoba.

I had the good fortune of being at the University of Manitoba during what I refer to as "The Golden Decade"—1946–1956. World War II was over, the economy had emerged from a searing depression, and federal support for veterans opened the doors of the university to individuals who would otherwise be unable to attend. There was only one university in Manitoba in those days, and as a result, whether you attended the university itself or the affiliated colleges, you were thrust into a venue where you met and you worked with individuals from a variety of social, racial, and religious backgrounds.

I was born and raised in Thunder Bay, Ontario, and I was aware of the existence of racial and religious prejudice, but I had not personally experienced the reality of prejudice. The nature of Thunder Bay, a small community with a large number of ethnic groups, eliminated meaningful exposure to real prejudice. It was on my arrival in Winnipeg in 1946 that I confronted that reality. The resentments engendered by the three issues that I have referred to still resonated. In addition, there had been a quota on the number of Jewish students admitted to the Faculty of Medicine, there was a "gentleman's agreement" as to the sale of property in Tuxedo, and restrictions on admission to certain clubs. It was difficult, I was told, for Catholics to obtain certain jobs, particularly in the public sector.

But these factors of race and religion were irrelevant at the university. There was an active interfaith counsel, there were drama clubs, glee clubs, and musical and debating societies, all of which took no notice of race or creed, and the same attitude applied to student government. It was the ability, character, and integrity of individuals that were valued, not their ethnic, religious, or economic background.

In the 50 years since my generation graduated, the social, economic, and cultural landscape of Winnipeg, and Manitoba, have changed dramatically. My belief is that the graduates of the University of Manitoba have helped bring about that change. And the change was the direct result of our university experience where individuals from different backgrounds learned to work together and learned not to tolerate, but to respect diversity.

So how have we measured up against those benchmarks that I established? Well, relative to the conflict between the French and English, there is now a monument to Louis Riel on the legislative grounds. We now have French immersion classes in our public schools, as well as heritage classes in other languages. And, since 1979, the proceedings of the Manitoba Legislature are published in both French and English.

As to the Catholic school question, since the Roblin government introduced shared services legislation, we now have financial support for both parochial and private schools regardless of religious affiliation.

And in contrast to the antagonistic attitude towards labour and immigrants reflected in the 1919 strike, we now have laws that enshrine employees' rights and a more conciliatory attitude towards labour/management relations. In addition, Winnipeg is a community that welcomes immigrants and celebrates diversity, best reflected in such festivals as Folklorama.

And as for the "gentleman's agreement" relative to the purchase of Tuxedo property, suffice to note that the Asper Campus is in Tuxedo, and now the Manitoba Club and the Glendale Golf & Country Club have joint membership provisions. I should have lived so long to see all this!

But I have the privilege of witnessing and participating in this amazing evolution, in which community is not defined solely in terms of economic growth, but rather a community that embraces a broad spectrum of society, and where giving is a condition of citizenship.

We have reason to be proud of this achievement, but the demands of social justice will not be corrected in a single generation. They require patience and continued commitment. If it is true that eternal vigilance is the price of liberty, history also has taught us that tyranny is the penalty for indifference. The world paid an incalculable price for the indifference to the racial vandalism of what was initially an insignificant group of German fanatics.

So while we have achieved much, much remains to be done. Not only in combating ethnic and religious prejudice, but also in the struggle against the dehumanizing impact of social injustice, both at home and abroad.

Here in Manitoba, we confront the corrosive conditions faced by members of our First Nations, especially on reserves. They must not become forgotten victims of jurisdictional infighting. Nor can we fail to deal with the difficulties faced by the new immigrants. For many of us in this room, our parents or grandparents faced similar problems in adapting to a new land and a new language. And it is in addressing these kinds of problems that agencies such as the Jewish Foundation act as a conscience of society. And I urge you as friends of the Jewish Foundation to continue your support for the services it continues to provide.

But all our efforts will not solve the historic and continuing wrongs throughout the world. But our efforts will be a sign that we are not indifferent to these evils. We can take pride in a city that has experienced human conflict and has adopted a process for reconciliation.

In my opening remarks, I set as my goal to give perspective to the past, purpose to the present, and hope for the future. Now what is that future? What are the needs of this brave new world of the 21st millennium? And what is the role of a new Geneva?

One of the critical factors that we face is the environment and the inequitable consumption of resources. We sometimes forget that we are only life tenants on this planet and that if we breach the terms of that agreement the lease might not be extended. But here in Winnipeg, we have the International Institute for Sustainable Development with world-wide representation on the Board, and it is dealing with this specific problem.

Another issue is world health, an ever-present concern. We had the SARS epidemic scare, and the current H1N1 flu threat. And it underlines the fact that the protection of health is global rather than local. And we have here in Winnipeg the International Centre for Infectious Diseases, a world-class facility dealing with the broad field of research in the area of communicable diseases.

enlargethispage-12ptAnd if we hope to reach the twenty-second century, we must harness the power of education in pursuit of peace. And here in Winnipeg, we have the Centre for Peace and Justice with students from Canada, the United States, Kenya, Iran, Azerbaijan, Nigeria, Botswana, Russia, Uzbekistan, and Laos. All working towards Ph.D. in Conflict Resolution and Peace Studies. Upon completion, they will return to their homes to train teachers and to participate in policy decisions, but they will take with them the Winnipeg experience.

In 2012, the Museum for Human Rights will bring physical reality to Winnipeg's role in this human drama. With the opening of the Museum, we should urge the Federal Government to locate the Canadian Human

Rights Commission here in Winnipeg. We should pursue the possibility of the United Nations opening a UNESCO office in Winnipeg to deal specifically with the issues confronting aboriginal people around the world.

In short, we have now in Winnipeg the framework that can be built on and prepare a profile of Winnipeg as a world centre in peace studies and human rights. Robert Kennedy articulated the credo of those determined to strive for social justice when he said, “Some men see things as they are and ask why; I dream of things that never were and ask why not.” We in Winnipeg have been blessed with dreamers. We have the dreamers who built wide boulevards and Assiniboine Park, and we have dreamers who built a tunnel from Shoal Lake in Ontario to bring fresh water—and still provide fresh water to Winnipeg. And we have dreamers, like Izzy Asper, who dreamt of a temple to human rights—and so long as that structure stands it will challenge us and it will challenge the world to the questions of: why not humanity instead of brutality, why not dignity instead of degradation, why not understanding instead of hate, why not peace instead of war.

And each of us has an obligation in this pursuit of peace and social justice. And if we stand mute in the face of injustice we stand convicted of the social crime of silence. As John Don Warren wrote, “Ask not for whom the bell tolls, it tolls for you and me.” And by our actions, we can determine whether that tolling bell is the sound of doom and approaching darkness, or the peal of hope and a new dawn. Therein lies both the message and the purpose of the Museum of Human Rights and the Centre for Peace and Justice. That hope will be turned into a process for reconciliation and that committed people of goodwill can achieve peace and justice.

enlargethispage-24ptWinnipeg has been declared the Cultural Capital of Canada for 2010. To declare Winnipeg as the Cultural Capital of Canada in the field of visual and performing arts is, for me, to state the obvious. But the fundamental culture of this city, which has sustained it in good times and bad, is a culture of hope. It is a hope that, in the words of Taier Jardin, “a day will come when we will harness for God the energies of love, and on that day, for the second time in human history, man will have discovered fire.”

My hope is that our individual efforts and the efforts of institutions such as the Jewish Foundation will help kindle that fire, and that in time that fire will become a blaze seen around the world. And just as the

Geneva Convention outlined the rules of war, there will be a Winnipeg Convention establishing the rules for peace and social justice. And then Winnipeg will become the New Geneva. Thank you.

Reproduced with permission.

Dr. Arthur V. Mauro, OC, OM, QC, Canada, is the former Chancellor of the University of Manitoba, the generous benefactor of The Arthur V. Mauro Institute for Peace and Justice at the University of Manitoba. His visions for peace and human rights have been foundational to the work within this collection.

Index

L. E. Reimer and K. Standish (eds.), *Perspectives on Justice, Indigeneity, Gender, and Security in Human Rights Research*,
https://doi.org/10.1007/978-981-99-1930-7

Printed by Printforce, the Netherlands